Broadcast Hysteria

BROADCAST HYSTERIA

Orson Welles's

War of the Worlds

and the

Art of Fake News

A. BRAD SCHWARTZ

Hill and Wang
A division of Farrar, Straus and Giroux New York

Hill and Wang
A division of Farrar, Straus and Giro
175 Varick Street, New York 100

Published in 2015 by Hill and Wa
First paperback edition, 20

Grateful aknowledgment is made for permission to reprint excerpts fr
the script of the *War of the Worlds* broadcast. Reprinted by permissio
ICM Partners. Copyright © 1940 by Howard E. Ko

e Library of Congress has cataloged the hardcover edition as fol
Schwartz, A. Bra
Broadcast hysteria : Orson Welles's War of the worlds and the art of fake
A. Brad Schwartz. — First editio
pages cm
Includes bibliographical references and ind
ISBN 978-0-8090-3161-0 (hardcover ISBN 978-0-8090-3163-4 book)
1. War of the worlds (Radio program 2. Welles, Orson, 1915–198Criticism
and interpretation 3. Science ction radio programsPsychological aspec
4. Radio broadcastingUnited States-History—20th century I. Title.
PN1991.77.W3 S48 20
791.44'72-dc23
201404051

ISBN: 978-0-8090-3164-1

Designed by Abby Kag

www.fsgbooks.com
www.twitter.com/fsgbooks • www.facebook.com/fsgbo

For Mom and Dad

Believe nothing you hear, and only one-half that you see.

—EDGAR ALLAN POE

Contents

Broadcast Hysteria

Introduction

Like many Americans in the fall of 1938, John and Estelle Paultz had come to depend upon their radio. With their country seemingly in free fall and their world spinning out of control, Americans in the thirties sought to lose themselves in entertainment as never before. And no form of escape could be had more cheaply or more readily than the radio. A set cost ten dollars, well within the reach of even very poor families, and the programming it broadcast cost absolutely nothing but time.[1] For the Paultzes, who were uninterested in Hollywood and unable to afford tickets to a stage play, radio was a godsend. They had exactly six dollars to their names, on the evening of Sunday, October 30, 1938, and so appreciated all the free entertainment they could get.[2]

The couple lived at 8 East Fifteenth Street, New York City, less than a block from Union Square. Theirs was a working-class neighborhood filled with low-cost amusements, where the stores were packed with cheap merchandise and the lunchrooms with cheap food. Between features in the movie theaters, patrons played "screeno," a variant of bingo created for the Depression. Winners walked away with a coveted bag of groceries.[3] But all the Paultzes wanted that Sunday evening was to curl up by the fireside and listen to their radio. When Estelle switched the set on, sometime after 8:30 p.m., it happened to be tuned to WABC, the New York affiliate of the Columbia Broadcasting System.

The Paultzes weren't really listening at first, but the ominous announcements pouring out of the loudspeaker soon captured their attention. The CBS announcer read bulletin after bulletin describing some kind of armed invasion of the Eastern Seaboard. Enemy aircraft were landing in New Jersey, and war machines were sweeping across the state toward New York. The army could do nothing to stop them, and more were coming all the time. As the Paultzes listened, CBS patched into a transmission from the 22nd Field Artillery, which had established a line of defense in the Watchung Mountains of northern New Jersey. The gunners opened fire on the invaders and scored a direct hit on one of the machines, but that barely slowed them down. The other invaders released a thick cloud of black smoke—poison gas—that swept over the artillerymen. The Paultzes thought they could hear the soldiers choking to death live on the air.

On the verge of terror, Estelle asked her husband what he thought they were listening to. "A news broadcast, surely," he replied.[4] It sounded so real, it couldn't possibly be anything else. Realizing that their city might be under siege at any moment, Estelle felt as though her blood were coagulating in her veins.

Now they were listening to a transmission from the leader of a bombing squadron, flying in over the invading machines as they crossed the Pulaski Skyway, the major artery leading into New York City. But before the airmen could release their bombs, the invaders sprayed the planes with some kind of death ray, bringing them all down in flames. The squadron leader managed to crash his plane into one of the machines, destroying it. But that still left five invaders moving rapidly toward Manhattan, trailing huge clouds of poison gas in their wake.

Another announcer broke in: "Newark, New Jersey. Newark, New Jersey . . . Warning! Poisonous black smoke pouring in from Jersey marshes. Reaches South Street. Gas masks useless. Urge population to move into open spaces. Automobiles use routes 7, 23, 24. Avoid congested areas. Smoke now spreading over Raymond Boulevard."

Estelle had family in Newark; her sister lived with young children just a few blocks from Raymond Boulevard. Now, Estelle reasoned, they were all probably drowning in poison gas. "The horror of it!" Estelle later wrote. "I couldn't listen any more." Her husband dashed upstairs to the roof and looked up at the sky, hoping to see the approaching invaders. Estelle remained by the radio, frozen, afraid to keep listening and afraid to shut the thing off. She didn't really know what was happening, but she knew she didn't want to die in Manhattan, trapped like a rat as she choked to death on the black smoke. "All the primitive fear of the unknown—awakened within me robbing me of all reason," she wrote. "Only one thing remained to do[:] *run fly*—get on the fastest thing on wheels, and go as far and as quickly as our (last) six dollars would take us."[5]

When the Paultzes burst out the front door of their building, they found the streets largely empty, apart from one lone "stranger peacefully leaning against the doorway." Rapidly they explained the situation to him: the invaders, the war machines, the poison gas. Then he took off in a panic down Fifteenth Street, desperate to reach the subway stop in Union Square. But the Paultzes, sprinting just ahead of him, got there first. They dashed down the stairs and through the turnstile, then jumped onto a train heading uptown. They got off at Forty-second Street, expecting to find Penn Station, but instead found themselves staring at the glittery brilliance of Times Square. They'd missed their stop. "Then we remembered that the Pennsylvania station is on 34th," Estelle wrote. "Back we went to 34th running all the way—heeding nothing—stopping for nothing flying for our lives—before this horrible unknown."[6]

Eight blocks and less than ten minutes later, John and Estelle made it to the massive neoclassical façade of Penn Station. They darted between the immense Doric columns and down into the cavernous waiting room, then spent most of their remaining six dollars on two tickets to Hartford, Connecticut. There they hoped they might be safe, or at least might be able to make it to the open spaces. They hurried to the platform and, "hand clenched in hand," got on their train shortly before it left the station. "Nothing to do but sit tense—white faced and wait," Estelle wrote, "while the train raced."[7]

The Paultzes shared their car with several other passengers, none of whom seemed at all concerned about the invaders menacing New York. Clearly, they had missed the news. John and Estelle congratulated themselves on making it to the train "ahead of the panic stricken mob that was sure to follow as soon as they heard!" But when, somewhere in Connecticut, the train suddenly and inexplicably slowed to a halt, the Paultzes "nearly went mad with anxiety." Apparently, none of the other passengers took notice of their terror. "*Why* had the train stopped?" Estelle wondered. "What had happened ahead?"[8] On the radio, she had heard that the invaders were tearing up railroad tracks and destroying power lines, in order "to crush resistance, paralyze communication, and disorganize human society." Had the invaders already reached Connecticut? Were they just ahead, bearing down on the train?

Unable to contain himself, John leaned toward two college students sitting nearby and explained the situation. Word of the invasion rapidly ricocheted around the car, and a crowd soon gathered around the Paultzes. One of the passengers went to find a conductor, to ask why they had stopped, and came back with an explanation. A woman on the train had fallen sick, he said, and an ambulance was coming to pick her up. But by now, the entire car was half convinced that the story of the invasion was true. Estelle was probably not alone in thinking that the conductor had made up the sick woman to keep the passengers calm.

The passengers in the car were growing restless, talking, debating, and shouting over one another. "The people began to wonder," Estelle wrote, "half fearing that we were *not* mad—that what we were saying might be true!" Finally, one of the passengers said something to John that Estelle could not hear over the rising commotion. John—perhaps panicked, perhaps relieved—turned to his wife and, shouting to make his voice heard over the ruckus, asked, "Who is Orson Wells [*sic*]?"[9]

Estelle knew very well who Orson Welles was. She had seen the young actor/director onstage in one of the revolutionary productions that had made him Broadway's golden boy. At the age of twenty, Welles had shocked the city with his "Voodoo *Macbeth*," set in Haiti and staged in Harlem with an all-black cast. At twenty-two, he had premiered the radical labor opera *The Cradle Will Rock* in direct defiance of the federal government, which tried to shut the play down on opening night. Later that same year, Welles debuted his own theatrical company, the Mercury Theatre, with a production of *Julius Caesar* in modern dress. He gave the show a fascist aesthetic that made Shakespeare's portrait of dictatorship seem chillingly relevant for 1930s audiences. Now, at twenty-three, Welles had his own radio series on CBS, where he adapted other literary classics as effectively as he had Shakespeare's plays. Estelle knew right away that Welles "was the one man capable of *imagining* and bringing to vivid life the kind of thing we had heard."[10]

After processing that revelation "for fully a minute," Estelle shouted out for a newspaper. "Someone dug up a much trampled Tribune," she wrote, and "we almost shredded the pages" in a frantic search for the radio listings.[11] Finally, there it was: in the 8:00 p.m. slot, on station WABC,

Welles and his *Mercury Theatre on the Air* in a dramatization of H. G. Wells's *The War of the Worlds*.

Desperate to make the forty-year-old novel about a Martian invasion of England seem relevant to modern American audiences, Welles, the producer John Houseman, and the writer Howard Koch had changed its setting to the United States and restructured the first part of the story as a series of fake news bulletins. Americans had grown accustomed, in recent months, to hearing radio programs regularly interrupted by distressing news from Europe as Nazi Germany pushed the world closer and closer to war. Welles and the Mercury Theatre copied the style of those bulletins as closely as they could, giving their invasion from Mars a terrifying immediacy.

Most people who heard the *War of the Worlds* broadcast that night loved it. Many considered it the Mercury's greatest triumph of the season, though Welles and his colleagues deemed it too silly to be taken seriously. But other listeners, like the Paultzes, tuned in late and greatly misinterpreted what they heard. The next day, newspapers nationwide reported that thousands of people across the country had taken the fake news to be true and fled their homes in terror—grabbing firearms, putting on gas masks, and clogging the highways in a mad rush to escape the imaginary Martians. John and Estelle likely didn't understand that the bulletins they had heard described an extraterrestrial, as opposed to an earthly, enemy; but, according to the press, they were far from the only listeners who made a break for it.

The New York Times described a "wave of mass hysteria" washing over the United States, even throwing some families in Newark, New Jersey, into such terror that they "rushed out of their homes with wet handkerchiefs and towels over their faces" and stacked furniture on their cars before heading for the hills. Frightened listeners supposedly jammed phone lines to newspapers and authorities, coast to coast, with one San Franciscan quoted as inquiring: "My God, where can I volunteer my services? We've got to stop this awful thing." A woman in Indianapolis rushed into a church and brought services to an abrupt halt, announcing that the end of the world had arrived. "You might as well go home to die," she cried. "I just heard it on the radio."[12] In the small town of Concrete, Washington, the power went out during the broadcast. Residents were just about to flee when the lights came back on.[13]

These anecdotal reports, and many more like them, prompted the Radio Research Project at Princeton University to investigate listener reactions to the broadcast. Published in 1940 as *The Invasion from Mars: A Study in the Psychology of Panic* by Hadley Cantril, their study documented the bizarre behavior of a handful of Americans in lurid detail. It quickly became a classic in its field. Cantril estimated that, of the six million people who heard the broadcast, at least one million believed it to be true.[14] The population of the United States at that time was somewhere around 130 million people.

Remembered as "a textbook example of mass hysteria," the *War of the Worlds* panic is still cited constantly by historians as evidence of the anxiety permeating the country just before World War II.[15] The broadcast itself has become shorthand for the dangerous power and influence of the media, not to mention the gullibility and ignorance of mass audiences. Whenever viewers mistake a mockumentary for the real thing, or a tweet is misinterpreted and spread, causing consternation, the incident is invariably referred to as another *War of the Worlds*.

Yet, after decades of accepting the mass-hysteria story at face value, scholars around the turn of the twenty-first century began to question whether the panic was really as large as Cantril and others suggested. A close reading of *The Invasion from Mars* reveals that Cantril's team deliberately oversampled people frightened by the broadcast, ignored survey data from listeners who knew it was fiction, and only interviewed listeners in New Jersey—where all accounts agree that the panic was most intense. Other researchers have called those very news articles into question, arguing that they were poorly sourced, highly repetitive, and largely inaccurate.[16] These reports and the book they inspired present an extraordinary claim: that a "tidal wave of terror . . . swept the nation" on the evening of October 30, 1938.[17] But they present little hard evidence to back it up.

In 2013, media coverage of the broadcast's seventy-fifth anniversary put the growing gap between the conventional wisdom and the more skeptical view on full display, with little hope of a consensus. Most news articles at least paid lip service to the idea that the media had exaggerated the panic, but Cantril's theory of widespread hysteria remained immensely popular—a cultural touchstone, frequently embellished. "It is so easy now to mock the millions who freaked out at the 'War of the Worlds,'" wrote the risk-management consultant and Harvard instructor David Ropeik in a piece for *The Huffington Post*. "Millions who heard it believed it, calling police stations in terror, fleeing their homes, gathering with families to wait for 'the end of the world.' "[18] Like many firm believers in the *War of the Worlds* panic, Ropeik wildly inflates the size and scale of its effects. Even Cantril estimated that the broadcast frightened only 1.2 million people, not the "millions" Ropeik claimed.[19]

On the other side of the argument were the communications and journalism professors Jefferson Pooley and Michael Socolow. They argued, in an oft-cited piece in *Slate*, that *War of the Worlds* was much ado about nothing—less significant, in the regulatory history of American broadcasting, than Janet Jackson's infamous "wardrobe malfunction" during the 2004 Super Bowl. "The supposed panic was so tiny as to be practically immeasurable on the night of the broadcast," they wrote. "Despite repeated assertions to the contrary... almost nobody was fooled by Welles' broadcast."[20]

This argument is true in a sense; the news media did embellish the panic, as Pooley and Socolow demonstrate. But these scholars try too hard to correct the conventional wisdom. They discount too easily the small but significant number of Americans who, like the Paultzes, did experience *War of the Worlds* as a news report and were indeed frightened by it. Those listeners may have been relatively few in number, and they may have held the historical spotlight for too long, but their stories are worthy of examination and explanation. We cannot fully understand the broadcast and its historical significance without them.

Learned and well-meaning academics can come to such widely varying conclusions about *War of the Worlds* because, for most of the past seven decades, reliable information on its effects has been largely unavailable. Apart from the problematic news reports, the only publicly available listenership data are found in Cantril's flawed study. "What should be said about what really happened?" wrote the Welles biographer David Thomson, as if throwing up his hands at the thought of trying to make sense of it all. "Is there anything as substantial as 'history' connected with such a legendary occasion?"[21]

Fortunately for history, many Americans who personally experienced *War of the Worlds* preserved their reactions in writing. In the wake of the broadcast, the Federal Communications Commission received more than six hundred letters regarding it, which are currently held by the National Archives II facility in College Park, Maryland. These letters have received limited attention from scholars, but they are incomplete without another, larger collection, long thought lost, that has only recently resurfaced. In the days following *War of the Worlds*, nearly fourteen hundred people—including Estelle Paultz—wrote to Orson Welles and the Mercury Theatre about the broadcast. Their letters were donated to the University of Michigan in 2005, and this book is the first to examine them.

Taken together, this extraordinary one-way correspondence—close to two thousand letters in all—presents a much fuller picture of the broadcast than has ever been published before. They capture the voices of men, women, and children from all walks of life and all but one of the forty-eight states, locked in time at that moment between economic collapse and world war, stamped onto foolscap by a typewriter or scrawled onto sheets of legal paper with a dull pencil. In letters dripping with invective or bubbling with praise, these listeners sent in newspaper clippings, wrote original poems, even drew cartoons. Frequently, they requested Welles's autograph. But above all, they wrote to take part in a national debate on the role of mass media in American life. They recognized that the radio, and the speed with which it transmitted information, presented great possibilities and even greater dangers to their society, and they revealed their anxieties about the power of the media in their letters. Although today we live in a world where information moves much faster than Americans in 1938 could possibly have imagined, these listeners' concerns about the radio are just as applicable to the Internet or social media in our own time.

In the 1930s, writing letters to broadcasters was common practice—as much a part of the radio experience as sending in box tops for a decoder ring. With few reliable means of judging the size and tastes of their listenership, broadcasters encouraged fan mail simply to find out who was listening.[22] But listeners wrote in for their own reasons—not just to give feedback or make suggestions, but to carry on an imaginary conversation begun over the airwaves.[23] "In a way," wrote the researcher Herta Herzog in 1941, "the radio seems to have taken the place of the neighbor."[24] Listeners treated the voices they welcomed into their homes each week as if they were friends, familiars, confessors. They were not afraid to share private, even embarrassing details in a letter to a celebrity who would probably never read it personally.[25] Frequently, listener letters betrayed opinions that their authors felt very keenly but would probably never have spoken aloud.[26] As one New Jersey woman explained to Orson Welles, "I am writing as a friend and hope you will regard me as such."[27]

The letters written to the Mercury and the FCC in the wake of *War of the Worlds* do provide evidence hinting at how many people were frightened, and how fear spread that night. But, more important, they also show how the country reacted to the *idea* that a radio show had supposedly panicked the nation. This, in some ways, was the real *War of the Worlds* panic: the fear the broadcast raised about the power of the media in American society. When combined with the newspapers, the Cantril study, and other firsthand accounts, these letters bring the night of October 30, 1938, and the days that followed—which decided the fate of Orson Welles and of American broadcasting itself—into focus for the first time.

War of the Worlds should not be defined by a single burst of blind, unreasoning panic. The broadcast caused a complex series of hysterias, ranging from hysterical praise to hysterical fury. The fear that saturates these letters is not of Martians, but of what damage the new instrument of radio might do to American democracy. For some, the stories of panic in the newspapers were proof that the nation was too stupid to survive the age of fascism. For others, a few loud calls for government censorship of radio suggested that the First Amendment, too, was under threat. These letters prove that the broadcast was, in the words of one letter written to the FCC, part of an ongoing "battle to control radio"—one that was also, fundamentally, a battle for America's future.[28]

When word got around that train car stuck somewhere in Connecticut that the invasion the Paultzes were fleeing was not real, the passengers dissolved into hilarity. Estelle went practically mad with relief. But she couldn't help noticing that one of the college students her husband had first talked to, a young man carrying "a book of Cervantes," wasn't sharing in the excitement.[29] In fact, he looked disappointed.

"Too bad really," he said with a shrug. "I'm almost sorry that it isn't true."[30] Evidently, he had enjoyed the thrill of imminent annihilation.

Before very long, the Paultzes also developed mixed feelings about their reprieve. When the train began to move again, they remembered they were on their way to Hartford "with fifty six cents between us—and *nothing* ahead!"[31] They asked the conductor for help, and were told there was nothing he could do. Around midnight, they got off the train in New Haven, where they had no friends or acquaintances. Each held a transfer that would only take them the rest of the way in the wrong direction. They didn't have nearly enough money for a train ticket home, or even for a place to stay in town. They were, to put it mildly, stuck.

Then the college students from the train stepped forward. "They had been going back to Yale," Estelle wrote, "and most gallantly offered to lend us the fare back to New York." The Paultzes gratefully accepted, though it is unclear how they could ever pay the students back. Perhaps they already had: they'd given the young men a wonderful story to tell and had broken, however briefly, the monotony of their existence. "And now," said the student who had been thrilled by it all, "back to the dull, the lifeless."[32] And he carried his Cervantes toward campus.

The next day, after she and her husband made it back to Manhattan, Estelle wrote a handwritten letter to Orson Welles. She strung together fifteen pages of breathless, loosely punctuated sentences describing what the broadcast had put her and her husband through. But she wasn't angry. If anything, she was appreciative.

"Now I write to you sir," she explained, "not bitterly, for you are doing a great work in breathing some life into the theatre and bringing it so close to home—but I thought perhaps you ought to know how well you've succeeded, and I hope that the next performance, and wish you many to come, will bring us great joy instead of great fear. Its [sic] easier on our minds and—pursestrings [sic]. We who spent our last dollar in tribute to the astounding performance of the Mercury Theatre of the Air. Salute!"[33]

1

"Journalism and Showmanship"

We have spent so much time in the past few weeks listening to "special dispatches from the Press Radio bureau" that it was a relief to hear a few of such bulletins over which one did not have to feel concern.

—Daniel C. Knickerbocker, Jr., of Syracuse, New York,
to Orson Welles, October 31, 1938[1]

With the household around him in chaos, Oliver Whateley picked up the phone and called the police in nearby Hopewell, New Jersey. "Colonel Lindbergh's son has been stolen," he said in his pronounced Scottish burr. "Will you please come at once?"[2]

It was the evening of March 1, 1932—five years after Whateley's employer, Charles Augustus Lindbergh, achieved international celebrity as the first man to fly solo across the Atlantic Ocean. Public fascination with the slim, handsome, and shy "Lone Eagle" had only continued to grow following his historic flight, as the decadence of the Roaring Twenties gave way to the despair of the early thirties. Lindbergh's quiet heroism and storybook family life gave Americans something to look up to as the world seemed to fall apart around them. Now the news that Lindbergh's twenty-month-old son had disappeared from his crib would shock a nation still suffering through the darkest days of the Great Depression.[3]

Within half an hour, newsrooms in three states had gotten word of the crime and begun frantically revising their front pages. A horde of reporters descended on Hopewell, and thousands of curiosity seekers soon followed, stampeding all over the Lindbergh estate and making a general mess of the crime scene. By the next day, when headlines nationwide screamed "LINDBERGH BABY KIDNAPPED," the daily routine of millions of Americans effectively ground to a halt.[4] "Did you ever see such a day?" wrote the prominent humorist and columnist Will Rogers a few days later. "Nobody don't feel like doing anything, taking any interest in anything. The attention of the world is on a little curly haired baby. Until he is found we can't get back to normal."[5]

Unable to focus on anything else, Americans hungered for news of the case. Newspapers, even though they printed countless extra editions, could never keep up. In one day alone, *The New York Times* answered over three thousand phone calls from people impatient for updates.[6] And so radio, a relatively untried news medium, stepped in to meet the demand. Station WOR, out of Newark, had broken the news first, with a bulletin at 11:35 p.m. on the night of the kidnapping. Meanwhile, CBS and NBC dispatched crews to New Jersey, setting up impromptu studios wherever they could—in a hotel room, above a store, even in a restaurant. Both networks broadcast virtually nonstop for the next 150 hours, passing every bit of news they received on to anxious and eager listeners.[7]

Broadcast journalism had been born twelve years earlier, in a hastily built shack atop a factory in East Pittsburgh, Pennsylvania. From that makeshift studio, station KDKA made history by reporting the results of the presidential election of 1920 as soon as they rolled off the news wires. But in the decade that followed, as the number of "radio homes" in the United States jumped from sixty thousand in 1921 to 16.7 million in 1930, broadcast news grew little beyond covering such special events.[8] The Lindbergh kidnapping saga marked the first period of extended news coverage in the medium's history, the moment when broadcast journalism came of age, and it changed forever the speed at which news traveled. But, as the historian Robert J. Brown has noted, listeners embraced radio news not just because it was fast, but because it was riveting. The powerful intimacy of radio, which broadcasters were just beginning to understand, conveyed the drama and emotion of the "crime of the century" in a way print media never could.[9] When, on May 12, 1932, police found the badly decomposed corpse of an infant and quickly identified it as the missing child, the entire nation mourned as one. Radio had helped create a collective loss of innocence; many would long remember exactly where they were and what they were doing when they learned that the Lindbergh baby was dead.[10]

This kind of shared national experience was an entirely new phenomenon. Never before in human history had such a great mass of people, spread over such a wide area, been able to follow events instantaneously. Radio allowed people to be both disparate and together, isolated yet involved; it helped foster a sense of national community at a time when economic and social turmoil threatened to tear the country apart.[11] And no one understood this power better, or harnessed it quite as well, as the newly elected President of the United States, Franklin Delano Roosevelt.[12]

When FDR took the oath of office on March 4, 1933, the American banking system had essentially collapsed. Thirty-eight states had temporarily closed some or all of their banks, forcing people to live off their pocket change or revert to the barter system as they waited to withdraw much-needed cash. Roosevelt had a plan to stabilize the financial system, but it had no chance of success if nothing was done to allay the nation's fears. So, on the night of March 12, he used the radio to make his case to the American people, reassuring sixty million listeners that their savings were indeed safe. In the first of what came to be known as his "fireside chats," the President explained, in simple and direct terms, why this crisis had occurred, how his administration planned to solve it, and what was required of the American people to make the plan work. Above all, he sought to dispel what he called "the phantom of fear," to prevent people from taking hasty or panicky action. "You people must have faith, you must not be stampeded by rumors or guesses," he said. "Let us unite in banishing fear."[13]

No president had ever spoken to the country like this, and the effects were immediate and unprecedented.[14] A flood of telegrams from grateful Americans overwhelmed the White House as soon as the speech ended. Thousands of appreciative letters soon followed, each testifying to renewed faith in the future.[15] Rather than rush to withdraw their savings first thing in the morning, people all over the country lined up to redeposit hoarded cash and gold. Within a month, $1.2 billion had returned to the banking system, and most of the shuttered banks successfully reopened. Roosevelt's address, and the cooperation of a nation, had staved off financial ruin. The radio had made it possible.[16]

Roosevelt's success on the radio is often ascribed to his plain and straightforward speaking style, and to the unique timbre of his voice, which carried well over the airwaves.[17] But that first fireside chat also showed his ability to capitalize on radio's immediacy, its "liveness," to spur listeners to action. In his speech, Roosevelt called directly on the American people to help pull themselves back from economic catastrophe. "We have provided the machinery to restore our financial system," he said; "it is up to you to support and make it work . . . Together we cannot fail."[18] Listeners responded to the urgency of his words because urgency is radio's defining characteristic. "What is heard on the air is transitory, as fleeting as time itself, and it therefore seems *real*," wrote the psychologists Hadley Cantril and Gordon Allport in 1935. By letting Americans hear history being made, radio came to represent the immediate present. Listeners learned to expect that what they heard over the loudspeaker was happening *now*, in the very moment of transmission. This quality of immediacy made momentous events seem even more pressing for radio listeners.[19]

Throughout that Depression decade, radio delivered news of tragedies and crises from every corner of the continent with ever-increasing speed and intensity. To read about a faraway disaster in a newspaper was, in some sense, to learn about it in safety, far removed from the actual experience of living through it. But the radio made each catastrophe intense and immediate. Listeners, notes Edward D. Miller, actually felt transported by the words of correspondents and commentators as they experienced these tragedies in real time.[20] Occasionally, the commentators themselves became a part of the story. In September 1934, when a devastating fire on the luxury liner SS *Morro Castle* killed 137 passengers and crew off the coast of New Jersey, radio broke the news first and covered the event throughout the day. As the announcer Tom Burley of WCAP in Asbury Park told his audience that the burned-out vessel was drifting toward shore, he looked out his window and saw the massive wreck sliding out of the mist. WCAP's studios sat right on the Jersey coast, and the *Morro Castle* was barreling straight toward his building. "My God," Burley blurted on the air. "She's coming in right here!"[21] The ship beached a few hundred yards from where he sat, and in the following days, scores of New Jerseyites came to view the wreck, many of them drawn by the radio.[22]

Other broadcasters stretched the medium's bounds far beyond New Jersey. Through transatlantic telephone wires and shortwave transmissions, radio regularly took Americans to Europe during one of the most tumultuous times in its history. H. V. Kaltenborn, the widely respected "dean of commentators" on CBS, recognized radio's ability to transport listeners and used it to educate his audience, whom he referred to as his "old traveling companions."[23] In mid-1936, Kaltenborn even let Americans listen in to the sounds of actual fighting during the Spanish Civil War, as he hid with a microphone in a haystack near the Battle of Irún.[24]

Two years later, when Hitler's Germany annexed Austria, commentators like William L. Shirer and Edward R. Murrow brought eyewitness accounts of the fascist advance straight into millions of American homes.[25]

All of a sudden, no crisis, disaster, or tragedy seemed truly remote anymore. Broadcast news kept Americans better informed about current events than they had ever been before, but it also kept the nation permanently on edge. "Instead of helping to relieve a disturbed people in time of war scares, floods, hurricanes, fires, etc., [radio] has taken the other side and for sensational 'scoops' kindled that fear with announcements breaking up programs," wrote one Connecticut man after the *War of the Worlds* broadcast. "Why, it is really sickening."[26] Americans wanted to believe that the Atlantic and Pacific could isolate them from any future European war, but radio demonstrated that the world was much smaller than they thought. The very instrument that many turned to for escape and entertainment also helped make a scary decade even scarier.

Yet listeners remained fascinated with the medium's ability to connect them with distant happenings. They saw radio not just as a constant stream of information and entertainment, but as a newfound link to the outside world. Although smaller stations often aired prerecorded music or programming, the networks rejected the practice, because it violated radio's immediacy. "Even though such transcriptions cannot be distinguished by the majority of people from real performances, listeners feel dissatisfied," wrote Cantril and Allport. "The thought of a whirling disk cannot create the sense of participation in actual events that is radio's chief psychological characteristic."[27] Or, as John Royal, vice president of NBC, put it in 1938, "The difference between a live program and a transcribed program is the difference between a pretty girl and her picture."[28]

For this reason, the major broadcast networks banned the use of prerecorded content in the 1930s. Everything listeners heard over NBC and CBS in that decade—every concert, every dramatic program, every comedy show—aired live, because of preference, not technical necessity.[29] The networks argued that the use of recordings in news broadcasts, even more than in musical or dramatic programming, was particularly deceptive—a "sort of hoax . . . on the listener"—because audiences had been trained to regard radio shows as live events.[30] By this logic, truth and liveness went hand in hand; one could not exist without the other. A recording, even of a real event, seemed less authentic to 1930s listeners than a live performance of a fictional program.

This posed a serious problem for broadcast journalists, since news rarely occurred within easy reach of a live microphone. Broadcasters often had to get creative in bringing news to their listeners with all the drama and immediacy that their medium allowed, without violating the ban on recordings. For example, when Bruno Richard Hauptmann went on trial for the Lindbergh kidnapping in early 1935, NBC re-enacted each day's testimony on air, with one announcer portraying the witness and the other the questioner. The judge had banned all microphones from his courtroom, so this was as close as listeners could get to "the trial of the century."[31]

One news event, more than any other, challenged the networks' stance on prerecorded content. On May 6, 1937, the German zeppelin LZ 129 *Hindenburg* completed the first transatlantic trip of its second flying season. It came in for a landing over the Naval Air Station in Lakehurst, New Jersey, just after 7:00 p.m., before a small crowd of reporters and photographers, as well as one radio correspondent.[32] Herbert Morrison and the sound engineer Charles Nehlsen had come all the way from Chicago to record the landing for station WLS. Because the program's sponsor, American Airlines, offered connecting flights to the *Hindenburg*, Morrison did his best to make the event sound exciting. He spoke of how tricky landing in the rain would be, and remarked on how the rays of the setting sun sparkled on the *Hindenburg*'s windows "like glittering jewels on a background of black velvet." But his tone betrayed the banality of the situation. Despite the rain, this was shaping up to be just another routine landing.[33]

Then a small jet of fire, shaped like a mushroom, burst from the top of the aircraft just ahead of its tail. In an instant, the highly flammable hydrogen keeping the ship aloft exploded, and the back half of the *Hindenburg* was ablaze. Fire consumed the entire ship in a mere thirty-four seconds. "It's burst into flame!" Morrison shouted into the mike before he was cut off—the shock wave from the explosion had knocked the needle off the recording disc. But Nehlsen replaced it quickly enough to capture Morrison's voice as it went rapidly from calm to panicked to racked with emotion.[34]

"Get this, Charlie!" Morrison screamed, forcing his way through the crowd to keep his eyes on the sinking dirigible. "It's crashing . . . it's crashing terrible! Oh, my! Get out of the way, please! It's burning, bursting into flames and—and it's falling on the mooring mast and all the folks between it. This is terrible, this is one of the worst catastrophes in the world . . . It's a terrific crash, ladies and gentlemen. It's smoke and it's flames now. And the frame is crashing to the ground, not quite to the mooring mast. Oh, the humanity, and all the passengers . . . I can't talk, ladies and gentlemen. Honest, it's just laying there, a mass of smoking wreckage . . . I'm going to step inside where I cannot see it. Charlie, that's terrible . . . Listen, folks, I'm gonna have to stop for a minute because I've lost my voice. This is the worst thing I've ever witnessed."[35]

After composing himself, Morrison continued to describe the scene and to interview survivors, stopping frequently to help people get away from the burning wreck. All the while, he kept addressing the audience as if he were broadcasting live, even though no one would hear the record for hours. Word of the disaster first reached radio audiences in New York about eight minutes after the explosion, with a news flash over station WHN. NBC interrupted programming nationwide with an announcement about fifteen minutes later.[36] Meanwhile, Morrison and Nehlsen rushed back to Chicago. Their forty-minute recording of the disaster and its aftermath first aired over WLS at 11:45 a.m. on the day after the explosion.[37]

Despite the newsworthiness of Morrison's recording, the major networks hesitated to put it on the air. They still regarded prerecorded content as inauthentic and potentially deceptive, likely to mislead the audience into thinking they were listening to a live event. But NBC eventually aired an edited version, coast to coast, four hours after it had aired over WLS, breaking their own ban on recordings for the first time. Other stations soon followed suit.[38] Each made sure to state carefully that they were about to air a recording and not a live report. But the piece was so vivid that many listeners still believed they were hearing the event as it happened.[39] The networks' concerns about the use of recordings had, in a sense, been validated.

However, many Americans had already listened in on the *Hindenburg* explosion hours before Morrison's recording first aired. The networks had another way of making past events seem immediate, a technique widely praised and immensely popular—yet, in many respects, infinitely more deceptive than just playing recordings. The historian Erik Barnouw has noted that, in more recent years, this method would probably be considered criminal, an early version of identity theft.[40] But in the 1930s, it was perfectly acceptable for radio stations to restage news events in a studio, complete with actors and sound effects, and broadcast them for later audiences, as long as the re-creation aired live. Broadcasters justified the practice by clearly stating that these were re-enactments, not recordings, and listeners embraced it as an entertaining way of reporting the news without breaking their connection to live events. The show that pioneered this technique was called *The March of Time*, and by 1937 it was probably the most popular news program on the air.[41]

Listeners tuned in to CBS just two hours after the *Hindenburg* explosion would have heard an in-depth report on the tragedy from *The March of Time*. After giving a brief history of the zeppelin's development, the show let listeners hear the terrible explosion itself, complete with the sounds of "frenzied cries, crackling flames, and crumpling girders." None of those noises were real. With scant information to work from, *The March of Time*'s writers and technicians had thrown together a re-creation of what they thought the event had sounded like, long before anyone had heard Herbert Morrison's recording.[42] But it would have been difficult for 1930s audiences to tell the difference between the recording and the re-creation. Although broadcasters clearly labeled both for what they were, their incredible realism made at least some listeners think of each as a live event. They seemed more real than reality itself.

This "new kind of reporting the news," as the first episode of *The March of Time* proclaimed itself, almost didn't get off the ground.[43] It began in 1931 as an advertising campaign for the young *Time* magazine, the brainchild of Roy Edward Larsen, general manager of *Time*, and the Ohio broadcaster Fred Smith. They felt that bringing the stories in a current issue of *Time* to vivid life on the air, using the techniques of radio drama, would greatly increase the magazine's circulation.[44] But Larsen worried about impersonating real people, because he knew that many listeners would believe the impersonations were real. Smith replied that they would take pains to portray the characters as accurately as any "serious" news show ever could. "How could the newsmakers object," wrote the radio historian John Dunning, "unless they objected to what they themselves had said?"[45]

Larsen pitched the concept to Time Inc. founder Henry Luce as a combination of "journalism and *showmanship*," but Luce did not care for it.[46] As the film scholar Raymond Fielding has noted, the two men had fundamentally different philosophies about the news business. "To Luce, journalism is a crusade," wrote one colleague in 1937, "to Larsen a game."[47] But Larsen's enthusiasm and cajoling eventually won out. Luce agreed to fund first a pilot episode and then a thirteen-week season on CBS. Because Larsen used only top radio talent—the best announcer, the best director, and the very best actors he could find, not to mention a full orchestra—the show proved exorbitantly expensive, costing about six thousand dollars per episode, equivalent to over ninety-four thousand dollars today. Luce strongly doubted that The March of Time, as it soon came to be known, would be worth it.[48]

The first episode of The March of Time—which brought listeners impressions of such figures as Mahatma Gandhi and Chicago mayor "Big Bill" Thompson, among many others—established the format that the show would follow for almost a decade.[49] Each script was based on the current issue of Time, expanding news items in the magazine into half a dozen dramatic scenes. The writers straddled the line between journalist and dramatist, drawing facts from the magazine as it was being put together. If the outcome of a story was uncertain, they wrote different versions and chose which one to air at the last minute. Although they used actual quotations where available, the format of the show required them to make up most of the dialogue. They wrote lines that fit the facts as they understood them, but which the people portrayed on the show had never actually said.[50] When this technique was later applied to a film series, also called The March of Time, Luce described it as "fakery in allegiance to the truth."[51] Much the same could be said of the radio show. It may not have been fake news, but it was certainly faking the news.

Tying these disparate scenes together was the booming, disembodied voice of a narrator, dubbed "the Voice of Time" and portrayed variously by Ted Husing, Harry Von Zell, and Cornelius Westbrook Van Voorhis. He commented on the action with godlike omniscience, and his shouted catchphrase, "Time . . . marches on!," cued the transitions from scene to scene. In effect, the Voice of Time embodied radio's power to transport listeners through space. At his command, the show whisked audiences across great distances as orchestral music blared.[52] This effect lent the fictionalized scenes another layer of credibility. "In annihilating auditory distance," wrote Cantril and Allport of The March of Time, "the radio has to some extent destroyed for the listener his capacity to distinguish between real and imaginary events."[53]

The Voice of Time also supplied the show's only commercials, brief statements at the beginning and end of each broadcast that extolled the virtues of *Time*. He read them in the same imperious tone as the rest of the narration, so they did not seem like ads. Instead, they helped enhance a false sense of the show's journalistic authority.[54] "A thousand new details, new facts in the world's history, come into being every hour . . . ," said the Voice of Time at the outset of that inaugural broadcast. "From every corner of the world come new facts about politics, and science, people, crime and religion, art and economics. There is one publication which watches, analyzes and every seven days reports the march of human history on all its fronts. It is the weekly newsmagazine—*Time*."[55]

Audiences responded well to the first episode—the book publisher John Farrar wrote to *Time* that the show was so powerful it almost brought him to tears—and the series built a following over its first thirteen-week season.[56] Listeners loved the fly-on-the-wall perspective it gave them on current events. Its producers (an advertising agency) built a sense of journalistic objectivity by never editorializing, and maintaining what *Radio Guide* later called "a positive mania for accuracy."[57] As its first season came to a close, a poll of radio critics found *The March of Time* to be the third-most-admired drama on the air, behind two different series based on the Sherlock Holmes stories.[58] But, despite all this goodwill, the show was still wildly expensive. All told, the season cost Time Inc. $211,000, the equivalent of over $3.3 million today—much more than Luce thought advertising was worth in those Depression days. And so, in early 1932, Luce announced that *The March of Time* would not be renewed for a second season.[59]

Over twenty-two thousand listeners wrote to *Time* in hopes of saving the show. The magazine printed several of their letters in a two-page spread that February. More than one listener pledged to let his or her radio be repossessed if *The March of Time* did not return. Another threatened simply to throw his out the window. People described the show as a public good, saying that it did much to keep Americans informed. "I realize that TIME, itself, may well dispense with this feature as an advertisement," wrote one listener from Astoria, New York, "but your radio audience can ill afford to lose such a pleasure and such a delightful source of information as to what is going on in the world." Time Inc. replied that they were not about to spend money on advertising that did not work, simply for the sake of educating the public. They asked their readers: "As an army marches on its stomach, so under existing circumstances a radio program can keep marching only on somebody's dollars. Whose?"[60]

Funding for radio programs, *Time*'s editors well knew, was a controversial subject in the early 1930s. Unlike in most European countries, broadcasting in the United States was run as a business, paid for by advertising. Broadcasters carved up the day into the now familiar system of hours and half-hours, creating standard units of time that could be sold to sponsors. Those sponsors, in turn, sought programs that appealed to as broad an audience as possible, in order to get their ads before the maximum number of potential customers. This meant that the prime-time hours, when most people listened to the radio, were dominated by light entertainments: musical programs, variety shows, and stories of drama or comedy, each liberally sprinkled with commercials.[61] Many people at the time saw this as a betrayal of radio's promise, its ability to enlighten and inform the public on a heretofore unimagined scale. The airwaves were held to be public property, licensed to station owners for a limited time. Broadcasters were expected to serve "the public interest," not just sell soap and cigarettes. As late as 1934, Congress seriously considered setting aside a quarter of all broadcast frequencies for noncommercial, educational use, though the proposal failed to make it out of the Senate.[62]

To placate these reformers, American broadcasters aired a considerable amount of unsponsored programming at their own expense. Referred to as "sustaining shows," these included symphonic concerts, lengthy discussions of major national issues, and experimental dramas. As the broadcasting historian David Goodman has noted, the major networks essentially bent over backward to avoid a government cleanup of their industry by airing so much civic, educational, and high cultural programming.[63] In the mid-1930s, stations typically gave between 60 and 90 percent of each broadcast day over to sustaining shows. But these were often the hours that could not be sold to advertisers anyway, such as those in the middle of the day or opposite a particularly popular program on another station, when few people would be listening. Most Americans still found their time with the radio constantly interrupted by ads for products like Jell-O and Pennsylvania Blue Coal.[64]

Officially, *The March of Time* was just another paid advertisement, the exact opposite of a sustaining show. But *Time*'s editors cast it as a public service. In an editorial, they echoed the arguments of radio reformers in criticizing what advertising had done to broadcasting. "For all its blatant claim to being a medium of education," they wrote, "[r]adio contributes little of its own beyond the considerable service of bringing good music to millions." They implied that CBS itself should pay for any further episodes of *The March of Time*, the better to serve the public interest.[65] And, after some behind-the-scenes negotiations, CBS did just that, reviving *The March of Time* in 1932 as a sustaining show.[66] The network stopped footing the bill after that year's presidential election, but other corporations soon stepped in to fill the void. Electrolux, Wrigley's Chewing Gum, and other advertisers kept *The March of Time* on the air until 1939 by essentially paying for Time Inc.'s commercials.[67] The show that blurred the line between news and entertainment, between fact and fiction, like none other on the airwaves, also managed to turn advertising into education.

Listeners, however, did not think of *The March of Time* as an advertisement, or even as a radio drama. They considered it a news program and trusted it as such. The show introduced many Americans to the most important figures of their day, from Winston Churchill to Joseph Goebbels, Haile Selassie to William Randolph Hearst—even if the voices were all fake.[68] But the impressions were uncanny, and easily mistaken for the real thing. The son of the King of Spain, for one, could not distinguish his father's voice from his *March of Time* impersonator. The show attracted the best actors in radio—notably Agnes Moorehead, who frequently portrayed Eleanor Roosevelt—and required them to research their subjects extensively until their impressions were exact. When prominent people died, even controversial ones like Bruno Hauptmann or Senator Huey Long, their doppelgängers on *The March of Time* often felt a unique sense of loss.[69]

The most popular impersonation by far, and perhaps the most exact, was a voice that Americans already knew very well: Franklin Delano Roosevelt's. As with the other impressions, many listeners assumed that the show somehow used the President's real voice. "Why don't you tell us when you are using a record?" one *March of Time* listener complained in 1932. "Everyone knows that was a gramophone record of Mr. Roosevelt you put on last night." *Time*'s editors always made clear that Roosevelt's voice, recorded or otherwise, never appeared on their show.[70] But many still believed that they regularly heard the President on *The March of Time*, and this became a matter of concern for the Roosevelt administration. FDR's voice was a powerful instrument, with the proven ability to calm a nation. Roosevelt worried that by constantly counterfeiting it *The March of Time* would dilute some of its power.[71]

Soon after Roosevelt's inauguration, the White House asked *The March of Time* to stop impersonating the President. After some hesitation, they complied, announcing that they would remove FDR from their cast of characters in early 1934.[72] More letters from dismayed listeners poured into their offices, asking both *The March of Time* and the President himself to change their minds. "Much as Mr. Roosevelt uses the radio, we still have little opportunity to hear from his own lips the living drama of the New Deal," wrote one Californian. "'The March of TIME' supplied the missing links. True, the Voice issued from the lips of an actor, but verisimilitude gave life to the conned lines."[73]

The loss of Roosevelt's voice did nothing to hurt *The March of Time*'s popularity. It remained beloved by listeners and critics, and its style of "fakery in allegiance to the truth" was widely influential.[74] Many smaller stations used the *March of Time* technique to dramatize local news stories. Detroit's WJR, for example, aired a *March of Time* clone called *News Comes to Life* that restaged news events just like its predecessor.[75] A poll conducted in 1939 found that the vast majority of radio listeners (95 percent) liked *The March of Time*'s style of "dramatized news" better than regular news reportage, and this should not be surprising.[76] Unlike straight news commentary, which was allowed to be dry, *The March of Time*'s primary goal was to entertain. And, of course, to sell magazines.

Throughout its run, *The March of Time* caused occasional misunderstandings and even serious confusion. The most notable incident occurred in 1937, when a Hawaiian radioman picked up an episode about the search for Amelia Earhart and took it for a transmission from the missing aviator.[77] But more dangerous, perhaps, was the way it turned current events into a kind of theater, by focusing on personalities rather than hard facts. This effect soon found its way into the political sphere. During the presidential election of 1936, the Republican National Committee produced their own *March of Time*-style program, titled *Liberty at the Crossroads*, dramatizing what they considered the negative consequences of the New Deal. Like *The March of Time*, it used an omniscient narrator—not the Voice of Time but "the Voice of Doom"—to warn Americans about the growing national debt. That same year, Michigan senator Arthur Vandenberg produced his own news "dramatization" called *A Fireside Mystery Chat.* It used clips from Roosevelt's speeches, taken out of context, to stage a mock debate with the President. CBS aired the show with reservations, only to cut Vandenberg off halfway through—because, they claimed, he had violated their ban on the use of recordings.[78] One wonders if he could have stayed on the air by employing an actor, and not the President's actual voice. Both shows foreshadowed the negative campaigning and theatricality that would define elections in the television era, and they show the clear influence of "fakery in allegiance to the truth."

The March of Time has a complicated legacy. Broadcasting historians often praise its artistry and ingenuity, and justifiably argue that it did much to get Americans interested in current events.[79] But it also mingled fact and fiction in a dangerous way, confusing public service with naked commercialism. Its fusion of news, entertainment, and advertising set the stage for other programs, less interested in accuracy or fair play, that were to follow.[80] Much of twenty-first-century news coverage owes more, perhaps, to Larsen's vision of "journalism and *showmanship*" than to the hard news coverage of H. V. Kaltenborn and Edward R. Murrow. And *War of the Worlds* owes *The March of Time* an even greater debt.

"*We take you now to Nuremberg, Germany . . .*"[81] For Americans listening to CBS at 2:15 p.m., Eastern Time, on September 12, 1938, so began eighteen days of anxiety as Europe teetered on the brink of war. Listeners heard Adolf Hitler demand that the Sudetenland, the German-speaking region of Czechoslovakia, be ceded to Germany immediately. If the Czechs refused to give it up, Hitler made clear that the Nazis would take it by force. Thanks to a quick translation from CBS, Americans knew that this territorial dispute thousands of miles away could, in the very near future, throw the world into another total war. Suddenly the "jitters" felt in England, France, and Czechoslovakia were felt just as strongly in the United States.[82]

In the following weeks, American radio networks routinely interrupted their regularly scheduled programming to deliver late-breaking news bulletins.[83] By the end of the crisis, rarely an hour went by on CBS without some kind of news report.[84] Listeners got used to hearing these interruptions, and to trusting them implicitly, because events were moving so fast that only the radio could keep up. "In the minds of the masses of

American people radio has grown to occupy a supreme place as the disseminator of accurate, unbiased, last minute news . . . ," wrote a Maine woman to the FCC after *War of the Worlds*. "During the recent war scare especially we came to depend on our radio . . . to interrupt regular programs for the most recent news." A few weeks later, when this listener and many others tuned in to what sounded like authentic news reports of an armed invasion of the East Coast, there was little reason to doubt them.[85]

Nine days after Hitler's ultimatum to the Czechs, another event paved the way for *War of the Worlds*. On September 21, 1938, one of the most devastating hurricanes in recorded history slammed without warning into New England. Whole seaside communities were swept away, and the topography of some areas was virtually rewritten. The "Great Hurricane of 1938," as it came to be called, left about seven hundred people dead and another sixty-three thousand homeless. It remains the deadliest storm ever to strike New England, because it caught the region entirely off guard.[86] Residents were left in a state of shock, reeling at the thought that such destruction could come so completely out of nowhere. Some who tuned in late to *War of the Worlds*, just over a month later, were ready to believe in yet another unexpected catastrophe. "The people of New England have just gone through a flood and hurricane and were particularly susceptible to this program . . . ," wrote a New Hampshire man to the FCC. "The flood and disaster [were] a fine example of radios [*sic*] ability to help in an emergency but after last night the people have lost faith, I believe."[87]

Yet so caught up was the rest of the country with developments in Europe that the Great Hurricane was largely ignored outside of New England.[88] On September 29, the four powers reached a deal. In exchange for peace, they gave in to Hitler's demands.[89] British prime minister Neville Chamberlain called the deal "peace with honor . . . peace in our time."[90] American broadcasters were also celebrating. Thanks to their coverage of the Czech crisis, radio listenership jumped almost 40 percent, and sales of radio sets increased dramatically.[91] No network benefitted more from the public's sudden taste for news broadcasting than CBS. The insightful commentary of H. V. Kaltenborn and others had turned it into America's most trusted source of news.[92]

On September 30, CBS broadcast a special announcement to acknowledge the work of their news staff, and to thank audiences for tuning in so frequently. The announcer said they had "received thousands and thousands of letters, [and] hundreds and hundreds of telegrams," praising their coverage. The statement closed with CBS's heartfelt promise to "continue to treat news of extreme importance in just this way, or, we hope, an even better way, because of the experience we have gained, and the heartening support *you* have given us."[93]

Exactly one month later, the work of a twenty-three-year-old actor/director would make many Americans strongly reconsider the faith they placed in CBS. That artist had gotten his big break in radio on *The March of Time*, and his name, as he so frequently reminded audiences, was Orson Welles.

2

Winged Mercury

Any man who can produce and act so well at twenty three should feel proud of himself . . . I think you are a wonder.

—Eleanor B. Craig of New York City
to Orson Welles, November 1, 1938[1]

It all began with that voice—deep, resonant, and powerful, booming off the walls of New York's Martin Beck Theatre in late December 1934. In the audience that night, for a road company production of *Romeo and Juliet*, sat a fledgling theatrical producer named John Houseman. Little from the show, not Katharine Cornell's Juliet or even Basil Rathbone's Romeo, left much of an impression on Houseman. But he was struck by the incongruity of that voice, erupting from an ungainly teenager who stormed about the stage in the role of Tybalt. Houseman sat entranced by this "monstrous boy," as he described him in his memoirs, with his baby face, flatfooted walk, and the voice that spoke, to Houseman, of some raging inner fire. When he went backstage to congratulate the cast, Houseman looked in vain for the young Tybalt and never found him. For the next few days, he could think of little else.[2]

Born Jacques Haussman in 1902, Houseman was thirty-two, with an urbane English accent that belied his Romanian birth and polyglot parentage. He had come to the United States as a successful grain merchant, only to lose his business in the stock market crash of 1929. Without a valid work visa or any money in the bank, he had turned that failure into an opportunity, remaining in the United States illegally to pursue his lifelong love of the arts. By 1934, he had written a few plays, worked in Hollywood, and earned some recognition in New York for producing Gertrude Stein and Virgil Thomson's *Four Saints in Three Acts* with an all-black cast. But his career had not taken off with the velocity that

Houseman, always a roiling mixture of ambition and self-doubt, would have liked. By that night in the Martin Beck Theatre, he felt his days in the arts were coming to an end. "Against all reason I continued to cherish the conviction that once again, any day now, some golden opportunity would present itself," Houseman later wrote, "and that I must be alert and resourceful enough to grasp it when it appeared." When it did, Houseman fixated on the young actor with what he later described as an almost romantic infatuation.[3]

At only nineteen, George Orson Welles was thirteen years Houseman's junior—reckless, undisciplined, and still very much an adolescent. The son of an alcoholic inventor and a passionately political musician, both of whom died before his sixteenth birthday, Welles had been acting since he was three.[4] From the earliest, he displayed a remarkable gift for the spoken word; he talked like an adult from almost the moment he could speak.[5] The family doctor, Maurice Bernstein, later recalled that at eighteen months Orson introduced himself with the words: "The desire to take medicine is one of the greatest features which distinguishes men from animals."[6] Like many stories from Welles's life, this one may or may not be true (and probably is not). But it reflects the astounding verbal precocity that, as Welles's biographer Simon Callow has noted, far outstripped the child's other natural abilities.[7] Whether or not he was really a born genius, Welles sounded like one. And Bernstein, who became Welles's guardian after his parents' death, did much to make reports of his brilliance a self-fulfilling prophecy.

At the Todd School for Boys in Woodstock, Illinois, Welles enjoyed a period of profound creative exploration under the guidance of the headmaster, Roger "Skipper" Hill. With Hill's blessing, Welles essentially commandeered the school's drama department, putting on his own productions of classic plays—including some, like Marlowe's *Doctor Faustus* and Shakespeare's *Julius Caesar*, that would later make him famous on the New York stage.[8] When he was thirteen years old, Welles even wrote his first radio drama for Todd's own radio station, based on the Sherlock Holmes stories.[9] Upon graduation at age sixteen, Welles fled the prospect of a college education by traveling to Ireland. Broke and very far from home, he wound up outside the Gate Theatre in Dublin and demanded an audition, claiming to be a famous stage actor from New York. That afternoon, he won a debut role that, one Irish critic wrote, "might have been written for him."[10]

After failing to find acting work in London and New York, Welles returned to Woodstock. He got his second chance at the stage in the spring of 1933, after meeting the author Thornton Wilder at a Chicago cocktail party. Wilder knew of Welles's work in Dublin and helped arrange an audition with Katharine Cornell's traveling company. Welles spent two seasons with them, pausing in between to produce a drama festival at Todd in the summer of 1934. There he made his first film, a grotesque little short called *The Hearts of Age*, and met his first wife, the young actress Virginia Nicolson. But by the time Houseman saw him as Tybalt, Welles's career had hit a lull. He had grown tired of the Cornell company, and his offstage antics during their first season—drinking, carousing, being late for call—had gotten him demoted from Mercutio to Tybalt for this, his Broadway debut.[11] Welles did not know it yet, but he was in dire need of the change that Houseman was about to supply.

It took Houseman three weeks to come up with a reason to approach Welles, and the one he found was something of a stretch. He had become attached as producer to a verse play titled *Panic*, by the poet Archibald MacLeish. It told of an arrogant, fifty-something tycoon named McGafferty, who met his downfall in the 1933 banking crisis. Welles was not yet twenty, but Houseman felt passionately that he would be perfect in the lead, and Welles jumped at the chance. Then they had to convince the playwright, who was frankly unimpressed by the teenage Welles. But all that changed when MacLeish heard that voice—"an instrument," Houseman wrote in his memoirs, "of pathos and terror, of infinite delicacy and brutally devastating power." MacLeish agreed; they had their McGafferty.[12]

Houseman mounted an impressive production, and Welles turned in an impassioned performance. But, overall, *Panic* was met with indifference. It ran for only three nights, and the reviews were somewhat tepid. As Houseman later realized, neither theatergoers nor critics were eager to revisit the dark days of the recent past.[13] But in order to get at least a fraction of their work before a larger audience, Houseman arranged for an extract from *Panic* to air on *The March of Time* on March 22, 1935, a week after the play closed. Since MacLeish edited *Time*'s sister magazine, *Fortune*, this would not have been a hard sell: *Panic* gave Time Inc. another chance to promote itself. But Welles was the real beneficiary. Though he had done some radio work before, he had never appeared on such a popular program as *The March of Time*.[14]

In rehearsal, Welles volunteered to take on an additional role that none of the show's impressionists could quite perfect: the "Baby Jabber" of five infants. That night, his voice made its *March of Time* debut, rapidly switching gears from the imperial tones of McGafferty to the meek babbling of babies, live on the air.[15] The show's producers were impressed, and they remembered his versatility. A year later, when they needed a voice for the munitions magnate Sir Basil Zaharoff, they brought Welles back in for an audition. He won both the part and a regular role in the series. And that episode—an obituary, describing how the once mighty Zaharoff had been reduced to a weak and wizened old man—later served as an inspiration for *Citizen Kane*.[16]

Welles loved doing *The March of Time*, delighting at the license it gave him to impersonate everyone from Fiorello La Guardia to Sigmund Freud.[17] He benefitted tremendously from the show as well, because it introduced him to the world of radio acting, where a voice like his could make a lot of money very quickly. At a time when much of the country was out of work, Welles earned between a thousand and fifteen hundred dollars a week by crisscrossing New York, from recording studio to recording studio, every day. He appeared on any show that would take him and usually went on air without rehearsal.[18] Like all successful radio actors, he had a knack for sight-reading and a willingness to work without credit, but that impossibly rich voice made him unique.[19] And as he worked, he learned everything he could about the medium, waiting for a chance to bring his own ideas to bear as its premier actor/director.

Compared with Welles's later, legendary productions, the three-night run of *Panic* seems a relatively minor event. But it was a crucial moment in his career. Its title was particularly appropriate, because *Panic* brought Welles to the radio and introduced him to three of the vital elements that would shape *War of the Worlds*: Houseman, MacLeish, and *The March of Time*.

Welles and Houseman could not have picked a better time to take New York's theater world by storm. With funding from Congress, the Works Progress Administration had just enacted a series of public-works projects, along with a smaller assortment of artistic endeavors. These arts programs—such as classical concerts put on by the Federal Music Project, or the testimony of former slaves recorded by the Federal Writers'

Project—took up a minuscule fraction of the WPA's budget, but they profoundly enriched American culture, both in the 1930s and for future generations. And no WPA unit got more attention, or garnered more controversy, than the Federal Theatre Project, thanks in large part to the work of its director, Hallie Flanagan.[20]

Depending on one's politics, Flanagan was either a visionary or a radical. She seized on the Federal Theatre Project as an opportunity to enlighten and challenge Americans, exposing them to ideas they would never encounter on the radio or in the movies. Typical of her approach were a series of "Living Newspapers," plays that dramatized current events with documentary realism, somewhat like The March of Time. The first, about the Italian invasion of Ethiopia, actually had to be scrapped after the White House refused permission to quote the President's speeches. But, unlike the radio series, these living newspapers focused exclusively on controversial subjects and encouraged audiences to take action. For conservatives, they were nothing less than left-wing agitprop. Critics of the New Deal used them to paint the Federal Theatre as a dangerous hotbed of radicalism. But, as the journalist Michael Hiltzik has noted, the project was less interested in politics than in diversity—both diversity of ideas and diversity of performers. And this was especially true in perhaps its most ambitious arm: the Negro Theatre Project.[21]

In sixteen American cities, the Federal Theatre established "Negro Units" for African American actors and stagehands. The New York unit was located in Harlem, and to run it Flanagan tapped Rose McClendon, a well-known black actress, and John Houseman, both of whom had worked on Panic. Houseman's main qualification was his earlier production of Four Saints in Three Acts, which had featured African American actors without condescension or reference to their race, and he planned something similar for the Negro Theatre. One wing would produce contemporary plays about the African American experience, written and performed by blacks, while another would put on classic works without acknowledging the actors' race. And Houseman had just the man in mind to direct the first of the Negro Theatre's classic plays: Orson Welles.[22]

They were not exactly the kind of men the WPA was meant to help. Welles was making money hand over fist in radio, and Houseman was an illegal alien living under an assumed name. But the WPA arts programs were allowed to hire some talent not in need of federal relief, in order to produce work that people would want to see. In that respect Welles and

Houseman were perfect for the project, because they could certainly create attention-grabbing theater. For Welles, it was a heaven-sent opportunity to direct his first play on the New York stage, and he immediately brought Houseman an exciting idea supplied by his wife, Virginia. They would do Shakespeare's *Macbeth* in Haiti, replacing the witches' black magic with voodoo. Instead of ignoring the actors' race, as Houseman had originally intended, Welles would foreground it. But Houseman raised no objection, and Welles set about transforming Harlem's Lafayette Theatre into an eerie Haitian jungle.[23]

The riskiness of this endeavor cannot be overemphasized. Welles was only twenty years old, and his directorial résumé consisted mainly of a few productions at the Todd School in Woodstock, Illinois. Yet suddenly he was leading a cast of dozens, most of whom were not professional actors and a few of whom could barely read, through one of Shakespeare's more difficult plays. All the while, he kept taking every radio job he could find, routinely working at least eighteen hours a day. Because of Welles's radio schedule, rehearsals for *Macbeth* always began after midnight and ran until dawn. The brusque and imperious manner Welles adopted, to compensate for his youth and inexperience, threatened at times to spur the cast to mutiny. And, to make matters worse, the play itself was at the center of a political firestorm. Before its premiere, many in Harlem assumed that the "Voodoo *Macbeth*" was meant as a deliberate insult to the African American community. Four Harlemites even attacked Welles one night outside the Lafayette.[24]

But, as later productions would prove, these were the conditions that brought out the best in Welles. Life at the edge of collapse thrilled him, and fueled his most memorable art. By opening night, April 14, 1936, Houseman's publicity had built up fervent anticipation throughout Harlem. A throng of ten thousand people clogged the streets around the theater for hours, and the play itself did not disappoint. Welles had drawn remarkable performances from his actors, professionals and newcomers alike, and the stagecraft, as in most of his productions, was exceptional.[25] No one had ever done Shakespeare like this, and although the reviews were tempered with a fair amount of racism, they were almost unanimous in praising the young director.[26] The next month, Orson Welles turned twenty-one.

Houseman knew the Negro Theatre could not hold on to Welles for long—his star was rising too fast. Since Houseman did not want to lose him, he convinced Flanagan to give Welles his own theatrical unit under the WPA aegis, devoted to modern productions of classic plays. And, with a twinge of guilt but not much regret, Houseman left the Negro Theatre so he could run it.[27] In Project 891, as it came to be called, Welles and Houseman produced some of the Federal Theatre's most innovative, arresting, and varied plays, from the zany farce *Horse Eats Hat* to Christopher Marlowe's *Tragical History of Doctor Faustus*. The latter was a particular triumph for Welles. With a ruthless editorial eye and liberal use of magic tricks, he turned the Elizabethan tragedy into a ninety-minute shocker that played to packed houses for months. Props flew across the stage, and actors disappeared before the audience's very eyes, thanks to clever applications of black velvet and lighting effects.[28] As Welles told a reporter at the time, his goal was "to create on modern spectators an effect corresponding to the effect in 1589 when the play was new. We want to rouse the same magical feeling, but we use modern methods."[29] That was the secret to Welles's early success—his talent for infusing classics with showmanship—and he brought much the same technique to radio.

In fact, Welles could not have done *Faustus*, or any of his early plays, without the radio. Although the government bankrolled Project 891, there was never enough money for the scenery and effects Welles wanted. So he acted regularly on the radio just to pour his considerable earnings into his stage productions.[30] To get from theater to recording studio and back as fast as possible, he began hiring an ambulance to speed him through traffic, claiming there was no law reserving ambulances for the sick.[31] Each night, before the curtain rose on *Faustus* at nine, he would dash across town for a radio broadcast at eight, perform before the microphone in full stage makeup, and then return to the Maxine Elliott Theatre just as the play got under way. Once the play was over, he later claimed, he then had to rush back to the studio to perform the radio show again for West Coast audiences.[32]

Around this time, Welles accepted the lead in a new pulp adventure series called *The Shadow*. He played Lamont Cranston, a suave playboy with the unique ability to "cloud men's minds" and render himself invisible. As the unseen crime-fighter the Shadow, Cranston solved mysteries alongside the plucky socialite Margot Lane.[33] Welles took the part purely for a paycheck, and he found the show enjoyable if hokey.[34] But *The Shadow* became a breakout hit, making Welles's voice famous, coast to coast. Although he wasn't credited on air until his last appearance in the role, Welles became indelibly linked with the character in the public mind.[35] Only after *War of the Worlds*, one Pennsylvania listener wrote, had he "successfully lived down the 'Shadow.'"[36]

Radio acting came easily to Welles.[37] As his collaborator William Alland later put it, these were jobs "that he blew through his nose."[38] But Welles's interest in the medium extended far beyond the financial. He learned much about the form in these early gigs, and benefitted greatly from working with its best practitioners on radio's premier artistic series: *The Columbia Workshop*. This was one of radio's unsponsored "sustaining shows," meant to earn CBS prestige where it could not sell advertising time. The network had given the director, Irving Reis, a worthless time slot against a popular variety show on NBC starring Jack Benny, and Reis devoted each hour to artistic experiment. Because ratings were not an issue, *The Columbia Workshop* could try anything, whether or not it worked—including letting a twenty-one-year-old actor adapt Shakespeare for the ether. It proved to be one of their more successful experiments.[39]

Welles's *Columbia Workshop* adaptations of *Hamlet* and *Macbeth* were his first professional radio productions. They also introduced him to the young composer Bernard Herrmann, then working on CBS's music staff, who factored heavily in his later career.[40] The two geniuses clashed almost immediately; Herrmann was notoriously prickly, and Welles threw out his carefully prepared score for *Macbeth* at the last moment. But despite their mutual resolve never to collaborate again, Herrmann would return for Welles's own radio series and later prove a crucial contributor to *War of the Worlds*.[41]

The Columbia Workshop also paved the way for *War of the Worlds* by reuniting Welles with Archibald MacLeish for *The Fall of the City*—a verse play in the form of a fake news broadcast. It told an allegory about a mythical metropolis, seemingly both ancient and modern, menaced by an approaching conqueror. The citizens decide to surrender to the invader, who turns out to be an empty suit of armor. Just like that of real fascist dictators, his authority is hollow. The message was powerful and timely—a parable about the collapse of free societies into fascism—and it resonated with audiences when *The Fall of the City* aired on April 11, 1937. Many critics hailed it as the first great work of radio art.[42]

Remembering Houseman's production of *Panic* two years earlier, MacLeish had written the lead expressly for Orson Welles.[43] Welles played an unnamed narrator who described and interpreted events like a news-caster, using words and phrases familiar from news broadcasts.[44] Radio writers had long avoided using such narrators, believing that they took audiences out of the play.[45] But MacLeish recognized that using the format and language of a news broadcast would make his allegory seem chillingly real for 1930s listeners, and the effect worked. Welles must have paid close attention: the following year, he built his own radio series around the same kind of "first person" narrative voice. He also drew heavily upon MacLeish's fake news style in making *War of the Worlds* sound as realistic as possible.

For the moment, however, Welles focused on the stage. There he and Houseman prepared to debut something very different from their earlier offerings: a left-wing labor opera by Marc Blitzstein called *The Cradle Will Rock*. This was a play ripped from the headlines, a provocative defense of organized labor that attacked every aspect of capitalist society.[46] It seemed too radical even for the WPA, whose budget was coming up for renewal in Congress. Conservatives would not look kindly on a piece of pro-labor propaganda paid for by the federal government. As opening night approached, the Federal Theatre Project saw its budget slashed by a third. The WPA put *Cradle's* premiere on hold, along with every other art project opening that month, in expectation of further cuts. Uniformed guards—"Cossacks," Houseman called them—even padlocked the Maxine Elliott Theatre to prevent the play from opening on time. But Welles and Houseman, believing that the federal government wanted to censor *The Cradle Will Rock*, refused to cancel the show.[47] "If they hadn't padlocked the theater, I would never have taken that strong a stand," Welles later told his biographer Barbara Leaming. "The padlock was an insult."[48]

On the evening of June 16, 1937, the cast and crew of *The Cradle Will Rock* led six hundred audience members to an empty theater across town. There Marc Blitzstein performed his entire libretto on a shabby upright piano while the performers, prevented from appearing onstage by union rules, played their parts in the aisles. Actors and audience alike were enthralled.[49] Archibald MacLeish called it "the most exciting evening of theater this New York generation has ever seen."[50] For Orson Welles, it was perhaps the most fortunate event in a run of remarkable good luck. The play would never have been such an event had the government not tried to shut it down, and there is every indication that Welles's elaborate production would have overwhelmed Blitzstein's message. But fate had handed him a fresh way of staging the play without frills, and the next day *The Cradle Will Rock* was front-page news.[51] The story even made it onto *The March of Time*, with Welles playing himself. That, he said many years later, convinced him that he had truly arrived.[52]

The publicity surrounding *Cradle* earned Welles an offer from the Mutual Broadcasting System, for whom he did *The Shadow*, to direct and perform in a seven-part adaptation of Victor Hugo's *Les Misérables*. It ran that summer, giving him an opportunity to build on the "first person" technique MacLeish had used in *The Fall of the City*.[53] He also began to experiment with sound effects, developing an innovative style of sound design that set his work apart from other radio fare. To get the proper sound for the sewers of Paris, Welles set up a microphone in the recording studio's bathroom to pick up the drip-drip-drip of its ancient plumbing. But the plan backfired when someone had to use the restroom during the show. As he inadvertently broadcast the sound of a flushing toilet, coast to coast, Welles, not for the last time, made radio history.[54]

But in the summer of 1937, Welles still thought of radio only as a sideline, an adjunct to his theater work. Now that further federal productions were an impossibility, he and Houseman decided to start their own company. They kept the personnel, apparatus, and ideals of Project 891, but they needed a new name. They found one on the cover of an old magazine in Welles's fireplace. Its title was *American Mercury*, and so their company would be the Mercury Theatre.[55]

On August 29, 1937, the Mercury boldly announced itself in *The New York Times*, pledging to keep producing "plays of the past—preferably those that seem to have an emotional or factual bearing on contemporary life." Their first would be Shakespeare's *Julius Caesar*, and as they had with *Faustus*, they hoped to recapture "much of the speed and violence it must have had on the Elizabethan stage."[56] This time, instead of using magic tricks, Welles relied on a bracingly modern aesthetic. He dressed his actors in military uniforms and business suits, and lit his bare stage with the "Nuremberg lights" familiar from Nazi rallies. These were bold choices, deliberately echoing the fascist dictatorships in Italy and Germany, and there was no telling whether they would work. Without money from the WPA, Welles and Houseman were constantly short of cash, and their first preview was a total disaster. George Coulouris, the production's Marc Antony, warned the cast that the Mercury's first performance would almost certainly be its last.[57]

But, once again, Welles walked his company back from the brink of disaster. He drastically reshaped the play in the days before its premiere, creating a production powerful in its timeliness. The Mercury made it to opening night, November 11, 1937, and astounded critics and audiences alike with their stripped-down, modern-dress *Caesar*.[58] "Move over and make room for the Mercury Theatre," proclaimed *The New York Times*.[59] The *New York Herald Tribune* agreed: "Here, after all of this waiting, is a production so imaginative, so completely fascinating in all its phases, that there is nothing to do but let ourselves go and applaud it unreservedly."[60]

Caesar was a smash hit, with people lining up outside for tickets. Had the Mercury run it for a year or more, their financial troubles would have been over. But Welles and Houseman would never have done anything so sensible. "We had gambled and won," Houseman later wrote; "intoxicated with success, we were moving much too fast, with our own special kind of reckless, whirling motion, to stop for any reason—good or bad."[61] As in the days of Project 891, they followed their bold reimagining of Shakespeare with a broad comedy, Thomas Dekker's ribald *Shoemaker's Holiday*, and a more serious work, George Bernard Shaw's *Heartbreak House*. Though neither quite reached the heights of *Cradle* or *Caesar*, both were very well received, and *Heartbreak House* earned Welles the cover of *Time* magazine on the week of his twenty-third birthday.* "The brightest moon that has risen over Broadway in years," *Time* wrote, "Welles should feel at home in the sky, for the sky is the only limit his ambitions recognize."[62]

By the time the Mercury closed its first season, in the spring of 1938, Welles's rapid rise had caught the attention of CBS. The network wanted to fill out their summer schedule with a sustaining show that might, if it picked up enough listeners, garner a commercial sponsor, and they saw promise in the Mercury. They offered Welles the chance to produce his own nine-week radio series, Mondays at 9:00 p.m., featuring the Mercury actors in fresh adaptations of literary classics. Welles could choose

---

* The following week, *Time*'s cover featured FCC chairman Frank McNinch, who later played a major role in the controversy surrounding *War of the Worlds*.

whatever source material he liked, though CBS strongly encouraged him to adapt public-domain adventure classics that were cheap to acquire and fun for the whole family. The budget was small—fifty thousand dollars—but the opportunity was priceless. Above all, Welles's authorship would be unquestioned. Unlike his earlier, anonymous radio jobs, this would clearly be labeled as the work of a single artistic genius: Orson Welles.[63]

CBS announced the new series in a press release on June 8, 1938, just over a month before its debut.[64] It took its title, *First Person Singular*, from the narrative technique Welles had borrowed from Archibald Mac-Leish. Using a narrator "brings more intimacy to the dramatic broadcast," he explained to *The New York Times*. "When a fellow leans back in his chair and begins: 'Now, this is how it happened'—the listener feels that the narrator is taking him into his confidence; he begins to take a personal interest in the outcome."[65] The role of the storyteller was, of course, almost always reserved for Welles, who often played more than one part in a given show. A common joke in the industry was that Welles "not only invented 'First Person Singular,' but he IS 'First Person Singular.'"[66] As Callow notes, most other radio shows still obeyed the rules of stage-bound drama, making them seem stilted and artificial. But Welles recognized that, as the "theater of the mind," radio worked best when treated like a novel or a short story. His effective use of a narrative voice inspired many other series.[67]

For the first episode of *First Person Singular*, Welles chose Robert Louis Stevenson's *Treasure Island*—just the kind of adventure story CBS wanted. But shortly before the premiere, he changed his mind. Long John Silver could wait until next week; they would do *Dracula* instead.[68] The resulting show was a triumph of radio drama, drawing critical praise and a small but respectable audience. It used multiple narrators to preserve the novel's epistolary structure, and Welles's talent for weaving together dialogue, music, and sound effects was on full display.[69] Welles himself considered it one of the Mercury's best broadcasts, and it remained vivid in the minds of some listeners for months.[70] "I don't think I shall ever forget it," wrote one listener that October, in a letter to Welles. "It thrilled me a hundred times more than the picture show ever did."[71]

Dracula set the tone for the rest of the Mercury broadcasts. Over dinner each week, Welles and Houseman would select a book to adapt.[72] Usually, they drew on their own interests, but sometimes they used suggestions from listener letters. Then Houseman would go off to script the show. Handling the Mercury's various ventures left him so exhausted that he wrote each episode in bed, either too tired or too busy to get up. Welles revised each script extensively, and recorded an early rehearsal on acetate discs to see how the show would sound.[73] The actors were some of the best in radio, including Ray Collins, Joseph Cotten, and Agnes Moorehead—people Welles had gotten to know on such shows as *The Columbia Workshop* and *The March of Time*. In fact, Welles's producer Richard Wilson later said that casting decisions were often made based on an actor's past performance on *The March of Time*. The wide variety of roles on that show gave Welles a good sense of each performer's range.[74]

On the day of the broadcast itself, Welles rehearsed the actors for hours and made innumerable changes. Often, he infuriated his collaborators by taking the script apart and putting it back together at the last minute.[75] These frantic edits usually left the show either much too long or much too short. With only an hour or two, or perhaps even minutes, before airtime, Houseman rapidly rewrote the script to bring the story in line.[76] But Welles had his own ways of getting the show to just the right length. Houseman later recalled that in his years as a radio actor, Welles had developed such control over the pacing of his speech that he could add or subtract minutes to a show, simply by slowing down or speeding up his voice.[77] Not that the episodes always came in on time. As Callow notes, Welles had to pad the ending of *Treasure Island* with an extended and almost desperate curtain speech to keep from leaving the audience with several minutes of dead air.[78] But in most cases, the shows came out perfectly paced and fitting the time slot exactly. No matter how chaotic it got, Welles always seemed to know what he was doing. He invariably succeeded in drawing art out of pandemonium.

In this atmosphere of what Houseman called "soul- and health-destroying pressure,"[79] the Mercury produced lively and polished adaptations of everything from Charles Dickens's *A Tale of Two Cities* to John Buchan's *The Thirty-Nine Steps*, Alexandre Dumas's *The Count of Monte Cristo* to G. K. Chesterton's *The Man Who Was Thursday*. Passions always ran high, but eventually the bedlam became somewhat routine. The performers and technicians grew adept at handling the caprices of their director, and Welles's involvement began to diminish. Often, he came in only on the day of the broadcast itself, having turned earlier rehearsals over to another director.[80] As the summer waned and the Mercury Theatre's second season of stage productions rapidly approached, Welles had plays to prepare. He had also fallen in love with a new medium: filmmaking.

Welles's first professional experiment with motion pictures would prove to be an unmitigated disaster. He planned to add filmed segments to the Mercury's first play of the season, a comedy by the renowned American actor William Gillette titled *Too Much Johnson*. He spent much of the summer of 1938 dashing about Manhattan and Haverstraw, New York, with Joseph Cotten and a small film crew, shooting a silent comedy in the madcap style of Buster Keaton or Harold Lloyd. Houseman was even pressed into service as a Keystone Kop, and wound up looking frankly ridiculous, like a man too old for the party he has been invited to.[81] The surviving film preserves some of the manic energy of those Mercury days, when it seemed Welles could do anything. So far, he had explored three media—theater, radio, and film—with total control and almost no restraints. He attacked them with all the inventiveness of youth, delighting in experiment and disdaining convention, because he was fortunate enough to have resources to match his genius. But this golden moment could not last forever. *Too Much Johnson* marked the first major turn in the Mercury's fortunes.

Thanks to the success of *Caesar* and their other productions, Welles and Houseman were briefly flush with cash that summer. But filmmaking is an expensive endeavor, and producing *Too Much Johnson* quickly drained the Mercury's finances. Then they discovered that they couldn't even show the film they had shot. Their theater lacked the equipment to screen it, and Paramount Pictures, who owned the movie rights to *Too Much Johnson*, demanded a hefty licensing fee that the Mercury could not pay. Furthermore, Actors' Equity forced Welles and Houseman to pay their actors extra salary for shooting the movie, and that expense almost bankrupted the company. With no alternative, Houseman decided to scrap *Too Much Johnson* and focus instead on producing the next show they had planned: *Danton's Death*, Georg Büchner's drama of the French Revolution. Distraught, Welles retreated to the hotel suite where he had been editing *Too Much Johnson*, and emerged only to heed the call of the radio. For, while the Mercury Theatre was in crisis, *First Person Singular* got better and better each week.[82]

Even though the show had so far failed to find a sponsor (the Mercury had pitched it to Campbell's Soup, without success), CBS was impressed enough to continue their run into the fall, with two changes.[83] One was the name; the show had long been known colloquially as *The Mercury Theatre on the Air,* and the new season made it official. The other was the time slot. Because it had no sponsor, the Mercury had to abandon its plum spot on Monday nights for an unsalable period against *The Chase & Sanborn Hour,* a variety show that aired Sundays at 8:00 p.m.[84]

Named after the coffee company that paid its bills, *The Chase & Sanborn Hour* starred the vaudeville veteran Edgar Bergen and his alter ego, the ventriloquist dummy Charlie McCarthy. Because the sponsor wanted a large audience, the show offered something for everyone: Bergen and McCarthy provided comedy sketches, and Nelson Eddy and other stars of the stage and screen sang the day's most popular tunes. The format worked, making *The Chase & Sanborn Hour* one of the day's most popular shows.[85] The Mercury could never compete with this ratings juggernaut. Week after week, Welles's inexpensive, artistic, and experimental show would serve as CBS's cannon fodder, earning the network critical praise and prestige where it could not make money.[86] But playing to a small audience also allowed Welles to do what he wanted, with fewer constraints.

The Mercury began its new season by revisiting a past triumph, Shakespeare's *Caesar.* Then they went on to present more classic works: *Jane Eyre, Sherlock Holmes, Oliver Twist,* and others. Most of these were books associated with youth. As the Welles biographer Frank Brady has observed, telling these stories gave Welles a chance to experience, however briefly, the childhood he had largely skipped over.[87] They also highlighted the remarkable precocity that, for many, was Welles's defining feature. A philosophy teacher from a small college in Illinois—who, like Welles, was only twenty-three years old—wrote him a fan letter that fall just to say that her own precocity paled in comparison with his. "If you've accomplished so much dramatically," she wrote, "my so called accomplishments aren't worth a pin." Then she mentioned, almost as an afterthought, that she had advanced so far despite being blind. Still, she wrote, Welles's genius seemed more remarkable than anything she had achieved.[88] Another young fan from Illinois—who assured Welles that she was no "silly school-girl" but actually "old enough to vote"—also sent her praise. "Of course, this probably will sound mushy," she wrote, "but I do think you're marvelous . . . and I do mean marvelous."[89]

Many others found Welles's early success intoxicating, but did not realize that his rise was unsustainable. Without another breakout hit on a par with *The Cradle Will Rock* or *Julius Caesar*, the Mercury would inevitably burn out. And their prospects, in the fall of 1938, looked very dim indeed.

When rehearsals began on *Danton's Death*, the play quickly developed into an even bigger mess than *Too Much Johnson*. The source material itself struck many as greatly inferior to Welles's earlier productions; one Mercury actor called the play "turgid," and another said it was "a piece of shit."[90] Its selection also offended the company's primarily left-wing audience, who thought that Welles planned to attack communism just as he had used *Caesar* to attack fascism. To get around the weaknesses in the text, Welles constructed an elaborate set, with a huge elevator at the center of the stage, which proved to be something of a death trap. Preview performances were canceled left and right as engineers struggled with the set, pushing the play's opening into the first week of November. Finally, the elevator crashed during one rehearsal, and an actor, Erskine Sanford, broke his leg. Another preview was canceled, Sanford was sent to the hospital, and Welles kept rehearsing his actors literally around the clock, desperately trying to avert a train wreck.[91]

From his "executive office" in the Mercury Theatre, Houseman could look down at the stage through a peephole and watch the company slowly falling to pieces. One day that fall, as Welles and the crew tore apart the stage to build the massive elevator, Houseman received a visit from a young playwright named Howard Koch, new to the city and looking for work. Koch had come recommended by one of the Mercury's backers, and Houseman knew that the Federal Theatre in Chicago had produced a few of his plays. One of them, imagining what Abraham Lincoln* might think of 1930s America, convinced Houseman that Koch had talent. Now Houseman quickly sized up the slim and somewhat lanky young man with midwestern good looks and decided he was just the writer for *The Mercury Theatre on the Air*. Koch knew nothing about radio, but Houseman knew that could be corrected. More important, Koch came cheap. He signed on for seventy-five dollars a week, blissfully unaware that his new bosses were about to put him through the wringer.[92]

At the start of each week, Koch received the book Welles and House-

---

* Played by the future film director and actor John Huston.

man had decided to adapt. He then had about six days to turn it into a sixty-page radio script. This kept Koch working day and night, writing page after page for Welles and Houseman to read, rehearse, and correct. Koch's pencil never stopped; nor did the requests for changes. To help move things along, Houseman lent Koch his secretary, a young college student named Anne Froelich, who typed up Koch's penciled pages almost as soon as they were written. Working for the Mercury, Koch later reflected, was not easy, but it built his writing skills and discipline.[93] After adapting *Hell on Ice*, a nonfiction work about a doomed Arctic voyage, and *Seventeen*, Booth Tarkington's novel of adolescent angst, Koch learned that his next assignment would be *The War of the Worlds* by H. G. Wells.[94]

Welles and Houseman had not chosen the novel because they particularly liked it, but because it fit a concept that Welles was eager to try. "I had conceived the idea of doing a radio broadcast in such a manner that a crisis would actually seem to be happening," he later said, "and would be broadcast in such a dramatised [*sic*] form as to appear to be a real event taking place at that time, rather than a mere radio play." Without knowing which book he wanted to adapt, Welles had brought the idea to Houseman and Paul Stewart, a veteran radio actor and director who codirected the Mercury broadcasts. They discussed various possibilities, including *The Purple Cloud*, by M. P. Shiel, and *The Lost World*, by Sir Arthur Conan Doyle, before settling on *The War of the Worlds*. Houseman doubted that Welles had ever read the story, but he passed it on to Koch anyway, with the instruction to convert it into late-breaking news bulletins.[95]

As soon as Koch read the novel and began trying to adapt it, he hit a wall. Even with the fake news conceit, he found it impossible to turn the fantastical story of an alien invasion into a credible radio drama in less than a week.[96] On Tuesday, October 25, after three days of work on *War of the Worlds*, he called Houseman to say the book was hopeless. He wanted to adapt something else, and suggested a story written by one of his friends.[97] Houseman was unconvinced, so Froelich got on the line to back up the exasperated writer. "It's all too silly!" she told Houseman. "We're going to make fools of ourselves! Absolute fools!"[98]

Ever the diplomat, Houseman rang off with the promise to see if Welles might agree to another story.[99] But when he called the Mercury Theatre, where Welles had been rehearsing *Danton's Death* for thirty-six straight hours, he could not get his partner on the phone.[100] All Houseman had to replace *War of the Worlds* was something he had written for the summer series and eventually given up on, an "extremely dreary" adaptation of R. D. Blackmore's *Lorna Doone*.[101] So, with no other options, he called Koch back and lied. Welles, he said, was determined to do the Martian novel this week. In fact, it "was Orson's favorite project."[102] After promising to help with the adaptation, Houseman hung up, leaving Koch to struggle with the ideas of Wells and Welles.[103]

3

Martians of the Mind's Eye

Incidentally, I tip my hat to the men who did the radio adaptation, and to men
behind the scenes who made each sequence click like clock-work.

—Abner I. Weisman of New York City
to Orson Welles, October 31, 1938[1]

In the spring of 1895, Herbert George Wells, a twenty-eight-year-old former science teacher turned theater critic, left the bustling city of London
for the tranquil county of Surrey. Ill health had forced him to seek a
kinder climate, and he hoped to devote more time to his burgeoning career as a writer.[2] The first of his "scientific romances," the novel *The Time
Machine*, was about to be published on both sides of the Atlantic.[3] *The
Island of Doctor Moreau* would follow a year later, and *The Invisible Man*
the year after that. Each drew upon the latest scientific discoveries to tell
stories that seemed fresh, exciting, and terrifying because of their plausibility. But powerful political undercurrents also ran through Wells's
work, reflecting his deeply held socialist beliefs. His fourth "scientific romance," inspired by his time in Surrey, would again be as much a work of
social criticism as of science fiction.[4]

Out for a walk one day that spring, Wells and his brother Frank discussed their country's colonial misadventures in Tasmania. European
settlers there had wiped out an entire indigenous population by trapping
some people like animals, giving others poisoned food, and shooting the
rest on sight.[5] Looking out over the quiet countryside, Frank Wells mused
aloud, "Suppose some beings from another planet were to drop out of the
sky suddenly, and begin laying about them here!"[6] The ironic reversal of
a colonial superpower's suddenly finding itself colonized fired H. G.
Wells's imagination. That summer, he began work on a novel about an
alien invasion of Earth—the first of its kind.[7] Upon its publication in

book form in 1898, Wells dedicated *The War of the Worlds* to his brother, crediting him for the offhand comment that established an entire genre.[8]

In the novel, hyperintelligent Martians attempt to colonize Earth in order to escape the slow death of their own planet. They launch themselves through space in metal cylinders fired from a massive cannon on the surface of Mars. The first cylinder lands in the small English town of Woking, where Wells lived at the time.[9] There the Martians construct three-legged fighting machines that allow them to move swiftly about the countryside. Using highly advanced weaponry—a "heat-ray" and poisonous "black smoke"—they sweep through England and conquer London, quickly decimating the military and reducing the British people to refugees. The novel's unnamed narrator, a scientifically inclined writer reminiscent of Wells himself,[10] struggles to reach his wife in London as more Martians arrive. Trapped in an abandoned house with an increasingly unstable clergyman, the narrator witnesses the invaders rounding up surviving humans to feed upon their blood. Eventually, the narrator escapes, reaches London, and discovers that the Martians are all dead or dying from earthly diseases against which they have no immunity. At the novel's end, the narrator reflects on how the war has cured humanity of much of its arrogance, and wonders whether the Martians will try to invade again.

Wells took great pains to make the story as realistic as possible. He wrote *The War of the Worlds* in a spare, journalistic style, as if it were a work of history or reportage. The book is packed with up-to-date scientific detail and frequent references to real newspapers and even actual scientific articles, one of which Wells wrote himself.[11] He used maps from the British Ordnance Survey to plot out every step of the Martian invasion, and often rode around Surrey on his bicycle, looking for "suitable places and people for destruction by my Martians."[12] Wells enjoyed the work quite a bit. He wrote to a friend of his delight in "killing my neighbours in painful and eccentric ways," and specifically selected for destruction parts of London that he did not like.[13] But these details made the book especially frightening for its first generation of readers. The novel seemed particularly prescient in the wake of World War I, which saw widespread destruction and chemical warfare much like what Wells described. "Our present civilisation, it seems, is quite capable of falling to pieces without any aid from the Martians," Wells wrote when the novel was reissued in 1924.[14]

Equally credible to fin-de-siècle readers was the idea that intelligent beings lived on Mars. In 1877, the Italian astronomer Giovanni Schiaparelli drew detailed maps of the Martian surface, showing a series of dark lines that he called *canali*, Italian for "channels." Schiaparelli was agnostic on what these lines actually were. But in English, *canali* got mistranslated to "canals," a word implying that these were not natural formations—that someone had built them.[15] The idea of a canal-building Martian civilization inspired the wealthy, self-taught astronomer Percival Lowell to build his own observatory in Arizona to study the Red Planet.[16] In 1895, he published his fanciful conclusions: that Mars was a dying and desiccated world whose inhabitants built massive canals to siphon water from their polar ice caps.[17] The scientific community never took Lowell's work seriously, but his book became a bestseller, convincing many of the plausibility of intelligent life on Mars.[18] H. G. Wells drew on it heavily in giving his own Martians a motivation to flee Mars and attack Earth, and his readers would have recognized the reference.[19]

All of these scientific and technical details made *The War of the Worlds* gripping reading in 1898. But forty years later, when Howard Koch set out to adapt the book for radio, he found it terribly dull and dated. In the 1930s, science fiction was largely the purview of children, with alien invaders confined to pulp magazines and the Sunday funnies.[20] Lowell's ideas about intelligent Martians still had some currency with the public, but the vast majority of scientists believed that Mars could support, at best, only "vegetable and low types of animal life."[21] Worse, from Koch's standpoint as a dramatist, was the fact that *The War of the Worlds* did not conform to the Mercury's "first person singular" format. Wells's narrator is a passive character, usually an observer of monumental events rather than a direct participant in the action. Koch struggled to inject drama into this largely impersonal chronicle.

For inspiration, Koch stopped at a gas station the Monday before the broadcast and picked up a road map to plot out the invasion. Because the gas station happened to be in New Jersey, he purchased a map of the Garden State. Later, when it came time to select the Martians' ground zero, he closed his eyes and dropped the point of a pencil on the map at random. It landed on the tiny hamlet of Grover's Mill, about six miles from Princeton. Koch had never heard of the place, but he liked the homespun sound of its name.[22] Then, like H. G. Wells before him, he set about gathering geographic details to lend credence to the story. But without knowing it, he had already taken his first major step toward making the broadcast sound real enough to be believed. Purely by happenstance, he had set the Martian invasion in New Jersey—a state that, from the Lindbergh kidnapping to the *Morro Castle* to the *Hindenburg*, had seen more radio crises that decade than perhaps any other. "Having lived in New Jersey all my life," wrote one listener after *War of the Worlds*, "and having listened to the descriptions of the explosion & fire of the Graf Zeppelin and the burning of the Morro Castle, I sincerely believed this was a momentous occasion."[23]

The following night, after calling Houseman to vent his frustrations, Koch finally began to warm to the material.[24] Houseman visited the writer long after midnight to offer what help he could, and found Koch gleefully wreaking havoc on the East Coast.[25] With suggestions from his producer, Koch worked through the night and the following day, filling countless yellow legal-pad pages with his elegant if frequently illegible handwriting.[26] Somehow, his secretary, Anne Froelich, made sense of these penciled hieroglyphics and typed them up into a script.[27] By sundown on Wednesday, Koch had finished a complete draft ready for rehearsal.[28]

Koch's script followed the plot of the Wells novel very closely, retaining its division into two parts. The first, before the station break at the middle of the program, relied primarily on a series of fake news bulletins to recount the arrival of the Martians and their rapid conquering of the United States. The second used the "first person singular" format to relate events from the perspective of Professor Richard Pierson, a fictitious astronomer from Princeton University. Like Wells's unnamed narrator, Pierson survives the Martians' initial attack and wanders about New Jersey and New York before finding the invaders dead from disease.[29] Koch's script benefitted from suggestions from Houseman and Froelich, but Orson Welles remained uninvolved. He had come up with the fake news idea before Koch received the assignment, but now he was too preoccupied with *Danton's Death* to give the radio show any attention.[30]

At this stage of his career, as his biographer Simon Callow has observed, Welles was a director more interested in big ideas than in the mechanics of storytelling. His genius lay in finding new and shocking ways to restage old and familiar classics.[31] The idea of doing *The War of the Worlds* as a series of fake news bulletins was not all that different from setting *Macbeth* in Haiti in a voodoo milieu, or setting *Caesar* in fascist

Italy. It was fresh, exciting, and current—just the kind of idea that would excite Welles creatively. He had no intention of making a statement; his only interest was in thrilling his audience. And although Welles had never done a fake news broadcast before, he had been working up to it for some time, with several shows that deliberately echoed current events.[32]

On August 15, 1938, *The Mercury Theatre on the Air* had performed John Drinkwater's *Abraham Lincoln*, just ninety minutes before a radio address by President Roosevelt. Welles made the contemporary parallels clear in his opening monologue. "Much of this you will recognize and much of it is news . . . ," he told his audience, "as if it were happening in the White House tonight."[33] For the Mercury's broadcast of *Julius Caesar*, their first show of the fall season, Welles had H. V. Kaltenborn read selections from Plutarch's *Lives of the Noble Grecians and Romans* in between Shakespeare's scenes, as if he were commenting on the action.[34] By using the voice of radio's pre-eminent newsman, Welles made the play sound like breaking news, just as he had made it look modern onstage. He probably sought a similar effect by applying news bulletin techniques to *The War of the Worlds*.

Of course, in later years, Welles suggested more than once that he had had a bigger goal in mind for his Martian broadcast. Its fake news bulletins, he claimed, were meant to be intentionally deceptive, in order to teach the public a lesson about their overreliance on radio.[35] But these comments were made with the benefit of hindsight, in an attempt to claim more credit for the broadcast's effects than he, or anyone else, deserved. No one else who worked on *War of the Worlds*, including John Houseman and Howard Koch, ever made such a claim. In fact, they denied it, long after legal reprisals were a serious concern.[36] And the notion that Welles deliberately planned the scare in order to draw channel-surfing listeners away from NBC, as at least one biographer has claimed, is, in Houseman's words, "absolute rubbish."[37] No one could have anticipated how audiences would react to *War of the Worlds*, and so no one realized just how cavalierly Welles and the Mercury were playing with fire. If anyone there had, CBS would have never allowed the show on the air.

Network executives had little reason to expect a problem, because, by late 1938, many other shows were blurring the line between radio news and radio drama. The growing popularity of news broadcasts and the melding of journalism and entertainment on programs like *The March of Time* had inspired other radio writers to experiment with using news techniques in fictional shows.[38] *The Fall of the City* was perhaps the earliest example of this trend in American broadcasting, but its success encouraged others to follow MacLeish's example. Even an episode of Welles's own *The Shadow,* which aired the previous December, had interrupted itself with a fake news bulletin to speed up the action.[39] "Don't overlook the fact that the radio audience responds heartily to news broadcasts," explained a 1937 guide to radio writing. "Capitalize on this desire for news whenever possible."[40] But no show on American airwaves copied the news bulletin format quite so closely, or pushed the boundaries between fact and fiction quite so far, as *War of the Worlds* would the following October.

In all likelihood, Welles's direct inspiration to do a fake newscast came from *Air Raid,* MacLeish's follow-up to *The Fall of the City.* It premiered on *The Columbia Workshop* on October 27, 1938—four days before *War of the Worlds.*[41] Inspired by the bombing of Guernica during the Spanish Civil War, MacLeish dramatized an aerial attack on a small European town with chilling realism. Once again, he told his story from the perspective of a news announcer, played this time by the Mercury actor Ray Collins. With the same language that had transported Americans across the Atlantic during the Czech crisis ("Stand by: we'll try to take you through . . ."), *Air Raid* brought listeners into the homes of these fictional Europeans as warplanes bore down on them, to vivid and powerful effect.[42] Although the play aired after Koch began scripting *War of the Worlds,* MacLeish had been writing it for about seven months, and Welles certainly knew about it before its debut.[43] He even sat in on rehearsals; a CBS photographer captured him in conversation with MacLeish, Collins, and the director, William N. Robson, as if he were a member of the cast.[44] Knowing what MacLeish had prepared for *The Columbia Workshop* very likely encouraged Welles to do something similar with *War of the Worlds,* though his approach would be less poetic than MacLeish's.

Welles, however, never acknowledged MacLeish as an influence on *War of the Worlds.* Instead, he told the film director Peter Bogdanovich that he had gotten the fake news idea from another broadcast, twelve years before, in the United Kingdom, which had generated headlines on both sides of the Atlantic.[45] Houseman, too, vaguely recalled the British show and the controversy it had caused, though he never imagined that the Mercury's broadcast could have a similar effect.[46]

Although he never laid claim to it, Father Ronald Arbuthnott Knox probably deserves credit for the accidental invention of fake news broadcasting. Born in 1888, Knox followed his father, an Anglican bishop, into the ministry of the Church of England at age twenty-four. But five years later, he converted to Catholicism, and soon became a prominent apologist for his adopted faith. In his spare time, Knox penned several successful detective novels that earned him membership in Britain's "Detection Club," alongside such lights of the genre as Agatha Christie. He also wrote several keen and biting satires,* and his puckish sense of humor would leave its mark on British broadcasting.[47]

Unlike in the United States, where national radio networks didn't emerge until the late 1920s, broadcasters in the United Kingdom had a national audience from the very beginning. The British Broadcasting Company (which only later became a corporation) was founded in 1922 as an offshoot of the Post Office, giving all Britons access to the same programming at the same time. But because it spoke both to and for the entire nation with uncontested authority, Knox grew concerned about its power to shape public opinion. Some years later, he wrote of an effect that he called "broadcastmindedness"—"the habit of taking over, from self-constituted mentors, a ready-made, standardized philosophy of life, instead of constructing, with however imperfect materials, a philosophy of life for oneself." Knox worried that listeners accepted whatever they heard on the radio without question; broadcasting, he believed, discouraged critical thinking.[48]

After listening to a broadcast of election returns in the mid-1920s, Knox decided to vent his frustrations with the radio by writing a satirical fake news show titled *Broadcasting the Barricades*.[49] A friend at the BBC station 2EH in Edinburgh allowed him to perform it on the air at 7:40 p.m. on January 16, 1926, when Knox was thirty-seven years old.[50] The show was duly listed in newspaper radio schedules, and prefaced with an announcement that what followed "would not be a serious lec-

---

* Knox is probably best known today for his 1911 essay "Studies in the Literature of Sherlock Holmes"—a satirical attack on Biblical Higher Criticism that, to his dismay, inspired generations of Holmes fans to pick apart Sir Arthur Conan Doyle's stories as if they were factual and sacred texts.

ture, but a skit on broadcasting."[51] But for listeners who tuned in late to Knox's pitch-perfect parody of a BBC newscast, complete with realistic sound effects, only a finely tuned sense of humor could have revealed these bulletins for what they really were.

Knox began by reading a series of fake news items, like sports scores and a weather forecast.[52] The last item concerned an unruly mob of unemployed workers massing in London. At the urging of their leader, "Mr. Popplebury, the Secretary of the National Movement for Abolishing Theatre Queues," the mob sacked the National Gallery, attacked government buildings, and roasted a prominent philanthropist alive.[53] In between the reports, the broadcast cut to a dance band at the Savoy Hotel—just as, twelve years later, *War of the Worlds* would frequently cut to dance music at the Park Plaza Hotel. Each musical interlude ended suddenly, as the announcer broke in again with another, more horrific bulletin. The mob, according to later reports, was now firing trench mortars at the Houses of Parliament. As listeners heard Big Ben crashing to the ground, Knox informed them that Greenwich Mean Time "will be given [instead] from Edinburgh on Uncle Leslie's repeating watch."[54] Uncle Leslie was the star of a popular radio program for children.[55]

In the BBC manner, Knox read each report blandly, without betraying any emotion or alarm. He also included a lot of needless yet educational detail, such as the year the National Gallery was founded, and the exact height of Big Ben. After reporting that the crowd had hanged "Mr. Wutherspoon, the Minister of Traffic . . . from a lamp-post in the Vauxhall Bridge Road," Knox interrupted himself for a correction:

> One moment, please. The British Broadcasting Company regrets that one item in the news has been inaccurately given. The correction now follows. It was stated in our news bulletin that the Minister of Traffic had been hanged from a lamp-post in the Vauxhall Bridge Road. Subsequent and more accurate reports show that it was not a lamp-post but a tramway post which was used for this purpose. A tramway post, not a lamp-post, was used by the crowd for the purpose of hanging the Minister of Traffic. The next three items in our programme are unavoidably canceled. You will now be connected up with the Savoy Band again.[56]

A brief musical interlude followed, only to be cut off by the sound of an explosion as the mob blew up the Savoy Hotel. Then Knox reported that the crowd was moving in on BBC headquarters. But, rather than sack that building as well, they remained "in the waiting room . . . reading copies of the 'Radio Times.' "[57] And, with that anticlimactic ending, Knox signed off. He had been on the air for barely twenty minutes.[58]

Less than half an hour later, while Knox ate dinner, he received word that hundreds of people were calling the Savoy Hotel, wanting to know if it had really been blown up. Some asked if they should cancel upcoming reservations.[59] Back at the station, the only employee left in the studio, a sound-effects technician, suddenly found himself answering calls from listeners who had thought the revolution was real.[60] Then a newspaper reporter called, asking rapid-fire questions that, to the sound-effects man, displayed "a certain lack of sympathy with the BBC and a natural desire to make the most of a good story."[61] The next day, newspapers throughout the United Kingdom reported receiving frightened phone calls from listeners seeking verification of the story. In some parts of the country, where heavy snowfall delayed delivery of the morning papers, rumors of a communist uprising in London supposedly swirled for hours or even days.[62] This despite the fact that, within hours, the BBC had broadcast an authentic bulletin telling listeners that the revolution was "imaginary," and reassuring them that "London is Safe. Big Ben is still chiming, and all is well."[63]

Broadcasting the Barricades cannot accurately be called a "hoax," because there is no indication that Knox intended to deceive anyone. Nor can the reaction from its audience be truly described as a "panic."[64] Apart from a report in *The New York Times* that "ladies in remote country districts . . . in great consternation barricaded themselves behind their bedroom doors," and *The Baltimore Sun*'s claim that "at least one woman fainted when she heard it," there is little evidence that Knox's confused listeners did much more than call up newspapers, radio stations, or government officials to find out if the news was true.[65] These people may have missed several cues that the whole thing was fiction, but they had good reason to be concerned. Nothing like a fake news broadcast had ever been done before, and the idea that the BBC might deliberately present as news something that was not would have seemed inconceivable. Also, radio drama was still in its infancy, and sound effects were not yet widely used.[66] The ones in *Broadcasting the Barricades* were humble— "an orange-box to be hacked, torn, and stamped to pieces, and a sack of broken glass to be dumped on the studio floor"—but they were apparently very realistic.[67] As one frightened caller told the *Daily Mail*, "We have heard it on the wireless. Why, we have even heard the explosions!"[68]

Most important, the content of the broadcast was not at all far-fetched. The Russian Revolution was not even a decade old, and there were rumblings that left-wing radicalism might gain a foothold in the United Kingdom.[69] Just four months after *Broadcasting the Barricades*, the nation found itself crippled by a massive nine-day general strike, which left virtually no strata of society unaffected.[70] In such a climate, hearing news over the radio that unemployed workers were attacking government buildings and lynching Cabinet ministers may have come as a shock, but not as a surprise. Knox's rioters were just as fictional as Welles's Martians, but their existence was infinitely more plausible.

Nevertheless, newspapers in both Britain and America made much of the incident, roundly criticizing the BBC for airing the program and the public for believing in it.[71] "Humour and satire are dangerous implements when they are applied to mankind in the mass," wrote *The Irish Times*. "The BBC will be wise if, in future, it takes no risks with the public's average standard of intelligence."[72] But, in researching press coverage of the event, the historian Joanna Bourke noted a curious quirk in this reportage. Newspapers tended to report that people in other parts of the country, outside their usual readership, were the ones most frightened by the show.[73] *The Times* of London, for example, implied that the fright was confined to Ireland, and the Scottish papers—and Father Knox himself—claimed that the English had been fooled but the more sensible Scots had not.[74] Viewing the incident from afar, *The New York Times* declared that a similar incident "could not happen in this country," and wrote that the furor "was thoroughly representative of this stodgy old country [Great Britain] and the dear old ladies who have abandoned knitting needles for wireless sets."[75] Everyone, in short, seemed to point the finger at someone else, all confident that they were too smart to be taken in by a broadcast that made their rivals look like fools. This suggests, perhaps, that these articles are tinged with a certain degree of either embarrassment or embellishment.

The press had their own motives for exaggerating the broadcast's effects. For years, British publishers had made a concerted effort to keep the BBC from regularly reporting the news. Several newspapers used Knox's broadcast as an opportunity to paint the BBC as reckless and radio as a dangerous instrument.[76] "Here is a means by which vast communities, susceptible to any sort of rumour, might be reached with swift and calamitous results," wrote *The Irish Times*. Other editorial pages argued that print news was infinitely more responsible than the wireless variety; as *The Star* noted, any false "broadcast alarm" could only spread panic "until the newspapers come out."[77] It seems likely that some papers, at least, played up the controversy surrounding *Broadcasting the Barricades* because of their growing rivalry with radio.

Undoubtedly, Father Knox's satire briefly fooled and even frightened listeners throughout the U.K. But, as with *War of the Worlds* twelve years later, press coverage overstated the fear and outrage it caused. Though the BBC received 249 angry letters protesting the program, it ultimately counted 2,307 in support of Knox and the BBC—a ratio of roughly nine to one.[78] John Reith, the BBC's managing director, credited much of the uptick in favorable letters to a public backlash against press criticism of Knox.[79] Many people who wrote in regretted having missed the performance, and it even convinced some to buy their first radios.[80] Knox and the BBC publicly apologized, but privately Reith encouraged the company to come up with similar programs.[81] Within months, Knox was back on the air with another satirical program: a "parody of a popular scientific talk illustrating the sounds, now made audible to the learned, of vegetables in pain."[82]

Readers of *The Times* of London got a reminder of *Broadcasting the Barricades* four years later, when Germany had its own fake news scare. On September 25, 1930, a radio station in Berlin aired *Der Minister ist ermordet!* (*The Minister Is Murdered!*), a two-hour radio play by the well-known writer Erich Ebermayer.[83] It began with a seemingly ordinary musical program, then suddenly interrupted itself with a bulletin about the assassination of the German foreign minister. Some listeners mistook this for an actual news flash and bombarded local newspapers and the German Foreign Office with telephone calls, asking for more information. According to *The Times*, some of those calls even came from outside the country.[84]

As with *Broadcasting the Barricades*, there is little evidence that listeners did much more than pick up the phone in response to *Der Minister ist ermordet!* The show may have caused some temporary fright, but no real panic. Yet it is easy to see why some listeners were misled. As the scholar Kate Lacey has noted, the broadcast drew heavily on political and social tensions in Weimar Germany. Ebermayer based his play on the real assassination, eight years earlier, of German foreign minister Walter Rathenau by political extremists. Since that event, Adolf Hitler and the emerging Nazi Party had tried and failed to overthrow the government, and their influence was growing. Just like Britons in 1926, Germans in 1930 had good reason to expect a revolution—not a left-wing labor uprising, but a right-wing putsch. And just three years later, the Nazis assumed control of the German government.[85]

At the time, Ebermayer came under fire from the German press for producing such a vividly realistic radio show. Right-wing newspapers, in particular, objected to his depiction of rightist political violence. Journalists from other countries also took note of the incident.[86] One of the reporters who questioned Welles the day after *War of the Worlds* mentioned having heard *Der Minister ist ermordet!* while living in Europe. He said that Welles should have anticipated the public reaction to his broadcast because of the response to that earlier show.[87] But Welles, Houseman, and Koch could never have imagined that their show would have such an effect. Father Knox and Ebermayer had both drawn upon current political tensions in making up events that seemed frighteningly plausible even when treated satirically. The Mercury, on the other hand, used fake news techniques to enliven a forty-year-old novel about Martians. They simply thought their story was too silly ever to be taken seriously.

On the Thursday before *War of the Worlds* was set to air, a handful of Mercury actors met to rehearse Koch's draft script.[88] Welles's collaborators Richard Wilson and William Alland were there, along with one or two other actors, and they performed all the parts.[89] Welles was not present. Paul Stewart led the rehearsal, as he had each week since the early days of *The Mercury Theatre on the Air*.[90] Houseman watched from the control room, keeping careful track of the timing. Everyone who heard it later agreed that this stripped-down production—with no music and only the most basic sound effects—was an unmitigated disaster.[91]

The youngest member of the cast that day was Richard Baer, a twenty-two-year-old Princeton grad with dreams of being an actor. Houseman had hired Baer right out of school because he was willing to work for practically nothing. *War of the Worlds* would be Baer's first professional acting job. For playing "a voice in the crowd," he received the princely sum of fifteen dollars.[92] But his primary job that Thursday was to record the rehearsal onto acetate discs for Welles to listen to later that evening. This was Welles's usual method; it freed him from having to read script drafts, and gave him some sense of how the show would sound.[93] Once the rehearsal was completed and the discs were finished, Baer brought them over to Welles's suite at the St. Regis Hotel. But Welles, still furiously rehearsing *Danton's Death*, was not there to receive them personally. Baer may very well have been relieved. The first time he had met his boss, to deliver fifty dollars to his hotel suite, Welles had answered the door completely naked, thanked him politely, and shut the door without another word.[94]

Later that night, when Welles finally managed to pull himself away from *Danton's Death* to return to the St. Regis, Houseman and Stewart were waiting for him. The room was still littered with discarded film from *Too Much Johnson*; Houseman later recalled that the three men had to sit on the floor as they listened to the recording. This was Welles's first exposure to any material from the broadcast, and he hated what he heard. Bone-tired and probably somewhat irritable, he condemned the script as too "dull" and improbable ever to hold an audience. Welles believed, and Houseman and Stewart agreed, that they could only save the show by making the fake news portions sound as realistic as possible. Beyond that general note, he offered few if any specific suggestions, and soon left to return to *Danton's Death*.[95]

In Welles's absence, Houseman and Stewart tore into the script, drawing upon the *March of Time* style of "fakery in allegiance to the truth" to make the story seem more credible.[96] Then Houseman passed their changes on to Koch and Froelich for frantic last-minute rewrites.[97] These revisions and deletions left the script somewhat lopsided. Unlike in most radio dramas, the station break would come about two-thirds of the way through, not at the halfway mark.[98] This meant that people who tuned in late would have to wait almost forty minutes before hearing an announcement that the show was fiction. Listeners expected that fictional programs would be interrupted on the half-hour for station identifications and advertisements. Breaking news, on the other hand, failed to follow those rules. People who believed the broadcast to be real would be even more convinced when the station break failed to come at 8:30 p.m.

Other revisions removed several clues that might have helped late listeners figure out that the invasion was fake. Two moments in the first draft that broke with the news-broadcast fiction to present conventional dramatic scenes were deleted or revised.[99] At Houseman's suggestion, Koch also removed some specific mentions of the passage of time, such as one character's reference to "last night's massacre."[100] The first draft had clearly established that the invasion occurred over several days, but the revised version made it seem that the broadcast was proceeding in real time. Having the Martians conquer an entire planet in under forty minutes made no logical sense, but Houseman wanted to make the transitions from actual time to fictional time as seamless as possible.[101] Each change added immeasurably to the show's believability. Without meaning to, Koch, Houseman, and Stewart had made it much more likely that some listeners would be fooled by *War of the Worlds*.

Before the script could be mimeographed and passed out to the cast, a draft was sent to CBS's legal department for review. It came back with almost thirty requested changes. Some involved standard issues of taste and decency: a line referring to fleeing mobs trampling one another was deleted, as was the Martian war cry "*Ulla, Ulla, Ulla,*" because both were thought to sound too horrific.[102] But the censors' main concern was changing the names of real institutions mentioned in the script to avoid libel suits. So "the United States Weather Bureau in Washington, D.C.," became "the Government Weather Bureau," "Langley Field" became "Langham Field," and so on.[103] The Mercury grudgingly complied, but the changes were so minor as to be almost insignificant. Apparently, no one at CBS had any idea how dangerous the show might be.[104] The network executive Davidson Taylor even offered suggestions on how to improve the news bulletin portions of the program.[105]

Other changes came from the cast and crew. Houseman later recalled that *War of the Worlds* was unusually collaborative, with almost everyone in the company, apart from Welles, pitching in to save the show.[106] Actors suggested ways of reworking the dialogue to make it sound more naturalistic, comprehensible, or convincing. One cast member pointed out a line, taken from the Wells novel, where a survivor of the Martian attack suggests hiding in "the drains." To Americans, who only associated "drains" with the bottoms of sinks and showers, that Britishism would make no sense. So the word was changed to "sewers."[107]

But no one in the cast took the show quite as seriously as Frank Readick, a veteran radio actor who had preceded Welles as the Shadow.

Readick played Carl Phillips, a hapless reporter who witnesses the arrival of the Martians and dies in their initial attack. His is perhaps the most crucial role in the broadcast, because it is through his eyes that the audience is first asked to accept, to whatever degree, the Martians' existence. The credibility of the show depends largely on his terrified reaction. For research, Readick hunted up a copy of Herbert Morrison's *Hindenburg* recording and listened to it again and again, studying the way Morrison's voice swelled in alarm and abject horror. In the broadcast, he replicated those emotions with remarkable accuracy.[108]

However, not everyone in the cast thought that the show could be saved. Ben Gross, radio critic for the New York *Daily News*, later recalled approaching one of the Mercury's actors during that last week of October to ask what Welles had prepared for Sunday night. "Just between us, it's lousy," the actor said. In his view, not even Welles could do anything with a story that belonged in the funny papers. He told Gross not to tune in. The show would, he said, "probably bore you to death."[109]

By Saturday, the script was locked and given to the sound engineer John Dietz for a technical rehearsal, directed once again by Paul Stewart.[110] Welles later credited Stewart with devising many of the tricks, such as the frequent musical interruptions, that made the show sound so realistic.[111] Ora Nichols, head of the sound-effects department at WABC, also contributed greatly to the broadcast's verisimilitude. She had the perfect background for the Martian broadcast, having created sound effects for both the science fiction of *Buck Rogers* and the fakery of *The March of Time*.[112] The exact tricks she used on *War of the Worlds* have been lost to history, but legend has it that she achieved the scraping sound of the opening Martian cylinder by unscrewing a pickle jar in a bathroom.[113] Welles admired her work so much that, after the furor died down, he sent her a handwritten note of appreciation: "Dear Ora: Thanks for the best job anybody could ever do for anybody. All my love, Orson."[114]

After the tech rehearsal ended, Welles called the studio from the Mercury Theatre to find out how things were shaping up. A soundman answered and told him that Houseman and Stewart had already left. Then Welles asked what he thought of the show. "Very dull. Very dull . . . It'll put 'em to sleep . . . ," he said. "Where's the love interest?"[115] That would not have been what Welles wanted to hear, since *Danton's Death* was not turning out much better. He now faced disaster on two fronts, and it may very well have seemed to him that his remarkable run of luck was at its end. But, as Houseman well knew, Welles did his best work with his back against the wall.[116] Finally, *War of the Worlds* had earned its director's full attention.

Midafternoon on the day of the show, the cast and crew began to assemble in CBS's Studio One.[117] Among the first to arrive was Bernard Herrmann, who composed and conducted the music for the Mercury broadcasts. Paul Stewart oversaw Herrmann's rehearsals with the CBS orchestra, suggesting popular dance tunes, such as "La Cumparsita" and "Stardust," to fill the spaces between fake news bulletins. But the classically trained Herrmann struggled to find the proper rhythm, and the orchestra did not sound right. Stewart had tried to get an actual dance band, but the Mercury could not afford one. So he was left with a collection of "symphony men," more comfortable with Toscanini than Artie Shaw. Finally, the notoriously irascible Herrmann lost his temper and suggested that Stewart conduct the music. Stewart calmly took the baton and led the orchestra through the piece perfectly, much to Herrmann's chagrin. The conductor eventually took back the baton and led the orchestra during the show, but he never did get the rhythm quite right. Stewart would later describe Herrmann's rendition of "Stardust" as "one of the most hysterical musical moments in radio."[118]

Meanwhile, Welles, his coat off and his sleeves rolled up, stepped up on his own podium to Herrmann's right. The script lay before him on a music stand, and the actors clustered around microphones directly in front of him. Through the large glass windows to his right, Welles could see Houseman and the others in the control room.[119] From that central spot, Richard Baer recalled, Welles directed the show like a conductor. He waved his arms in the air and threw cues to Herrmann and his actors as if they were musicians in an orchestra.[120] And, like Herrmann, he quickly began to lose his temper with the material. Baer remembered him describing the script as both "corny" and "the worst, silliest thing he had ever done; just a Halloween prank."[121] Welles's assistant Richard Wilson, also in the cast that night, recalled that Welles at one point dropped his script to the floor and called it "the worst piece of crap I've ever had to do." The entire company, feeling much the same way, could not help laughing.[122]

But according to Houseman, such outbursts were typical of Welles in the frantic hours before each Mercury Theatre broadcast. He routinely berated his collaborators—calling them lazy, ignorant, incompetent, and many other insults—all while complaining of the mess they'd given him to clean up.[123] He delighted in making his cast and crew scramble by radically revising the show at the last minute, adding new things and taking others out. There were even times, as William Alland recalled, when he cut up the script with scissors and pasted it back together in the precious few hours before airtime.[124] Houseman once called radio "a hysterical medium,"[125] and Welles did his best to make it that way. But out of the chaos came a much stronger show.

One of Welles's key revisions on *War of the Worlds*, in Houseman's view, involved its pacing. Welles drastically slowed down the opening scenes by adding dialogue and drawing out the music to the point of tedium. Houseman objected strenuously, but Welles overruled him. He believed that listeners would only accept the unrealistic speed of the invasion if the broadcast started slowly, then gradually sped up.[126] Once the interplanetary war began, the pacing became chaotic, rudely jerking listeners from location to location, and event to event, without giving them any time to get their bearings. As the radio scholar Neil Verma has observed, the broadcast moved listeners swiftly through space, much like *The March of Time*, but without that series' central narrator the effect was wildly disorienting.[127] By the station break, even most listeners who knew that the show was fiction would be carried away by the speed of it all. For those who did not, those forty minutes would seem like hours.

One of Welles's most effective revisions came directly from his experience on *The March of Time*. Koch's first draft had included a speech from "the Secretary of War," reassuring listeners that their government was doing everything possible to combat the Martians. But it had been eliminated, likely at the behest of CBS's lawyers, before the script was mimeographed.[128] Welles put it back in and reassigned it to a less inflammatory Cabinet official, "the Secretary of the Interior," in order to appease the network. But he gave the character a purely vocal promotion by casting Kenneth Delmar, a *March of Time* actor who could do a pitch-perfect impression of Franklin Roosevelt.[129] Impersonating the President on air, on almost any show that was not *The March of Time*, was still expressly forbidden.[130] But Welles suggested, with a wink and a nod, that

Delmar make his character sound presidential, and Delmar happily complied.[131]

These kinds of ideas only came to Welles at the last minute, when disaster waited in the wings. As Richard Wilson observed decades later, radio brought out the best in Welles because it "was the only medium that imposed a discipline Orson would recognize, and that was the clock."[132] With the hours and then the minutes before airtime ticking away, Welles was forced to come up with innovative ways to save the show, and he invariably delivered. The cast and crew responded in kind. Everyone began to take the show more seriously, and to give it their best efforts for perhaps the first time.[133] A few may even have realized that the show might not prove disastrous after all—at least, not in the way they had anticipated.

When the revisions were complete, the cast and crew ran through the full script twice. Their first performance was almost eight minutes too long, a typical problem for the Mercury Theatre. Last-minute cuts and changes were made, and sometime after 6:00 p.m., a final "dress rehearsal" came in at about fifty-eight minutes—a perfect length.[134] With less than an hour left before they were set to go on, the cast scarfed down a hurried dinner while Welles and Houseman made whatever revisions they thought were necessary.[135] Finally, just two minutes before airtime, Welles resumed his place at the podium, drained a bottle of pineapple juice, and donned his headphones. The script that lay before him—heavily marked up, torn apart, and hurriedly thrown back together—was at last ready for an audience.[136] When Welles cued the announcement that the night's show would be an adaptation of H. G. Wells's *The War of the Worlds*, he could have had no idea how powerful the broadcast would prove to be—or that it was about to make him an international celebrity.

4

"Yours In Terror"

At any rate, you are to be congratulated on this marvelous piece of work as its realism was too much to describe. I was scared to death.

—Henry Clark of New York City
to Orson Welles, October 30, 1938[1]

It was 8:00 p.m. on the East Coast, 5:00 p.m. on the West. All across the continent—from Orono, Maine, to Fort Stevens, Oregon; Aberdeen, South Dakota, to Round Rock, Texas; and throughout southern Canada[2]—radios tuned to one of CBS's many affiliated stations poured out the stately, descending chords of Tchaikovsky's Piano Concerto No. 1 in B-flat minor. Since the past July, this dignified melody, given a full-bodied treatment by Bernard Herrmann's in-house orchestra, had signaled the beginning of each broadcast of *The Mercury Theatre on the Air*.

Most radio series used classical music because it was in the public domain and therefore cheap—*The Lone Ranger*'s use of the *William Tell Overture* being the most famous example.[3] But the Mercury's opening theme came as a specific suggestion from Davidson Taylor, the network executive in charge of the program. Slim, eloquent, and culturally refined, Taylor had chosen the piece over objections from CBS's marketing department, which wanted something more up-tempo and accessible to a mass audience.[4] The Tchaikovsky, on the other hand, seemed to package the show for a more refined listenership. As Theodor Adorno once noted, radio listeners had been trained to take that piece as a banner of high culture; it made them think, "Aha, serious music!"[5] But this ran somewhat counter to Welles's own hope that the show would, like his stage work, appeal to a wide audience.[6] After all, many of the Mercury's best episodes—from *Dracula* to *Sherlock Holmes* to tonight's *War of the Worlds*—were meant to be crowd-pleasing thrillers.

After twenty seconds of Tchaikovsky, the music cut out and the announcer, Dan Seymour, came on to introduce Orson Welles. Typically, at this point in the program Seymour trumpeted the accomplishments of the Mercury, and Welles spoke a little about the author whose work would be dramatized that night. But *War of the Worlds* began with very little preamble. Welles launched right into a monologue taken almost verbatim from the novel, his voice sonorous and sinister as he described how the Martians had been watching humanity for some time.

None of the other Mercury shows had gotten under way quite this quickly, or carried such a foreboding tone. But tonight there was no time for kidding around. With source material this fantastical, Welles knew he had to play it as straight as he could. From its very outset, this would be a different kind of program—serious, unsettling, and scary. Then Welles set the scene: an optimistic future, exactly one year from that night, in which all of the nation's anxieties were a thing of the past. With a segue into a prosaic weather report, the show established a fictitious broadcast within a broadcast. It was now about 8:02 p.m. in CBS's Studio One. The Mercury would not break this news-broadcast fiction for another thirty-eight minutes.

Not many people were listening. *The Mercury Theatre on the Air* had built a small but dedicated following since its premiere that summer. But, because it was geared "more to the classes then [sic] to the masses," as one New Jersey listener expressed it, the show had so far failed to make much of a mark on the radio landscape.[7] Its audience fell into what the sociologist Herbert J. Gans has called the public with "upper-middle culture" taste—well-educated, well-read, and artistically inclined listeners.[8] They were not quite at the forefront of avant-garde high culture, but they rejected the melodramatic thrillers, soap operas, and comedy/variety shows most popular with listeners and sponsors. They embraced *The Mercury Theatre on the Air* as high culture with mass appeal. "After six days of listening to moronic, asinine radio plays," a Brooklyn couple wrote to Welles the day after the broadcast, "your plays come as a refreshing, cool drink in an arid desert."[9]

This is not to say that all of the Mercury's regular listeners were radio snobs, though more than a few of them were.[10] Most simply enjoyed good drama and good literature. Those outside major cities particularly appreciated the show as a rare opportunity to experience Broadway-caliber theatrical productions.[11] "At the end of each broadcast," wrote a woman from Orange, New Jersey, in a letter to Welles, "I feel somehow that I should send you the price of a theater admission for an hour well spent."[12] And for young listeners with a love of the theater, many of whom were aspiring actors or writers themselves, Welles was an inspiration. "You seem to symbolize that youth *has* a place in the legitimate theatre," wrote a fifteen-year-old fan in Milwaukee.[13]

Most Americans, however, were not so discriminating. They were perfectly happy with what one of Welles's fans called the "frothy crap-peroo" available on other stations.[14] Each week the Mercury reached only 3.6 percent of the radio audience, or about four million listeners. By contrast, its time-slot rival, *The Chase & Sanborn Hour* on NBC, regularly commanded a whopping 34.7 percent of listeners at the same time.[15] Many of Welles's fans found *The Chase & Sanborn Hour* moronic and inane, yet it remained immensely popular thanks to the comedy sketches featuring ventriloquist Edgar Bergen and his dummy, Charlie McCarthy.[16] This could create a fair amount of conflict in households (or even within individual listeners) whose loyalties were divided between Bergen and Welles.[17] "I want you to put your programes [*sic*] on earlier because I have to battle with my family at eight in order to be able to listen to you," wrote a New York City listener to Welles. She added, perhaps with disdain, "They like that McCarthy dummy."[18] Others found themselves switching back and forth in a vain attempt to catch the highlights of both programs.[19]

Each episode of *The Chase & Sanborn Hour* began with two songs from Nelson Eddy, one of the nation's most popular singers. That evening, he lent his rumbling basso profundo voice to the "Song of the Vagabonds" and the "Canadian Logging Song." Then came the witty repartee of Bergen and McCarthy. In keeping with the holiday, this Halloween-eve program found Bergen struggling to describe a night spent in a haunted house, with constant interruptions from his wooden costar. "And then, without warning, a horrible figure pounced upon me," Bergen said. "Something tugged at my memory. Where had I seen that ghostly face before?" Flipping into his McCarthy persona, Bergen offered his own retort: "In a mirror?" After giving up on the ghost story, Bergen turned the show over to the screen star Dorothy Lamour, who sang Hoagy Carmichael's "Two Sleepy People."[20]

Very soon after *War of the Worlds*, it became commonly accepted that many of the people panicked by the broadcast were *Chase & Sanborn* listeners who lost interest in the show during one of its musical inter-ludes.[21] They spun the dial, so the story goes, and landed on CBS in the midst of the Martian invasion. This kind of channel surfing, or "dial twirl-ing," was common practice in the 1930s. The *New York Post* called it "di-alitis," defined as "a disease of the hand which makes it impossible for some folks to stay with any one program."[22] Welles's fans, and others who took radio drama seriously as an art form, deplored "dialitis." They felt that the medium could only mature when audiences learned to pay attention. *War of the Worlds* became an opportunity for them to chastise people who listened to the radio carelessly, distractedly, without giving good drama the respect they felt it deserved.[23] "Perhaps this will be a lesson for those asinine individuals who blithely spin their dials haphazardly from one program to another," wrote one Arizonan to Welles. "Hereafter they will probably refrain from jumping to conclusions before they know all the details."[24] But these "dialitis" critics jumped to some untenable conclu-sions of their own. All the hard evidence suggests that *The Chase & San-born Hour* was only a minor contributing factor to the Martian hysteria.

People who wrote in to the Mercury Theatre or the FCC after *War of the Worlds* were often very specific about when and how they had tuned in.[25] For those who were frightened, it was important to establish how they had been deceived in order to prove they were not silly, stupid, or superstitious. For those who were not, it was a way of showing that any-body who listened correctly would not have been fooled. Yet, of all the nearly two thousand surviving letters written in the broadcast's wake, only six came from people frightened by *War of the Worlds* because they channel-surfed away from Bergen and McCarthy.[26] Additionally, an au-dience survey taken after the broadcast found that only 12 percent of listeners who heard *War of the Worlds* tuned out *The Chase & Sanborn Hour* after the first comedy routine, as the "dialitis" myth suggested. The Mercury, therefore, only captured a small sliver of Bergen and McCarthy's audience, and over 80 percent of the people who heard *War of the Worlds* missed *The Chase & Sanborn Hour* entirely.[27]

The "dialitis" theory survives because it offers an easy explanation for how a show with such a small audience could have panicked a large num-ber of people. Most historians still blame Nelson Eddy and his suppos-edly lackluster rendition of the "Neapolitan Love Song," even though Eddy never actually sang the "Neapolitan Love Song" that night, and his first musical interlude ended a good five minutes before *War of the Worlds* began to heat up.[28] But many if not most of the people frightened by the broadcast did not suffer from "dialitis." The idea that they did is a distortion born of 1930s cultural elitism, of disdain for a mass audience dumb enough to trust a ventriloquist that they could not see. One Toledo man echoed the views of many, in his letter to Welles, when he wrote that the panic "serves America genuinely, jolly right for her moronic taste—to a nation of Charlie McCarthy listeners last night terror flew Westward upon gleeful wings."[29] But, in truth, there was no mass exodus from Charlie McCarthy to Orson Welles that night.

Instead, the broadcast's accidental audience came in dribs and drabs. They began to tune in soon after Welles's introduction ended and the fake weather report began. Some were people who had been listening to CBS earlier and left their dials on it when they shut their radios off. When they switched them back on after 8:00 p.m., they stumbled into *War of the Worlds* without knowing what they were listening to.[30] Others were people who wanted to hear *The Mercury Theatre on the Air* but were, for whatever reason, delayed. And because Boston's CBS affiliate did not carry the broadcast, listeners in New England who picked up *War of the Worlds* often did so on faraway stations, plagued with poor reception and heavy static. This made it nearly impossible to understand what was going on.[31] When these latecomers heard the fake news reports, at least some of them believed, however briefly, that Welles's program had been pre-empted by news of a disaster or some other urgent program.[32]

But there was one musician on the air that night whose listless performance did more to bring late listeners to CBS than perhaps anything else. Not Nelson Eddy, or even Dorothy Lamour, but Welles's own Bernard Herrmann.

After Welles set the tone, the broadcast got off to a very slow start. One accidental listener, in his letter to the FCC, called it "a mild, insidious beginning."[33] After reading the fake weather bulletin, the announcer told listeners that he was transferring them "to the Meridian Room in the Hotel Park Plaza in downtown New York," where they would enjoy the musical stylings "of Ramón Raquello and his orchestra." On Welles's cue, Herrmann led his musicians into a plodding, slightly off-key rendition of "La Cumparsita." It was intentionally bad, a parody of the slow dance music popular on the airwaves at that time. But on this quiet Sunday evening, that was exactly the kind of music that a lot of Americans wanted to hear.

In rehearsal, Houseman had worried that such a slow start would drive away many listeners.[34] But the exact opposite happened: the show's audience grew as soon as the music began. A Gallup poll later found that 60 percent of those who heard the broadcast tuned in after it started.[35] People all over the country were reading, studying, doing the dishes, or putting the kids to bed, and they wanted to hear something that would help them relax.[36] Some spun the dial and stopped when they found the Spanish strains of Herrmann's orchestra.[37] Others had been using their radios as background music, listening without really paying attention, and missed the initial announcements.[38] "Well I can't say definitely that the announcer did *not* mention the fact that the following was a play," wrote one woman in her letter to the FCC; "still I heard no mention of it. I did hear the announcement that a program of dance music would follow."[39] Because radio shows often began with a commercial at the top of the hour, many people only half listened to the first few minutes of any program anyway. Most of Welles's audience did the same that night.[40]

Then the music faded away, and the audience heard: "Ladies and gentlemen, we interrupt our program of dance music to bring you a special bulletin from the Intercontinental Radio News." The report that followed—that astronomers in Chicago and Princeton had seen "several explosions of incandescent gas, occurring at regular intervals on the planet Mars"—was not really the stuff of a late-breaking news flash. Some listeners may even have wondered why the network bothered to interrupt the music at all. For at least one listener in California, this first mention of Mars was enough to make clear that he was listening to a play.[41] But barely a month earlier, Europe had come within a hairsbreadth of world war, while the East Coast of the United States suffered its most destructive hurricane in generations. The words "we interrupt our program" and "a special bulletin" were still powerful enough to make people sit up and take notice, or to wake up listeners who were half dozing.[42]

"Quick, listen, Mars is exploding," shouted Lucile McLain, a patient in a tuberculosis sanitarium in Oregon, to the other convalescents resting nearby. Each patient had headphones to listen to the radio, and so all seven women sitting on the front porch that "gloomy, rainy Sunday evening" put on their sets just in time to hear "Ramón Raquello" segue into

Hoagy Carmichael's "Stardust."[43] Almost a thousand miles to the south, in Los Angeles, Mrs. Johanna Wilizenski was so intrigued by the news that she "called to friends & neighbors, as we were told, to listen in for further reports."[44] Other listeners, less interested in what was happening on a dead planet millions of miles away, ignored the bulletin or switched over to something else.[45]

Still more were tuning in. Edward A. Callan of Elmhurst, Long Island, missed these opening announcements because of a debate with his seventeen-year-old daughter and eleven-year-old niece: they could not decide on what to listen to that night. "We are all lovers of all radio stories," he later wrote to Welles. "We also love Edgar Bergen. So we flipped a coin to determine which we would listen to and the coin decided on 'Orson Welles.'"[46] They tuned in about five minutes after the hour and heard the music interrupted for another announcement. According to this bulletin, "the Government Meteorological Bureau" found the Martian explosions significant enough to ask observatories nationwide to keep an eye on the Red Planet. "Due to the unusual nature of this occurrence," the announcer said, "we have arranged an interview with the noted astronomer Professor Pierson, who will give us his views on this event."

With a promise to connect listeners to the Princeton University Observatory as soon as possible, the announcer gave them over to another twenty seconds of "Ramón Raquello" and "Stardust." Callan could have been forgiven for thinking he'd tuned in to the wrong station, or that Welles's program had been pre-empted for some reason. But he knew immediately that he was listening to a radio drama—a particularly boring one, but a radio drama nonetheless. "At this point," he wrote to Welles, "it was anything but interesting, but as we have enjoyed your stories before, we decided to hang on and [are] glad we did."[47]

When the connection to Princeton came through, listeners first heard an echoing, clocklike ticking. Then the reporter Carl Phillips, played by Frank Readick, introduced himself. After explaining that the ticking came from the machinery of the observatory's massive telescope, Phillips began to interview Professor Richard Pierson. The astronomer's deep voice, a bit gruff and self-satisfied, marked him as a man entirely confident in his understanding of the universe and his place in it. With a bit of a chuckle, Pierson derided the popular notion that there were canals on the Martian surface, assuring Phillips that there was almost no possibility that the planet was inhabited. He could not, however, offer an explanation for the strange explosions seen on Mars.

"By the way, Professor," Phillips asked, "for the benefit of our listeners, how far is Mars from the Earth?"

"Approximately forty million miles," Pierson responded.

"Well," Phillips said, laughing, "that seems a safe enough distance."

In the affluent Cleveland suburb of Solon, Ohio, E. C. Parmenter was just tuning in. His entire family, "including a ten-year-old girl who should have been in bed but wasn't," were all circled around the radio. At first, they did not understand what they were hearing. "This is funny," Parmenter said. "I haven't got the Mercury Theater [sic]. It's just some astronomer giving a scientific talk."[48] Even though Parmenter and his family were presumably regular listeners of *The Mercury Theatre on the Air*, none of them recognized Orson Welles as the voice of Professor Pierson.

Then Phillips interrupted the interview to say that Pierson had gotten a telegram. With Pierson's permission, Phillips read it on the air. It described a "shock of almost earthquake intensity" detected outside Princeton. Pierson assured listeners that this event, possibly a meteor strike, had nothing to do with the explosions on Mars, and Phillips brought the interview to a close. After a brief piano interlude, the announcer came back on the air to confirm "that at 8:50 P.M. a huge, flaming object, believed to be a meteorite, fell on a farm in the neighborhood of Grover's Mill, New Jersey." He then told listeners that Phillips and Pierson were en route to the site. In Ohio, the Parmenter family settled in to hear more. The words "Mars" and "meteorite" were all they needed to realize that what they were listening to was fiction.[49]

Two minutes later, Phillips was back on the air, claiming to have "made the eleven miles from Princeton in ten minutes." The impossible speed of Phillips's arrival convinced some late listeners that the broadcast was fake, but not many.[50] More were swept along by Phillips's rapid-fire description of the impact site. The "thing," as Phillips described it, that had fallen from the sky had plowed into a farmer's field, digging itself a massive crater. It was cylindrical, roughly thirty yards in diameter, and made of a bizarre "yellowish-white" metal unmarred by its fiery descent through the atmosphere. In short, it looked like no meteor Phillips had ever seen. Police were on the scene, keeping bystanders from getting too close to the object. The wailing sirens of their squad cars wove an eerie tapestry of sound for radio audiences. Phillips complained that a cop blocked his view, and the mike picked up the shouts of spectators and police talking over one another. It all sounded loud, messy, and real.

"Imagine tuning in on some dance music," wrote one Coloradan to the FCC the next day. "Suddenly it is interupted [sic] by a news flash, later by another. This is quite a common occurance [sic], isn't it? Then a radio commentator comes on with an interview with a Princeton proffessor [sic], and later an eye-view account. Isn't that all happening in reality almost every day?"[51]

Phillips began to interview Mr. Wilmuth, the farmer who owned the land where the "thing" fell. Gently, he prodded Wilmuth to describe what had happened when it crashed. But Wilmuth, given a folksy country dialect by the actor Ray Collins, spoke with an awkwardness that made it clear he had never been on the radio before. Phillips had to ask him twice to get closer to the mike, and kept interrupting him when he strayed off topic. When the interview was over, Wilmuth, enjoying his newfound fame, asked, "Want me to tell you some more?" But Phillips talked right over him, shuffling him off the proverbial stage: "That's quite all right, that's plenty." The dialogue in fictional radio shows was never this rough or jumbled, and the characters never, ever struggled with the mike. For listeners who were just tuning in now, or who did not know what they were listening to, this exchange (and Wilmuth's vanity) had the unmistakable ring of truth.[52]

As Phillips went back to describing the scene around him, he began to notice a strange sound coming from the object. "Do you hear it?" Phillips asked his listeners, telling them he was bringing the microphone closer to the object. "Now we're not more than twenty-five feet away. Can you hear it now?" And there it was: a low, rumbling, *scraping* sound. Pierson grumbled something about that sound's having to do with the "unequal cooling" of the object, but he was about to be proved wrong.

Phillips cut the professor off, exclaiming that he could see the top of the cylinder rotating. The object was *opening*. Listeners heard police shouting at the crowd, telling them to stay back, and then a dull thud as the top of the "thing" fell off and hit the ground. Rapidly, breathlessly, Phillips told his listeners that he could see something emerging from the cylinder: a strange tentacled creature, "large as a bear" and with skin "like wet leather." It could barely move—it was "weighed down," Phillips explained, "by . . . possibly gravity or something"—and the reporter was both fascinated and repulsed by its horrendous face. "I can hardly force myself to keep looking at it . . . ," he said. "The eyes are black and gleam like a serpent. The mouth is V-shaped with saliva dripping from its rimless lips that seem to quiver and pulsate."

This was radio's theater of the mind at its most vivid. Koch had breathed new life into H. G. Wells's words, and Readick's delivery made listeners see the horror Phillips was describing. "I only wish I could forget it," one Washington woman later wrote about the broadcast, "especially how the monsters emerged from the cylinder."[53] Phillips told listeners he was moving the microphone to a better vantage point. "Hold on, will you please," he said, "I'll be right back in a minute." And he left listeners with thirty seconds of eerily calm piano music as they tried to process what, exactly, they had just heard.

This was the first major leap of faith the broadcast asked listeners to make. The slightly compressed time frame aside, everything up until this point had been more or less credible. But here things moved clearly into the realm of science fiction. Many late listeners, upon hearing Phillips's description of the slimy, tentacled alien, finally realized what was up. "Of course, when the Martians appeared, the horror element became comedy for me in the realization that I had been *had*," wrote one Connecticut listener.[54] Another wrote to Welles that Phillips's description of the Martian's face "was all to [*sic*] much for me. I picked up a paper and saw your listing. And my heart returned to normal."[55]

But thousands of others were listening in astonishment and stunned disbelief. They may not have trusted the message, but they saw no reason to distrust the messenger. "We, the American people, look to radio as our most reliable and quickest source of news," wrote one listener to the FCC. "We depend upon the authenticity of this news."[56] If it seemed hard to believe that aliens had landed in New Jersey, it was even harder to accept that CBS, America's "news network," would so violate the public trust.[57] "There have been articles by scientists published from time to time which say that they believe Mars to be inhabited by people," wrote one listener in her letter to the FCC. "When one considers the advances and progress that have been made, which our forefathers would not believe, even a sane person might believe such a thing possible."[58] The brilliant use of music and sound effects, to say nothing of Readick's impassioned performance, made it even easier to accept the broadcast as genuine.

"There was of course the thought that such a thing could not happen, it could not be so," wrote one Arkansan to CBS, "but there it was, presented as fact by the Columbia Broadcasting System as News, there being no way for a late tuner, or a tuner otherwise occupied at the beginning of the program, to know that it was drama and not a bona-fide News Bulletin."[59]

In struggling to reconcile the fantasy they were hearing with the realism of the program, some listeners relied on an accepted frame of reference, whether factual or spiritual, to interpret what they heard. "My husband thought it the end of the world and I thought it was Germany coming over here to destroy us," wrote one Californian to the FCC.[60] Another listener wrote that she was briefly "puzzled" by the broadcast, but then there was "a flash in my mind 'suppose this was a german [sic] war plan disguised [as] make believe a fairy tale some new stunt.'" So she flipped to other stations, heard their regular programming, and realized that she had been deceived.[61] Also, earlier references to the crashed spacecraft as a "meteor" led some listeners to believe they were hearing reports of destruction caused by a falling meteorite.[62] There had been a spate of "falling star" sightings reported in the press that summer, and it was easy to imagine that another had landed in New Jersey.[63] People, even now, were not necessarily listening attentively to each and every word of the program. They were filtering it through their own assumptions, and making it fit with their own understanding of the world.

The broadcast did not give listeners much time to reflect. Phillips was soon back on the air, words tumbling out of him as he explained that three police officers were approaching the pit with a white flag of truce, hoping to parley with the strange creatures. Then listeners heard a weird, unearthly whine as Phillips described a mysterious device rising out of the cylinder: "a small beam of light against a mirror." As the Martian weapon opened fire on the crowd, Phillips's voice swelled with alarm— just like Herbert Morrison's in the Hindenburg recording. "There's a jet of flame springing from that mirror, and it leaps right at the advancing men!" he cried. "It strikes them head on! Lord, they're turning into flame!" In the background, people could be heard shrieking in pain and terror. Then the beam of fire ignited the gas tanks of nearby parked cars. As Phillips breathlessly announced that the flames were spreading in his direction, he was suddenly and violently cut off.

And then . . . silence.

In CBS's Studio One, Welles held the pause like a conductor for a full six seconds, while his cast and crew waited anxiously to get on with the show.[64] In their New York City apartment, Mrs. Anna Farrell and her nephew, who had tuned in only a few minutes earlier, were absolutely horrified. "I was crying so hard," Farrell later wrote, "[that] my sister woke up and wanted to know what I was crying for, well she listened."[65] No radio drama had ever used dead air to artistic effect like this. Farrell and her family were absolutely convinced that they had just heard Phillips and countless others burned to death live on the air.

Finally, the announcer returned: "Ladies and gentlemen, due to circumstances beyond our control, we are unable to continue the broadcast from Grover's Mill. Evidently there's some difficulty with our field transmission. However, we will return to that point at the earliest opportunity."

It was now about 8:19 p.m., seventeen minutes after the fake news began, and the broadcast began to pick up speed. A brigadier general from the New Jersey State Militia came on, announcing that the governor had put large swaths of the state under martial law. The announcer said that the Red Cross had sent emergency personnel into Grover's Mill, where the State Police reported that all fires started by the Martian "heat ray" had been contained. At 8:23 p.m., someone claiming to be "vice-president in charge of operations" told listeners that the network was "turning over our facilities to the State Militia at Trenton." Then the broadcast patched into a transmission from "Captain Lansing of the Signal Corps." Listeners heard him describe the scene at Grover's Mill, where seven thousand soldiers surrounded the Martian spacecraft. "It looks almost like a real war," Lansing said, confident of an imminent victory. But then he saw something, "a shield-like affair rising up out of the cylinder"—standing up, in fact, on three massive metal legs—and the transmission cut out once more.

Then the announcer came back on the air: "Ladies and gentlemen, I have a grave announcement to make. Incredible as it may seem, both the observations of science and the evidence of our eyes lead to the inescapable assumption that those strange beings who landed in the Jersey farmlands tonight are the vanguard of an invading army from the planet Mars." He went on to report that the Martians, in their massive tripod fighting machine, had already decimated the seven thousand soldiers sent in to destroy them. Now they were moving north, ripping up railroad tracks and lines of communication, with a horde of refugees fleeing before them. It was about 8:26 p.m. The New Jersey State Militia had been called up and wiped out in less than seven minutes.

For those who knew that they were listening to fiction, it was clear that events were moving much too quickly to be real. "Before 30 seconds, of course, the nature of the program is obvious," wrote one New Yorker to the FCC. "I am not convinced that the entire land forces of the American army in the East here can be mobilized in a few seconds, much less wiped out."[66] But for those listeners who believed in what they heard, even those listening with rapt attention, it was not so clear that things were happening sequentially. As the sociologist David Miller has noted, the broadcast came to them as a blur of information, flying by too fast to be fully understood, and they had no way of going back to verify what they had just heard.[67]

Dozens of letters written by the frightened mention that they were listening to the broadcast in the company of others, often in groups of more than five or six people.[68] "My family were panic stricken," wrote one woman from New York City, "my mother, father, sister, brother[,] nephew, cousin, brother in law and myself were crying and we just didn't know what to do."[69] It was, after all, Sunday evening, a time for dinner parties and family gatherings, when the entire household would be clustered around the radio. In that environment, people simply cannot have heard every word of the broadcast. They were talking to one another, shushing one another, theorizing, trying to figure out what was happening, and they came away with a patchy understanding of what the announcers were saying.

These listeners only picked up key words and phrases, such as the movements of the military and reports of fleeing refugees. People tuning in just in time to hear that "forty people, including six State Troopers, lie dead in a field east of the village of Grover's Mill" had no understanding of the context, and had heard nothing about aliens. Wrote one anonymous listener to Welles: "As we listened it was some time before Mars, or Martians, was mentioned, or we caught such mention."[70] All they knew was that something horrible was happening on the Eastern Seaboard—and that, perhaps, it was coming their way. When the broadcast said that the Martians were filling the countryside with huge clouds of poisonous black smoke, against which gas masks offered no protection, that was all many listeners could focus on.[71] "I tuned the dial to K.N.X. and a voice said there are five enemy planes flying high over New Jersey dropping big steel tanks of gas and germs," wrote one Californian to President Roosevelt.[72] Poison gas had been used to devastating effect on the battlefields of

World War I, and there was every indication it would return in the next major conflict. Now the broadcast made it seem that that prediction was coming true.[73]

For late listeners in New York and particularly in New Jersey, what stood out most were the familiar place names. "All we could hear was the news of a Martian volcano and 'a meteor has struck in New Jersey,'" wrote a Newark woman to Welles. "Being New Jerseyites, we immediately pricked up our ears."[74] With his careful attention to geographic detail in plotting out the Martian invasion, Howard Koch had given his script great credibility. The broadcast described the spread of the poisonous black smoke down to the individual streets it crossed. Listeners were told exactly which highways they should use to evacuate, all of which were real. "I tuned in just in time to hear the announcer say: 'This radio station has been turned over for the services of the N.J. State Militia,'" wrote a New Jersey listener to CBS. "When names such as 'Trenton,' 'Plainfield,' 'Watchung,' 'Newark,' 'Raymond Boulevard,' [and] 'South Street' are mentioned, I think a radio program of that type is being carried too far."[75]

Above all, what late listeners heard and understood were the references to real organizations and figures of authority. Their ears pricked up at the mentions of the governor of New Jersey, the Red Cross, the vice president of CBS, and Princeton University. This, more than perhaps anything else, made the broadcast seem real to those that it deceived.[76] "It was *not* because of superior acting that the listening audience became hysterical," wrote one anonymous listener to Welles, "but, because you used government departments and news flashes which people have always placed faith in, prior to your broadcast."[77] Listeners regarded the names of these institutions and officials as essentially trademarks, falsely assuming that they could not be invoked without the government's permission.[78] Therefore, if the broadcast said that the governor of New Jersey had proclaimed a state of martial law, then it must be so, no matter what. "Truly, the broadcast seemed incredible," wrote a Maine woman to the FCC. "But not as incredible as the thought that our government would allow its name to be used to disseminate such a lie."[79]

At about 8:27 p.m., Kenny Delmar came on as "the Secretary of the Interior." In a voice almost identical to Franklin Roosevelt's, he urged the country to "confront this destructive adversary with a nation united, courageous, and consecrated to the preservation of human supremacy on this earth." Some listeners did believe that they were hearing a speech from the President, though perhaps not as many as is commonly supposed.[80] The letters and telegrams sent in the following days to Harold Ickes, the real secretary of the interior, suggest that not everyone was taken in by Delmar's impression.[81] But the speech carried the full weight of the Department of the Interior and, for some people, that was enough. "It might just as well [have] been the President of the United States addressing the country," wrote one Massachusetts man to the FCC, "it meant the very same to me."[82] Many listeners believed that impersonating a Cabinet official on air simply could not be legal—even though such impersonations were the stock-in-trade of *The March of Time* and other similar programs. One man, in a letter to Ickes, wrote that the impersonation was a forgery, no less than if Welles had signed Ickes's name to a check. And if *that* was illegal, then why not this?[83] Much the same could be said of *The March of Time*. By drawing upon their shared experience with that show to add realism to *War of the Worlds*, Welles and Delmar had unwittingly revealed the dangers of "fakery in allegiance to the truth."

In their letters, the frightened often stressed that they were not unintelligent or otherwise hysterical people. They mentioned their level of education, professional qualifications, and, in one instance, the number of books they owned.[84] "Here we're both college graduates, both level-headed, and really not silly at all," wrote a married couple from Michigan, "yet tomorrow the whole town will be giving us the laugh."[85] But they need not have felt so self-conscious. With its many markers of authenticity, anyone who tuned in on the broadcast at the right time could have been taken in, no matter how well educated or sensible people felt they were. And after about 8:20 p.m., when the tempo of the broadcast sped up dramatically and the references to "Mars" and "Martians" grew fewer and fewer, anyone just tuning in could fall for the news flashes without believing that aliens were attacking Earth.

"You may question my sanity, you may wonder what was the matter with me, a man supposed to be educated and experienced, that I did not realize that such could not possibly be true," wrote a Long Island listener to the FCC; "my only answer is that I am, or was, a person who believed in the integrity of the basic honesty of a Press Radio News bulletin, and that I know that never in God's world would any high government official, sane or insane, drunk or sober, ever play such a practical joke."[86]

At 8:30 p.m., any other radio program would have stopped for a station break. But the announcer on CBS kept reading bulletin after bulletin describing the advance of the Martian tripods, now numbering six. He reported that another Martian cylinder had landed near Morristown, New Jersey, and that the army was trying to destroy it before it released more fighting machines. Listeners were connected to an artillery unit in the Watchung Mountains, only to hear it overrun by a cloud of the poisonous black smoke. Then they heard a transmission from the leader of a bombing squadron flying low over the tripods as they approached New York City. Before the planes could release their bombs, the Martians opened fire with their heat ray, shooting them all down. As the last surviving pilot shouted that his plane was about to crash into one of the fighting machines, he, too, was cut off.

Then came what sounded like a brief exchange between ham-radio operators, describing the spread of the black smoke throughout New Jersey. A cacophony of sirens, bells, and far-off whistles faded in—the clamor of a city being evacuated. Another announcer came on the air, reporting that he was standing atop the "Broadcasting Building, New York City." He described the scene as frantic citizens fled Manhattan. "Streets are all jammed," he said. "Noise in crowds like New Year's Eve in city." He explained that most major roadways leading out of the city were blocked by a crush of refugees, while others tried to flee on dangerously overcrowded boats in the East River. But they had nowhere to run. "Martian cylinders are falling all over the country," the announcer said. "One outside of Buffalo, one in Chicago, St. Louis . . . seem to be timed and spaced."

Ray Collins, the actor who had earlier played the farmer Wilmuth, read these lines with just the right amount of restrained desperation. His tone made it plain that the situation was entirely hopeless. "No more defenses," he said. "Our army wiped out . . . artillery, air force, everything wiped out. This may be the last broadcast." It was 8:37 p.m. in New York. "The rout of civilization . . . the massacre of mankind," as H. G. Wells described it in the original novel, was almost complete.[87] It had taken roughly thirty-five minutes.

Then the announcer said he could see the Martian machines approaching Manhattan over the Palisades, "wading the Hudson like a man wading through a brook." There were five of them now, one having been destroyed when the crippled bomber crashed into it. Step by step, the announcer described their approach. Once they were all marshaled "like a line of new towers on the city's west side," the Martians began filling the concrete canyons with poison gas. The announcer told listeners that New Yorkers were diving into the East River in droves, trying to swim to safety, and he called out the approach of the black smoke, street by street.

"It's reached Times Square," he said, the terror in his voice barely contained. "People're trying to run away from it, but it's no use. They're falling like flies. Now the smoke's crossing Sixth Avenue . . . Fifth Avenue . . ." He began to cough. "A hundred yards away . . ." He was struggling for breath now. "It's fifty feet . . ." Then listeners heard a sigh and a thud as the announcer's body hit the floor. That left them with nothing but the banshee wail of boat whistles and car horns far below.

Finally, listeners heard the voice of a single ham-radio operator, played once again by Frank Readick, trying to establish contact with another station. "Isn't there anyone on the air?" he asked into the void. "Isn't there anyone?" But there was no one left alive for him to talk to.

This was the dramatic climax of the broadcast. Listeners nationwide, whether they believed in what they heard or not, were on the edge of their seats. Even though the vast majority of Welles's listeners knew that they were listening to a play, some felt themselves being pulled in by the realism of it all.[88] "I could feel the world reeling around me," wrote one Philadelphian later that night. "It was almost too realistic."[89] Another listener, who knew full well that the show was a fiction, wrote to Welles that she still could not help covering her nose and mouth with a handkerchief as the Martians gassed New York.[90] For these listeners, and many others, the broadcast had achieved the ultimate goal of any dramatic production: it had drawn its audience completely and totally into its fictional world.

For the fraction of Welles's audience who thought the broadcast was real, this illusion went far beyond playful suspension of disbelief. The relentless Martian advance, so meticulously plotted by Howard Koch, effectively encircled listeners in New York, New Jersey, and Pennsylvania. They were stuck, with nowhere to run, in the path of a vicious and swift invader. And when the announcer mentioned that more Martians were landing in the Midwest, frightened listeners in Illinois, Missouri, and other states knew that they were next.[91] This sense of being hopelessly trapped, with death an absolute and imminent certainty, was what made the broadcast such a terrifying experience for those it deceived. In their letters, these listeners vividly described how the show had them praying, sobbing, or shaking uncontrollably—and sometimes all at once.[92]

"I could not stop crying," wrote a listener in Ohio the day after the broadcast. "Every muscle in my body became tense and today I am unable to go to my work, because I feel like I had been beaten all over. My head aches all over, too."[93] A New Yorker wrote to Welles, "A few years ago I nearly drowned but God only knows those few minute[s] were nothing at all compared with the torture I went through last night."[94] And a Pennsylvania man, describing his family's experience, captured the feelings of many when he wrote: "We all suffered a thousand deaths."[95] This intense, often visceral fear can only be called hysteria.

Because these letters were usually written immediately after the broadcast, when emotions ran high, it can be difficult to separate genuine physical terror from hyperbole. Ten letters, for example, report people suffering "heart attacks" or near heart attacks during the broadcast, and a few more say that doctors were called to calm down frightened listeners.[96] But it is not at all clear how serious these incidents really were. Though speculation swirled for weeks that *War of the Worlds* had caused one or two fatal heart attacks, no deaths were ever definitively tied to the broadcast.[97] Undoubtedly, the show was powerful enough to make some listeners feel ill with fear—even leaving them bedridden for hours, yet unable to sleep. For perhaps a few listeners, weakened by illness or old age, the shock could be serious.[98] But rarely did the effects last more than a day or two.[99] Those whom the broadcast frightened, it terrified—but not for very long.

What is clear is that, however terrifying the broadcast was, it was rarely enough on its own to send people fleeing into the streets. Later reports of listeners who abandoned their homes en masse or took arms against the Martians were greatly exaggerated. Only six listeners who wrote to Welles mentioned having fled their homes because of the broadcast, though at least another thirteen were ready to do so.[100] And although the number of angry letters written to the FCC was ultimately much higher than those written to the Mercury, the number of writers who admitted fleeing in advance of the Martians is almost the same. Five letters came from individuals who abandoned their homes, and one man sent the FCC a newspaper clipping describing how his young son had hurt himself by falling into a ditch as he ran for safety.[101] Even for truly terrified listeners, panic was the exception, not the rule.

"I don't even know whether your name is spelled this way," wrote a Michigan woman to "Orton" Welles, "but I do know that fifteen minutes ago, my husband and I, our two sleeping little ones, cherubic in pink 'cuddly' blankets, were racing downtown to get the car tanked, yes darn you! 'tanked' with gasoline. We were off for the 'open spaces' after putting in a $1.50 long distance call to say goodbye to my mother."[102] At a gas station in rural Virginia, a lawyer from the District of Columbia reported seeing a car pull up with an entire family piled inside. The driver "jumped out of his car, his face white as a sheet," the lawyer later wrote, "and asked me if I had heard about the terrible thing that had happened. I told him no." As the driver rapidly explained that "monsters" from Mars had killed thousands of people in New Jersey, other people at the gas station, who knew nothing of the broadcast, began to grow alarmed. "Of course, with an elementary knowledge of science I knew the story couldn't be true," wrote the attorney in his letter to the FCC, "but you must realize that the overwhelming majority of the American people do not have even an elementary knowledge of science."[103]

In Philadelphia, Alvesta C. Flanagan was listening to Bergen and Mc-Carthy on NBC when her downstairs neighbors rang her doorbell. "Come down!" they said. "There's something on the radio. It's serious!" Flanagan went to their apartment, where her neighbors were debating whether to wake their young children and flee the city. "Between their questions I was catching words from their radio," she later wrote to Welles, " 'bombing planes—martial law—destroying bridges—communication.' " But as soon as she caught a mention of Mars, Flanagan realized that it was *The Mercury Theatre on the Air* and quickly told her neighbors. "Color came back into their faces; fear began to drain out," Flanagan wrote. Her neighbor's husband "went next door to tell his brother everything was all right. His brother had kissed his little girl good-bye and was going out for his car—whether he intended to combat the Martians by automobile, I don't know."[104]

These panicked scenes of flight and near flight, which turned *War of the Worlds* into the stuff of American legend, did happen, but they were very, very rare. Even among the people frightened by the program, most stayed close to their radios, listening intently for twenty, twenty-five, or thirty minutes before they figured out it was fake (as many did) or heard an announcement that it was fiction. As they would in a real emergency, people did not want to miss any important information, and there was not much time to do anything but listen. "Unable to move, we sat and listened to the astounding announcements," wrote a woman from New York State. "Breathlessly we listened! We were like flies that had become stuck to their fatal paper."[105]

Instead of panicking, many frightened listeners fell prey to a more common, and perhaps more dangerous, impulse. The historian William Manchester called it "an instinct older than the invention of language"— the need to spread the news.[106] In dozens of letters, frightened listeners describe calling up or going to see friends or relatives, telling them to turn on CBS or to get out of the path of the invaders.[107] Dozens more came from people who tuned in only because they were on the receiving end of those calls, or because their next-door neighbors burst in to warn them of the catastrophe in New Jersey.[108] As one Maryland woman wrote to Welles, her frightened neighbor "couldn't stand to listen alone."[109] Listeners who tuned in on *War of the Worlds* this way—without an understanding of the unrealistic pace of the broadcast, or even knowing that it was about Martians—were some of the people most frightened by it. Yet, as the journalism scholar W. Joseph Campbell has noted, their fear had more to do with how they were told about the show than with the show itself.[110]

In their Manhattan apartment, Anna Farrell and her sister decided to warn anybody they could about the invasion. Farrell's sister threw a coat on over the pajamas she was wearing (which "were of the male species," with the "fly up the front") and donned "a pair of flamingo red gloves and a broken pair of spectacles," and together they headed out onto West Fifty-fourth Street. They missed an announcement that the program was fictitious by mere seconds. After telling a cabdriver, who thought they were crazy, and the owner of a local delicatessen, who grabbed a can of dog food and fled into the night, Farrell grew despondent. She started toward a nearby drugstore, intending to buy poison because she did not "want to die by fire." But she stopped when her sister suggested, in what Farrell described as "her sweet voice," that they should "go get a drink first." They found a local bar, had three Scotch highballs apiece, and decided that "the Lord had sent us to the right place." Farrell later sent Welles a "bill for the amount of $2.10"—the cost of the six highballs she and her sister had consumed.[111]

Other listeners had more success in convincing people that the world was coming to an end. In Los Angeles, Johanna Wilizenski gathered a crowd of friends and neighbors around her radio as soon as she heard the first bulletins about Mars. Soon, these listeners were crying and shaking with fear, or running home to tell their own families. Wilizenski later wrote to President Roosevelt of her heartbreak at seeing a fourteen-year-old girl "trembling, her eyes almost bugging out of her head," clinging to her mother, because she was so afraid of being killed by the Martians. If she felt embarrassed, or otherwise remorseful for leading these people astray, Wilizenski did not write those feelings down. "I only wished I could get my hands on the one who caused all this," she wrote; "I don't know what I would have done to him."[112]

Many of the people whose evenings were rudely interrupted by hysterical neighbors never even heard the broadcast.[113] "Across the street from my home is a church," wrote one New Jersey woman to the Mercury. "And while the services were going on, so was your program. To me, it was so real that I ran across the street, burst in on the service and warned the people to proceed in all available cars to the highlands of New Jersey along route 23. Before I had complited [sic] my excited speech the church had cleared and everyone was on their way home to gather their loved ones to safety." Only after she had scattered these poor parishioners to the four winds did this listener realize her mistake. "I now feel that I'll never be able to show my face outside my door again," she wrote, "thanks to you."[114] A listener in New York State, who wrote in protest to the FCC, was similarly shamefaced: "As matters now stand, I am an ass, for I had called many of my friends and suggested that they leave their homes immediately and am being ridiculed for my actions."[115]

In college dormitories, fraternities, and sororities, this need to spread the word could easily create small outbreaks of hysteria. The broadcast terrified large groups of people on college campuses in at least ten states, including New Jersey.[116] In his letter to Welles, an Oregon student described the scene in his own fraternity house: "Twenty college students, all of above-average intelligence, gathered about a radio—Pale, trembling, nearly paralyzed with fear and hysteria, listening to reports of an invasion of the world by 'mysterious monsters from Mars.' "[117] In Kansas, another fraternity boy tuned in late to the broadcast and, believing it to be true, gathered everyone in the house around the radio. Soon he realized that the broadcast was fiction. But all of his brothers still believed, and he and another student decided to have a little fun with them. "We went upstairs and found a fire-cracker," he wrote to Welles.

"When . . . reports were coming in from Chicago and St. Louis of the Men from Mars arriving, he lit the firecracker and I turned off the electricity. Mr. Wells [sic] I'm telling you I never have seen such a scared bunch of college boys in my life."[118]

In such tight quarters, fear spread like a virus, rapidly infecting dozens of other people. "The quiet bell had just rung and someone came crying out 'a rocket is coming from Mars—We're all going to be killed!' " wrote a student in Morristown, New Jersey. "The news spread like wildfire!"[119] Anywhere a lot of people lived close together, especially in this kind of institutionalized housing, fear could easily become contagious. An inmate in a Michigan prison wrote to Welles that, while listening to the broadcast, his "fellow inmates . . . did everything from reforming to getting prepared to be released by the invaders from Mars and a more plain scared bunch of boys you never saw in your whole life."[120] As Hadley Cantril later noted, concentrated fear among a large group of people could create a kind of echo chamber. People were more likely to believe in the broadcast because everyone around them believed in it as well.[121]

This viral effect is essential to understanding reports of panicked people running in the streets that night. Listeners in apartment buildings or dense neighborhoods, often in the path of the Martian invasion, could be seized with the impulse to spread the news.[122] They ran next door or across the street to warn friends and neighbors, or to seek confirmation of what they had heard. Soon wild rumors about invaders and poison gas were spreading far beyond the radio's reach. One New Jersey listener, for example, wrote to the newspaper columnist Dorothy Thompson that during the broadcast "a policeman arrived at our front door and warned us to evacuate." But this officer had not actually heard the broadcast "and could give no reasonable explanation for the warning he was giving all throughout our neighborhood, except that there had been a radio alarm broadcast of impending catastrophe."[123] On the other side of the country, a California listener wrote to Welles that during the broadcast his son had "heard people in the streets, where he was spending the evening, [say] that a comet had fallen in New Jersey and [there were] many killed."[124] This hysteria had as much to do with the power of rumor as it did with the power of radio.

It was also a localized phenomenon—intense where it was felt, but not felt very widely. One street in East Orange, New Jersey, "was unusually quiet" during the broadcast, but elsewhere in the state that same night a woman wrote Welles that she saw "many people in the streets scared to death that that black cloud of gas would probably drift towards us soon."[125] And the vast majority of Americans, even those living in New Jersey, saw no panic and had no idea anything unusual was going on. "The infernal machines passed within a few blocks of my house coming up the highway from South Jersey . . . and I didn't think to step outside and see them," wrote a man in Elizabeth, New Jersey. "After New York was destroyed we all went to bed."[126]

Listeners who picked up a phone, instead of bursting in on a next-door neighbor, were better able to spread fear far and wide. In the small neighboring towns of Meckling and Gayville, South Dakota, a telephone operator somehow heard about the broadcast and believed it to be true. Then she began calling up everyone in the area, telling them all to tune in. Two listeners later wrote to Welles about the experience, explaining that before she realized her mistake "the telephone operator had practically the entire town alarmed!"[127] Several other listeners wrote to Welles complaining of the charges they had incurred by calling up friends and relatives. Some even demanded that CBS pay their phone bills. One Philadelphian, who spent a dollar phoning relatives in New York and New Jersey, wrote: "We'll look for a check."[128]

As the broadcast got under way, telephone switchboards coast to coast began lighting up like mad. They stayed lit throughout the remainder of the hour and into the next.[129] Northern New Jersey saw a 39 percent increase in its usual phone traffic between 8:00 and 9:00 p.m.—or roughly seventy-five thousand to a hundred thousand additional calls—and a 25 percent increase from 9:00 to 10:00 p.m.[130] The United Press reported that, at the time of the broadcast, operators in San Francisco suddenly found themselves bombarded with "requests for cross-continent telephone connections with New York and New Jersey."[131] At least some of those calls were meant as warnings to friends and relatives on the East Coast. One Philadelphia man, for example, who had been listening to the broadcast and enjoying it as fiction, accepted a collect call from his terrified mother across the continent. Later, he discovered a long-distance charge on his bill in the amount of $12.75—or about $215.52 in today's dollars. "I heard the entire program and think it was a splendid presentation," he wrote to Welles, requesting reimbursement, "but the $12.75 telephone call from California left a dent in my purse."[132]

Apart from these ill-advised warnings, many if not most of the calls that night appear to have been to newspaper offices, and police and radio stations. *The New York Times* logged 875 calls related to the broadcast, and the *Newark Evening News* over a thousand.[133] "I want a gas mask!" demanded one caller to police in Brooklyn, New York. "I'm a taxpayer!"[134] Paul Morton, city manager of Trenton, New Jersey, wrote in an official complaint to the FCC that the Trenton Police received "two thousand phone calls . . . in about two hours, [and] all communication lines were paralyzed" during the broadcast.[135] Many radio stations that carried the program later reported a dramatic influx of calls at the same time, some receiving as much as 500 percent over their usual Sunday night traffic.[136] These frantic inquiries convinced about 60 percent of the stations carrying the show to break in and explain that it was all fiction.[137] After a certain point, the telephone operators at some newspaper offices began simply greeting callers with the words "It's just a radio show."[138]

This flood of phone calls indicates how quickly news of the "invasion" spread, not the existence of a widespread panic. As Campbell notes, calling a reliable institution was, for many, the only way they could verify what they had heard on the radio or from a terrified neighbor.[139] Even the newspaper radio listings were not always reliable. At least one paper—in, of all places, New Jersey—incorrectly listed that night's *Mercury Theatre* episode as a dramatization of Dickens's *Pickwick Papers*.[140] When frightened listeners did call the police, operators were usually able to calm them down. According to the *St. Louis Post-Dispatch*, some people even called back later to apologize for phoning in the first place. But the false news spread so fast by word of mouth that authorities in several cities received inquiries about the broadcast for hours after it ended. The morning after the show, a reporter for the *Post-Dispatch* overheard one St. Louisan still "unconvinced by denials" state that the invasion "might really have happened."[141]

"Within a few hours," wrote *The Baltimore Sun*, "there were almost as many versions of what was believed to have taken place as there were listeners, the stories colored and embellished as they were told and retold."[142] The logbook of the Trenton headquarters for the New Jersey State Police that night recorded about fifty calls "inquiring as to meteors, number of persons killed, gas attack, military being called out and fires."[143] All were reasonable assumptions, given the hearsay flying around the state during the show. "Confused reports resulting from the broadcast led to many rumors," wrote the *New York Herald Tribune* the next day, "including one that a meteor had struck near Princeton and that many persons had been killed."[144]

Indeed, many if not most of the calls to press offices and police stations were not about Martians. The majority of callers quoted in the next day's newspapers inquired about either a catastrophic meteor strike or some kind of "gas raid" or bombing attack on the East Coast.[145] The New Orleans *Times-Picayune* even quoted people calling in to say "that an earthquake had shaken Montana."[146] The lack of detail about Mars or Martians in these calls suggests that many people picked up the phone almost immediately after hearing a rumor or fake news flash, with little understanding of what was being "reported." Their first instinct was to verify what they had heard—and, in some cases, to ask if they should get out of the way of the gas.[147]

Even calling a reliable institution was not always successful. "My brother phoned Jersey City Police Headquarters to verify the statements that came from W.A.B.C.," wrote one listener to the FCC. "He was told to call back later."[148] Others could not even get through. One Florida listener, eleven years old, wrote to Welles that her local CBS affiliate "was busy all the five times I called."[149] A Pennsylvania woman captured her experience in verse:

> Six state troopers were lying dead,
> When my auntie lost her head.
> She dashed to the phone and called the local station,
> But after sun-down it ceases operation![150]

At the very least, this cross-continental flood of phone calls suggests that, far from losing their heads, many people stopped to think before heading for the hills.

Combined with random accounts of listeners piling into their cars or threatening to commit suicide, reports of overburdened telephone exchanges and people rushing about in New Jersey give the impression that much of the country panicked during the broadcast. But that is not really what happened. Listeners nationwide did everything they could to confirm half-heard reports or rumors that were not necessarily implausible, or to spread the word to those they felt might be in danger. Under certain volatile conditions, this could create pockets of hysteria, but it cannot accurately be called a mass panic. As defined by sociologists, a panic requires "mobilization," in which people flee en masse or take other action against a real or imagined threat.[151] Apart from a few scattered instances of flight, this did not happen on the night the Martians landed.

Howard Koch wrote with relief in his book on the broadcast that "miraculously no one actually died in the mad scramble to escape the Martians."[152] A simpler explanation is perhaps that the "mad scramble" never took place. The next day's New York *Daily News* featured a front-page photo of Caroline Cantlon, an actress employed by the WPA, with the broken arm and skinned knees she sustained while hurrying down a flight of stairs, trying to escape the "smoke in Times Square."[153] But apart from that, as Campbell has noted, no major papers reported any deaths or serious injuries caused by panicked flight.[154] There were no car accidents, no miscarriages, no suicides. Nobody took potshots at a water tower, thinking it was a Martian fighting machine, or disappeared into the mountains, never to be seen again.[155] And if the highways really were clogged with people trying to flee the cities, nobody said so at the time. It was only later, once the "panic broadcast" entered American folklore, that stories of jammed streets and groups of farmers roaming the Jersey countryside, shotguns ready to perforate the first spaceman they saw, began to spring up.[156]

This does not mean that no one was frightened. A small but significant number of people were—terribly so. We can never know exactly how many Americans were terrified by the broadcast, though Cantril's guess of around one million is as good as any.[157] Out of a country of 130 million people, and a total audience of perhaps six million, that is not insignificant. But saying that *War of the Worlds* panicked one million people would be as inaccurate as saying that it frightened none. One million Americans may indeed have briefly believed Earth was under attack from the Martians that night—or, at least, that something horrible was happening in New Jersey—but almost none of them actually panicked.

Forty minutes after the hour—and about ten minutes after it would have been expected—*War of the Worlds* finally paused for a station break. "Then, out of the clear blue sky, we heard, 'You are listening to the Mercury Theatre's presentation,' etc. etc.," wrote a frightened listener in Brooklyn. "What a downslide my heart took! What a load off our minds!"[158] Many other frightened listeners shared her delight in this sudden reprieve. "Such a relief when they announced what it was," wrote a Georgia woman to Welles. "Then we all laughed+laughed. It had given us a thrill we hadn't had in ages."[159]

After the station break, the show dropped the news-broadcast fiction entirely, and Welles narrated the rest of the story as Professor Pierson. His character wandered through the desolated countryside, encountered a megalomaniacal survivor, and eventually discovered that the Martians had all died from bacteria—"slain, after all man's defenses had failed, by the humblest thing that God in His wisdom's put upon this earth." Houseman later praised Welles's performance, but claimed that no one heard it, with so many listeners panicked in the streets.[160] But all evidence suggests that he was mistaken. A Gallup poll later found that 71 percent of people who heard the broadcast listened until the end, and more probably listened at least until the station break.[161] However, even with all this excitement, the Mercury's audience remained pitifully small. A telephone survey conducted during the broadcast found that only 2 percent of homes with radios were tuned in to *War of the Worlds.*[162]

Those few who had believed that they were hours or perhaps minutes away from a horrible death now found themselves with powerfully mixed emotions. For some, the best way to process those feelings was to pour them all out on paper.[163] "This may be incoherent and rambling," Lucile McLain wrote to Welles that night, "but this letter will be a salute to your genius."[164] Even before the broadcast was over, or only minutes after it ended, listeners were filling page after page with their experiences. Often, they did not really know why they were writing.[165] "It's 9 o'clock now and I'm writing this letter, and my legs are still a little shaky," wrote a Wisconsin man to Welles. "For a Halloween scare it couldn't be beat."[166]

Some listeners felt the need to lash out. "To you the assholes of the earth and Mars," wrote an anonymous listener from Pennsylvania, "WE THE PEOPLE IN THE WESTERN PART OF PENNA. THINK THAT YOU ARE A *PISSPOT* BASTARD AND ALL THE REST OF THE WORDS WE CAN'T THINK OF SAYING."[167] Others had no trouble coming up with a few choice words for Welles and company. "I would not insult a female dog by calling you a son of such an animal," wrote one South Carolinian to Welles. "Your conduct was beneath the social standing of and would be unbecoming and below the moral perception of a bastard son of a fatherless whore."[168]

These listeners wanted badly to get back at the man who had tricked them, but there was little they could do besides call him names. Writing a letter of protest to CBS or the federal government, in the hopes that it might get Welles kicked off the air, gave them the feeling of taking action without actually doing so. That, in itself, was reassuring. A few listeners even threatened Welles—such as one "southerner" who wrote, "If this Orson Welles ever finds himself below the Mason-Dixie [sic] line—we will string him to a tree."[169] But it is difficult to take these threats seriously. What the frightened needed, more than anything else, was to vent, and many did so in writing.

But, however intense this anger was, it did not last very long. In some letters, it failed to get to the bottom of the page. One New Jersey woman began her letter to Welles, "You horrible, terrible person," and ended by writing, in words somewhat cramped to fit them on the page, "After thinking about it I must say it was marvelous and accept my congratulations."[170] An Ohio man appended to his letter to CBS—a "letter to protest such broadcasts" after what he called "the worst scare of my life"— a postscript: "P.S. Swell program. I'll be listoning [sic] next week. I have come to the conclusion that I have a sound heart."[171] These sentiments capture in brief how many frightened listeners changed their minds about the broadcast in the hours and days that followed. One can only imagine how many similar letters were begun in haste, yet abandoned or left unsent, because their writers had a change of heart.

About fifty-two letters of protest were written to the Mercury Theatre on the night of the broadcast, most if not all from people who had been frightened. Another twenty-six, all from frightened listeners, can only be described as ambivalent. "If any one of us had been in your presence at the conclusion of the story, we can truthfully say, we would not know whether to congratulate you or kick you," wrote one ambivalent listener to Welles. "We, however, are certainly glad to be alive."[172] But, even combined, these seventy-eight letters are still less than the eighty-two pro-Welles letters written to the Mercury that same night. And about twenty-five of those came from people who had been frightened yet praised the broadcast anyway. "I am writing to give you a laugh," wrote one listener to Welles. "I am laughing now too, but—I wasn't twenty minutes ago."[173]

The day after *War of the Worlds*, Welles told reporters that the Mercury had already received "many telegrams" from appreciative listeners who wanted to say "how much they liked the show."[174] The positive telegrams sent that same night to station WABC, the CBS affiliate in New York, numbered in the hundreds. Many came from frightened listeners who, according to the *New York Herald Tribune*, "laughed it off and took the attitude that 'the joke's on me.'" They wired the station not to complain or threaten lawsuits but instead to applaud "the extreme vividness of the presentation."[175] Even more supportive letters from frightened listeners came in the following days. Some simply enjoyed the thrill: "For what is more worthwhile in this life than a well rounded fund of experiences?" wrote one Ohioan.[176] But others found the experience thought-provoking and immensely valuable. As a Wisconsin woman put it on November 3, "Your broadcast took my safe little life in its King Kong hands, juggled it around carelessly for the space of fifteen or twenty minutes, and allowed it to settle gently—again with proper perspective and in normal proportion."[177]

Some of the drop-off in angry letters sent to Welles can be attributed to people's writing to the government instead. Newspaper coverage of the broadcast gave the FCC sudden national prominence, leading many angry listeners to write directly to them. "The only reason you didn't receive this complaint last night," wrote one Maryland man, "is because I didn't know with whom to communicate."[178] Indeed, angry letters written to the government peaked a day later than those sent to the Mercury, with sixty-three penned on October 30 and 185 on Halloween. But they dropped off just as sharply. Fifty-three were sent on November 1, and only fourteen on November 2. And on both of those days, as well as the next two, more pro-Welles letters were sent to the FCC than anti-Welles letters.

Ultimately, the Mercury received 115 protests related to *War of the Worlds*, and the FCC received 353. Not all of these were from people frightened by the broadcast. Once it became a national controversy, many who had not heard the program felt the need to weigh in. But even so, these totals are not especially high. One episode of the horror series *Lights Out* was supposedly so scary that it generated fifty thousand angry letters, and over twenty-two thousand people wrote in to save *The March of Time* from cancellation.[179] Most of the letters written after *War of the Worlds*—which were penned in praise and defense of Welles—were not responding to the broadcast itself. Rather, they were responding to the reports of panic in the following day's newspapers. The national controversy that followed had very little to do with the opinions of people actually frightened by *War of the Worlds*.

The broadcast garnered very strong reactions, both positive and negative, from the people who heard it firsthand. But for most, as with even the best theatrical productions, those feelings dissipated very soon after the performance was over. If a few frightened listeners were left with lingering resentments, more came to appreciate their brush with imaginary death. "I was profited [*sic*] very much by it, and I am sure if we would all confess, it did us good," wrote one frightened listener to the FCC. "I just can't find words to say how I do feel about this broadcast, but I feel better by it."[180] It's a testament to the artistry of Welles and the Mercury that the program was such a remarkable experience for those who heard it firsthand. But if the press had not fanned the flames of controversy surrounding the show, the whole incident could easily have been forgotten.

At 8:48 p.m., while Welles was still on air as Professor Pierson, the Associated Press issued its first bulletin about the broadcast: "Note to Editors: Queries to newspapers from radio listeners throughout the United States tonight, regarding a reported meteor fall which killed a number of New Jerseyites, are the result of a studio dramatization."[181] Less than forty-five minutes later, Walter Winchell began his nightly newscast by reassuring listeners that "America has *not* fallen."[182] For many, this was the first they heard that anything unusual had happened that night. The real *War of the Worlds* panic—an upswell of anxiety over the power of the media and the future of American democracy—was about to begin.

5

"Public Frightener No. 1"

[The] wave of terrorism ... In the paper in all probability is just a shiver.
—Joe Smith of Chicago to FCC chairman
Frank McNinch, October 31, 1938[1]

Several minutes into the *War of the Worlds* broadcast, as the show grew more and more intense, the phone in Studio One's control room began to ring. It was Welles's wife, Virginia, calling to praise the "absolutely marvelous, and hair-raising" program. Her compliments were met with laughter; all in the Mercury still thought they had a turkey on their hands.[2] But as Houseman watched through the control-room window, and heard the broadcast coming to life under Welles's directorial hand, his concerns about the material and the pacing disappeared.[3] For maybe ten or twenty minutes, until about 8:30 p.m., Houseman enjoyed the only real respite he would have that night.

Then, about the time Kenny Delmar gave his speech as the "Secretary of the Interior," the phone in the control room rang again. The CBS executive Davidson Taylor picked it up, listened for a few moments, and, without explanation, rushed out of the room. He returned, face pale and drawn, as Ray Collins narrated the fall of New York City, and tried to force his way into the studio. When Houseman intervened, Taylor told him in no uncertain terms that they had to stop the show. CBS's switchboards were overwhelmed with calls from frightened listeners, he said. He'd even heard rumors that people were killing themselves because of the broadcast, or trying to flee from the Martians in droves. They had to announce that it was all fake immediately.[4] But Taylor must have known that by this point the damage, whatever it was, had already been done. He was looking beyond the station break, fearful that Welles was about to dig himself in even deeper.

Earlier, Welles had made a late addition to the script, a closing curtain speech in which he appeared out of character and described the broadcast as a Halloween prank—"the Mercury Theatre's own radio version of dressing up in a sheet and jumping out of a bush and saying Boo!" Welles often closed the Mercury broadcasts this way, with a bit of light-hearted fun that helped establish an easy, conversational rapport with his audience. At the end of *Dracula*, for example, he reassured listeners that the horrors they'd just heard were only sound effects—before hinting that vampires really *do* exist.[5] But with the vague and horrifying rumors Taylor had just heard—of panicked mass flight, injuries, and even suicides—the speech at the end of *War of the Worlds* took on much darker implications. Calling the broadcast a prank implied intent to deceive the audience. As Welles later explained to Peter Bogdanovich, he would be, in effect, "admitting malice."[6] And it would be difficult to convince a jury otherwise if the reports of deaths and injuries were true.

When the station break finally came, Taylor rushed into the studio and urged Welles to change the curtain speech. But Welles, completely oblivious to the firestorm brewing outside Studio One, blew him off.[7] Meanwhile, the phone in the control room was ringing yet again. On the other end of the line, a group of angry listeners in Michigan, who claimed to be hunkered down in their basement with shotguns, threatened to shoot Welles if they ever met him face-to-face. When a CBS page dutifully brought that message into the studio just before the station break ended, Welles and his actors got their first inkling of how their broadcast had been received by its audience.[8]

But the show must go on. Welles gave the cue for Herrmann and his orchestra to strike up a slow, haunting melody that set the tone for the broadcast's languid second half. All of the energy of the first half evaporated. Without the fake news flashes, the Mercury troupe were left with the dull, lifeless broadcast they had worked so hard to avoid. This sedate tone, however, masked a growing tension in the studio. Several minutes in, Welles glanced over at the control-room window and saw two blue-uniformed men looking back at him.[9] When one of the police officers tried to enter the studio, a member of the Mercury pushed him away from the door.[10]

The cops were not there to arrest anyone. Concerned about the sudden torrent of phone calls, and unable to get through CBS's tangled switchboards, the local precinct had sent them over to see what was going on.[11] But Welles had no way of knowing that. When he came on at the end to read his curtain speech, his voice sounded stiff and strained, barely betraying his nervousness. Uncharacteristically, he tripped over his words, turning "the next best thing" into "the best next thing." As he signed off that night, there must have seemed a good chance that he was bidding farewell not just to his audience, but to his radio career—and possibly even to his freedom. "So goodbye everybody," Welles said, "and remember, please, for the next day or so, the terrible lesson you learned tonight. That grinning, glowing, globular invader of your living room is an inhabitant of the pumpkin patch, and if your doorbell rings and nobody's there, that was no Martian . . . it's Halloween."

Then Dan Seymour signed off, and all hell broke loose. CBS employees burst into the studio, snatching up every bit of evidence they could find before the police or the press got their hands on it. All the scripts and recording discs were either locked away or destroyed on the spot.[12] Meanwhile, the phones were ringing off the hook. Another angry listener phoned in a bomb threat, and someone at CBS called the police. Soon cops were everywhere, hustling the cast and crew into a nearby restroom for safety while they swept the studio for explosives. "Houseman denies this," the cast member Richard Baer later wrote, "but I distinctly remember a group of frightened men squeezed in the ladies' room of the CBS building."[13] Welles and Houseman were not among them: network employees had hurried them downstairs and locked them in a back office. There they waited, completely cut off, with only a horribly vague sense of what their broadcast had done to the country.[14]

Their first contact with the outside world came in the form of a gaggle of reporters, who bombarded them with misleading questions implying that the broadcast had killed as many people as a small war. The newshounds repeated rumors of mass stampedes, fatal traffic accidents, and suicides with absolute certainty, even though none of these had any basis in fact. When Welles and Houseman finally made it out the back way and into a car, Houseman was shocked to see that the streets were calm. The reporters had completely convinced him that the broadcast had thrown the country into chaos, and that he and Welles "were mass murderers."[15]

Bedlam did reign that night, but only in newsrooms across America. Reporters and switchboard operators expecting a quiet evening suddenly found themselves overwhelmed by calls about a disaster in New Jersey. In his memoirs, the radio critic Ben Gross described how the broadcast threw the offices of the New York *Daily News* into chaos. Phones rang everywhere, as confused reporters struggled to get a call in to CBS. Photographers dashed out in search of the story—whatever it was. At the "blazing" switchboard, a telephone operator rapidly reassured caller after caller that "there ain't no men from Mars."[16] Similar scenes played out in other areas of the country. As far away as Memphis, journalists at the *Press-Scimitar* were "swiftly mobilized" to tackle the late-breaking story. "The managing editor, city editor and a number of reporters sped to the office after receiving wild reports that 'cities are being bombed,'" wrote the *New York World-Telegram*.[17]

News staffs had little reason to doubt the story, because most of the early calls were not about Martians. The next day's newspaper articles quote many inquiries about a catastrophic meteor strike in New Jersey, and very few about aliens.[18] Without knowing that they were hearing the garbled plot of a science-fiction story, journalists on the receiving end of those calls immediately sought to verify the information. Many contacted the regional offices of the major news services for confirmation, spreading word of the "meteor" even further. This explains why the first AP bulletin about the broadcast concerned a "reported meteor fall" and not an alien attack.[19] Some newspapers even reached out to the radio stations directly. Inquiries from the press and others prompted the CBS affiliate in Providence to tell its listeners that the source of the false bulletins was "a drama with a meteor in it."[20]

Other papers sought confirmation closer to the source. *The Philadelphia Inquirer*, for example, called the Princeton Press Club for details on the supposed meteor at Grover's Mill. Excited by the news, a young student working there contacted the chair of the geology department at Princeton University, Dr. Arthur F. Buddington.[21] Without having heard the broadcast, Buddington believed he had been given a rare chance to view a fresh meteorite. As he later told the *New York Herald Tribune*, such opportunities come around "only once in a man's lifetime."[22] So he and another professor, Dr. Harry Hess, went looking for it. They drove around Grover's Mill for about an hour, but only found several other people on a vain hunt for the fictitious space rock.[23] The next day, their folly found its way into newspapers all over the country. Usually, those stories left out the fact that Buddington had heard of the "meteor" through a well-meaning but misinformed newspaper reporter.[24]

As the hour of the broadcast went on, the character of the calls coming into newspaper offices began to change. Now the callers wanted to know if the bulletins describing a "gas raid" or bombing attack on the East Coast were real, and whether they should do as the announcer said and evacuate the area.[25] To the operators, these callers often sounded agitated, even hysterical—"obviously in a state of terror," as *The New York Times* described it.[26] In some areas, the callers included police who also faced a sudden influx of calls about the "invasion." With no information on their end, these cops called their local newspaper to find out what they knew.[27] By this point, most news staffs knew the source of the false alarm and were able to explain that it was "just a radio show."[28] But the sheer number of inquiries, and the hysterical nature of many of them, convinced the press that something momentous was going on, even if the "war" was not real.

Many papers composed bulletins describing the phone calls they had received and sent them out on the major news wires. Soon teletype machines in newsrooms coast to coast were chattering with bizarre reports of hysteria and panic. One bulletin said that in Pittsburgh a man called in to say that he had barely stopped his wife from drinking poison before the Martians got her. "I'd rather die this way than like that," she was quoted as saying. *The Boston Globe* sent out a report that one of its callers believed she could "see the fire" and that she and her neighbors were "getting out of here." According to another bulletin, an unnamed man called the Kansas City AP bureau to say that he had piled his family into his car, gassed it up, and was ready to evacuate. "Where is it safe?" he asked. The bureau sent his query around the country.[29]

As the media critic W. Joseph Campbell has noted, these were isolated, scattered instances of hysteria, often coming in second- or third-hand.[30] But, taken together, they seemed to paint a picture of a nation in headlong flight from imaginary aliens. "As the AP, UP and the Chicago *Tribune* News Service wires in our office gave evidence, the panic's coils had also clutched most of the cities, towns and hamlets from coast to coast and down south to the Mexican border," Gross, the *Daily News* critic, later wrote. "The people of the United States had succumbed to an unprecedented mass hysteria."[31] That was the way it seemed to most newspapers, even though they had no way of accurately judging the size of the disturbance. So they extrapolated, based on these extreme examples of fright, a nationwide panic that never actually existed.

"Americans knew today the chilling terror of sudden war, of meeting invasion from another world, unsuspecting and unready," began a front-page story in *The Washington Post*. "So unnerved were Americans at the prospect of invasion that at least two persons suffered heart attacks, hundreds fainted, men and women fled their homes, would-be fighters volunteered, [and] hysteria swept the nation for a long and fearful hour."[32] The *Los Angeles Times* began its own front-page article with a series of similarly alarming images: "Residents of New Jersey fled their homes tonight, squad cars and ambulances roared through Newark, and newspaper and press association offices throughout the country were besieged with telephone calls demanding to know about a 'meteor which fell in New Jersey.'"[33] AP papers in many different cities claimed that "the anxiety [the broadcast] created all over the country was immeasurable."[34]

Yet, below these alarming pronouncements, the articles offered little evidence that the broadcast caused truly widespread fear and panic. Most newspapers focused on disturbances in New York and New Jersey.[35] Reports that rumors of war had spread throughout Harlem during the broadcast—with people showing up in police stations, ready to evacuate, and church services turning into "'end of the world' prayer meetings"—were reprinted all over the country.[36] Many papers, even those far from New York City, quoted Samuel Tishman, a resident of Riverside Drive, who described receiving a call from his terrified brother about the broadcast, tuning it in briefly, and then hurrying outside to find "hundreds of people milling around in panic."[37] There were also several reports of individuals who showed up in police stations, seeking information or asking to be evacuated, and of people who tried to warn others, often by running into crowded theaters or churches.[38]

But there were few similar reports coming out of other cities. Papers from Detroit to Atlanta and New Orleans to Los Angeles all printed the same anecdotes coming off the news wires—the near suicide in Pittsburgh, the woman in Boston who could "see the fire," the evacuee in Kansas City, and a handful of others. This, Campbell notes, made their articles all virtually identical, often word for word.[39] But no paper provided more than a few local details of panic, often just a sidebar about the number of phone calls received in that particular office.[40] *The Milwaukee Journal* even ran an article stating that the supposedly nationwide hysteria had left their city largely untouched. "Only a small number here took the broadcast seriously," they wrote. They went on to claim that, because "Milwaukee is a Charlie McCarthy town," few people there even heard the show, and because "Milwaukeeans are a canny lot, given to sharp appraisal of anything," few of those who did believed it.[41] There seemed ample evidence of fear and confusion in New York and New Jersey, but not of the "wave of mass hysteria" that supposedly "seized thousands of radio listeners throughout the nation," as *The New York Times* put it in their lead.[42]

However, *War of the Worlds* did not make the front pages everywhere. The New Orleans *Times-Picayune*, for example, ran a three-column story on the panic, but they kept it on page 3 with barely a mention on page 1. They also reported receiving relatively few calls from frightened listeners.[43] Indeed, it seems that, for many newspapers, the broadcast merited extensive coverage simply because of all the calls from people wanting to know if it was real. Where there were few calls, *War of the Worlds* got less attention.

Rather than acknowledge that their information was spotty and incomplete, most newspapers wildly generalized. They focused on isolated cases of extreme hysteria and, by either implication or overstatement, made it seem that that behavior was widespread. Many newspapers reported on an incident in Newark, in which rumors of "a gas-bomb attack" convinced over twenty families in a single neighborhood, at the corner of Heddon Terrace and Hawthorne Avenue, to flee their homes.[44] Police cars and an ambulance were called to the scene, where they found people loading furniture onto cars and wearing "wet handkerchiefs and towels over their faces" as impromptu gas masks.[45] *The New York Times* and the *Los Angeles Times* prominently featured this alarming anecdote, but made it clear that they were describing a single, isolated instance at a specific location.[46] The New York *Daily News*, on the other hand, falsely applied it to the entire region: "Without waiting for further details, thousands of listeners rushed from their homes in New York and New Jersey, many with towels across their faces to protect themselves from the 'gas' which the invader was supposed to be spewing forth."[47] By projecting the absurd behavior of a handful of people onto the broadcast's entire audience, the *Daily News* suggested the panic might be larger and more severe than it actually was. Other papers did much the same thing.

With little solid information to go on, reporters filled in the gaps with their own assumptions. They had no way of accurately knowing whom the broadcast frightened or how many, yet several papers implied or even claimed outright that most of the panicked people were women. "Mothers whose sons are National Guardsmen called tearfully to learn if the District Guard would be called out," wrote *The Washington Post*. "Women, frantic with fear, voices betraying their terror, asked if they could remain in their homes."[48] *The Milwaukee Journal* claimed to know of "several cases of women becoming hysterical with fear as a result of the broadcast," including two who were terrified even though their husbands knew it was fiction.[49] And, most egregiously, *The Washington Post* and the *Detroit Free Press* incorrectly described Arthur Buddington and Harry Hess as "women members of the geology faculty" at Princeton, who went "equipped with flashlights and hammers" to "Grovers Corners" on a hunt for the fictitious meteor.[50]

Outside of these articles, there is little hard evidence that the broadcast frightened more women than men. The Princeton psychologists who later studied *War of the Worlds* found that the two sexes were equally likely to believe under the right conditions.[51] But these articles are full of accounts of frightened women because "hysteria" is a very gendered word. It derives from the Greek *hystera*, meaning "uterus," and refers to the ancient belief that an unoccupied womb could drive a woman insane. For millennia, "hysteria" was a medical diagnosis that applied only to women.[52] In the 1930s, it was still primarily considered a female problem. To the journalists compiling these articles in 1938, it would have seemed natural to assume that most hysterical listeners were women. Instead of admitting their ignorance, they relied on a familiar stereotype.

That was the danger of "fakery in allegiance to the truth." The journalists who wrote these stories—in the very early hours of Halloween morning, under encroaching and inexorable deadlines—felt free to make things up or stretch the truth in a way that agreed with the facts they thought they knew. They believed they were merely enhancing the truth, adding details where none existed. But they didn't understand the story as well as they thought they did, and they passed their misconceptions on to the public. These half-truths, generalizations, and mistakes add up to a different kind of fake news—one born of sloppiness and haste, but deceptive nonetheless. The newspapers took a complex, multifaceted event and drastically oversimplified it. In the process, they created a false narrative of a nationwide mass panic.

It should not be surprising that many news staffs developed an exaggerated sense of the broadcast's effects, since a large portion of the calls from frightened listeners were directed at them. But several observers, in 1938 and since, have seen more than confusion and sloppiness in these misleading articles. Instead, they have argued that newspapers deliberately played up the event to attack their newfangled rival, the radio. "Having worked for a newspaper whose publisher['s] . . . resentment toward radio was so strong that he for some months would not even allow us to use the word 'radio' in a news story," wrote one Tennessean to the FCC, "I realize that much of the hue and cry is being created or aggravated by newspapers who see a chance to strike again at a news and advertising medium they fear."[53] Years later, Welles also asserted more than once that print journalists were out to get him after the broadcast because radio had siphoned off much of their ad revenue in the 1930s.[54] Houseman, too, often claimed that the reporters who assailed him and Welles that night were out for blood because radio had scooped them time and again during the recent Czech crisis.[55]

This has become the standard argument for those who doubt that War of the Worlds really caused widespread panic. After studying dozens of news articles about the broadcast, W. Joseph Campbell came to the conclusion that the press's "delight in chiding an upstart rival" prompted them to blow the panic out of proportion. Like Houseman, he suggested that radio's successes during the Czech crisis particularly rankled print journalists. "American newspapers thus had competitive incentives to denounce radio and characterize it as irresponsible and unreliable," he wrote. "Many newspapers seized the chance to do so with enthusiasm."[56] This idea has grown into a kind of counter-myth to the story of nationwide panic—an easy way of explaining why and how the hysteria became exaggerated. But, like the panic itself, it does not stand up to close scrutiny.

It is certainly true that, in the early days of radio, newspapers fought hard to keep broadcasters from reporting the news by restricting access to the wire services. Hostility between the two media bubbled up in the early 1930s in a series of legal battles that historians call "the Press-Radio War."[57] For the first time since Gutenberg, new technology had prompted a major realignment in how people consumed news and information. Those in more established media struggled to adapt. Some were scared to death of it. "Newspaper publishers had better wake up," warned one Tennessee publisher in 1932, "or newspapers will be nothing but a memory on a tablet at Radio City."[58] But not every print journalist saw radio as an existential threat. The Press-Radio War was more complex—and, in some sense, less contentious—than is commonly held.

In the early days of radio, many newspapers contributed greatly to the medium's development by founding their own stations. They used radio largely as advertising, airing brief news bulletins, cribbed from the major wire services, that teased the stories in that day's paper. The wire services allowed this, according to the radio historian Francis Chase, Jr., because it kept broadcasters from doing their own news-gathering. As long as the press maintained control of the news itself, they believed that radio posed no threat to their business.[59] But not all print journalists agreed. Smaller newspapers without a direct connection to radio viewed the medium as a dangerous competitor. And so, as the historian Gwyneth Jackaway has noted, a rift began to grow, not just between radio and the press, but between newspapers big and small. The big papers saw radio as a promotional tool, a way of stimulating interest in printed news, whereas the small papers worried that radio's speed and immediacy would rob them of customers. Only one thing, Jackaway notes, could bring the two sides together: concern over advertising revenue, the lifeblood of both publishing and broadcasting. And after the stock market crash of 1929, when advertising dollars, like dollars of all kinds, suddenly became scarce, the character of the conflict changed dramatically.[60]

Radio was one of the few industries that saw unparalleled growth during the Great Depression. Its advertising revenues rose dramatically, even in the toughest years of the early 1930s, while newspapers' ad revenue dropped sharply during the same period. Publishers that owned or were affiliated with radio stations tended to ascribe that loss to the Depression. But those with no ties to broadcasters, who were decidedly in the majority, blamed it solely on their newfound competition.[61] At the same time, radio began to flex its muscles as a news medium, covering first the Lindbergh kidnapping in 1932, and then the presidential election later that same year. On Election Day, Roosevelt took the country in a landslide, and radio's coverage of the returns roundly trounced its print competitors.[62]

Suddenly radio seemed to be hitting the press from all sides, and the press panicked. In April 1933, members of the American Newspaper Publishers Association (ANPA) resolved to stop printing radio listings unless stations paid for them as advertising. Later that same month, the Associated Press and other wire services stopped selling news content to the major networks. Under the headline "A.P. and A.N.P.A. Declare War on Radio," the trade journal *Broadcasting* noted the shortsightedness of this decision. The press, they wrote, were "casting aside entirely the proved fact that they can use radio cooperatively to their own promotional ends and profit" in an effort to stem the tide of progress.[63] Indeed, this decision backfired almost immediately. To feed the public's appetite for news, NBC and CBS did exactly what the press did not want them to do: they set up news-gathering apparatuses of their own. In no time at all, they became adept at it.[64]

The two sides finally met to talk peace at the Biltmore Hotel in New York City, on December 11, 1933.[65] The major networks agreed to stop gathering news and to limit themselves to two five-minute newscasts a day, one in the morning and one at night. These, the agreement noted, were mainly intended for "thousands of radio listeners, invalids, shut-ins, and the blind, who are unable to read the newspapers."[66] The wire services would provide content for those broadcasts through a new office: the Press-Radio Bureau. But the networks would have to pay for it, and would always refer listeners to their local papers for more details. They were also prohibited from selling advertising time for these newscasts or reporting on events that had happened within the last twelve hours.[67]

The "Biltmore Agreement," as it came to be known, handicapped the two elements of radio most concerning to many newspapers: its advertising revenue, and its immediacy. But these qualities were also what attracted some publishers to the new medium. The industry as a whole could not decide whether to embrace radio or to tame it, and this tension would prevent the Press-Radio Bureau from ever catching on. The tumultuous events of that decade had left Americans hungry for news, and advertisers began to sense great promise in sponsoring news broadcasts. Hoping to cash in on this demand, two of the major wire services, the

United Press and the International News Service, went back on the Biltmore Agreement and resumed selling news to the networks. This made the Press-Radio Bureau essentially superfluous, and it "died quietly" in 1938. In less than five years, the newspapers' assault on broadcasting had entirely broken down. As Jackaway put it, "There was just too much money to be made in radio."[68]

As early as May 1937, *Broadcasting* reported that newspaper publishers had largely resolved to end their hostility toward radio. They decided it would be better to work with broadcasters than to keep fighting them. One publisher referred to radio as a "sister business" to the newspapers; *Broadcasting* called it "a hand-maiden of the press."[69] The gendered language is notable. Newspapers saw themselves as an older, wiser, and stronger industry, trying to win over a young and inexperienced competitor. They did so mainly with money. By 1938, newspapers owned or controlled about 30 percent of American radio stations.[70] And just six months after *War of the Worlds*, the ANPA signaled their newfound harmony with broadcasters by electing a pro-radio publisher as their president. In their annual report, the ANPA further encouraged members to give "continued cooperation" to broadcasters.[71]

Publishers still had some reasons to fear the rise of news broadcasting. Survey data suggested that a majority of Americans favored radio as their source of news, feeling that it lacked the bias and inaccuracies of print media.[72] But all indications are that, if anything, broadcast journalism increased the American appetite for the printed variety. As news programming on the radio increased, so did newspaper circulation.[73] An experiment conducted at the end of the decade by Hadley Cantril and the Princeton Radio Project found that people who regularly read newspapers were loath to give them up in favor of the radio.[74] One medium could not simply replace the other. Reports of the newspaper's demise had been greatly exaggerated.

More than anything else, the Czech crisis highlighted the constructive relationship built by the two media in the latter half of the 1930s. Like most Americans, print journalists stayed close to their radios during those tense weeks, covering the event from afar.[75] Print journalists on the ground in Europe also came to depend on the facilities set up by broadcasters to send their stories back to the United States.[76] But the Czech crisis also demonstrated just how much money the newspapers could save thanks to radio. With the entire nation hearing events as they happened, the press had no reason to print costly extra editions that would be out of date as soon as they hit the streets.[77] Instead, they focused in their regular editions on supplementing the information people had already heard on air. And because radio had gotten Americans so intensely interested in events overseas, readers snapped those papers up. Newspaper circulation jumped during the Czech crisis, with sales spiking each time there was a major development in the story.[78]

Houseman and others were wrong, then, to suggest that the Czech crisis had left American newspapers particularly embittered toward radio. On the contrary, it made the two media more interdependent than ever. "The dramatic Munich crisis last fall recorded a new high point of cooperation between radio, newspapers and newspaper press services," wrote the ANPA in April 1939.[79] Americans still depended on newspapers for detailed reportage and elaboration of events briefly covered on the air. Radio could get there first, but it could not give the full picture. It stimulated interest that the newspapers were ready and willing to entertain. Once the press realized this, thanks to events just weeks before *War of the Worlds*, their sense of competition with the radio largely evaporated.[80] Some journalists may have harbored lingering resentments against broadcasting on the night the Martians landed, but there is absolutely no reason to suppose that a desire to discredit radio led the industry as a whole to exaggerate the panic. By that point, so many newspapers had a hand in broadcasting that in attacking the radio they would, in effect, have been attacking themselves.

As the historian Michael Stamm has argued, the Press-Radio War was not really fought between broadcasters and publishers. Instead, it was a conflict between newspapers themselves, over whether radio was a benefit or a threat. Ultimately, they decided to embrace it—provided they had some measure of control over it. And much of the industry came to this conclusion long before *War of the Worlds*.[81] The long view shows that the press-radio battle fought in the early to mid-1930s was less of an existential fight than a momentary break in a steady process of media consolidation. Misguided fears about advertising losses, brought on by the Great Depression, drove the two media apart, but not for very long.

In this respect, it would be wrong to say that the press lost the war. The real losers were the smaller newspapers who could not or would not affiliate with radio stations. As the Princeton Radio Project noted in

1940, the growing power of companies that owned both newspapers and radio stations, combined with an overall decline in advertising revenue, would make it impossible for smaller papers to compete. The Radio Project predicted that someday there might be only one major newspaper in a given city or media market—a situation that has, by and large, come to pass.[82]

On September 30, 1938—the day after the Czech crisis came to an end, and newspapers and radio reached their new détente—the Chicago station WGN debuted a new pulp adventure series called *The Crimson Wizard*. Its title character was a strange hunchbacked scientist named Peter Quill, on the run from a communist spy ring called "the Red Circle."[83] In the first episode, the Red Circle stole plans for a new class of "super-dreadnaught battleships" from a fictitious naval archives building in Chicago. Then they set the building on fire to cover their tracks.[84]

The Crimson Wizard was fairly standard radio melodrama in every respect except its format. Like *War of the Worlds*, that first episode was a broadcast within a broadcast, set in WGN's studio. In the story, one of the Red Circle's spies, the villainous Ivan Molokoff, worked undercover in the studio as an engineer. Listeners heard a report on the new battleships interrupted by a police shortwave transmission about the fire in the naval building. Then a woman began to sing, in what sounded like a regularly scheduled musical program. But she was quickly cut off by more transmissions, including a request for fire engines. In the dead air between interruptions, listeners heard a "lugubrious, monotonous, hollow voice" repeating the name "Peter Quill" over and over. That voice supposedly belonged to Molokoff, who created this mishmash of transmissions in order to cause chaos in Chicago.[85] And according to the next day's *Chicago Tribune*, the show had that effect in real life as well.

In a front-page story, the *Tribune* reported that hundreds of people had called their offices, as well as "state, county, and city police stations," asking if the reports were true. "Wasn't there even any fire in the naval building?" one listener asked. Another told the *Tribune*: "I didn't think it was true at first but I watched my wife's face and decided it must be."[86] As would be the case with *War of the Worlds* one month later, it appeared that many people had tuned in late to WGN and missed the opening announcement that the show was fictitious. Hearing what sounded like plausible reports of a disaster in their city, they sought confirmation from the press and the police. Welles's broadcast had a wider impact because its reach was wider and its intensity was greater. But the "panic" it created was not dissimilar to the one caused by *The Crimson Wizard*.

Yet the article left out one important point: the *Chicago Tribune* owned WGN. The station's call letters were an acronym for "World's Greatest Newspaper."[87] In fact, *The Crimson Wizard* was essentially a joint production between WGN and the *Tribune*, co-created by the station's program director and the paper's managing editor. After each episode aired on Friday, it was "permanently recorded" in print in the Color Graphic Section of the following Sunday's *Tribune*.[88] Rather than explain exactly what *The Crimson Wizard* was about, the front-page story about the fright it caused directed readers to pick up the next day's Color Graphic Section for more information. It also ran just two columns away from an advertisement for the printed *Crimson Wizard* stories.[89]

Right in the middle of its front page, among articles on such pressing matters as the march of German troops into the Sudetenland and alleged corruption within the CIO, the *Tribune* had run an ad for its own radio series dressed up as a legitimate news story. And the fake news did not stop there. Just over a week later, on October 9, the *Tribune* ran a short piece alleging that the President was suddenly "jittery about spies." They claimed that he had called up "all the counterespionage forces of the United States government to prevent foreign nations from learning our national defense plans." According to the *Tribune*, the only possible explanation was that the President had been listening to *The Crimson Wizard*. "It is perhaps too late to demobilize our fighters of spies," they wrote. "But the President must be told that the story of the Crimson Wizard is fiction. Little did we imagine that the combination of radio and a serial story was being done so realistically that the government itself would take it seriously."[90] In many ways, this seems more dangerous and irresponsible than the earlier story. It mixes alarming news, concerning a real government official, with a barely disguised advertisement. And it is not entirely clear that readers were supposed to know that it was, in fact, fake.

Rather than declare war on the radio, the *Tribune*, like a lot of large newspapers, opted for synergy. They used their paper to promote their radio station, and vice versa. This, in the long run, was wise from a commercial standpoint, but it led to playing dangerously fast and loose with the rules of journalism. As the *Tribune* reported, *The Crimson Wizard* probably did prompt a few phone calls from confused listeners. It seems unlikely that they would make up such a story out of whole cloth, though no other Chicago newspaper reported on the incident.[91] But the *Tribune* also chose to put it on their front page when it had no business being there, in a rather shameless attempt to sell papers. Despite radio's challenge, newspapers were still the dominant news medium of their day, with the power to create or direct widespread conversation. The *Tribune* tried to use that power to focus undue attention on a radio show. Much the same could be said of how other newspapers handled *War of the Worlds*.

One month later, the *Tribune* buried their coverage of *War of the Worlds* on page 3, among articles on child brides and ads for ladies' clothing. The piece, a three-paragraph squib, described only the large number of phone calls received by police and the press. It gave no anecdotes of panic, and failed to mention Welles's name.[92] Almost certainly, awareness of their own journalistic shenanigans kept the *Tribune* from giving the broadcast much coverage. As one Chicago man put it in a letter to the FCC: "The self-professed World's Greatest Newspaper . . . gave this SCARE such little space" because of "their own radio SCARE" a few weeks previously.[93] But this conspicuous near-silence made the *Chicago Tribune* one of the few newspapers in the country to treat the story with anything approaching restraint.

Writing in 1947, Paul W. White, managing director of CBS News, argued that headlines, by their very nature, push newspapers toward sensationalism. Alarming headlines, or "scareheads," increase a paper's circulation, even if they exaggerate the stories they are supposed to advertise. "Not in every case, but in too many cases," White wrote, "news stories are written to justify headlines which will make people want to buy newspapers."[94] This fact, along with the flood of frightened phone calls, helps explain why *War of the Worlds* wound up on so many front pages nationwide. Like most Sundays, October 30, 1938, was a slow news day. At the time, there were rumblings that the press played up the panic because they lacked good copy for their Monday editions. As one observer noted, controversial radio shows that aired on Sundays got much greater press attention than broadcasts on other days of the week.[95] The *Crimson Wizard* incident proved that some newspapers, at least, were not averse to using the radio to drum up their circulation. And nothing sells newspapers like massive headlines about Martians and panic.

Indeed, the press seems to have had little interest in the story beyond those headlines, because they did almost no follow-up reporting after the front-page stories on Halloween. Newspapers nationwide covered the show for at least two weeks after it aired, but these were generally reports on the FCC investigation, human-interest stories, and editorials.[96] Few papers bothered to question their initial reports or correct their mistakes.[97] No journalist made a serious attempt to figure out how much of the country had even heard the broadcast, much less how many in its audience were frightened. It fell to the Princeton Radio Project to commission a Gallup poll, six weeks after the broadcast, to find out how many people had believed it to be true.[98] Had they not done so, we would not today have even the faintest idea of how many people were frightened.

Instead, news staffs and editorial boards accepted the panic immediately and wholeheartedly, seeing it as proof of a wide variety of social ills.[99] Many papers commented on radio's supposed power to deceive. "No hoax in print could be misunderstood and suddenly stir masses to panic as did this radio blunder," wrote the *New York Herald Tribune.* "This vice of halfway comprehension or even whole-way miscomprehension is inherent in the medium and must plainly be zealously guarded against."[100] *War of the Worlds* had proved that radio's speed and immediacy were a liability as well as a benefit. Staid newspapermen saw the virtue in stopping to think before jumping to conclusions. A few newspapers even congratulated themselves on being the resource frightened callers turned to for verification or reassurance.[101]

But it would be wrong to read these editorials as a wholesale attack on the medium. Papers with particularly close ties to radio tended to lay blame for the panic elsewhere. The day after the show, *The Detroit News,* itself a radio pioneer, condemned the broadcast but not the radio itself. In a front-page editorial, they made sure to remind readers "that the blame for what happened rests with the broadcasting chain, not the local station, such as WJR in Detroit, under contract to carry the program."[102] The *Chicago Tribune* took things a step further by harshly criticizing the people who had been frightened. "No harm has been done," they wrote; "on the contrary, the incident may have jolted a few persons into a realization of their intellectual limitations."[103]

Above all, what characterizes many editorials is their patronizing tone. "Radio is young and has not yet learned all its lessons," wrote *The Milwaukee Journal.* "But it is time radio began to grow up."[104] The *Detroit*

Free Press called the broadcast "childish smart aleckism" and suggested that Welles and the Mercury "receive some sound spankings as rewards for their efforts."[105] Here again is the sense that newspapers saw themselves as older, wiser, and able to teach radio a thing or two. They often sound like a parent reprimanding a wayward child. *The New York Times*, for one, gave radio an extended lecture on how to behave. "Radio is new but it has adult responsibilities," they wrote. "It has not mastered itself or the material it uses. It does many things which the newspapers learned long ago not to do, such as mixing its news and its advertising."[106] Evidently, the *Times* editorial board had never heard of *The Crimson Wizard*.

Stamm has noted that many in the newspaper business saw *War of the Worlds* as an opportunity to increase their influence over broadcasting. The radio, they argued, could regulate itself, but only under the calmer and wiser hands of print media. As one industry official put it the following year, the panic proved that "newspapermen, who know public reactions, should own and control radio stations."[107] This made it essential that newspapers demonstrate their wisdom and years of experience. Like *The New York Times*, many editorials claimed that newspapers had outgrown these kinds of youthful indiscretions. To prove it, some cited a century-old newspaper hoax that bore superficial similarities to *War of the Worlds*.[108]

In 1835, the fledgling *New York Sun* ran a six-part series of articles purporting to prove that the moon was inhabited. Through a new and immensely powerful telescope, astronomers were said to observe several fanciful species on the moon's surface. Most notable was a race of intelligent winged apes dubbed "Vespertilio-homo," or "bat-men," who behaved much like humans but lacked Victorian sexual inhibitions. The hoax was the work of a young reporter at the *Sun*, Richard Adams Locke, but he attributed the "discoveries" to a real and well-known astronomer to give them an extra layer of credibility. The story was widely believed, both in the United States and abroad, and the "Moon Hoax" quickly became a sensation. "Not one person in ten discredited it," wrote Edgar Allan Poe, a successful hoaxer in his own right, "and (strangest point of all!) the doubters were chiefly those who doubted without being able to say why . . . because the thing was so novel, so entirely out of the usual way." The truth only came out when Locke told a friend, who worked at a newspaper that was about to reprint his articles, that the whole thing was fake.[109]

Both the "Moon Hoax" and *War of the Worlds* dealt with extraterrestrials, and both relied on the credibility of an academic astronomer, but there the similarities ended. *War of the Worlds* lasted for only an hour, whereas the "Moon Hoax" went on for weeks. And, unlike Locke and the *Sun*, Welles and the Mercury never meant to deceive anyone. They just used news techniques to dress up something they believed was clearly labeled as fiction. The *Sun*, on the other hand, used its journalistic authority to lend credence to fiction clearly labeled as fact, in a blatant attempt to increase its circulation. But what contributed more to the hoax's believability than anything else was that many prominent publications reprinted and endorsed the story. Even *The New York Times* wrote that the details "of the wonderful discoveries in the moon . . . are all probable and plausible and have an air of intense verisimilitude."[110] As with people who listened to *War of the Worlds* in groups, this created a powerful echo effect. Those who doubted were surrounded with unassailable belief. No newspaper bothered to check up on the pseudo-scientific details that any informed observer would have seen right through.

The story of the *War of the Worlds* panic grew out of a similar bandwagon effect. Since the Czech crisis—and probably even before—the press had come to understand that radio gave them a new function. Broadcasters would always beat them to the scoop; it fell to the newspapers to explain and elaborate. But with *War of the Worlds*, the system broke down. The press went with the surface reality of the story without bothering to dig any deeper. Rather than honestly examine what had happened, they helped fuel a phony controversy that made them look good at the radio's expense. The "fog of war," as one researcher calls it,[111] that still swirls around the events of October 30, 1938, is due in large part to the press's shirking of their basic journalistic responsibilities in the wake of the broadcast. In that respect, America's print media proved the biggest dupes of Welles's unintentional Halloween prank.

As they sped from the CBS building to the Mercury Theatre, Welles and his associates noticed a commotion in Times Square. A crowd had gathered outside the *New York Times* building at Forty-second and Broadway, watching the illuminated news ticker. Welles and company got out of their car just in time to see news of the panic gliding in lights along the side of One Times Square. For everyone connected with the Mercury, this was a terrifying sight. Welles may have wanted to see his name in lights, but this would not at all have been what he had in mind.[112]

Richard Baer made it back to the theater ahead of Welles, where he found the cast of *Danton's Death*—including Joseph Cotten, Martin Gabel, and Arlene Francis—still waiting for their perpetually tardy director. Baer tried to explain what had happened, but no one believed him. It seemed like only the latest of Welles's wild excuses.[113] Then Welles arrived, and his attitude dispelled their doubts. He seemed hounded, afraid—like a fugitive from the law. Francis later recalled that Welles said he might be arrested at any moment, and others felt the same way.[114] Soon after the broadcast, Bernard Herrmann called his wife, the writer Lucille Fletcher, to tell her what had happened. "He was like a kid, terribly thrilled," Fletcher said many years later. "He thought Orson was going to be arrested. I think he wanted to be arrested too."[115] No one in the Mercury, least of all Welles, could quite believe what had supposedly happened.

Soon a crowd of press photographers arrived at the theater. One of them snapped Welles's picture as he stepped up onto the stage.[116] He stood with his arms at his sides, palms out, and a weary, forlorn look on his face, as if beseeching his tormentors to leave him be. The camera flash lit him from below, casting the glow of innocence on his features and throwing a long shadow onto the curtain behind him. He looked weak, pathetic, and eminently remorseful—"like an early Christian saint," as Welles said with a laugh many years later.[117] And that was how many Americans first met Orson Welles, staring out at them plaintively from the front page of a newspaper over the caption "I Didn't Know What I Was Doing!"[118] *The Detroit News* ran a similar picture, proclaiming him "Public Frightener No. 1."[119] "I can't tell you how sorry I am for you," wrote a New Jersey woman to Welles, two days after the broadcast. "What made me decide this mostly, was the very pitiful picture of you in one of the current newspapers. You looked so frightened and bewildered that I decided to write immediately."[120]

Welles looked just as shocked as the nation felt. "When I opened the morning paper, I was astounded (that is the only word to use) at what I saw," one Oregonian wrote to Welles. "I couldn't believe my own eyes."[121] The vast majority of Americans had neither heard *War of the Worlds* nor seen any evidence of the hysteria it caused. Yet the headlines that Halloween morning made it clear that something monumental had happened. "FAKE RADIO 'WAR' STIRS TERROR THROUGH U.S.," screamed the front page of the New York *Daily News*, in the kind of heavy, bold type usually reserved for the beginnings and endings of actual wars.[122] The banner headline of *The Boston Globe*—"RADIO PLAY TERRIFIES NATION"— stretched across the paper's full eight columns, pushing a story about the treatment of Polish Jews in Germany below the fold.[123] In a letter to Welles, one listener described a Massachusetts newspaper that had given most of its front page to *War of the Worlds*. "And way down at the bottom of the page, crowded into little letters, it gives an article about Hitler and his troubles," this listener wrote. "Boy, when you can crowd that guy off the front page, you're doing something."[124]

With their huge headlines and alarmist prose, America's newspapers turned *War of the Worlds* into a national event. Suddenly everybody was talking about it, from grade-school classrooms to college campuses.[125] "Not in many a day have I heard radio discussed at restaurants, in offices, on street railway cars, as I have since Sunday night," wrote one Chicagoan.[126] Another listener wrote to Welles that the broadcast "is the topic of New York this morning, and yet I seem to be in the minority in having listened to it all the way through. I have heard innumerable people today in my office and in restaurants in New York wishing aloud that they had heard the play all the way through or could hear it again."[127] Indeed, many people who missed the show wanted to know what all the fuss was about. So many, in fact, that requests for a repeat performance poured into the Mercury and the FCC.[128] The CBS affiliate in Washington, D.C., reported that it had received two hundred calls about the show the next day, five out of every six asking that it be aired again that night.[129] In response, CBS emphatically denied that they had any intention of ever presenting *War of the Worlds* again.[130]

A handful of people doubted the press accounts—like one Ohioan who wrote to Welles that the "newspapers have made 'much of nothing' in hysterical accounts of attempted suicides and all the other rubbish that has been printed"—but not many.[131] Most accepted the panic at face value, because it reinforced their beliefs about the power of the media and the state of the country. And for those who had been frightened, the headlines were an affirmation that they were not alone. "If we were the only ones misled by the broadcast," wrote a New York City woman to the FCC, "you might be justified in regarding this as a letter from a 'crank.' But, according to newspaper reporters, people by the thousands all over the nation, were petrified."[132]

Within a few hours, the facts no longer mattered. This heightened version of events, born in newsrooms under assault from a flurry of incomplete and misleading information, became accepted as the new reality. Even the specific details of these news stories—that panic was rare and limited, and that many of those who were frightened did not understand that the broadcast was about aliens—would be forgotten or ignored. All that mattered were the startling headlines and inaccurate summaries that news staffs put together at the eleventh hour. By common consent, *War of the Worlds* had in fact "convinced untold thousands that the end of the world was at hand—that monsters from Mars actually had landed a great cylinder near Princeton and that they were advancing on New York City, spraying fire and poisonous gases," as the *New York World-Telegram* put it. "Perhaps no similar wave of terror ever swept so rapidly across the country, for it drove hysterical men and women from their homes, fleeing across the countryside in their fear of the awful invasion."[133]

Many Americans found that narrative much more frightening than the Martians ever could be. It would form the basis for the national debate that followed—even though, in its exaggerations and sensationalism, it was almost as fictitious as the Martian invasion itself.

6

"Air Racketeers"

I respectfully request that Station WABC be warned to eliminate this man Orson
Welles and his programs from the air, until he can restrain himself so that his
stuff may be fit for the ears of women and children.

—James A. Higgins of New York City to FCC chairman
Frank R. McNinch, October 31, 1938[1]

While his collaborators dodged hordes of reporters, fearing arrest or attacks from angry listeners, Howard Koch lay asleep in his apartment. The exhaustion from the previous six days of frantic work had finally caught up with him. He had listened to the broadcast without incident and fallen into a deep and peaceful slumber soon after. When Houseman called later that night, to explain what had happened or to warn him about the press or the police, Koch never even heard the phone ring. He awoke the next morning looking forward to a haircut on his day off, entirely unaware that anything was wrong. He left his apartment without even bothering to check the morning papers.[2]

As Koch walked along Seventy-second Street, he sensed what he later called "an air of excitement among the passersby." Hearing people talk about "invasion" and "panic" convinced him that Hitler had finally started another world war.[3] But when he arrived at the barbershop and asked what all the excitement was about, the barber simply smiled and handed him a newspaper. On the front page, Orson Welles stared plaintively up at him, over a transcript of the broadcast. For Koch, this was a surreal moment. His life and his career would never be the same again. But if he was at all concerned to read that the Federal Communications Commission had asked to see a copy of his script, presumably in order to determine if it had broken any laws, he left that out of his recollections.[4]

Later that morning, Koch arrived at the CBS building about the same time as Welles. The director had only just been roused from a three-hour rest after rehearsing *Danton's Death* until dawn.[5] Welles had had no time to read the morning papers, so his understanding of the situation remained vague. Yet suddenly he found himself alone, red-eyed and un-shaven, before dozens of reporters, photographers, and newsreel camera-men. All he had for protection was a prepared statement, likely written by CBS's lawyers. It expressed Welles's "deep regret over any misappre-hension" caused by the show, but maintained that the Mercury had done nothing wrong.[6] Fixing the newsreel cameras with his best pathetic, doe-eyed stare, Welles apologized to the country and claimed to be "deeply shocked and deeply regretful about the results of last night's broadcast."[7]

The prepared statement gave four reasons why the fictional nature of the show should have been obvious. None were particularly convincing. Welles repeatedly emphasized that the broadcast had been set in 1939, based solely on a fleeting reference in its first few minutes. He also claimed that listeners should have recognized *The Mercury Theatre on the Air* because it had been airing for seventeen weeks. But he failed to mention his series' low ratings and new time slot, and the fact that none of the previous episodes had resembled the fake news format of *War of the Worlds*. The most important giveaway, according to the statement, was the broadcast's subject matter: "conflict between citizens of Mars and other planets," Welles said, was "a familiarly accepted fairy-tale" from many radio shows and comic strips.[8] This may have been true, but a close reading of that morning's newspapers would have shown that most frightened listeners were concerned about falling meteors or poison gas, not about Martians.

By far the most disingenuous claim, widely quoted in many news-papers, was that there had been four announcements explaining that the show was fiction.[9] This was technically true, if highly misleading. It counted the introduction at the very beginning, which most frightened listeners missed, and Welles's curtain speech at the very end, which came too late to do much good. The other two announcements came during the single station break, when the announcer said twice that the show was based on *The War of the Worlds*. In other words, there was really only one interruption, forty minutes in, though many stations had inter-rupted the show at some point.[10] But for listeners who had been deceived, and who had heard no interruptions until the station break, it sounded as if Welles were lying to cover his tracks. The claim that there were four announcements "is a deliberate falsehood," wrote one West Virginian to the FCC, "as at no time during the broadcast was anything of this kind said excepting at the finish when the damage had all been done."[11] Reading the prepared statement, designed to get him off the hook, had only made Welles look even guiltier.

Many years later, Welles would imply that he really was feigning innocence, hiding his delight in order to dodge twelve million dollars in lawsuits.[12] On the *Today* show in 1978, he claimed to have gotten "a huge laugh" out of the whole incident, and said he "never thought it was anything but funny."[13] But there is every indication that here again Welles embroidered the truth, because he had very little to laugh about that Halloween morning. Threats of legal action were still pouring in. One anonymous man called CBS and promised to sue them "for every cent you've got," and the FCC had heard rumors that a hundred-thousand-dollar suit was in the works.[14] Sara Collins, an actress living in Los Angeles, received a fair amount of press later in the week for actually filing suit against CBS, claiming fifty thousand dollars in damages for a "nervous shock" caused by the broadcast.[15] Ultimately, the damages alleged in lawsuits would not quite reach into the millions; Houseman later estimated the total at about $750,000.[16] But that would still have been enough to make anyone think twice about letting Welles near a microphone again.

Then there was the FCC. They refused to pass judgment immediately but left open the possibility of punitive action against CBS.[17] And if Welles had bothered to read any of the angry letters mailed to him or the FCC that day, he would have found a lot of support for kicking him off the airwaves permanently. "I think you are nothing but an impossable [sic], sawed-off *nincompoop* who should be barred for life from Radio, and I shall work towards that end," wrote one Rhode Islander. "I only wish I could have my hands on you for 5 minutes."[18] An anonymous New Jerseyite suggested "that your days of fame are just about over *Mr. Orson Wells* [sic] . . . Perhaps hundreds of people who listened to your program either died or at this very moment are suffering a nervous breakdown. And to think the blame will all be placed on *you*."[19] Yet another angry listener suggested that Welles leave the country.[20]

Even H. G. Wells was against him. The author of the novel *The War of the Worlds* had his American representative, Jacques Chambrun, demand that CBS publicly apologize for "rewriting" his book. Wells had just released a new novel, *Apropos of Dolores*, and feared that people would think the broadcast had been a publicity stunt to promote it.[21] In truth, Wells had no involvement in the show, but he soon reaped the benefits of his newfound notoriety. Demand for the novel skyrocketed, as did interest in the Red Planet. *The Baltimore Sun* reported that all copies of *The War of the Worlds* were checked out of that city's public library before noon on Halloween. "Astronomy books were open on many library tables," they wrote. "Questions on the 'inhabitants' of Mars were phoned to the information desk."[22] Within a few months, Dell released a new illustrated edition of Wells's novel in paperback. "WHEN THEY TOLD IT ON THE RADIO," the cover proclaimed, "IT TERRIFIED THE WHOLE COUNTRY."[23]

For Orson Welles, on the other hand, things looked very bleak indeed. Everyone who knew Welles thought that *War of the Worlds* had ruined him.[24] There is absolutely no reason to believe that he felt any differently. "If I'd planned to wreck my career," he told several people at the time, "I couldn't have gone about it better."[25] When he went before reporters at what he later called "a terrifying mass press interview," he knew exactly how high the stakes were.[26] So he did everything he could to seem pitiful, to convey remorse and regret. Given the immense stress he must have been under, he handled himself remarkably well. He appeared both calm and conciliatory, contrite yet unafraid. But there were moments when the mask cracked, revealing not glee but exhaustion, and even hints of fear. Welles, as several biographers have alleged, gave a truly masterful performance that morning.[27] But in no way did he enjoy the attention. On the contrary, he was fighting for his professional life.

After giving his statement, Welles took questions from the reporters surrounding him on all sides. As flashbulbs popped and movie cameras rolled, he chose his words with extreme care. He made sure not to insult the intelligence of those he had deceived, even as he expressed shock and surprise that anyone could believe in men from Mars. He was evasive without seeming to be, giving few specific answers and dodging difficult questions with all the adroitness of a politician. The reporters kept coming back to the question of why the broadcast had been done so realistically. Welles maintained that, as with the Mercury's earlier production of *Dracula*, he wanted to give listeners the kind of thrill they might experience in a horror movie, and nothing more. "You can never tell how a thing will catch on, can you?" he asked.[28]

In general, Welles tried to minimize the inventiveness of *War of the*

Worlds, describing it as just another radio drama.[29] He said truthfully that many other radio shows used fake news techniques, and so he had not expected to frighten anyone.[30] His only concern, he told the press, had been "that perhaps people might be bored or annoyed at hearing a tale so improbable."[31] When asked why the Mercury had used the names of real places rather than fictional cities and towns, Welles responded that the original novel had used actual British locations; using American locations for an American audience simply made sense.[32] He also went out of his way to praise the novel—"the fine H. G. Wells classic,"[33] as he called it—in order to mollify its outraged author. He refused to say that he would never do another fake news broadcast, calling it "a legitimate dramatic form," and he offered no comment on whether there should be laws prohibiting similar shows.[34] "The wisdom of radio executives and of an organized public will decide these things for us," Welles said. "It's not up to me to speak. I'm the, uh . . . the accused."[35]

For those whom the broadcast had frightened, it seemed hard to believe that such shows were not illegal. They assumed that some censorship mechanism already existed to keep people safe from terrifying hoaxes.[36] "The CBS + Orson Wells [sic] may call a play like that censored," wrote one Indiana woman to the FCC. "Well it is time the censors are given a chance to explain which of them are crazy and how many of them are crazy."[37] Some letter writers knew that the FCC was empowered to prohibit "false or fraudulent signals of distress,"[38] and they wrote in arguing that *War of the Worlds* constituted a false SOS.[39]

The legal scholar Justin Levine has noted that if the Radio Act of 1912 had still been in place, forbidding any "false or fraudulent signal, call, or other radiogram of any kind," Welles's broadcast could very well have been considered illegal. But because the Communications Act of 1934 narrowed that language, limiting it only to "signals of distress," *War of the Worlds* had not actually broken the law.[40] This apparent lack of any legal restrictions on fake news infuriated frightened listeners. Some considered the broadcast itself to be a crime—"assault by a radio," one Pennsylvania lawyer called it.[41] "Had it occurred through misuse of the mails, there would be legislation to cover it; is there similar legislation to cover misuse of radio?" one Virginian asked the FCC. "If not, there should be."[42]

In their letters, outraged listeners frequently asked for some kind of "censorship" to protect them from future hoaxes.[43] "How will we know when news is news, or when it is just fiction, if that is an example of future radio programs?" wrote one Mississippian to the FCC. "Evidently the program departments needs [*sic*] a little more censorship."[44] But that word, "censorship," with its connotations of political or moral control, obscures what most of these people really asked for. "Regulation" would be a better term.[45] As one Coloradan put it, *"Where are our policemen of the air?"*[46] Others used the same analogy, comparing the FCC to the police, and broadcasters like Welles to common criminals.[47] "We do not believe this should be permitted," wrote one Californian to the FCC, "any more than we should permit any *other* hoodlum or gangster or criminal in our homes to talk in the presence of our parents or our children or those who are ill."[48] A few listeners went even further—arguing, in the words of another Californian, that "the Government should take over the Broadcasting Companies and stop a lot of this dam [*sic*] foolishment."[49]

These were the knee-jerk and slightly hysterical reactions of a handful of people, not legal opinions. The complexities of abridging the First Amendment went largely unaddressed. "Always a believer in freedom of expression in the press, over the radio, and at assembly," wrote one New Jersey listener to Welles, "your direction and rendition of such a program holds no place in America."[50] But these letters do reflect a belief that the government should have some power to regulate the airwaves, in order to protect people from misleading broadcasts. "How can people be expected to heed any radio-warning of danger of floods, storms etc. if this 'joke' goes unpunished[?]" wrote one Indiana listener. "It will be repeated by *someone*."[51] That was a perfectly valid point, and one that could have led to a fruitful public discussion on where exactly to draw the line between fact and fiction on the radio. But that debate never happened, in part because the incendiary connotations of "radio censorship" created something much more contentious and even uglier.

Although *War of the Worlds* may not have actually panicked the United States, radio itself created what could be called an ongoing "moral panic" throughout that decade. As defined by the sociologist Stanley Cohen, "moral panics" occur when a society perceives a threat to its established value system. Usually, that threat is a new behavior or technology believed to corrupt the young. Society then rushes to defend itself in a disorganized, disproportionate, and often hysterical manner. As Cohen put it, "The moral barricades are manned by editors, bishops, politicians and other right-thinking people," all believing they know how best to deal with the problem. Cohen wrote about youth culture in 1960s Britain, but others have seen "moral panics" in the controversies surrounding everything from comic books to violent video games.[52] The term applies just as well to the way parents and reformers reacted to radio in the 1930s.

War of the Worlds came at a time of general moral panic over the influence of radio on American society. Those fears magnified public outrage caused by the show, even as they obscured the actual factors that frightened some listeners. Many Americans saw the stories of panic in the newspapers as further proof that radio harmed the developing minds of children, though the connection is specious at best. In particular, these people objected to horror, thriller, and crime dramas—"youth-poisoning programs," as one New York listener called them.[53] A United States senator, Democrat Clyde L. Herring of Iowa, even used the controversy to try to legislate against such shows. His attempt created a secondary hysteria over fears of the media's power that had little basis in fact.

Solemn, soft-spoken, and unassuming, Clyde LaVerne Herring was no stranger to the spotlight. Like Orson Welles, he had previously graced the cover of *Time* magazine, when it covered the Iowa State Fair in 1935. The article recounted Herring's rise from humble beginnings in rural Michigan to wealth and political success. As a teenager, Herring had befriended the young inventor Henry Ford, who later put him in charge of all the Ford dealerships in Iowa. By the time Herring left the company after World War I, he had amassed a personal fortune of around three million dollars. He used that money to embark on a rocky political career, losing elections for governor in 1920 and senator in 1922. But the anti-Republican landslide that swept Franklin Roosevelt into the White House also got Herring elected governor in 1932. Four years later, he ascended to the U.S. Senate.[54]

None of Herring's previous accomplishments earned him the kind of attention he received in the wake of *War of the Worlds*. The day after the broadcast, newspapers around the country quoted Herring's vow to pass a law "controlling just such abuses as was [sic] heard over the radio tonight."[55] Herring argued that the FCC should establish an office to review radio scripts for violent or indecent material. They would not have direct censorship power, but they would inform the FCC if any station aired something "contrary to public interest, convenience or necessity." It would then be up to the FCC to decide whether that station deserved to keep its license.[56] "There is no freedom of the press or radio involved at all," Herring told reporters. "It is merely a move to tell radio what we want to come into our homes."[57]

Herring took his inspiration from the Motion Picture Production Code, a set of guidelines governing the content of Hollywood films. The major film studios voluntarily adopted the code in 1930, and set up their own censorship board—known as the "Hays Office," after its founder and chief proponent, Will Hays—to police themselves.[58] They did so mainly to forestall the kind of government regulation that Herring had proposed for radio. But Herring felt that *War of the Worlds* proved the need for broadcasting restrictions that carried the full force of federal law. "Radio has no more right to present programs like that than someone has in knocking on your door and screaming," he said. "Programs like that are an excellent indication of the inadequacy of our present control over a marvelous facility."[59]

Herring jumped on the broadcast so quickly—he spoke to reporters the very night that it aired—that some people saw ulterior motives in his outrage. "I think terror inspired this morning's outburst," wrote one listener to Orson Welles. "Or else he has a phenomenally alert mind and is seizing this opportunity to make 'Senator Herring' a household word. Personally, I never heard of him before."[60] Herring was undoubtedly ambitious; he later made a failed attempt to get on the Democratic presidential ticket in 1940.[61] But there is a simpler explanation for his sudden support of censorship: he had proposed an identical bill earlier in the year, yet failed to introduce it.[62] *War of the Worlds* gave him an opportunity to push the legislation again. His concerns had almost nothing to do with the broadcast itself, but he became by far the most vocal advocate of government censorship in its wake, thanks to the attention given him by the press.

Herring had no intention of censoring fake news or broadcast hoaxes. Instead, he wanted to ban what he called "sleepy-time nightmares," radio shows that excited children with scenes of horror, bloodshed, or suspense.[63] "Some of the bedtime stories which are supposed to put children to sleep—but involve murder and violence—are an outrage and should be stopped," he told the press soon after *War of the Worlds*.[64] Like many parents, he worried that such programs harmed children, wrecking their nervous systems, interfering with their sleep, and creating a generation of mental cases.[65] Even worse, in Herring's view, were crime melodramas, such as *Gang Busters*, a thirty-minute show that dramatized real police cases.[66] Herring believed that these "air racketeers," as he called them, inspired countless youngsters to take up a life of crime.[67] The alleged results of *War of the Worlds* supported Herring's belief that radio could compel those with weak and developing minds to behave irrationally or immorally.

Many of these charges were identical to those lobbed for decades at the movies. Almost since its introduction, film had been decried as a corrupter of youth. Because motion pictures were so new, their effects were understood poorly, if at all. Parents worried that by making sex and crime seem appealing, film would inevitably draw kids down the path to immorality.[68] That idea was first tested scientifically from 1929 to 1932 in a series of studies financed by a philanthropic group called the Payne Fund. Their work found that film had a more complex and limited effect on youth than most people thought at the time.[69] But that message did not reach the general public, thanks to the work of Henry James Forman, a freelance journalist hired to condense the Payne Fund studies into a mass-market book.

First published in 1933, Forman's book, *Our Movie Made Children*, was "an antimovie diatribe" that confirmed every parent's worst fears about film.[70] Forman called Hollywood movies "a veritable school for crime," and cited one neurologist who said that the thrills kids experienced in horror films were "virtually the same as shell-shock"—what today we would call PTSD. "Scenes causing terror and fright are sowing the seeds in the system for future neuroses and psychoses—nervous disorders," the neurologist said.[71] Most of the Payne Fund researchers were unhappy with *Our Movie Made Children*. Many were even embarrassed by it. But the book became a bestseller, because it reinforced what many Americans believed about motion pictures.[72]

Inevitably, this outsized view of the mass media's impact on children was applied to the radio as well. Reform groups and parent-teacher associations argued throughout the 1930s that kids' shows were "making neurasthenics of their youngsters" and prompting them to commit innumerable crimes.[73] In 1937, for example, a twelve-year-old boy shot first his teacher and then himself at an Ohio school. The incident was immediately blamed on a radio show, *The Green Hornet*, even though the connection later turned out to be false.[74] Many adults found violent and horrifying radio programs even more worrisome than the movies. As Herring put it, "Radio invades the sanctity of the home," making it difficult for parents to monitor what their kids were being exposed to.[75] "We do not permit our children to attend 'horror' movies," wrote one New Jersey man to the FCC after *War of the Worlds*. "The radio obligingly barges into our homes, with nauseating details, without at least giving us a warning . . . What is radio trying to do to America?"[76]

As with the movies, children tended to like best the shows that frightened and thrilled them.[77] These were the kind of programs that parents hated but advertisers loved. Companies selling breakfast cereals and other children's products knew their audience. They made sure to sponsor programs that were violent and exciting, so more kids would listen and send in box tops to get the decoder rings and other toys promised on air.[78] The radio show most popular with children was also the one most disliked by parents' groups: *Little Orphan Annie*. Its suspenseful cliffhangers were believed to cause "unnatural over-stimulation and thrill," and its advertising was so effective that kids nationwide indignantly demanded that their mothers buy them Ovaltine.[79]

In many ways, *The Mercury Theatre on the Air* was the exact antithesis of the programs believed to harm children in the 1930s. It was an unsponsored show featuring great works of literature—about as far from *Gang Busters* or *Little Orphan Annie* as one could possibly get. Rather than making children crave Ovaltine, it inspired them to read. One Massachusetts family with three teenage children wrote to Welles that they always made sure to read the book he was adapting each week, the better to appreciate his show.[80] "All of the literature professors of the University of Houston think it is a good influence on the youth of America," wrote one Texan to the FCC, in praise of the Mercury broadcasts. "Many of them otherwise would not become interested in good books. I, myself, have been spurred on to better reading by this program!"[81] And yet Senator Herring was far from alone in lumping *War of the Worlds* in with the crime and horror programs so controversial at that time.

"Children insist on listening to that variety of shock and are being developed into a race of morons and jitter bugs," wrote one Missourian to the FCC.[82] Others suggested that the government should use this controversy to make radio safe for young ears.[83] A woman from Washington described *War of the Worlds* as too "harrowing. And that is the word that describes many, many such broadcasts (beginning with 'Orphan Annie,')—harrowing," she wrote. "Anything to keep suspense alive and at topmost pitch, and little or nothing to make one happy, and this writer is no Pollyanna either."[84] Despite the broadcast's scary subject matter, more letters refer to crime shows like *Gang Busters* than to horror series like *Lights Out*.[85] "We wonder why this world is becoming corrupt," wrote one Vermonter to the FCC. "There is no question in my mind! Some of the programs our children listen to are making criminals of the present generation."[86]

Similar sentiments can be found in press coverage of *War of the Worlds*. Some newspapers, including *The New York Times*, compared the fright caused by the broadcast to the "creeps" Welles had given kids as the Shadow.[87] The *Detroit Free Press* applauded Herring and called for a general cleanup of children's shows. "If thousands of grownup men and women could be thrown into panic . . . what must be the effect on millions of boys and girls in America . . . of tales of disaster and crime which greet their ears daily and nightly . . . ?" they asked. "The radio simply must be cleansed of its evil sensationalism, and if there is no other way to perform the job, it must [be] through some sort of government action."[88] Like Senator Herring, these newspapers and listeners misunderstood entirely why *War of the Worlds* frightened some people. Yet they made up a significant portion of the calls for radio censorship in the broadcast's wake.

Behind this outrage lay a generation gap. As the "theater of the mind," radio particularly fascinated young imaginations. Parents who grew up in the age of print struggled to understand its appeal.[89] One Ohio father wrote with dismay to the FCC of how his son loved "some of these wild, shrieking mystery stories" so much "that he gets up in his sleep and screams and walks around the room, dreaming about the thrills he has heard on the radio." The father found these youthful displays of imagination so worrisome that he had the child "regularly examined by the doctor," and gave him his own radio so he could listen to those "disgusting" programs on his own. As with several like-minded letters, there is no indication that this man actually heard *War of the Worlds*. He referred to it as the "Martian Adventurers" program, as if it were a science-fiction serial for children.[90] But that did not stop him, and others, from using the controversy to attack a medium that they knew next to nothing about. Their misdirected anger made it seem that the broadcast upset more people than it actually did.

This overly protective attitude toward children may have done more than just inflame the controversy surrounding *War of the Worlds*. Orson Welles later claimed that it indirectly caused the panic itself. He told *The Saturday Evening Post* in 1940 that "mistaken theories of education" had led too many parents to shelter their children from stories of terror and bloodshed. These tales, Welles argued, "used to be a part of the routine training of the young," helping them build up resistance to real-life horrors. Without them, Welles believed that "most of the population" had grown up "without any protection against fee-fi-fo-fum stuff."[91] Welles was speaking of the current generation of adults, most of whom had not grown up with radio. But broadcasters had eagerly taken up the mantle of sharing violence and horror with children, and it seems that, as Welles suggested, this left some kids less susceptible to panic than their elders.

Very little evidence survives as to how children actually perceived *War of the Worlds*. Of the nearly two thousand listener letters in existence, only twenty-four are definitely from people under the age of eighteen.[92] But there are tantalizing indications that, if anything, children were better able to understand *War of the Worlds* than their elders were. Most letters written by children approved of the broadcast,[93] and the vast majority, nineteen, show no evidence of fright. Only five letters came from kids who believed that the show was real.[94] "Now don't think I scare easy because I am a child," wrote one young South Dakotan to Welles; "the whole nighborhood [sic] had . . . their radios on too and were scared too."[95] One schoolteacher in Illinois gathered the reactions of some of her students to *War of the Worlds* and sent them to the FCC. "The twelve year olds seem to be able to take it," she wrote. "I wonder if nature is going to supply them a set of cast iron nerves."[96]

Credit was due, perhaps, not to nature, but to all those thrilling radio programs that parents hated so much. Because kids knew the medium better than adults, they would have been more likely to pick up on cues that *War of the Worlds* was fiction. One eleven-year-old girl, for instance, apparently recognized Welles's voice from *The Shadow*.[97] Children also knew more about the broadcast's science-fiction subject matter than their elders did. Comic-strip heroes like Buck Rogers and Flash Gordon regularly took youngsters to Mars and beyond. A thirteen-year-old girl from Minnesota wrote to Welles that even though she knew the show was fiction when it started, "the dramatization put me in a sort of coma in believing the facts. But by studying the Solar System in school, if any such thing would happen scientists would know about one year before the incident."[98] And, of course, the broadcast was a Halloween prank, something many children knew very much about. "Didn't any of our so called adults realize that Sunday night was Halloween and that is the night for scary things?" wrote a fourteen-year-old girl from New York City.[99]

Even at the time, some observers suspected "that the children would have understood the fantasy if their parents hadn't gone off the deep end," as *Variety* put it three days after the broadcast.[100] "By the way, the paper tells about adults who were scared, but nothing about kids," wrote one New Yorker to the FCC. "The kids probably remembered Buck Rogers. Maybe they have more sense than we have, after all."[101]

After Welles answered all the reporters' questions and apologized several times on film, the press conference finally ended. He had given a masterful display of contrition, and Howard Koch didn't believe a word of it. As Welles and Houseman left the room, Koch saw them silently congratulate each other. He found this gesture highly suspicious—proof, perhaps, that Welles really did pull the wool over everyone's eyes.[102] But Houseman was probably just pleased with how Welles had handled himself, and relieved that he had not gotten them into any more trouble. It must have seemed, for the first time, that the Mercury might actually survive this flap intact.

Welles stayed largely in seclusion for the next several days, and it took a while for his mood to improve. His biographer Simon Callow reports that on November 1, Welles was still so upset that he fired someone simply for eating a Mars bar in the Mercury Theatre.[103] But, gradually, Welles began to realize that he had not committed career suicide. The newspapers treated him more kindly than he may have expected. Some editorials did lambaste him, but others forgave him because they accepted the persona he presented to the press—that of a baffled young man who knew not what he did. At some point, too, Welles remembered an all-important rider his lawyer had attached to his contract with CBS. Because

War of the Worlds had not plagiarized anything or libeled anyone, Welles could not be held responsible for any lawsuits brought against the network because of it.[104]

On the evening of October 31, shortly before the curtain rose on a preview performance of *Danton's Death*, Welles gave a surprisingly candid interview to a couple of student journalists from *The Daily Princetonian*. He remained overtly remorseful and apologetic, and initially refused to poke fun at the incident. "When you cause pain, you can't laugh about it," he said. "Ordinarily I might be indignant with people for their gullibility, but as the unwitting agent of the suffering, I feel a little like one accused of murder." Then an unnamed Mercury actor burst into the room in full costume, overflowing with excitement. "Look at the Boston papers," he told Welles. "You throw sevens all the time. Anyone else would be thrown off the air for a performance like that and you get credit for the biggest publicity stunt in years. This show will be a sellout." The news lightened Welles's mood even further, to the point where he could finally joke about the broadcast.[105] Even then, he must have known that the incident would not destroy him. But he could never have imagined just how many people were about to rush to his defense.

In their coverage of the fallout from *War of the Worlds*, many newspapers reported on Herring's censorship bill alongside word that the FCC would investigate the broadcast.[106] This made the two actions seem connected, whereas in fact they had nothing to do with each other. Some Americans assumed that the federal government would use the broadcast to tighten its control over the airwaves, or even to take over radio itself. "Senator Herring's statement . . . is most alarming," wrote one Arizonan to the FCC. "There are certain interests in this country who have been hammering at the doors of radio's freedom of action for some time. I fear they will attempt to make a mountain out of the 'Great Martian Invasion' molehill in an effort to gain an opening wedge in the battle to control radio."[107] This fear of censorship prompted most of the letters written in response to *War of the Worlds*, by Americans striving to protect free speech as they understood it.

7

"The Public Interest"

I am not afraid of an invasion from Mars. I am afraid of a non-intelligent public in a democracy.

—Ellen B. Nash of Tacoma, Washington,
to Orson Welles, November 3, 1938[1]

The Federal Communications Commission had more than enough problems in the fall of 1938 without having to worry about Orson Welles. Its sixty-five-year-old chairman, Frank R. McNinch, had just embarked on an aggressive drive to streamline the agency at the President's request. Two of its most prominent members, Commissioners T.A.M. Craven and George Henry Payne, had publicly clashed with McNinch over those reforms earlier that month.[2] But even as it started to split apart, the commission spent months investigating whether the major broadcast networks were illegal monopolies. Public hearings, featuring testimony from the heads of NBC and CBS, were set to begin in two weeks.[3] The broadcast, then, found the young FCC at one of the stormiest times in its history, as it struggled through serious growing pains. No one, not even its seven members, could quite agree on just how much power the commission should wield.

The day after the broadcast, the commissioners seemed bewildered by the incident, unsure whether they should act or even whether they could.[4] Although U.S. law banned from the air all "obscene, indecent, or profane language," it said nothing about fake news.[5] None of the commissioners had even heard the show; several told *The Washington Post* that they had listened to Charlie McCarthy instead.[6] But the stories of panic in the newspapers demanded an official response. Suddenly all eyes were on the FCC.

McNinch told the press that Halloween morning that his commission had only received ten or twelve telegrams protesting *War of the Worlds*.[7] This was enough to warrant an official investigation, but it was hardly the "shower of complaints from nerve-shaken dial twisters" that *The Washington Post* and other papers described.[8] However, more were sure to come; letters posted that morning would take at least a few days to arrive, and some people were only moved to write after reading that the FCC had received few protests. "Mr. McNinch says he has not received many telegrams, [but] there are probably millions like myself, who cannot afford the price of a telegram," wrote one Iowan. "I have heard several people say 'if they could write well enough, they would write concerning that Broadcast. I do not consider myself good at writing letters, [b]ut I think I can express myself so anyone with average intelligence can understand."[9]

Every letter sent to the federal government about the show—whether to the White House, the Commerce Department, or even the FBI—was forwarded to the FCC for review.[10] Hundreds more poured in directly in the following days, many from people who just guessed at which agency they were supposed to write to. If a citizen wrote "Radio Commission, Washington, D.C.," on the back of a postcard and dropped it in the mail, that card inevitably found its way to the FCC.[11] Many demanded immediate action, putting the commissioners in a difficult position. If they bowed to public pressure (as amplified by the press) and somehow punished CBS, they would be widely scorned as censors. If they did nothing, they would seem like "a bunch of spineless swivel chair holders," as one Tennessean described them in his letter to the agency.[12]

The FCC existed mainly to keep order on the airwaves. Broadcasters could only use a limited number of radio frequencies, and so some restrictions were needed to prevent them from overcrowding the ether. To that end, the Communications Act of 1934 empowered the FCC to issue licenses to individual radio stations, giving them use of a certain frequency for six months at a time. Because these were the public airwaves, owned by the American people, the act stated that the FCC should only license stations operating in "the public interest, convenience, or necessity," without specifying what that phrase meant. If a station failed what one lawyer called the "vague and confusing test of 'public interest, convenience, or necessity,'" the FCC could refuse to renew its license, effectively taking it off the air.[13] But the Communications Act also denied the FCC "the power of censorship," and forbade them from doing anything to "interfere with the right of free speech by means of radio communication."[14] In other words, the law gave the FCC the power to silence radio stations for not acting in the public interest, but only if doing so did not constitute censorship or interference with free speech.

This contradiction left the extent of the FCC's authority very much in doubt in the late 1930s. Stations rarely lost their licenses for not serving the public interest, but broadcasters still lived in constant fear of getting kicked off the air. For that reason, they took great pains to avoid airing anything that anyone might find offensive. As David Sarnoff, president of the Radio Corporation of America, put it in the spring of 1938, "Fear of disapproval can blue-pencil a dozen programs for every one that an official censor might object to."[15] In many instances, speakers were denied access to the airwaves, or even cut off in midsentence, for touching on such uncomfortable subjects as atheism, socialism, or birth control.[16]

Often, the real censor was not the radio station, or even the FCC, but the audience. As *American Mercury* noted in 1934, broadcasters feared to upset a "hypothetical listener" who "is twelve years old and bristles with prejudices."[17] Anyone could write a letter to the FCC protesting something on the radio, and the commission took each letter very seriously. Occasionally, they even acted upon one. In the summer of 1938, the FCC received a single complaint about the use of phrases like "hell," "damn," and "for God's sake" in a radio production of Eugene O'Neill's play *Beyond the Horizon*. Later, when the licenses for several stations that had aired the show came up for renewal, the commission voted not to renew them—based on that one complaint. The incident caused a public outcry, and the FCC eventually reversed its decision. But many still feared that the commissioners wanted to set themselves up as America's thought police.[18] "If we don't want totalitarianism here, we must keep the FCC within bounds, and narrow bounds at that," wrote the *New York News* less than one month before *War of the Worlds*.[19]

The sole dissenting vote came from Commissioner Tunis Augustus MacDonough Craven, a retired naval commander and the FCC's only technical expert.[20] Craven firmly believed that broadcasters should be left to regulate themselves, and he publicly criticized his fellow commissioners for trying to "censor the air."[21] The day after *War of the Worlds*, he again came out strongly against federal censorship, warning the FCC "to avoid the danger of . . . censoring what shall and shall not be said over the radio." He argued that if the commission did not tread lightly, they could easily frighten other stations away from airing more creative and artistic programs. "The public," he said, "does not want a 'spineless' radio."[22] Yet, as the broadcasting historian David Goodman has noted, fear of the FCC's power had actually inspired some of radio's most creative programs. Broadcasters desperate to prove that they served the public interest aired scores of unsponsored, high cultural shows—including *The Mercury Theatre on the Air*—at their own expense. This strange mixture of free enterprise and fear of reform gave radio's "golden age" its unique character. The medium would have been much more "spineless" without it.[23]

Craven's laissez-faire attitude had a strong opponent in the FCC's most vocal member: George Henry Payne. Like Senator Herring, Payne had long protested radio programs that "produced terrorism and nightmares among children," and he held a dim view of the industry in general.[24] "The broadcaster enters our homes stealthily," he told the press in May 1938, "and often does much harm to our children by his blood-curdling programs and to adults by his propaganda."[25] For Payne, *War of the Worlds* called for swift action even if it had not broken any set laws. "Certainly when people are injured morally, physically, spiritually and psychically, they have just as much right to complain as if the laws against obscenity and indecency were involved," he told the press.[26]

Rather than the vague requirement that stations operate in "the public interest, convenience, or necessity," Payne believed that broadcasters should be made to obey a specific set of "program standards." These standards, carrying the full force of law, would prevent them from airing anything too lewd or shocking. If a station refused to abide by them, it would lose its license to operate.[27] The airwaves, Payne argued, belonged to the people, and so broadcasters had no right to offend or otherwise disrupt their listeners. "People who have material broadcast into their homes without warnings have a right to protection," he said the day after *War of the Worlds*. "Too many broadcasters have insisted that they could broadcast anything they liked, contending that they were protected by the prohibition of censorship."[28]

No one else on the FCC voiced similar views the day after the broadcast, though there was some agreement that "horror" programs should be regulated.[29] The other commissioners were more circumspect, willing to say generally that something should be done but not to offer any ideas.

The *Beyond the Horizon* controversy had left them all a little gun-shy.[30] One unnamed commissioner told reporters that although he believed *War of the Worlds* had earned "the booby prize for the year" for being a "prize boner," it would be unfair to punish the network for making a single mistake.[31] Another, Paul A. Walker, told *The New York Times*, "Probably the broadcasters are as anxious to straighten things out as anybody."[32] But Chairman McNinch, who after a year on the FCC remained something of a wild card, refused to pass judgment, and this gave broadcasters reason to worry. McNinch was short and slight, by no means an imposing man, but he had earned a reputation as a born reformer who took no prisoners. The entire radio industry was terrified of him.

Owlish and elderly, with ears like rearview mirrors, Frank Ramsay McNinch had the hardscrabble look of a Dust Bowl refugee. He was born into poverty, the son of a Confederate veteran wounded at Gettysburg, and he worked his way through college, then earned a law degree from the University of North Carolina at Chapel Hill. In 1917, McNinch became mayor of Charlotte, where he ended a streetcar strike by arming private citizens against the strikers. Voters tried to recall him for it, but he kept his seat and went on to serve a second term. Here, it seemed, was a man who got things done. Herbert Hoover appointed him to the Federal Power Commission and lived to regret it, because McNinch soon displayed a penchant for regulation. *Time* called him "a New Dealer before the New Deal began,"[33] and said that this avowed teetotaler kept a jug of milk on his desk to sip on throughout the day. Franklin Roosevelt bonded with McNinch soon after entering the White House, and, in the late summer of 1937, appointed him temporary head of the FCC. McNinch told reporters that the President had given him "a free hand" to clean up that bloated and inefficient agency, and there was some speculation that he'd try to clean up the airwaves as well.[34]

The FCC regulated the telephone and telegraph in addition to the radio, but McNinch made clear that his first order of business would be "to straighten out" the broadcast division. He told *Broadcasting*, the radio trade journal, that he planned to carry over much of what he had learned from his previous job, regulating power companies. Communications technologies, he believed, were also "public utilities," and their first duty was to serve the people. "Making money is to be included through fair profit when earned by this service," he said, "but profiteering on public utilities to me is hateful, undemocratic and anti-social."[35] This took the idea of the public airwaves one step further than many Americans were willing to go. A growing movement in Washington argued that radio should be "an organ of government if not a direct arm, as in Great Britain," and McNinch appeared to be leaning in that direction.[36]

Commercial broadcasters, on the other hand, had no desire to become an American version of the BBC. And so the networks mounted what Goodman has called "a sustained and sophisticated public relations campaign" to endear the public to the "American system" of broadcasting. American radio, they argued, was better and freer than any in the world; even commercials were held up as a product of democracy. Broadcasters told the public that government regulation inevitably led to tyranny. As proof, they cited the state-owned radio systems of European dictatorships like Germany and Italy. Only the free market, they claimed, could keep American radio free. Above all, they sought to entwine their business with the First Amendment freedoms of speech, press, and religion.[37] "These are the cornerstones of our American democracy," David Sarnoff told the Town Hall of New York in mid-1938. "What helps one helps all; what injures one is an encroachment upon all; what destroys one destroys all, and thereby destroys democracy itself."[38] But McNinch, it seemed, had different ideas, and he was shaping up to be a formidable opponent.

Just two months into his tenure, McNinch significantly streamlined the FCC, collapsing its three separate divisions—one each for the telephone, telegraph, and radio—into one unit. The press melodramatically termed this a "purge," because it put the heads of each division, who were all politically well-connected men, out of work. Clearly, McNinch was unafraid of offending the powerful. More reforms, even less popular, were soon to come.[39] Then, in April 1938, the FCC sent detailed financial questionnaires to every radio station in America. This marked the start of their monopoly investigation, and left the major networks feeling very nervous.[40] When CBS president William S. Paley went on air later that month to address his stockholders, *Time* reported that the investigation had left him so shaken that he suffered "a bad case of microphone fright."[41]

Broadcasters worried, too, over McNinch's views on censorship. He gave them reason to be concerned after coming into conflict with the nation's reigning sex queen, Mae West. On December 12, 1937, West made a guest appearance on *The Chase & Sanborn Hour* with Edgar Bergen and Charlie McCarthy. She performed in two comedy skits, showcasing her unique brand of double entendre. Like all the show's female guest stars, West bantered with McCarthy, but this time she was the one who took the lead, leaving the usually lustful dummy somewhat flustered. "Tell me, Miss West, have you ever found the one man in your life that you could really love?" Bergen asked. "Sure," West replied, "lotsa times." Later, she invited Charlie McCarthy into her "woodpile."[42]

More provocatively, West played Eve in a skit parodying the biblical story of the Garden of Eden. In this version, Eve tempts the serpent, not the other way around, and tricks Adam into eating the forbidden fruit by making it into applesauce. Poking fun at the Bible (on a Sunday, no less) was sure to offend some listeners, especially when Mae West, always a lightning rod for controversy, was involved.[43] But although observers at the time reported that the show caused "a storm of protest," in truth it only prompted four hundred angry letters to the FCC, out of an audience of twenty-three million people.[44] And these were not spontaneous responses. The scholar Steve Craig has studied those letters and found that most were part of a coordinated campaign by the Catholic Legion of Decency to get Mae West kicked off the air.[45] The real controversy only came one month later, when the FCC stepped in.

After reviewing the show and the protests, McNinch sent an open letter to NBC president Lenox Lohr condemning the Mae West skits. The commission, he said, found their content "far below even the minimum standards which should control . . . the selection and production of broadcast programs." Broadcast licenses carried "a social, civic and moral responsibility" to protect listeners "against features that are suggestive, vulgar, immoral or of such other character as may be offensive to the great mass of right-thinking, clean minded American citizens." Echoing Commissioner Payne, McNinch told the press that the FCC should create "standards of programs" clearly stating what could and could not be said on the air. But, rather than punish NBC, McNinch stated that the incident would be held against each of the fifty-nine individual stations that had aired the program the next time their licenses came up for renewal. He said it was their responsibility, not the network's, to "monitor" every show and "cut off those which are objectionable." If, in the next few months, they aired nothing else that was offensive, then, McNinch said, "there will be no further action."[46]

This veiled threat to pull the licenses of fifty-nine NBC affiliates "shook the industry," according to Craig, even though it was never carried out. Mae West would not appear on radio again for another fourteen years, and Paramount Pictures soon announced that they would produce no more of her movies, which sent her film career into decline.[47] But most of the public outcry fell on the commission, not Mae West. The FCC received two hundred more letters in the wake of McNinch's statement, 125 of them protesting what McNinch had threatened to do.[48] Several newspapers also harshly criticized the FCC, and the incident alienated some of McNinch's New Deal allies. General Hugh S. Johnson, formerly the head of FDR's National Recovery Administration, called the letter "a bold and outright prelude to censorship." The editorial board of the New York *Daily News*, a "militantly pro–New Deal" newspaper, agreed, telling the FCC to "keep its hands off." The American broadcasting system, they wrote, "is the world's only free one . . . If we want to keep our democracy, we must keep our radio free."[49]

McNinch, for his part, emphatically denied any interest in censoring the radio. In a speech before the National Association of Broadcasters in February 1938, he restated his belief that radio stations had the responsibility to censor themselves. "You know as well as the members of the Commission what is fair, what is vulgar, what is decent, what is profane, what will probably give offense," he said. "It is your duty in the first instance to guard against these." His words were overtly friendly, yet mildly threatening, since McNinch made clear that he had no intention of remaining hands-off. "If something has been broadcast that is contrary to the public interest, is vulgar, indecent, profane, violative of any rules of fair play ordinarily recognized, or that might be reasonably anticipated to give offense," he said, "I conceive it to be the duty of the Commission to do something about it."[50]

Those words, and his record of strong if unpopular action, made it hard to predict McNinch's reaction to *War of the Worlds*. A case could easily be made that Welles's broadcast was "contrary to the public interest," and many who wrote in to the FCC made just that case. "Some time ago, there was much ado over a broadcast that featured Mae West and Charlie McCarthy," wrote one New Yorker to McNinch. "If anything was made over such nonsense, then something drastic should certainly be meted out to [this] Station."[51] The radio industry, expecting punishment, immediately began to backtrack. CBS pledged never to air another fake news show "when the circumstances of the broadcast could cause immediate alarm to numbers of listeners," and the National Association of Broadcasters said in a statement, "Those of us in radio have only the most profound regret."[52]

But, despite his fearsome reputation, McNinch was not hasty.[53] The day after *War of the Worlds*, he sent a telegram to CBS asking for a copy of its script and a recording of the broadcast for the FCC to review. "I withhold final judgment until later," he said in a statement, "but any broadcast that creates such general panic and fear as this one is reported to have done is, to say the least, regrettable."[54] That, for some frightened listeners, was putting it mildly.[55] But those in the radio industry would have recognized the strong words at the end of McNinch's statement. The panic, he said, "points out again the serious public responsibility of those who are licensed to operate stations."[56] This reminded station owners of McNinch's power to take them off the air for not acting in the public interest. It must have seemed he was contemplating the same action he had suggested after the Mae West broadcast: punishing not the network itself, but each affiliated station that had aired *War of the Worlds*.

For broadcasters whose livelihoods depended on their licenses, that was a scary prospect. "The radio industry viewed today a hobgoblin more terrifying to it than any Halloween spook," wrote the Associated Press, adding that *War of the Worlds* had made "increasing Federal control of broadcasts" a distinct possibility.[57] The *Los Angeles Times* also led with the suggestion that "new standards defining what type of radio entertainment is 'in the public interest'" might come about as a result of the broadcast.[58] These were wild speculations, reflecting the panic of an industry desperate to avoid further regulation. But the press validated them by printing them, making it seem as if the entire American system of broadcasting—even "free radio" itself—was under threat.

Welles, too, appeared to be on the chopping block. The newspapers, wrote one Illinois woman to Welles, implied "that there might be need for [a] rally of forces to your side," and so listeners came to his defense the only way they could—through the mail.[59] They wrote to CBS and the Mercury, urging them not to take Welles off the air, and they wrote to the FCC, protesting any moves toward regulation or censorship. They knew that broadcasters paid close attention to their fan mail, and they used their power as consumers to try to save Welles's program. "If, because of your drama of Sunday, the Mercury Air Theater [sic] is discontinued or molded into the nauseatingly familiar pattern of the other radio theaters," wrote one couple, "there will be a good radio for sale cheap at our house."[60]

Listeners who wrote to Welles directly often tried to cheer him up with advice or moral support. They offered a " 'ray of sunshine' midst the 'angry clouds,' " as one New Yorker put it.[61] A thirteen-year-old boy in Chicago sent Welles a letter on behalf of his classmates, explaining "how sorry we all are that the people didn't like your play 'War of the Worlds.' " All of his fellow students "liked it very much," he wrote, "and what ever happens because of your radio play you will know that a dozen children will stick by you."[62] Other listeners falsely assumed that Welles would be deluged with angry letters; they wrote in to save him from a hysterical mob that did not actually exist.[63] In fact, so many people wrote to the Mercury, trying to offset protests from angry listeners, that their letters ultimately outnumbered those protests ten to one.

Fifty-two of the complaints sent to the Mercury were written on the night of the broadcast itself, more than on any other day. But that number dropped to thirty-six on October 31, even as the number of pro-Welles letters shot up to 440. On November 1, listeners sent another 253 supportive letters and only five protests. Meanwhile, the FCC also received an influx of letters from Welles's supporters. Complaints sent to the government topped out a day later than the Mercury, but they dropped off almost as sharply. In fact, on October 31 alone, more pro-Welles letters were sent to the Mercury and the FCC (513) than the total number of protests each would receive combined (468). As with the Mae West controversy, the initial reaction to *War of the Worlds* was not as negative as the press implied. It had a second wave, prompted not by the broadcast itself but by the stories about it in the newspapers.

Many of these letters praised Welles's artistry, describing *The Mercury Theatre on the Air* as one of radio's few worthwhile shows. "Nine-tenths of the other dramatic programs are plain saw-dust; they devitalize the existing intelligence of the unwary listener," wrote one man to Welles. "We need quality."[64] These Mercury fans argued that too many radio shows—crime dramas, adventure serials, variety shows—catered to low-brows and children. "Must we allways [sic] listen to 'swing' and low class comedians?" wrote a listener from Utica, New York. "Can't we have a little drama, realistically done, for a change?"[65] By defending Welles, they hoped to save a place for high culture on the radio dial. "Radio is too big a thing for any branch of it to be preempted for the use of any one class or age of persons," wrote an Indiana woman to McNinch. "All have a right to their own form of entertainment."[66]

No one, however, acknowledged that many of radio's most refined shows existed largely because of the FCC's public interest requirement. Instead, they argued that any government action would hinder radio's growth as an art form. The singer and radio personality Eddie Cantor wired the FCC three days after the broadcast to urge them "NOT TO GARROTE RADIO WITH EXCESSIVE CENSORSHIP." Doing so "WOULD RETARD RADIO IMMEASURABLY AND PRODUCE A SPINELESS RADIO THEATER," he wrote, echoing the words of T.A.M. Craven.[67] Others, expecting that Welles would be forced to tone his show down, wrote him directly to ask that he not "humor the whims of the stupid," as one Ohioan put it.[68] Instead of the FCC, these listeners imagined a dim-witted audience to be the real censors attempting to silence a program that was too smart for them to understand.

Intelligence tests done by the U.S. Army during World War I had found that the average American soldier had a mental age of less than thirteen years. On its face, the result was ridiculous; as Walter Lippmann pointed out, the average from such a large group would statistically represent normal adult intelligence. But the finding changed how people thought about the mental health of the United States, prompting many to wonder how democracy could survive in a nation beset by such idiocy.[69] And because radio spoke to the masses, the idea that most Americans had a thirteen-year-old mind came to define how broadcasters understood their audience.[70] Radio shows with commercial sponsors tried to appeal to listeners of average or below-average intelligence, so as to reach the greatest number of people.[71] Some observers, such as George Henry Payne, argued that this would inevitably create "a Nation of grown-up children."[72]

The *Chicago Tribune* captured this dim view of radio listeners in an editorial shortly after *War of the Worlds*:

> By and large the radio audience isn't very bright. Perhaps it would be more tactful to say that some members of the radio audience are a trifle retarded mentally, and that many a program is prepared for their

consumption. Newspapers, books, magazines, the stage, and even the movies strain the fat boys' powers of understanding and appreciation, but they can generally find something on the air which is within their comprehension.[73]

Like the *Tribune*, many of Welles's defenders assumed that those frightened by *War of the Worlds* did not or could not read—or else that they only read comic strips.[74] "It is my personal opinion," wrote one Maryland listener, "that the average American, not-withstanding his public free education, is a humbug, a blatherskite and a moron. He cannot sit to read a book for two hours, could give you no review if he read it, and cannot sit for ten minutes to hear what is said, proof being, that at least four times 'War of the Worlds' was announced as fiction."[75]

For Welles's supporters, then, the panic had everything to do with intelligence and nothing to do with mixing news and entertainment. Therefore, they dismissed out of hand the idea that fake news broadcasts were in any way dangerous. "'The Men From Mars' was not a hoax," wrote one Texan. "If some of the radio audience failed to listen to the clear announcements that it was fiction, and got jittery in consequence, the rest of us should not be penalized by having such clever dramas prohibited."[76] These listeners so resented their country's mass culture that they were more than ready to jump to the conclusion that most radio listeners were stupid. "You can't protect a pig from wallowing and scratching his back, nor can you protect the human mental pigs who, in spite of the millions spent in education, refuse to be educated," wrote one astronomer to the FCC. "Why not put the blame where it belongs—on the so-called comic strips, such as 'Buck Rogers,' 'Flash Gordon,' or others—and not on the Mercury Theater [*sic*]?"[77] This elitism explains why few of Welles's defenders suggested that the press exaggerated the panic. Most accepted the story without question, because it confirmed their disdain for the American mass mind.[78] "Since your fine production last Sunday evening," wrote one listener to Welles, "I have been ashamed that I am an American."[79]

This pessimism about the national intelligence led to some disturbing conclusions about the future of the country. As one Detroiter put it in his letter to the FCC, the panic had seemingly revealed "the uncertain foundation upon which our American democracy rests."[80] Americans knew all too well how propagandists in Nazi Germany and other dictatorships used the radio to control their citizens. The panic story made it seem as if the United States was just as vulnerable to mass-media manipulation. "I think you have proved conclusively what could happen in any nation whose radio system is government controlled," wrote a Michigan man to Welles. "We can easily see that if the government decided to scare the nation as we believe Hitler does in Germany that it would be impossible for anyone to convince the public that after all it was just a play. We are thankful that we still have free speech, whether in the pulpit or on the radio."[81]

No one in the FCC actually advocated a government takeover of radio, but many Americans believed that censorship or regulation could have no other end. A Gallup poll taken earlier that year found that 59 percent of respondents opposed "direct Federal censorship" of radio because it would lead to "a dictatorial usurpation of power" and the loss of freedom of speech.[82] "I can't understand why anyone in our free United States should want or encourage censorship of the air," wrote one Montanan to Welles. "It would ruin our democratic radio system and there is no telling what efect [sic] it would have on our democracy."[83] Many other listeners closely tied American broadcasting to American democracy in their letters. Violating one, they argued, would inevitably violate the other. "If censorship of Free Speech is in the 'offing,'" wrote one Wisconsin man, "how will we identify ourselves from any of the European Dictatorships?"[84] To others, it looked as if the country was already heading in that direction.

The Great Depression brought American democracy closer to outright failure than at any point since the Civil War. President Roosevelt's emergency actions in the spring of 1933 walked the country back from the brink, but by 1935 the nation had begun to backslide. The Supreme Court declared some of FDR's biggest achievements unconstitutional; business interests began to pick apart the New Deal even further. As unemployment continued to grow, many wondered if democracy had proved itself incapable of solving the problems of the modern world. The fascist states of Europe seemed, to all outward appearances, remarkably successful, their iniquities and shortcomings carefully hidden from view.

Many argued that unless the United States took similar steps toward a dictatorship, it would inevitably collapse into communism. There seemed no alternative.[85]

In the early days of his administration, Roosevelt had refused the suggestion of the columnist Walter Lippmann and others that he take "dictatorial" powers to solve the national economic crisis.[86] But when, in his second term, FDR tried and failed to add seats to the Supreme Court, some Americans worried that he had changed his mind. "It is probably too much to say that there exists any actual fear of dictatorship," wrote *The New York Times* in 1937, "but there is much disquietude, whether justified or not."[87] As late as 1939, the educator Lyman Bryson wrote that each and every American was "at the center of a battle" between communism, fascism, and democracy. These ideologies were "struggling to control the world" by appealing to "the ordinary citizen, the man on the street"—the very reader Bryson addressed. "The final choice—the way the world goes—is up to you," he wrote.[88]

The radio made it hard for Americans to make that decision honestly. In the mid-1930s, it empowered two voices that many believed could have pushed the nation into a dictatorship. The first belonged to Father Charles E. Coughlin, a Catholic priest broadcasting from the Shrine of the Little Flower in Royal Oak, Michigan. Coughlin began by giving children's talks over Detroit's station WJR, but as his audience grew, so did his political ambitions. Under the cover of religion, he railed against "international bankers"—eventually making clear that he meant Jews—and urged the creation of a crypto-fascist "corporate state." Some of his ideas were taken directly from the work of the Nazi propagandist Joseph Goebbels. As Coughlin's rhetoric grew increasingly political, the networks refused to carry his speeches, so he bought his own airtime on stations nationwide, essentially building his own network with money from his followers. And he had very many followers: during the bleakest days of the Depression, as many as thirty million people heard his broadcasts. He received three thousand letters each week, more than anyone else in the country, and many arrived with money in the envelope.[89]

Radio also introduced Americans to an equally charismatic—and, some argued, equally dangerous—orator in Senator Huey Long of Louisiana. Like Coughlin, Long was a populist who became a national figure thanks to his skill with the microphone. Americans loved Long's homespun speaking style, and especially his promise to cap large incomes and "share the wealth," guaranteeing that all citizens would earn at least two thousand dollars a year—or almost thirty-five thousand in today's dollars. When people asked for specifics, or questioned his logic, Long refused to elaborate. Yet soon there were "Share Our Wealth" clubs in more than eight thousand cities nationwide, with over seven million members—a ready-made network for an inevitable presidential campaign. The radio had made it all possible; Long was so popular with audiences that the networks gave him free airtime in order to boost their ratings. This gave Long, a United States senator, a platform to speak to the entire country as if he were already president. Some even said he was a better speaker than FDR.[90] One of Long's political rivals called him "the most persuasive man living."[91]

Like Father Coughlin, Long went from being a supporter of the New Deal in its early days to a fierce critic of Roosevelt by the middle of the decade. Many believed that the "Radio Priest" would join forces with the "Louisiana Kingfish" to challenge FDR in the 1936 election. But that possibility died in 1935, with Long's assassination in the Louisiana State Capitol. Coughlin tried to keep the movement alive by creating a new political party to run against Roosevelt that November. As his speeches became ever more vitriolic, his hatred for the President became plainer and plainer. But without the powerful persuasiveness of Huey Long, the movement went nowhere.[92]

Long's potential and even desire for dictatorship remain debatable. But at the time, many seriously considered him a possible American Hitler. "If you don't think Long and Coughlin are dangerous," General Hugh S. Johnson said in a speech in 1935, "you don't know the temper of the country in this distress!"[93] The writer Sinclair Lewis pursued this possibility in his 1935 bestseller It Can't Happen Here, in which fictional versions of Long and Coughlin push the country into fascism.[94] As in real life, Lewis's demagogues—Bishop Peter Paul Prang and Senator Buzz Windrip—rise because of the radio. "No man in history has ever had such an audience as Bishop Prang, nor so much apparent power," Lewis wrote. "By the magic of electricity, Prang made the position of any king in history look a little absurd and tinseled."[95] Windrip's message, like Long's, is one of wealth redistribution, full of twisted facts and logical fallacies. But his folksy and charismatic speaking style, amplified by the radio, wins over the country and carries him to the White House. Once there, he shuts down Congress, silences dissent, and opens a network of concentration camps staffed by his own band of storm troopers, the "Minute Men." In the novel, democracy collapses almost immediately—thanks in large part to the radio.

From its very title, *It Can't Happen Here* satirizes those who saw the United States as somehow immune to the spread of fascism. "Why, there's no country in the world that can get more hysterical—yes, or more obsequious!—than America," Lewis's protagonist says early in the book. "Where in all history has there ever been a people so ripe for dictatorship as ours!"[96] Listeners' hysterical reactions to *War of the Worlds*, as reported in the newspapers, seemed to suggest that Lewis was right, that Americans were just as susceptible to radio demagoguery as those in any European country. "It has been said that 'it can't happen here' and the same has been said by other nations, but it is happening just the same," wrote one New Yorker to Welles. "After your interpretation of last night's play, I think that a lot of us will realize that it can happen here, and the demonstration that followed might give us just a hint of what is going on on the other side and that we want no part of it." Like many listeners, this one expressed the hope that the panic might convince America to stay out of any future world war.[97]

Several of Welles's defenders brought up fascism in their letters, comparing the broadcast to the way Hitler and Mussolini used radio to manipulate the masses. "It's little wonder the much discussed 'isms' have gained such a foothold," a Maine listener wrote to Welles. "If the American people are as gullible and excitable as that a smooth tongued orator could soon turn their head."[98] A few even suggested that Welles had proved himself a potential dictator. "I congratulate Mr. Welles on his dramatic ability to sway mobs," wrote a Missouri woman to CBS. "Maybe he is to be our Hitler and control us with the sway of his radio voice. He must feel tremendously complimented by the evidence of his power."[99]

Such comparisons are specious at best. As the historian Michael Stamm has noted, Welles did not appeal to listeners with persuasive oratory, nationalism, or racial pride; he momentarily startled some of them by faking a news broadcast.[100] The effects of *War of the Worlds* were much more limited, and much less dangerous, than those of the radio speeches of Adolf Hitler or even Father Coughlin. But listeners made that connection because the panic story reinforced their fears of radio's power. They saw it as a hypnotic instrument, letting men like Hitler or Huey Long mesmerize whole countries into taking leave of their senses. As one

Washingtonian put it in his letter to Welles, "Maybe Hitler is on the right track in his opinion of the mentality of the masses."[101] More than Martians or even Nazis, these Americans feared their own countrymen.

In playing up the stories of people evacuating their homes or contemplating suicide because of the Martians, the press had badly caricatured those frightened by *War of the Worlds*. Welles's defenders distorted that caricature even further in their letters. They pictured countless Americans tuning in to the show, hearing something about aliens, and immediately rushing outside in a panic, never imagining that the fright was actually more complex and more measured than that. "This reaction of many of the American public entire[ly] changes my conception of our nation as a people of clear and intelligent thinkers," wrote one listener from Staten Island. "It is almost unbelievable to think that this nation would act in such an unbalanced maner [sic]."[102] The panic, as these listeners understood it, essentially sounded the death knell for self-government. How could Americans withstand a homegrown dictator, much less an invasion from outside enemies, if this was how they responded to a radio show about Martians? "Anyone who turns on a radio—catches a few sentences—and then turns off the radio and rushes out to die—is too much of a fool to be let at large," wrote one Pennsylvanian to the FCC. "They are positively a danger to the community."[103]

Later researchers and historians would see in the panic only evidence of America's "jitteriness" after the recent Czech crisis. But, as David Goodman has noted, most people at the time simply saw it as proof of mass stupidity.[104] "*No*, it was not the result of 'jitters' over the war situation," wrote one Californian to the FCC, "it was the result of ignorance, undeveloped intellects, [and] unrestrained emotionality which is the only resort low mentality has in a crisis."[105] This preoccupation with the national intelligence, Goodman wrote, reflects concerns about radio's power to spread propaganda. Welles's supporters felt that frightened listeners had failed in their civic duty to process everything they heard critically, and so they blamed them, and not Welles, for the hysteria caused by the broadcast.[106] "Please note that I write, 'the panic created by the public,'" wrote one Canadian to Welles. "I have read of, and heard this public blame governments, the author, the producer, the radio network and individual stations for the national hysteria, but not one of the panicky persons place the blame where it belongs—upon himself."[107]

Other listeners wrote, rather haughtily, that those who were frightened should learn a thing or two from the experience. "I have no sympathy . . . with those who demand punitive or restrictive action," wrote one Floridian. "It seems to me that those who were duped deserved and needed the lesson they got, and that the lesson was a good one."[108] Some even suggested that if frightened listeners didn't learn their lesson they should have their radios taken away from them—or worse.[109] But most agreed that, with despotism on the rise and democracy seemingly on the wane, the government should leave broadcasters alone. "I believe that just now we shall do well to protect really basic liberties," wrote one Kansan to McNinch. "Fundamental in that aim is the freedom of radio to act without restraints so long as it shows consciousness of its immense power and responsibility. That, to my mind, it is now doing, and doing admirably."[110]

This, of course, was exactly the argument broadcasters had been making for some time—that their "American system" produced a "free radio" unlike any in the world. The *War of the Worlds* letters suggest that they had succeeded in convincing the country that free speech and free-market capitalism were one and the same. Some listeners even argued that the radio industry could be trusted to regulate itself without government interference. As one New Yorker put it, "No regulatory body can ever work as effectively as public opinion."[111] Speaking for the entire industry, the trade journal *Broadcasting* agreed, calling *War of the Worlds* "as strong an argument as has yet been advanced in favor of Radio by the American Plan." For this reason, they thanked "Messrs. Wells and Welles" for giving "another contribution to better radio."[112]

Many newspaper editorials also defended the radio against further regulation. Even when they chastised Welles and CBS, most were firmly against any government censorship.[113] Instead, they argued that this controversy would teach broadcasters greater responsibility. "Censorship is not the answer," wrote *The Milwaukee Journal* on November 1. "It never is the answer in a democracy. The answer lies in the use of better judgment on the part of those who have freedom of communication."[114] The next day, the New York *Daily News* wrote that they had received nearly two hundred letters regarding *War of the Worlds*, half from people angered by the broadcast and half furious at those who were frightened. But the *Daily News* forgave both Welles and those he had fooled, reserving its own wrath for the FCC and Senator Herring. "We wish the FCC would relax and go on back to sleep," they wrote. "We hope the next Congress, and as many Congresses thereafter as necessary, will smack flat all radio censorship bills with the avalanche of NO's they deserve in a free-speech, free-press, free-religion, free-assemblage country."[115] There is every indication that most Americans felt the same way.

Instead of leading to calls for government intervention, as broadcasters had feared, *War of the Worlds* had the opposite effect. It pushed the United States further away from censorship. The panic story inflamed fears that radio might tip the country into tyranny. And in such a climate, Americans were liable to see any FCC action as a step toward totalitarianism. "The very fact that [the broadcast] frightened so many people makes it all the more plain that the Government should not control the radio," wrote one Texan to the FCC, "for if radio can make people think as the radio says, why then, each ruling power could make them think and believe anything, true or not!!"[116] But the government takeover that these listeners feared was largely illusory. Despite its many missteps, the FCC existed in a delicate balance with broadcasters. It acted as a check on radio's commercial interests, ensuring that the medium truly acted in the public interest. By rejecting the FCC's oversight, Americans gave the public airwaves over to commercialism. In so doing, they helped hasten the end of radio's golden age.

As early as two days after the broadcast, it was clear that the FCC would take no action in response to *War of the Worlds*. When the commissioners met on November 1, they discussed only routine matters.[117] None of them had listened to Welles's broadcast yet; they still awaited delivery of a recording from CBS. But, according to *The New York Times*, "There were fairly definite indications that no action would be taken beyond a possible statement of regret that the program was staged in too realistic a manner." Even the redoubtable George Henry Payne pivoted back to his pet cause. He complained again about "radio terror programs [that] are frightening children," and told the press that the FCC should investigate such shows.[118]

The commissioners knew that they had no legal authority to act. Some members told *The Washington Post* off the record that they were essentially "powerless," unable to do more than issue a stern reprimand to CBS.[119] Unlike in the cases of Mae West and *Beyond the Horizon*, no one could make the argument that *War of the Worlds* included "obscene, indecent, or profane language." Everything else fell into a very gray area, into which the FCC was hesitant to venture.[120] As McNinch explained to *The Baltimore Sun*, "There is censorship now, with the responsibility on the stations themselves. To put such responsibility on the commission— no, I would be opposed to that."[121] The FCC had gotten the message. They would exercise their regulatory powers more loosely from now on, because they knew broadcasters would keep radio under control.

On November 7, McNinch called an "informal" meeting with the heads of NBC, CBS, and the Mutual Broadcasting System to discuss the issues raised by *War of the Worlds*. McNinch suggested, and the network heads agreed, that news terms like "flash" and "bulletin" should be kept out of fictional programs, to avoid "general alarm." News broadcasting itself, however, would not be changed. There was also some discussion of "program standards," which McNinch encouraged the networks to impose upon themselves. Because of the prohibition on FCC censorship, McNinch made clear that he was not speaking on behalf of the commission or suggesting any further government regulation. This meeting, which lasted about three hours, marked the federal government's only direct response to the *War of the Worlds* broadcast.[122]

Orson Welles later claimed that "they passed a lot of laws" prohibiting future fake news hoaxes, but this appears to be untrue.[123] Although as many as thirty congressmen and senators, including Clyde Herring, prepared radio-censorship bills in the wake of *War of the Worlds*, none made it into law.[124] And according to the legal scholar Justin Levine, there is no indication that Herring even brought any legislation regulating radio before the Senate. Widespread press and public condemnation of his idea, Levine suggests, kept Herring's long-promised censorship bill from ever materializing.[125] The following year, Herring published an article on the subject directly contradicting his earlier view that government regulation was an immediate necessity. "Just as I am a staunch believer in the capacity of business to run itself," he wrote, "so I believe that the radio industry is able to regulate itself." Only if they failed to do so, he suggested, would there be a push "to impose some sort of governmental censorship"—by other hands, presumably, and not his own.[126]

The radio industry moved quickly to forestall any government censorship. Motivated by *War of the Worlds*, the National Association of Broadcasters met in Washington, D.C., in December 1938 to discuss self-regulation. They began drawing up their own program standards, focusing on advertising, "cuss" words, and children's shows. While such self-censorship was ostensibly voluntary, the association also provided for a code of enforcement that would make stations toe the line.[127] But even without a set code in place, "jittery" broadcasters immediately began policing themselves. "On guard against government censorship," wrote *American Magazine* in March 1939, "radio has clamped its own hand over its own mouth in a self-censorship as rigid as, if not more rigid than, anything the government could offer." Mae West and *War of the Worlds*, they wrote, had left the industry "scared silly" and determined to prevent any more controversial programs.[128]

Many stations consciously toned down their news coverage, making it as dry as possible, in order to avoid overexciting listeners. Re-enactments of news stories and impersonations of real people were banned. *The March of Time* went off the air in 1939 and returned two years later as a straight news program. Stations also scaled back their use of loud and violent sound effects. *Gang Busters*, that frequent target of Senator Herring and others, had to quiet the sounds of police whistles and gunfire in its opening sequence, but the content of the show apparently remained unaffected.[129] The industry and the general public welcomed such restraint. Speaking before the FCC in November 1938, RCA president David Sarnoff called "self-regulation . . . the American answer to an American problem."[130]

The FCC, meanwhile, never turned out to be the censor that many feared they would become, just as McNinch failed to live up to his reputation as a formidable cleanup man. Events conspired against him, forcing him toward the uncomfortable question of censorship. He badly overreacted to the Mae West incident, painting himself as a would-be censor and a bit of a puritan. Even though he proceeded more cautiously with *War of the Worlds*, the public outcry still left the FCC with yet another black eye.[131] At the same time, McNinch's drive to make the agency more efficient only led to more bickering with Payne and Craven. The "unrelenting war," as *Time* called it, between these three men came to a head late in McNinch's tenure, when he tried and failed to eliminate Payne's and Craven's jobs. In 1939, he left the commission because of ill health. *Time* suggested that instead of cleaning up the FCC, McNinch's efforts had left his successor, James Lawrence Fly, with a new mess of his own to deal with.[132]

Fly, a forty-one-year-old attorney, had worked for the federal government for a decade, most recently as general counsel for the Tennessee Valley

Authority.[133] Like McNinch, he emphasized that broadcasters' freedom of action came with a duty to the public. But Fly pursued this idea further, seeking to turn the airwaves into a true "market place of ideas," as he put it. "Freedom to listen is an essential counterpart of freedom of speech," he said in 1943. "Those who control this mechanism of free speech must treat free speech not as a right but as a duty. They must hold this mechanism of free speech in trust for the people—the listeners."[134] Rather than interfering with individual stations, as McNinch had done, Fly sought to open access to the airwaves. He saw the networks, not the government, as the real threat to free speech: by consolidating the power of broadcasting, he believed, they restricted access to information.[135]

In 1941, Fly concluded the monopoly investigation that McNinch had begun three years earlier. His *Report on Chain Broadcasting* made it illegal to own more than one radio station in a single community. NBC would have to separate into two companies, one for each of its radio networks. This, as Erik Barnouw has noted, was actually in their best interests; NBC vice president Mark Woods had argued privately for years that both networks would be more profitable if run separately. But Fly's report violated the sacred notion of "free radio" that so many had rushed to defend after *War of the Worlds*, and it proved extremely controversial. Broadcasters, journalists, and politicians attacked Fly from all sides, charging him with dismantling the American system of radio. The commission soon found itself under investigation by the House Un-American Activities Committee as a supposed nest of communism. Fly and the FCC survived the onslaught, however. The Supreme Court upheld their reforms, and NBC sold one of its networks to the American Broadcasting Company (ABC). Fly hoped that by scaling back network control, he would ensure that Americans were exposed to diverse opinions and ideas.[136] But his action only forestalled the inevitable. In the years since, the number of American media outlets has increased dramatically, but the number of companies controlling them has only gotten smaller.

When he asked the commission to approve the new ABC network, Mark Woods of NBC stated repeatedly that his company was more interested in profit than in ideas. "We are in the advertising business, gentlemen," he said, "and that business is the business of selling goods to the American people."[137] This philosophy explains a central irony of the *War of the Worlds* incident: even though the FCC did nothing in response to the broadcast, radio censorship grew much stronger in the program's wake. The American system of commercial radio was, in the end, an out-let for advertising. The companies paying for that advertising had no de-sire to alienate potential customers. Because sponsors controlled the purse strings, they controlled content. Broadcasters literally could not afford to offend their listeners. As late as 1948, Jack Benny had to refuse a request to mention a cancer charity on air because his sponsor, a ciga-rette company, forbade any use of the word "cancer" on his program.[138] Such commercial censorship was more than typical in radio's golden age—it was how the industry worked.

In the months after *War of the Worlds*, broadcasters cracked down on anything that might offend, especially humor. Jokes about George Wash-ington and Abraham Lincoln were banned outright. A line in a comedy script about a skunk that entered a church ("he brought his own pew") had to be reworded so as not to rub pious listeners the wrong way. The popular radio comics Jack Benny and Fred Allen had to stop calling each other "anemic" after a few people who actually suffered from anemia wrote in to complain. Just a few days after *War of the Worlds*, Allen even had to ditch a joke based on Welles's broadcast: a facetious warning meant for listeners who believed everything they heard on the radio. "Ladies and Gentlemen," he would have said, "before this radio presenta-tion starts, I would like to announce that this is a comedy program. Any dialogue or sound-effects heard during the next hour will be purely imaginary and will have no relation to any living sounds." But NBC, fearful of making any reference to the show that had inflamed the na-tion, cut those lines from the script.[139]

Such controls seem silly and arbitrary—attempts to cure the symp-tom and not the disease. But they were more than just an annoyance to radio's gagmen. They also kept listeners from hearing more provocative works of art like *War of the Worlds*. A few months after Welles's broad-cast, Standard Brands backed out of sponsoring a thought-provoking drama by Arch Oboler, author of Mae West's "Garden of Eden" skit, be-cause they found it "too hot" to broadcast. It imagined a meeting be-tween Jesus Christ and Benito Mussolini, in which Christ, with lines right out of the Bible, convinces the dictator not to bomb a helpless town. In hopes of making the play palatable to everyone, Oboler changed Christ to Lincoln and made Mussolini a generic despot, but to no avail. In fact, the drama had already been turned down five times, by multiple net-works and multiple sponsors.[140] This seems like just the kind of intelligent, adult entertainment many of Welles's supporters had praised in their letters, yet the American system of "free radio" kept it off the air. The argument implicit in many letters, that radio could only grow as an art form if the government left commercial broadcasters alone, is demonstrably untrue.

"Now the truth of the matter," wrote the psychologists Hadley Cantril and Gordon Allport in 1935, "is that radio drama has made more progress in countries where profits are not the prime motive in broadcasting." Broadcasters in Canada and England, they argued, had greater freedom to try costly experiments because they were not beholden to sponsors.[141] American airwaves saw an explosion of similar, if limited, creativity in the 1930s because the FCC's public interest requirement forced broadcasters to pursue quality, not just profits. Fear of government regulation, notes Welles's biographer Simon Callow, turned the networks into great patrons of the arts. They subsidized the work of artists like Orson Welles and Archibald MacLeish, even when their shows were unprofitable, in order to serve the public interest. Those artists, in turn, created what has come to be called the "Golden Age of Radio."[142] But after 1938, as the idea of "free radio" supplanted broadcasters' duty to the public interest, commercialism took over and creativity diminished.

The radio scholar Neil Verma has noted that by 1943, all of CBS's great unsponsored programs, such as *The Columbia Workshop* and *The Mercury Theatre on the Air*, had either "been cut or sold to sponsors." The networks began to exert greater control over the shows they aired, shaping content more and more to fit the needs of advertisers. Artists like Norman Corwin, perhaps the medium's greatest writer, found themselves facing the choice of either working in soap operas or not working in radio at all.[143] Television usually gets the blame for killing the radio, but advertising stunted its growth long before that. And when TV did arrive on the scene, it came without any of the unsponsored shows that had made radio so exciting decades earlier. Its job, first and foremost, was selling products. "Television," Corwin later said, "was born without a conscience."[144]

Americans struggled with the question of broadcast censorship in the 1930s because radio, like all new media, exposed them to new ideas and new art forms. Some, whether presented by Mae West or Orson

Welles, were uncomfortable, but free speech often comes with discomfort. Advertising, on the other hand, has to be inoffensive, at least to its intended audience. Listeners were right to associate government censorship with tyranny; dictatorships can only exist with tightly controlled mass media. But *War of the Worlds* was by no means a total victory for free speech. Instead, Americans simply chose one censor over another.

8

"The Story of the Century"

It makes one wonder if after all we aren't a nation of mice and not men.
—Mrs. Michael Conovich of Queens, New York,
to the FCC, November 1, 1938[1]

Grover's Mill sits about five miles and a world away from Princeton University. It's little more than a bump in the road, a small knot of clapboard buildings tucked away in the farmlands of central New Jersey. At its center is the town's namesake, a pale-blue gristmill predating the Revolutionary War, which stands at the edge of a placid millpond. In the fall of 1938, its millstones still turned, slowly grinding out grain, as they had for nearly two centuries.[2] Life in the little town went on without incident, as residents enjoyed their last few days and hours of anonymity quietly. If Howard Koch had not discovered the place by accident, it's doubtful anybody else could have found it on purpose.

Koch first visited Grover's Mill in 1969, thirty-one years after his script made it famous. He found the town as quiet as ever, largely unchanged since 1938—or 1838, for that matter. The residents, with practiced reluctance, spun wild stories of the night the Martians landed, tall tales that would not seem out of place in the works of Washington Irving or Mark Twain. The former fire chief of nearby Cranbury told Koch that he had spent that night chasing false reports of fires set by the aliens, and described a herd of shotgun-toting farmers searching the woods for invaders. More than a hundred state troopers, he said, had to be called in to disarm them. He also spoke of a panicked resident so eager to escape the Martians that he piled his family into his car and backed hurriedly out of the garage—without putting the door up first. Later, Koch examined a small water tower, behind a barn across the street from the mill, that legend says residents mistook for a Martian and riddled with buckshot. Apparently, he failed to spot any bullet damage.[3]

Even Koch had some sense that his leg was being pulled. After three decades of questions from reporters and curiosity seekers, the people of Grover's Mill had their stories down pretty pat. The *War of the Worlds* panic, aided and abetted by the press, had passed immediately into folklore, and memories frequently gained color in the retelling. But in the days following the broadcast, reporters searched eagerly for reports of mass panic near the Martians' ground zero and came up largely empty-handed. The *New York Herald Tribune*, for example, reported that during the show, a forest fire fifteen miles away had sent up a cloud of smoke "that was easily mistaken for some sort of Martian activity."[4] But they failed to specify whether anyone actually made that mistake. Such a sight should have sent the community into headlong flight if they believed the broadcast to be true. Yet, according to locals quoted at the time, no one in town took much notice.

James Anderson, a tenant farmer who lived at the Wilson farm in Grover's Mill, said he caught snatches of *War of the Worlds* while listening to *The Chase & Sanborn Hour* with his wife. The news that a "bomb or a meteor or something" had landed at the "Wilmuth farm" gave him pause, but no cause for alarm. "Oh," he told a reporter the next day, "I just looked out of the window and saw everything was about the same and went back to sleep." Anderson shared the Wilson farm with another family of tenants—Wyatt Fenity, and his wife and two children—but all of them were already asleep.[5] If any of their neighbors had fallen for the broadcast, they almost certainly would have spread word of the invasion, as others did all over the country. But the residents, it seems, saw or heard nothing amiss—at least until the broadcast was over.

Then the invaders began to arrive. The State Police headquarters at Trenton received so many calls about a catastrophe at Grover's Mill that they sent six men, carrying gas masks and riot guns, to investigate the scene. Along the way, the troopers stopped Philip Wassun, who lived in Cranbury, to ask if he knew what was going on. "I couldn't convince them it must be a fake," Wassun later told the press, "and two hours later I saw them, still riding around looking for whatever it was supposed to be."[6] But, according to the *Trenton Evening Times*, when the state troopers arrived in Grover's Mill, "they found nothing more than a dilapidated mill overrun with hundreds of would-be rescuers and thrill-seekers."[7]

It seems that many people had, like the Princeton professors Arthur Buddington and Harry Hess, gotten word of a meteor strike and come to see what they could see. The owner of a local drugstore even put out a sign directing people "to the meteor," probably because he was tired of having people ask about it. At least fifty sightseers parked their cars in a nearby field, destroying the crops of the hapless farmer who owned it. *The Daily Princetonian* reported that the farmer spent the rest of the night on his back porch, impotently waving a torch at anyone who got too close.[8]

The state troopers soon learned that the meteor was fake and quickly told the crowd, but by then it was too late. Tiny Grover's Mill sits at the juncture of four country thoroughfares, making it a potential bottleneck. Most of the time, people could pass through without even noticing the town, because few ever stopped there. But a crowd of "hundreds" of sightseers, many of whom brought their own cars, would immediately snarl traffic. And if there really was a forest fire in the area that night, it would only have added to the activity. Sure enough, the state troopers reported that the roads around Grover's Mill were "virtually impassable" for miles that night. Newspapers, such as the *Trenton Evening Times*, readily assumed that drivers "either trying to reach the scene of the 'invasion' or to get away from it as fast as possible" had caused this jam-up.[9] But eyewitnesses like Buddington, Hess, and the state troopers described sightseers looking for a meteor, not residents fleeing in a panic.[10]

Newsmen only added to the commotion.[11] By the next day, Grover's Mill was a veritable circus, packed with reporters and press photographers from New York and Philadelphia. William Dennison, son of the man who ran the old mill, couldn't believe all the activity. He had heard part of the broadcast the night before and, like everyone else he knew in town, had seen no one trying to escape. Yet suddenly the eyes of the world were on his workplace. "We couldn't operate the mill because of the newspaper reporters and sightseers coming to see [it]," he said fifty years later. "That was the first time I had seen an airplane taking aerial photographs."[12]

There was, however, very little to photograph. After all, how does one capture the aftermath of an event that never actually took place? So the cameramen improvised. They snapped photos of the mill with a small crowd of locals chatting in front of it. They heard about the nearby Wilson farm and, quickly substituting it for the "Wilmuth farm," took pictures by land and by air of the "Martian landing site." The Andersons even posed on the front porch of their farmhouse, looking up at the sky with conflicted expressions—on guard for another attack, presumably, from either aliens or newsmen. But no one in Grover's Mill was quite as picturesque as seventy-six-year-old William Dock, a decrepit old man in battered clothes who, shotgun in hand, left his unlikely mark on the pages of history.[13]

There is no way of knowing whether Bill Dock actually heard news of the invasion that night, grabbed his double-barreled shotgun, and went out hunting Martians—or "foreigners," as Koch had it. Some newspapers said that he did, but they were guilty of other embellishments.[14] What is certain is that the next day, a photographer from the New York *Daily News* convinced Dock to pose in the warehouse across the street from the old mill, re-enacting how he had supposedly defended Grover's Mill from the invaders.[15] The picture perfectly captured how people imagined the panic, and it went the 1930s equivalent of viral. Two weeks after the broadcast, *Life* ran it in a spread of images from popular science-fiction stories, putting old Bill Dock right alongside such stars of the silver screen as King Kong, Flash Gordon, and Boris Karloff in *Frankenstein*.[16]

Dock, who worked in the mill, soon grew to resent his newfound celebrity. According to the local researcher Bruce Clark, he died seven years after *War of the Worlds*, still feeling that the press had "made a joke of" him, and he rests in an unmarked grave.[17] But in death, Dock's image gave birth to folklore. He multiplied in local legend into an entire legion of shotgun-wielding farmers mistakenly blasting the Grover's Mill water tower. *Skeptical Inquirer* has tied the source of that myth—which first appeared in print in 1970, when Howard Koch published it—pretty conclusively to Dock's picture.[18] And the story has remarkable staying power. Nearly fifty years after the broadcast, Dock even appeared in a DC comic book, using his famous rabbit gun to shoot a robber who's capitalized on the panic by dressing up as a Martian.[19]

Dock's image helped legitimize the *War of the Worlds* panic. It became instant visual shorthand for all the bizarre behavior that newspapers reported but could not back up, and it sticks in the mind because it's strikingly composed and deeply funny. Dock was a small man, bent slightly by age, with a bushy white mustache. His clothes were as worn-out as his body: a threadbare suit coat, baggy pants, and clownish shoes with upturned toes, like Charlie Chaplin's, all of which seemed too big for him. The shotgun he held looked heavy enough to tip him over. But the eyes behind his rounded spectacles were steely, and the set of his jaw, tightly clenching a pipe, spoke of determination. Surrounded by sacks of grain from the mill, he seemed to have fortified the place with sandbags in preparation for a siege.

The image carries something of the American spirit: Dock would fit right in at the Alamo, ready to go down swinging. Yet he is, in the end, just a weak old man with nothing to shoot at. The picture lampoons his frontier courage, making him look ridiculous. And that is exactly how many Americans felt about their country in the aftermath of *War of the Worlds*. Dock's photo encapsulates not just the panic story, but how that story reflected back on the United States.

Several listeners who wrote to Welles or the FCC saw the panic as proof that "Americans have lost some of the 'guts' we once had," as one New Yorker put it.[20] "So America at heart is not as on the surface—yes?" wrote one listener to Welles. "Aren't ya a sort of a *modern* Paul Revere?"[21] Others bemoaned the loss of America's frontier toughness. They argued that the pioneers who had won the West never scared as easily as radio listeners apparently did. "Where are our true Americans that were invaded by Indians, in covered wagons and stood up and took it like men[?]" wrote one Michigan woman. "No place to run for protection then. But these molli coddled jitterbugs show what they're made of. Just a bunch of *cry babies*."[22] Modern life, these listeners felt, had sapped some of America's strength. They believed that, somewhere between the covered wagon and the radio, the United States had lost its grit.

This made some protest the idea of a government investigation all the more, because it drew attention to a national embarrassment. "As a staunch and loyal young American," wrote another New Yorker to Welles, "I resent the fact that the rest of the world has been made conscious of the many morons we harbor in our country."[23] Radio's wall-to-wall coverage of the Czech crisis had piqued public interest in foreign affairs as never before.[24] Just when many Americans began to wonder about their place in the international community, the panic made it seem they'd been caught with their pants down.[25] Hitler and Mussolini, some listeners imagined, would be delighted. "By what has been written, said and acted—Mr. Hitler must be laughing his head off (if he ever laughs) to think what cowards we are," wrote one New Jersey woman to Welles. "Well, he knows now, and I imagine is filled with his own particular brand of joy!"[26]

Newspapers in many European countries had a great deal of fun with *War of the Worlds*, but none more so than in Nazi Germany. The press there inflated the panic even further to make a mockery of the United States.[27] "Death Ray Panic in New York—Half of America Flees to Bomb Proof Cellars," ran a headline in *Der Angriff*, a German newspaper run by Joseph Goebbels.[28] The *Völkischer Beobachter*, the official newspaper of the Nazi Party, claimed that tales of German atrocities reported in the American press were just as fictitious as the Martian invasion. Americans, they snidely suggested, were apparently ready to believe anything.[29] Even Hitler made a crack about the incident in a speech one week after the broadcast. "I have to do everything—and will do everything—to keep Germany so well armed and equipped that her peace can never again be threatened," he told a crowd in Munich on November 8. "That does not mean that I will start a war scare in the world, a panic, perhaps, about an impending invasion of Martians."[30] It had taken only days for the panic story to ricochet around the world and get repurposed into Nazi propaganda.

Some letters suggest that the broadcast had given the Nazis more than just an opportunity to ridicule the United States. Perhaps, some thought, it had given them a few ideas. "Now, if a foreign power were making plans to invade [the] U.S.," wrote one Pennsylvanian to Welles, "why shouldn't they include in their plans a radio broadcast of such proportions and content as to destroy the morale of the citizens and perhaps that of our defense forces as well."[31] A woman from Texarkana wrote that this "disgusting display of much-boasted American 'Courage' . . . must furnish Messrs. Hitler and Mussolini with immense satisfaction." She added, "It is as well, perhaps, that the American public, so smug in its selfish but false feeling of security, get used to the idea of invasion. Sooner or later we will likely be faced with the real thing."[32] The United States, as it turned out, would be spared a Nazi invasion, but other countries would not be so fortunate. And when the war came, the announcement came over the radio.

On the evening of August 31, 1939, a top-secret SS unit staged a mock attack on a radio station in Gleiwitz, Germany, just across the border from Poland. They pretended to seize the station while wearing Polish uniforms. Then one of them broadcast a short speech in Polish claiming that they were part of an invading Polish army. To add verisimilitude, the SS men fired guns in the air and left behind a dying concentration camp inmate, dressed in civilian clothing and riddled with bullets. The event—which William L. Shirer later called "one of the most bizarre incidents ever arranged by the Nazis"—had been planned weeks earlier by Heinrich Himmler and others in the Gestapo. They wanted to make it seem as if Poland had attacked Germany, in order to justify an immediate invasion. Staging an attack on a radio station, and broadcasting a false message far and wide, could create the appearance of an incursion with the help of only a few actual troops.[33]

The next day, September 1, the Nazis invaded Poland, with Hitler claiming before the Reichstag that Polish troops had attacked Germany. American newspapers reported on the Gleiwitz attack as if it were real, though few were fooled for long. But it didn't matter: two days later, on September 3, 1939, Britain and France declared war on Germany. The Second World War had begun, and it all started with a radio hoax.[34]

By the fall of 1938, many Americans realized that another European war was all but inevitable. The question then became whether or not the United States would get involved. Some isolationists hoped that Welles's broadcast, and the panic it had supposedly created, would convince the country to mind its own business. "The nationwide hysteria is a healthy indication that the people of this country want peace," wrote one Connecticut man to CBS. "They got a small taste, a very minute taste of the horror of war, yet that was enough to arouse a fear and hatred for war and a deep desire for peace."[35] Another listener wrote that the broadcast had made him "more sympathetic to the peace . . . secured without honor" during the Czech crisis. He called *War of the Worlds* "good red meat for thought in the cause for peace."[36]

However, the case for isolationism was an increasingly difficult one to make. Hitler's relentless march across Europe had already convinced most Americans that it would be impossible to stay neutral forever. Support for aiding Britain and France in a war against the Nazis was growing, even though most Americans were not yet willing to go into battle themselves. Instead, they believed that the United States should be prepared for any future conflict, but take no steps to initiate it.[37] Many saw

War of the Worlds as a valuable dry run for an invasion or some other catastrophe; more than one listener compared it to a "fire drill."[38] Its alleged effects on the nation gave them reason to worry. "In one hours [*sic*] time [CBS] have proven conclusively that this country is totally unprepared for invasion of any kind," wrote one Pennsylvanian to the FCC. "That is more than anyone else has accomplished in twenty years."[39]

The panic story made it seem as though America would dissolve into chaos at the first sign of an emergency. "Not one in a hundred persons in the United States knows what to do in case of a sudden attack by invaders," wrote one Minnesotan to Welles. "This fact is proven one hundred per cent by the fact that fear-crazed persons went to CHURCHES TO PRAY, ran wildly into the streets, drove aimlessly away from their supposed doom, jammed telephone switchboards by crying hoarse questions at bewildered operators, and acted in similar unintelligent, ignorant ways."[40] Many suggested that this confusion and terror proved the need for national civil-defense drills. They argued that if people had known where to get gas masks or find a bomb shelter, the panic would not have been so severe.[41] "I do not admit without a little decrease of pride that I fainted," wrote a military cadet frightened by the broadcast. "But today I realize the importance and teaching that the program taught—to be prepared for such an emergency."[42]

War of the Worlds had shaken the United States out of its complacency. It served as a reminder that the Atlantic and Pacific offered little protection in the age of bombing planes and radio.[43] Many Americans began to rethink their stance on isolationism. "The apathy of we Americans is appalling in the light of what is happening," wrote one New Jerseyite to Welles. "Not by the Martians but the three monster Frankensteins: Germany Italy+Japan."[44] Franklin Roosevelt, who had not heard the show, laughingly told reporters on November 1 that it would have no effect on the nation's defenses, but this turned out to be untrue.[45] The broadcast, noted General Hugh S. Johnson, had given "unintended assistance to the President's great defense program."[46] Army strategists took note of the panic and reconsidered how radio might be used in a future war, either as a tool to keep the public informed or as a psychological weapon.[47] *Variety* reported that some in the federal government believed *War of the Worlds* "has inadvertently done a lot for national defense."[48]

This helped sway the country in Welles's favor. Instead of a dangerous hoax or a national embarrassment, people began to think of *War of the*

Worlds as "a public benefaction," worthy of thanks and praise.[49] And there were other silver linings to be found in the panic story. Many pious Americans, concerned that their country was losing its religion, were pleased with reports that frightened listeners had fled into churches, desperate to save their souls before the Martians claimed their bodies. They gave Welles credit for starting a brief but significant religious revival.[50] "There were some old moss back sinners who prayed that night, who had not prayed in forty years," wrote one South Carolinian to Welles.[51]

Welles had planned for none of this; he had only hoped to make the broadcast convincing enough to hold his listeners' interest. But for some the very panic that threatened Welles's career actually became an argument to keep him on the air. "For God's sake stop apologizing for that thing," wrote one listener to Welles. "It was the greatest service you've ever done or ever will do for mankind."[52]

The closing argument in Welles's defense came by way of America's most opinionated newspaperwoman, Dorothy Thompson. This "blue-eyed tornado," as one journalist called her,[53] had made her name as a foreign correspondent, one of the first to recognize how dangerous the Nazis truly were. At a time when most Americans still saw Hitler as a Chaplinesque clown, Thompson's fierce criticism of "the Little Man" got her kicked out of the Third Reich. Back in the States, she became a widely influential radio commentator, with a regular audience of six million people.[54] Her thrice-weekly column in the *New York Herald Tribune*, "On the Record," rivaled the popularity of Eleanor Roosevelt's. In a style one critic described as "gutsy and fresh," Thompson left her mark on the issues of the day, both foreign and domestic.[55] It was only a matter of time before she tackled *War of the Worlds*.

Thompson's column of November 2, 1938, titled "Mr. Welles and Mass Delusion," poured superlatives on the broadcast and its results. She wrote that the panic had proved the failure of American schools and laid bare "the primeval fears" behind the modern mask of civilization. Above all, she saw it as a perfect demonstration of demagoguery. "If people can be frightened out of their wits by mythical men from Mars," she wrote, "they can be frightened into fanaticism by the fear of Reds, or convinced that America is in the hands of sixty families, or aroused to revenge against any minority, or terrorized into subservience to leadership because of any imaginable menace." Thompson believed that Welles had earned the thanks of a grateful nation, not to mention "a Congressional medal," for revealing the roots of fascism.[56]

"Mr. Welles and Mass Delusion" is an odd mixture of insight and ignorance. On the one hand, Thompson deftly showed how dictators wield fear like a weapon. But, in making that case, she went out of her way to deride those who had believed in *War of the Worlds*. She claimed that the broadcast was obviously fictional, no matter when listeners tuned in, and that the only parts at all realistic were the names of real places. That anyone could have fallen for it, she wrote, proves "the incredible stupidity, lack of nerve and ignorance of thousands."[57] And this is where her argument breaks down. She dwelled on the show's fantastical elements and left out almost everything that made the broadcast convincing. Her entire argument is based on the assumption that *War of the Worlds* made much of its audience believe in an alien attack, but there is ample evidence that many frightened listeners understood the broadcast as something quite different, reports of either a natural disaster or an earthly invasion.

One New Jersey man briefly fooled by *War of the Worlds* wrote Thompson a letter objecting to her "blanket indictment of" radio listeners. He agreed with her basic premise, but said that she had failed to consider the many ways people could stumble onto the broadcast by accident. All this listener had heard of the show was that the governor of New Jersey had instituted martial law. He believed it was true because a relative had told him to tune in and then a policeman had come to the door warning him to evacuate. In those circumstances, he argued, anyone would have been concerned, no matter how logical he thought he was. For Thompson "to overlook the obvious negligence in permitting the use of the precise designation of public officials and the use of an existing locale and to pay unqualified tribute to Mr. Welles in providing us with this clinical demonstration of mass hysteria," he wrote, "is taking an untenable position capable of incalculable harm." He saw dangerous possibilities in her knee-jerk condemnation of the masses.[58]

Like everyone else, Thompson saw the panic that she wanted to see. Because of her longtime concern with Nazism, she imagined panicked listeners to be the same sort of people who had fallen under Hitler's sway. After lambasting those listeners for believing in the broadcast, she lambasted them again for protesting to the FCC about it. "The deceived were furious and of course demanded that the state protect them," she wrote, "demonstrating that they were incapable of relying on their own judgment." This, for Thompson, was the most sinister aspect of the whole episode. She was appalled that Americans might willingly give up their free radio at a time when so many dictatorships used broadcasting to spread propaganda and fear. The panic, she wrote, had proved that "no political body must ever, under any circumstances, obtain a monopoly of radio."[59]

She was not wrong, but neither was she entirely correct. Like a lot of Welles's defenders, Thompson equated any FCC action with fascism and wildly overestimated public gullibility. She warned against fear-mongering politicians even as she stirred up false fears of her own by mischaracterizing a few thousand Americans as an unthinking mob. And she did so with a certainty and conviction entirely typical of the rest of her work, not to mention that of the many media pundits from her day onward. "Once her mind is made up," one journalist wrote of Thompson, "she plunges."[60] In railing against the supposed ignorance of the public, Thompson failed to recognize that she was speaking from a position of ignorance herself.

Orson Welles, John Houseman, and Howard Koch all later gave Thompson great credit for turning public opinion their way.[61] She was one of the first prominent voices to speak out in their defense, and after her column was published the outcry essentially ended. But the public had already spoken in support of Welles; by November 2, over twice as many letters had been written to the Mercury and the FCC in praise of him than in protest of him. Just about every point in Thompson's column had already been articulated—perhaps less eloquently or acerbically—in dozens of those letters.[62] She was simply the first to speak loud enough for everyone to hear. Her influence and her way with words helped cement the way in which people understood the *War of the Worlds* panic, from then until now. Her false assumptions helped define the event.

In one respect, at least, she proved out of step with public opinion. "The newspapers are correct in playing up this story over every other news event in the world," Thompson wrote. "It is the story of the century."[63] But the papers did not keep playing it up for long; *War of the*

Worlds fell out of the headlines almost immediately after her editorial. The story offered a momentary reprieve, a distraction from the grim onward march of history, and fodder for "some good jokes from the columnists and the comedians," as one Philadelphian put it.[64] But when the laughs died away, the world moved on to other things. In surveys of both the press and the public the following December, the broadcast failed to rate as one of 1938's top ten most important news stories.[65] With the Czech crisis and the Nazi persecution of German Jews weighing on their minds, Americans had a very short memory for fake news. They had too much real news to worry about.

As early as two days after the broadcast, Welles had a very definite sense that the country would laugh the whole thing off.[66] The press coverage was encouraging, and the Mercury's mailbag even more so. "Young man, you are a genious [*sic*]," wrote one Pennsylvanian. "What might have been a catastrophe will probably turn out to be the best possible publicity for you."[67] Another listener wrote that Welles had "put to shame the alleged master-minds of Hollywood and now they will be beseeching you with offers."[68] For years afterward, Welles displayed in his office a cheerful telegram from Alexander Woollcott. The critic, well known for his way with words, playfully referenced Charlie McCarthy: "This only goes to prove, my beamish boy, that the intelligent people were all listening to a dummy, and all the dummies were listening to you."[69] Welles badly needed the support, because even after surviving *War of the Worlds*, the Mercury Theatre seemed ready to implode.

On November 2—the same day Dorothy Thompson defended Welles in her column—the Mercury finally opened their much-delayed *Danton's Death*. Welles later claimed that one angered listener had telephoned, threatening to kill him when he took the stage that night, but he needn't have worried.[70] The only attacks came from the critics, who were almost unanimously unimpressed.[71] The Mercury's debut had been "dynamic, exciting and enormously impressive," wrote the *New York Herald Tribune*, but *Danton* was "mannered, stately and artificial . . . effective neither in ideas, narrative nor production." The review summed things up bluntly: "For the Mercury Theater [*sic*], the honeymoon is over."[72] Welles was suddenly one of the most famous people in America, but all the publicity in the world couldn't save *Danton's Death*. It died onstage after twenty-one performances, and it took the Mercury down with it.[73]

Simply put, the company was broke. Houseman had sunk all their operating capital into *Danton's Death*. When the play flopped, he had no cash to make good on the worthless checks he had been writing for weeks.[74] But the Mercury had survived financial failure before; what it could not survive was indifference. "In the grandiose and reckless scheme of our lives," Houseman wrote, "the Mercury had fulfilled its purpose." It had made its founders famous and earned them a ticket to Hollywood. They had no interest in it beyond that.[75] Welles kept the name alive for almost a decade, until Mercury Productions ran out of money and folded in 1947.[76] But the scrappy little theater formed in defiance of the WPA was no more, after an *annus mirabilis* beginning with *Caesar* and ending with *War of the Worlds*.[77]

Even the radio show was about to change, and not for the better. Campbell's Soup, which had earlier passed on sponsoring the program, was now only too happy to have their product associated with "the men from Mars."[78] "I guess they figured, if Orson could make *The War of the Worlds* credible and the Martians credible, he could make Campbell's chicken soup credible," Houseman later said. "So we became *The Campbell Playhouse*."[79] With the change in title came a change in format, because Campbell's ad agency, Ward Wheelock & Co., wanted Welles to adapt fewer classics and more bestsellers. Now he found himself forced to banter with celebrity guest stars on air and bicker with his sponsor behind the scenes.[80] Not for the last time, Welles had changed an entire art form, only to lose control over it.

But Welles was already looking westward, and so were his collaborators. In March 1939, Howard Koch, the newest member of the Mercury triumvirate, became the first to leave. He accepted a job offer from Warner Brothers and moved to Los Angeles to become a screenwriter. His six months with the Mercury had been exhausting but immensely valuable—the stepping-stone to a brilliant career.[81] Offers from Hollywood poured in for Welles, too, but only George Schaefer, president of RKO Radio Pictures, could give the twenty-four-year-old novice what he really wanted—total control. Campbell's insisted that Welles stay in New York to do their show, but he went out to L.A. anyway and flew back one day each week for the broadcasts. In no time at all, he became TWA's most frequent flier.[82]

That summer, Welles signed the most legendary contract in movie history. He would produce two films, from idea to execution straight through to final cut. RKO had to sign off on the stories, but after that Welles would do everything—write, direct, act, and hire whomever he wanted. The entire town hated him for it, but that was all right; Welles didn't much like the town, either. He lived the high life, spending money he didn't have and burning through ideas, but all he came up with were a series of false starts. Once again, he was moving toward crisis, but now the stakes were infinitely higher.[83] As one fan had warned him back in November 1938, *War of the Worlds* had placed him "in the public eye," and he needed to be more careful. "You are a very young man who has gone far in a short time," this Ohioan wrote, "and apparently there are others in the world who do not like your quick progress. I mean this in all seriousness, as that is the way it looks to me. Maybe I'm wrong."[84]

Welles and the Mercury had moved on, and *War of the Worlds* had disappeared from the headlines. But the panic story remained, stuck in the minds of millions. In their letters, many listeners compared the broadcast "to the old story of the boy who cried wolf," arguing that it would make people distrust news bulletins in the future.[85] They were wrong: the American appetite for news coverage continued to grow after the outbreak of World War II. But, as the historian Robert J. Brown has noted, there are definite indications that *War of the Worlds* taught people not to believe everything they heard on air—at least, for a while.[86]

One hint of this national skepticism can be found in the first issue of the comic book *Batman*, published in 1940. The Joker, in his debut appearance, announces over the radio that he will commit a crime at a certain time and dares the police to stop him. The next panel shows an elderly couple listening to his broadcast and not believing a word of it. "That's just a gag," the husband tells his wife, "like that fellow who scared everybody with that story about Mars the last time!"[87] They are, of course, wrong; the Joker pulls off a murder and a jewel theft right on time. But it's all a trick. Before going on air, he has already injected his victim with a slow-acting poison and replaced the gem with a fake. Just like the demagogues Thompson warned her readers against, the Joker uses the radio to stir up false terror, to make himself seem bigger than he really is. Almost two years after *War of the Worlds*, Americans had not forgotten that demonstration of radio's power. One can only imagine how many times the scene between the elderly couple was acted out in real life, as people stopped to question a late-breaking news bulletin.

Another reminder came on December 7, 1941, when the Empire of Japan attacked the U.S. naval base at Pearl Harbor, Hawaii. Americans on the mainland first heard the news at 2:26 p.m., Eastern Time, when the Mutual network broke into a football game with a bulletin from the White House.[88] At least some listeners, and maybe very many, refused to believe it. "My first question was, 'Is this another Orson Welles "War of the Worlds" broadcast?'" one listener recalled. Later that day, when NBC began broadcasting from the scene, their commentator went out of his way to tell listeners that he was being serious, that this was not a hoax.[89]

This was a particular feather in Welles's cap. He liked to claim, in later years, that people doubted the first bulletins because he was on air when the interruption came. In truth, he was not, but there is every reason to suspect that, even without hearing his voice, many Americans still thought that he was at it again.[90] The panic story had entered the zeitgeist as a constant reminder not to believe everything you hear on the radio. It may be too much to say that it taught people to think critically about the news, but it did teach them to question a specific kind of reportage—the news flash. Even twenty-five years after the broadcast, on November 22, 1963, lingering memories of *War of the Worlds* caused at least one American briefly to doubt a radio report that President John F. Kennedy had been shot in Texas.[91]

A few weeks after the broadcast, as the national hysteria died down, some began to apply this newfound skepticism to the panic itself. "After calmer reflection, it is now apparent that most of the hysteria allegedly promoted by the 'Martian invasion' was actually headline-bred," wrote *Broadcasting* in mid-November 1938.[92] Later that same month, *The Wall Street Journal* agreed, asserting it was a "fact that the effects of the recent 'Martian' performance were undoubtedly exaggerated," presumably by the press.[93] The panic had taken on the flavor of a fable or an old wives' tale, the kind of folklore Howard Koch encountered in Grover's Mill thirty years later. It was an enjoyable and instructive story, but not something to take too seriously.

However, a brilliant team of scholars at Princeton University were about to breathe new life into the myth. On November 28, 1938, the General Education Board of New York City awarded a three-thousand-dollar grant to the Princeton Radio Research Project to look into the effects of *War of the Worlds*. There remained two unanswered questions that they hoped to address: just how many people had the broadcast frightened, and why?[94] In trying to find the answers, the Princeton researchers produced one of the twentieth century's most influential and controversial works of social psychology, one that changed forever how people understand the media's power.

9

"A Matter of Psychology"

As an experiment in psychology, basic instincts, and the effect of propaganda, it couldn't be surpassed—!

—Emmet Riordan of Corvallis, Oregon,
to Orson Welles, October 30, 1938[1]

Because it focused on events so close to Princeton University, *War of the Worlds* threw that campus into a special kind of chaos. While Professors Buddington and Hess went out in search of the "meteor"—followed soon after by Princeton's ROTC unit—anxious mothers swamped the local Western Union office with telegrams, asking if everything was all right.[2] One Princeton undergrad who had spent the day at Harvard, visiting the future president John F. Kennedy, returned "to find the college practically in flight due to an invasion of rocket-ships from Mars," as he later wrote to Kennedy's sister Kathleen.[3] The next day, waggish students formed a "League for Interplanetary Defense" to unite the world in response to the alien threat. By telegram, they asked Orson Welles if he would lead it.[4]

A young social psychologist at Princeton named Hadley Cantril took note of all the excitement. Cantril was thirty-two years old, an up-and-coming scholar with a background in radio research and a fascination with mass psychology. And, thanks to the wandering point of Howard Koch's pencil, the Martians landed practically in his backyard. Suddenly the entire country became his laboratory. Three days after the broadcast, he threw out whatever he had prepared for his course that term, Psychology 303, and lectured instead on *War of the Worlds*.[5]

By all accounts, Cantril cut a dashing figure on campus. He was handsome and charismatic, and he carried a certain aura of importance.[6] This may have been western swagger—he came from Hyrum, Utah, and always considered himself a westerner at heart[7]—or it may have been the product of his Ivy League background. Cantril graduated as a valedictorian at Dartmouth in 1928 and earned a Ph.D. from Harvard in 1931. After a brief stint at Columbia, he arrived at Princeton in the spring of 1936 and soon became one of the university's most popular professors.[8] Students responded well to his energy and enthusiasm; for years, they ranked him one of Princeton's best lecturers.[9] There is every reason to suspect that he brought that same energy to Room 10 of Guyot Hall on the morning of Wednesday, November 2, 1938.[10]

In his lecture, Cantril assured students that almost anyone could have fallen for *War of the Worlds*. The recent Czech crisis, he said, had "conditioned" Americans to believe in radio news flashes. Furthermore, comic strips and pulp magazines made a Martian invasion seem far from impossible. But that only partially explained the bizarre behavior reported in the newspapers. Cantril went on to claim that years of economic turmoil and fear of war had left Americans unsure of "the basic and fundamental meaning of it all anyway." Because they were ready to believe in yet another catastrophe, they were particularly vulnerable to suggestion. This, Cantril claimed, allowed the broadcast essentially to hypnotize its listeners, making them see things that were not really there. Hearing that the invaders couldn't be stopped, and that they were killing everything in their path, "increased the feeling of individual desperation" for each listener. This led, inevitably, to panic.[11]

Cantril had not had time to do much research beyond reading the newspapers before coming to these conclusions. Instead, he drew upon the common understanding of media effects at that time. No one had ever proposed a set theory of the media's influence, but scholars like Cantril worked under a set of assumptions that came to be called the "magic bullet" theory, or the "hypodermic model." They believed that evolution had conditioned human beings to react instinctually, rather than rationally, to certain stimuli. By playing upon those instincts, the media could essentially bypass the intellect, addressing audiences at their most basic, primitive level.[12] As Professor Walter B. Pitkin, a Columbia University psychologist, explained it to the *San Francisco Examiner* shortly after *War of the Worlds*, "The spoken word, especially when the sounds are made emotional as in a drama broadcast, stirs up the primitive angers, fears and other instinctive reactions." He compared the radio to "a sort of hypnotic drug," relaxing listeners' inhibitions and leading to a "sudden release of emotionality"—in this case, panic. "Whatever the intelligence might do to check fear and similar reactions," he said, "the ear neutralized."[13]

This theory led to serious concerns about the power of propaganda. If the media addressed people at a subintellectual level, then a clever propagandist could inject ideas straight into their minds. And if advertisers and demagogues could only find the right mental buttons to push, then supposedly they could make people believe anything. Memories of World War I, when the major powers used propaganda to tremendous effect, lent credence to these fears.[14] "Let us think," Pitkin told the *Examiner*, "of what might happen if some charlatan in politics, for instance, suddenly got control of the radio facilities of America. What might not he do! What a peril he might bring!"[15] By amplifying the media's voice, radio seemed to make propaganda unstoppable.

Like a lot of academics, Cantril shared these concerns. As a grad student in Germany, he had seen the roots of fascism firsthand, even witnessed Adolf Hitler speaking to a small group in a Berlin café.[16] When he returned home, he remained on alert for similar stirrings in the United States.[17] In 1937, he and several other scholars founded an Institute for Propaganda Analysis in New York, and Cantril served as its first president.[18] "America is beset by a confusion of conflicting propagandas," he said at the time, "a Babel of voices . . . assailing us continually through press, radio and newsreel."[19] The institute sought to help create an informed, intelligent, and skeptical mass public, able to make sense of that Babel. They issued regular newsletters to schools and colleges, filled with tips on how to detect, interpret, and resist every kind of media persuasion. Only by viewing all media critically and unemotionally, they argued, could the average citizen overcome the appeal of propaganda.[20]

Because of their concern with fascism and propaganda, Cantril and the Institute saw something sinister in the reported results of *War of the Worlds*. The panic, they wrote in a research proposal, proved that America carried the same kind of "free-floating anxiety" that had given rise to Nazism in Germany.[21] But the institute members would not investigate the broadcast themselves. Instead, work was already being done by another organization that Cantril had cofounded: the Princeton Radio Research Project. Theirs would be a kind of academic detective work—chasing down leads, interviewing witnesses, and following up on rumors. And it would all be done at breakneck speed, before the trails began to grow cold. They would fail to crack the mystery they set out to solve, but their work unlocked much greater truths about the media's influence on society.

Though Cantril was a pioneer in the study of radio, he came to the subject somewhat by accident. He had less interest in the medium itself than in its effect on the American mass mind. His lifelong fascination lay in what he called the "psychology of everyday life"—the ways ordinary people form attitudes and opinions. The radio, he believed, wielded greater influence over the mass public than anything yet known, but no one really understood its effects. This led him and the Harvard social psychologist Gordon Allport to publish one of the first major studies of the medium, *The Psychology of Radio*, in 1935.[22] They wrote with concern of "the tenacious grip that radio has so swiftly secured on the mental life of men" and gathered reams of data to judge its effect on listeners. But they also saw great potential in radio's ability to enlighten the public, writing that it might turn out to "be the greatest single democratizing agent since the invention of printing."[23] By charting "the new mental world created by radio," Cantril and Allport hoped to suggest how the medium might live up to its democratic promise.[24]

Broadcasters also wanted to understand better how listeners engaged with radio, but for very different reasons. If they knew what people listened to and why, they could better serve both listeners and, more important, advertisers.[25] Crude methods for measuring audiences existed, but, because they relied on telephone surveys and listeners' memories, they were largely inaccurate. Frank Stanton, a grad student at Ohio State University, demonstrated just how inaccurate they were in his doctoral dissertation in 1935. The work impressed CBS, who gave Stanton a job in their research department. Like Orson Welles, he soon proved something of a "boy genius." A decade later, at age thirty-eight, Stanton would succeed William Paley as president of CBS.[26]

Cantril and Stanton met in the mid-1930s and bonded over their similar interests. They were both young scholars seeking to read the mind of the radio audience, yet dissatisfied with the methods already in place. Stanton tried to interest CBS in funding new experiments in research methodology, but the network failed to see the value of such speculative work. Then Cantril suggested they apply to the Rockefeller Foundation for a research grant.[27] They submitted their proposal in the spring of 1937, asking for funds to develop new techniques for understanding radio's appeal. Key to their approach was understanding not just who listens, but *why* they listen.[28] "To date, we have merely counted noses, so to speak," Stanton said in a speech around this time; "to-morrow we must find out what makes the listener tick!"[29]

The Rockefeller Foundation approved their grant that summer, giving sixty-seven thousand dollars to the School of Public and International Affairs at Princeton to set up a radio-research office.[30] But Stanton and Cantril were not planning to devote themselves to the project full-time. Stanton did not want to leave CBS,[31] and Cantril had found other work that interested him more. The previous year, he had met George Gallup and become greatly intrigued by the new science of opinion polling. With Gallup's support, Cantril began to dig into this new line of research. In time, it became his life's work.[32] Both he and Stanton were, however, willing to serve as the Radio Project's associate directors if someone could be found to run it day to day. Cantril had a man in mind, but he also had some reservations about him. This scholar was his opposite in almost every respect—background, management style, and temperament—yet there was no more qualified candidate. In the summer of 1937, Cantril offered the job to a man whose work would redefine the American media landscape: Paul Felix Lazarsfeld.[33]

Lazarsfeld, a Jewish refugee from the rise of fascism in Austria, had come to the United States on a Rockefeller fellowship in 1933. From the earliest, he devoted himself to exploring the reasons why people make decisions. What factors, he wanted to know, led people to choose one candidate, radio program, or brand of toothpaste over another? He didn't distinguish between topics; they all came down, in his view, to the same psychological processes of choice and action. After his fellowship expired, Lazarsfeld set up a research center at the University of Newark to delve further into applied psychology. Because money was scarce, he often accepted research contracts from private industry. Businesses were more than willing to fund his work if the results helped them better understand their customers. Lazarsfeld called this "Robin Hooding"— stealing from the rich to give to the poor academics. In the process, he essentially invented what has come to be called market research.[34]

Lazarsfeld had heard about the formation of the Princeton Radio

Project, and he knew that he was not Cantril's first choice to run it. But he remained intrigued by the job's possibilities, and Cantril did everything he could to win him over.[35] In a letter written that summer, Cantril promised Lazarsfeld a free hand in shaping the project to fit his interests. "When I write this, I'm almost tempted to take the job myself," Cantril wrote. "Really I don't see any drawback to it except that it will end."[36]

Lazarsfeld could hardly say no, but he would only run the project on his own terms.[37] His disdain for convention and his openness to new ideas made the Radio Project an exciting place to work.[38] He eagerly pursued new lines of research, new methods and techniques—often branching out in several directions at once. One of his more successful innovations, developed with Frank Stanton, was a "Program Analyzer" that recorded listener responses to each moment of a radio show. It resembled a lie detector, with a long sheet of paper slowly spooling beneath two pens. Listeners in another room pressed a green button when they heard something they liked and a red button when they heard something they disliked, leaving marks on the paper. By comparing that sheet to the recording being played, researchers could tell which parts their subjects enjoyed and which they had not. Stanton and others affectionately referred to the device as "Little Annie."[39]

At least initially, Cantril and Stanton were happy to let Lazarsfeld take the project in his own direction. Stanton, in particular, loved Lazarsfeld's energy and ideas.[40] But relations between Cantril and Lazarsfeld soon grew strained over Cantril's concern about the project's budget. "Lazarsfeld," writes the radio scholar Susan Douglas, "was a disaster with money"—a man who elevated "deficit spending to an art form."[41] His passion for research drew him to many different projects at once, and he often overspent what Princeton had given him. The university blamed Cantril when this happened, and he repeatedly urged Lazarsfeld to rein in his expenditures. These appeals soon grew into heated arguments, with much resentment on both sides.[42]

More and more, Lazarsfeld went outside the academic bureaucracy for research funds, turning instead to his contacts in the radio industry. Stanton and CBS could always be counted on to provide quick cash for urgent "firehouse research," as Lazarsfeld called it, when work needed to be done immediately.[43] This allowed Lazarsfeld to pursue projects he could not have done otherwise. But his close ties to broadcasters often shaped his research along commercial, instead of purely academic, lines—turning "the ivory tower into the knowledge factory," as the scholar David Jenemann put it.[44]

The project could not long accommodate the divergent interests of its directors. Cantril remained focused on radio's potential effects on democracy. He sought not just to read the American mass mind but to change it, even to enlighten it. Lazarsfeld, on the other hand, was content simply to understand how it worked. His research was an end in itself; it mattered less what that research was used for. And Stanton had a very clear purpose in mind for the project. By learning more about listeners' likes and dislikes, he hoped to help CBS catch up with NBC in the ratings.[45] Much like the medium itself, then, the Radio Project found itself struggling to serve both commercial and civic ends. Lazarsfeld and Cantril's quarrels over money sharpened this conflict, because research funds would help decide the project's direction. And *War of the Worlds* would strain it to the breaking point.

The Radio Project's study of the Martian broadcast began as time-sensitive "firehouse research," with Lazarsfeld calling Stanton for money on the day after the show. Stanton was already keen to find out the broadcast's effect on the country. He had listened to *War of the Worlds* at home with his wife, and they were among the few listeners who rushed outside, jumped into their car, and sped away before it was even over. But they had not been frightened. Rather, Stanton realized that some listeners were likely to be misled, and that his employer might get in trouble for misleading them. Sensing a research opportunity, he rushed to CBS to compose an audience survey meant to reveal the extent of the fright and the reasons for it. He called Lazarsfeld for help in composing the questions, then contacted an insurance investigation firm in Atlanta that he often used for such surveys. The next morning, they began interviewing listeners all over the country. By the end of the week, they had talked to nearly one thousand people.[46]

Lazarsfeld also wanted to have some members of the Radio Project interview frightened listeners, but he lacked CBS's resources. A quick infusion of cash from Stanton, however, allowed him to send a small team to New Jersey immediately.[47] Their goals would differ somewhat from the CBS survey. Since Stanton wanted a rough sense of how many people had been frightened, his interviewers talked both to people who had believed and to those who had not.[48] Lazarsfeld and the Radio Project, on the other hand, were interested mainly in *why* people had been frightened, and so his team only went out in search of listeners who had believed.[49]

To lead the work and conduct most of the interviews, Lazarsfeld relied on his wife, Herta Herzog. She had done groundbreaking research on radio in the early 1930s, while studying under Lazarsfeld at the University of Vienna. During that work, she contracted polio and permanently lost the use of her right arm. But, learning to write with her left, she completed her research and earned her Ph.D. in 1932. Three years later, she followed Lazarsfeld to the United States, where they married.[50] When Cantril tapped Lazarsfeld to run the Radio Project in 1937, he also offered Herzog an assistantship, likely to entice her husband to come aboard.[51] But she proved an invaluable researcher in her own right, skilled in interviewing and qualitative analysis.[52]

Herzog and her team began their work in Orange, New Jersey, not far from the Radio Project's old offices in Newark. Though they seem to have chosen the location purely for convenience, they could not have picked a better place to hunt for frightened listeners. Orange fell almost directly in the path of the Martian invasion. The broadcast had "reported" that Newark, right next door, was overrun by poisonous black smoke. One would expect to find a greater degree of fright there than perhaps anywhere else in the country. But Herzog did not worry about selecting her subjects scientifically. These were preliminary interviews, meant to reveal the causes of fright, not its degree or spread. With little time in which to work, she remained in her immediate area. By talking to friends and neighbors of the frightened, Herzog and her team soon found thirty interviewees.[53]

Herzog hoped to find factors or trends that she could follow up on in other interviews, perhaps in other areas of the country.[54] Without knowing exactly what they might find, she and the other interviewers had to remain flexible. They asked open-ended questions and allowed the subjects to digress if they felt like it. Lazarsfeld had developed a similar technique for market research. He encouraged interviewers to stay "loose and liberal," in order to keep the conversation fluid and revealing.[55] And, given such a potentially embarrassing topic, the questioners had to build a rapport with their subjects.[56] Herzog was better at this than perhaps anyone else.[57] The responses she and the other interviewers elicited were detailed and revealing.

Herzog summarized her results in a memo to Stanton sometime that November.[58] Each interviewee, she wrote, carried some "potential anxiety," such as concerns about the rapid advances of science or memories of the recent New England hurricane. The vast majority were anxious about war because of the recent Czech crisis, and this, Herzog suggested, left them vulnerable to becoming frightened.[59] When asked why they found the broadcast believable, many listeners mentioned the use of real placenames. This is not surprising, since all of them lived in New Jersey. But most listeners (twenty-three out of thirty) found the references to government officials and scientists particularly convincing. Only five said that they believed simply because they placed great trust in the radio.[60] Like the letters to Welles and the FCC, Herzog's findings suggest that, for most frightened listeners, the content of the show was more important than the medium itself. They reacted to specific elements that they found believable, instead of trusting blindly in the radio. They processed what they heard and came up with the wrong answer. And not just one wrong answer—Herzog's research shows that they interpreted the broadcast in a variety of ways.

Only four of the interviewees understood that the fake news reports described a Martian invasion. Another four thought the aliens were "animal monsters." But ten thought there had been some kind of a natural catastrophe, and eight thought the Germans or the Japanese were invading. Herzog noted that the reaction broke down roughly into thirds— a third of the listeners thought it was an attack from an earthly enemy, a third thought it was some other kind of disaster, and a third believed in supernatural invaders.[61] Again, this suggests that the reaction to *War of the Worlds* was much more complex than news reports indicated at the time. If the trends Herzog noted were representative, and there is every reason to believe that they were, most frightened listeners understood the broadcast to be about something other than Martians. Its realism convinced them that something serious was up, but they missed the parts about aliens.

Herzog also recognized that the fright caused by the broadcast was contagious. In the memo, she called attention to the fact that exactly half

Orson Welles (*top*) and John Houseman (*bottom*) circa 1937, the year they founded the Mercury Theatre. (Top: Library of Congress, Prints and Photographs Division, Carl Van Vechten Collection, LC-USZ62-119765; bottom: Billy Rose Theatre Division, New York Public Library for the Performing Arts, Astor, Lenox, and Tilden Foundations)

A Martian tripod machine (*top*) decimates the English countryside, as depicted by the artist Henrique Alvim Corrêa for a 1906 Belgian edition of *The War of the Worlds*, by H. G. Wells (*bottom*). (Top: Spencer Collection, New York Public Library, Astor, Lenox, and Tilden Foundations; bottom: Library of Congress, Prints and Photographs Division, LC-DIG-ggbain-21320)

Welles (far left) visits rehearsals for *Air Raid*, a "fake news" radio play by the poet Archibald MacLeish (far right). The Mercury actor Ray Collins (center, standing) starred in *Air Raid* and later played multiple roles in Welles's *War of the Worlds*. (Billy Rose Theatre Division, New York Public Library for the Performing Arts, Astor, Lenox, and Tilden Foundations)

The Mercury Theatre on the Air reached only a small fraction of radio listeners because it aired opposite one of the day's most popular shows: *The Chase & Sanborn Hour*, starring the ventriloquist Edgar Bergen and his dummy, Charlie McCarthy. (New York World's Fair 1939–1940 records, Manuscripts and Archives Division, New York Public Library, Astor, Lenox, and Tilden Foundations)

DAILY ✪ NEWS

FINAL

NEW YORK'S PICTURE NEWSPAPER

Vol. 20, No. 109   New York, Monday, October 31, 1938   48 Pages   2 Cents

FAKE RADIO 'WAR' STIRS TERROR THROUGH U.S.

Story on Page 2

"War" Victim

Caroline Cantlon, WPA actress, listening to this radio in West 49th St., heard announcement of "smoke in Times Square." Running to street, she fell, broke her arm.

"I Didn't Know".

Orson Welles, after broadcast of expresses amazement at public reaction. He adapted H. G. Wells' "War of the Worlds" for radio and played principal role. Left: a machine conceived for another H. G. Wells story. Dramatic description of landing of weird "machine from Mars" started last night's panic.

—Story on page 2.

The day after *War of the Worlds*, the front page of the New York *Daily News* featured photographs of Caroline Cantlon, an actress who broke her arm fleeing after she heard reports of the "black smoke," and Welles, looking like "an early Christian saint," as he put it many years later. (New York Daily News Archive / Getty Images)

Hoping to protect children from frightening radio programs, the Iowa senator Clyde L. Herring used the *War of the Worlds* controversy to promote legislation that would censor the radio. (Library of Congress, Prints and Photographs Division, photograph by Harris and Ewing, LC-DIG-hec-21210)

In her popular newspaper column, Dorothy Thompson argued that the panic showed how fascism might gain a foothold in the United States. (Library of Congress, Prints and Photographs Division, photograph by Harris and Ewing, LC-DIG-hec-26561)

The Federal Communications Commission in 1937. Front row (left to right): Eugene O. Sykes, Chairman Frank R. McNinch, and Paul A. Walker. Back row (left to right): T.A.M. Craven, Thad A. Brown, Norman S. Case, and George Henry Payne. (Library of Congress, Prints and Photographs Division, photograph by Harris and Ewing, LC-DIG-hec-23448)

Many broadcasters feared how FCC chairman Frank McNinch, with his reputation as a strong and formidable reformer, would respond to *War of the Worlds*. (Library of Congress, Prints and Photographs Division, photograph by Harris and Ewing, LC-DIG-hec-23334)

Seventy-six-year-old William Dock of Grover's Mill, New Jersey, posing for a New York *Daily News* photographer on the day after the broadcast. This photograph remains an enduring symbol of the *War of the Worlds* panic, though it's unclear whether Dock actually took up arms against the Martians. (New York Daily News Archive / Getty Images)

Dr. Hadley Cantril, a professor of social psychology and a cofounder of the Princeton Radio Research Project, led the first investigation into *War of the Worlds*. (Princeton University Library)

Richard Wilson, a former member of the Mercury Theatre who performed in *War of the Worlds*, regards the monument that was installed at the "Martian Landing Site" in Grover's Mill on October 29, 1988, to mark the fiftieth anniversary of the broadcast. (Nicholas George Skroumbelos / Richard Wilson–Orson Welles Papers, University of Michigan Special Collections Library)

of their interviewees tuned in late after encountering someone who already believed. "It probably would need a lot of strength to keep one's head clear in the face of other people's fear," she wrote.[62] And although she did not mention it explicitly, she came close to realizing the importance of listeners' desire to spread the news. Near the end of the memo, Herzog described one woman who "behaved as a messenger of great importance," running around to tell everyone she could that the Germans had invaded New Jersey.[63] Given a few more interviews, perhaps Herzog would have noted the large role such behavior played in spreading fear.

These interviews also offer further evidence that actual panicked behavior was rare. Only two subjects fled their homes immediately without trying to find out whether the invasion was real.[64] Most (twenty out of thirty) tried to verify the fake news, but Herzog noted that only ten did so successfully. The rest saw or heard something that convinced them the disaster was real, such as a glow in the sky that they mistook for the fires of battle. Herzog highlighted two listeners who looked out the window to see if people were fleeing the invasion. One saw a street "black with cars," and imagined that her neighbors "were running away." The other saw an empty street and assumed there were traffic jams elsewhere in the city. "There was no way out," Herzog wrote. "Many cars or no cars at all seemed equally to indicate the worst."[65] This, for Herzog, was the key question raised by the interviews: why some people "checked up" correctly and others did not. She encouraged further study of this finding, in order to learn more about how fear distorts one's senses in a crisis.[66]

Herzog refrained from drawing general conclusions from such a small and unscientific sample, but her memo is still a remarkably accurate assessment of the true causes and degree of the fright created by *War of the Worlds*. She recognized that listeners' reactions were complex and varied, and had as much to do with how and when they encountered the show as they did with the show itself. Her analysis is of course incomplete, because she spoke only to frightened listeners, but her work was meant to be preliminary. Much remained to be done, particularly in determining how widespread the fright really was. Herzog's memo paved the way for that later research and provided a framework for the book that came from it. Other hands than hers, however, would write that book.

Herzog was one of several female scholars and graduate students on whom the project relied for research. Women did much of the work on the *War of the Worlds* study, and conducted all of the interviews with frightened listeners. However, because of the times in which they lived, their work received scant acknowledgment. The legwork fell to them, but little of the credit.[67] As Cantril lectured to his class on why people fell for *War of the Worlds*, Herzog and others pounded the pavement to see whether or not he was right. Their work suggests that he may have spoken too soon. But a year and a half later, when the study was published, it carried Cantril's name first and foremost.

After Herzog completed the initial interviews, the Radio Project went in search of funds to complete the study. On November 21, Hadley Cantril submitted a grant request to the Rockefeller Foundation's General Education Board for a "PROPOSED STUDY OF 'MASS HYSTERIA.'" By examining newspaper articles, checking telephone records, and interviewing people who were frightened, the Radio Project hoped to determine how many people had believed the broadcast to be true. Then they would find the "psychological, educational, and cultural factors" that made them believe. "How do the personal characteristics, traits, and capacities of those who believed the drama to be real differ from the characteristics, traits, [and] capacities of those who heard the broadcast under the same conditions but who did not believe its reality?" Cantril asked.[68] The implication seems to be that some people were mentally predisposed to fall for *War of the Worlds*, and the study would find out why.

Cantril sought to quantify what made individuals vulnerable to propaganda. He reasoned that people whose fears led them to believe in the Martians would easily fall prey to a dictator manipulating those fears for his own gain. In this respect, his study foreshadowed a major work of postwar psychology, *The Authoritarian Personality*, co-authored by another member of the Radio Project, the German sociologist and theorist Theodor Adorno. Concerned that fascism might reappear on American soil, Adorno and his co-authors attempted to find its psychological roots by identifying personality traits, such as aggression and submission to authority, that left people susceptible to fascist thinking. Certain individuals, they wrote, are "easily fooled" by fascist propaganda "because of long-established patterns of hopes and aspirations, fears and anxieties that dispose them to certain beliefs and make them resistant to others."[69] Cantril was motivated by similar concerns. He saw listeners frightened by *War of the Worlds* as weak links in the chain of democracy, and he wanted to know how to strengthen them.

One week after Cantril submitted his proposal, the General Education Board agreed to fund the *War of the Worlds* study.[70] Herzog and Cantril then began to plan the rest of the research. To determine the extent of the panic, they would gather data anywhere they could—from radio stations, newspaper offices, pollsters, even high school principals. Frank Stanton gave them access to the CBS survey and other information from the network. They also reached out to the Mercury and the FCC for any listener letters they had received. From these sources, Herzog and Cantril planned to create a "spot map" showing which areas saw the greatest concentrations of panic.[71] But their data must have proved insufficient, because the "spot map" never materialized. In the end, they could only provide a general estimate of the panic, based largely on a single Gallup poll taken about a month and a half after the broadcast.[72]

On December 16, 1938, Gallup's American Institute of Public Opinion called about three thousand members of the "voting public" to ask if they had heard *War of the Worlds*. Twelve percent said that they had.[73] By applying that result to the estimated U.S. population, Cantril got an audience of twelve million people. But, as he admitted in the published study, that number is far higher than every other estimate of how many people heard *War of the Worlds*. The ratings company C. E. Hooper, Inc., which regularly estimated the size of broadcast audiences, put the Mercury's listenership at only about four million people.[74] This discrepancy might indicate how much fear spread by word of mouth, or it could indicate, as some have suggested, that the broadcast's national prominence made some respondents say that they had heard it when in fact they had not. Noting the lengthy lag time between broadcast and poll, the Welles scholar Paul Heyer suggests that the Hooper figure of four million is more reliable.[75] But Cantril roughly averaged the two figures to get a total estimated audience of six million people.[76]

According to the Gallup poll, just over a quarter of the people who heard *War of the Worlds* took it for a real news report. Of those listeners, 27 percent reported being "very much" frightened by it, 42 percent reported being "somewhat" frightened by it, and 30 percent reported being "not at all" frightened by it.[77] Cantril took this to mean that 1.7 million people had believed the broadcast to be true, and 1.2 million of them "were excited by it."[78] Most sources cite this estimate as proof that over a million people panicked. But these categories are entirely subjective, and they offer no information on whether the listeners took any panicked action because of the show. Nor did the poll ask how long each respondent believed in the broadcast, or what any of them believed it to be about. With the crude statistical tools of the day, there was simply no way of accurately judging how many people heard *War of the Worlds*, much less how many of them were frightened by it. But all the evidence—the size of the Mercury's audience, the relatively small number of protest letters, and the lack of reported damage caused by the panic—suggest that few people listened and even fewer believed. Anything else is just guesswork.

However, accurately judging the size of the panic was really only incidental to Cantril's purposes.[79] The main thrust of the study would be more interviews with frightened listeners, probing their psyches to find their "intellectual maturity" and any anxieties that might have led them to panic. Herzog and Cantril drew up a questionnaire that asked subjects about their political views, phobias, prejudices, what they read and listened to on the radio, and "the extent to which . . . [they] attempt to give meaning to life." In effect, they put listeners' minds under a microscope, gauging their vulnerability to propaganda. Interviewees would not be selected scientifically, but Herzog and Cantril meant to keep their sample diverse. They would talk to men and women of different ages, living in both the city and the country, from a variety of socioeconomic and educational backgrounds.[80] And yet they made no attempt to gather diverse reactions. As Cantril later wrote, they "deliberately sought out more people who were frightened."[81]

Their research also lacked geographical diversity. Herzog and Cantril planned to interview listeners all over the country—in New England, Chicago, Iowa, California, and somewhere in the South.[82] But, like the "spot map," these interviews never happened; the investigators talked only to listeners in New Jersey.[83] The bulk of the study's data would come from the area that the Martians had supposedly attacked, where every source agrees that the fright was most intense.[84] The researchers did have access to a wider and more diverse data set: the survey that Frank Stanton had hurriedly commissioned on the night of the broadcast. It included testimony from nearly one thousand listeners, both frightened and nonfrightened, living all over the country. But Cantril's team treated it in a similarly blinkered fashion, selecting exactly half of the interviews for analysis and ignoring over two-thirds of those because the subjects either knew the show to be fake or learned the truth by coincidence.[85] This narrow focus ensured that Cantril's portrait of the audience would be woefully incomplete, giving undue weight to those who had panicked.

With no time to waste, the researchers rented an office in Newark and began hunting for listeners in December 1938.[86] Cantril remained in charge of the study from afar, but the work of finding interview subjects fell to Herzog, Stanton, and another researcher, Hazel Gaudet.[87] Gaudet was the project's top statistician—the person, Herzog later recalled, who handled much of their number crunching.[88] Her resourcefulness proved invaluable, because finding a large number of frightened listeners turned out to be somewhat difficult. Press reports were largely a dead end; news articles only led to a handful of interviews.[89] The Mercury Theatre was more helpful, graciously lending its listener letters to the project. But, fearing lawsuits, they expressly forbade Cantril from trying to contact any of the writers.[90]

Undaunted, Gaudet chased down whatever leads she could find. She talked to reporters, found police officers who had encountered panicked listeners, even came up with "leads to whole families or neighborhoods which were frightened," as she wrote in a memo to Herzog.[91] Yet, in some ways, she faced a Sisyphean task. After reading that some listeners had been hospitalized for shock in Newark, she called six other hospitals in New York and came up with nothing.[92] She also told Herzog that the *Newark Ledger* had recently held an essay contest about *War of the Worlds*, receiving nine hundred letters from people describing their experiences. But just two weeks before Gaudet contacted them, the newspaper staff threw all the letters away. "If we had only started work sooner we could have had them!" Gaudet wrote.[93]

Ultimately, the Radio Project interviewed 135 people who heard *War of the Worlds*. All of them had tuned in late, and only twenty-eight figured out that the show was fake.[94] When the interviewers asked about their fears, many of these people expressed concern about a future European war. This reaffirmed Herzog's preliminary finding that most of the frightened had believed in the show because of the Czech crisis. But Cantril rejected this idea, arguing that war jitters were, at most, only a minor contributing factor to the hysteria.[95] He focused instead on the other anxieties that the interviews turned up. Many of the frightened said that they worried about keeping their jobs or securing their financial futures. Others had more personal concerns. "I'm so worried about my looks," one young woman remarked. "I wish I were better looking."[96] These results seem self-evident; after all, everyone is anxious about something. But Cantril saw such ordinary, everyday worries as the main cause of panic. *The Princeton News* summarized his conclusion in February 1939: "In almost every case fright was based on psychological insecurity due to worry over jobs, health, religion, family problems and so on."[97]

Cantril had come to this conclusion while the study was still in progress, after less than three months of work. But he would not change his mind substantially between this interview and the study's publication in 1940. If anything, he focused more closely on the idea of economic insecurity, arguing in the published study that it was the driving force behind the panic.[98] But this seems a very broad conclusion to draw from such a small and unscientific sample. When asked about their worries, any randomly selected group of people in 1938 would display a certain level of economic anxiety. Cantril's explanation speaks as much to his anxieties, perhaps, as it does to the nation's.

Like Dorothy Thompson and many people who wrote pro-Welles letters, Cantril drew a false connection between the supposed panic and America's susceptibility to fascism. He blamed the fright on the very factor—widespread economic insecurity—that had made Hitler's rise to power possible.[99] Rather than a demonstration of radio's power or of the danger in mixing news and entertainment, Cantril saw the panic as proof that the Great Depression had left American democracy fundamentally unstable.[100] Like those frightened listeners who mistook the Martians for Germans, Cantril saw his own fears reflected in the panic.

This focus on individual anxieties blinded Cantril to the social aspects of fright, the viral spread of fear. His reliance on the "magic bullet" theory—the idea that people respond instinctually, rather than rationally, to media messages—led him to the false assumption that people believed because of their own inherent traits. Insecure people, he suggested, were prone to falling for the broadcast, whereas "psychologically secure" people were not—no matter how and when they tuned in.[101] By reading his own expectations into the data, he exaggerated the size of the panic and missed its true causes.

As work progressed on the *War of the Worlds* study, the rift between Cantril and Lazarsfeld continued to grow. The Radio Project remained chaotic and financially disorganized, and Cantril found the situation intolerable.[102] Lazarsfeld began to fear that Cantril wanted to usurp him as the project's head, though Cantril claimed to be losing interest in the work. "If the project could go on completely without me I should honestly be much happier," he wrote to Lazarsfeld in January 1939. "Few people would go on with this when they were so anxious to focus spare energies on other things."[103] According to Frank Stanton, relations between the two men finally collapsed when Lazarsfeld made advances on Cantril's wife—advances she did not entirely rebuff.[104]

Cantril had had enough. Instead of publishing the *War of the Worlds* study as a pamphlet through the Institute for Propaganda Analysis, as had always been the plan, he arranged to release it as a book through the Princeton University Press.[105] He was so desperate to separate himself from the project that he agreed to pay the costs of publication himself. "I shall have to underwrite my study to the extent of $900 and hope to hell I get most of it back," he wrote to Lazarsfeld later that year.[106] In today's dollars, adjusted for inflation, that meant Cantril would have had to spend over fifteen thousand dollars to bring the book to print.

But even as Cantril separated himself from the Radio Project, he retained some of its biases. The project's studies often betrayed a certain elitism; as Susan Douglas has observed, the researchers tended to scrutinize listeners in the lower economic classes without questioning the habits of those who shared their social status.[107] Cantril brought much the same attitude to bear on *War of the Worlds*. His first draft of the study, completed in August 1939, cast the panic as a class-based phenomenon. Hazel Gaudet, in her notes on the manuscript, urged Cantril to rethink this assumption. "You say that we should expect that individuals in the lower income brackets would be particularly perplexed and feel particularly involved in these days of economic confusion, but is this necessarily true?" she wrote. "You might make a case for the opposite as well, individuals who have enjoyed a certain amount of economic security may be much more upset in these times than those who have always been insecure."[108]

Because he saw economic anxieties as the main cause of panic, Cantril assumed that lower-income, lower-status people were more likely to be scared. But other evidence from the study suggests that people in rural areas were less vulnerable to panic, perhaps because they were not living in concentrated spaces, where fear could easily spread.[109] "City people may be more sophisticated, of higher education, have more social contacts, be more acquainted with drama, listen to drama less on the radio or listen more—how do we know?" Gaudet asked. She encouraged Cantril to look at how low income correlated with low education, a factor he had apparently left out of his analysis.[110] This focus on education would become a major part of the published version.

Gaudet also questioned Cantril's focus on individual traits and neuroses. This draft included commentary from a psychoanalyst who examined a few frightened listeners, but Gaudet found his ideas unconvincing and "a little silly." "Some psychoanalytic theories are bad enough when they have all the facts in the world behind them," she wrote, "so I think its [sic] pretty risky to base an analysis on no facts." At other points, Gaudet encouraged Cantril to broaden his view and look at the larger forces at play, not just the reactions of individual listeners. She noted, for example, that Cantril mentioned "that more were frightened in large groups" and "few were frightened in public places," but failed to explain why. She also suggested that people might be more likely to believe in the broadcast if listening with others. "Here is a group of people listening and if one person is skeptical of a point, there may be another who strengthens the subject's belief," she wrote.[111]

Gaudet was not alone in her concerns. In mid-October, Lazarsfeld sent Cantril a memo—with copies to Stanton, Herzog, and Gaudet—encouraging him to rethink the main thrust of the study. He believed that focusing on individual anxieties missed the point of the whole episode. "If you center the study around the fact that we are all full of anxiety and therefore believe everything, you can't help much because our anxiety will remain for a long time and dangers will happen all the time," he wrote. Rather, Lazarsfeld felt that "what is so extremely interesting . . . is the fact that after people were scared they were not able or not willing to check up to see whether it was true or not." This, he wrote, had major implications in the study of mob psychology. He used the example of race riots, where people do not stop to question rumors that a rape has taken place before they lynch the alleged perpetrator. As Lazarsfeld put it, "One could make a good case to show that not the belief, but the lack of check-up is the real danger."[112]

Cantril resisted making major changes, but he eventually agreed to reshape the study around the question of "checking up."[113] The work of gathering the necessary data fell to Herta Herzog. "God knows what her reward will be," Cantril wrote in a memo to Lazarsfeld, "except my continued admiration for her ability and a eulogistic footnote in the last chapter."[114] Yet, even with this new material, Cantril failed to probe his subjects' psyches in the way Lazarsfeld had suggested. Lazarsfeld, like Herzog, wanted to know how listeners processed the fake news, how individual attitudes and circumstance led them to interpret the reports in different ways. Cantril, on the other hand, was determined to find a way of preventing listeners from falling for similar false reports in the first place. He sought, in effect, a bulletproof vest for the "magic bullet" theory, a mental armor that could protect people against propaganda. This kept him from capturing the event in all its complexity.

To explain why some people "checked up" correctly and others did not, Cantril created catchall terms for two conflicting personality traits. On the one hand was "critical ability"; on the other, "susceptibility-to-suggestion-when-facing-a-dangerous-situation."[115] Listeners who figured out that the broadcast was fake had "critical ability." These tended to be better-educated, higher-status individuals, but not in every case. Cantril wrote that some people had certain anxieties or beliefs—like poor self-confidence or religious faith—that prevented them from thinking rationally. Therefore, they were susceptible to suggestion. Only with the bulletproof vest of "critical ability" could they steel themselves against future manipulation. "Critical ability" became, in effect, an antidote to media persuasion—a teachable trait that allowed people to resist propaganda. Cantril argued that if, through education, "critical ability" became more widespread, future panics would be much less likely.[116]

This is why the study downplays the viral spread of fright. Although Cantril acknowledged that being surrounded by fear could convince listeners that the invasion was real, he argued that people endowed with true "critical ability" would be "invulnerable in a crisis situation and . . . impervious to extraneous circumstances."[117] But this holds listeners to an impossibly high standard. As the sociologist Herbert J. Gans has noted, perfectly rational people immune to circumstance and media persuasion are not found in real life.[118] Cantril was chasing an imagined ideal. Under the right circumstances, anyone—no matter his or her income, anxieties, or level of education—could have fallen for *War of the Worlds*.

The historian Michael Denning has observed that the whole discussion of "critical ability" seems like "an elaborate attempt to explain why working people and poor people were more likely to be frightened" without condemning them outright. "Behind this argument," Denning writes, "lay a deep contempt for working-class culture."[119] The frightened listeners Cantril describes are often working-class people—the kind of ordinary folks who drop their "g"s and talk openly of God. Like "Mrs. Joslin," a poor woman who heard *War of the Worlds* as she "set by one window, prayin', listenin', and scared stiff," while her husband sat "by the other snifflin' and lookin' out to see if people were runnin'."[120] Just like many others who had not been frightened by the broadcast, Cantril had very definite ideas about what kinds of people had believed, and they did not resemble him.[121]

Despite its scientific language, Cantril's argument is not dissimilar to the one made in many letters to Welles and the FCC. In their review of the published study, *The New York Times* bluntly summarized its thesis by writing "that the less gullible listeners were not taken in, and that those taken in were the more gullible."[122] Like many of Welles's defenders, Cantril overestimated the size of the panic and blamed it on an ignorant mass public. But he also underestimated his own susceptibility to media persuasion. Rather than critically examining the newspaper accounts of a nationwide panic, he hunted for evidence proving them true and ignored several hints that they had been exaggerated. In the end, he proved somewhat gullible himself.

On April 10, 1940, four months behind schedule, the study went on sale as *The Invasion from Mars: A Study in the Psychology of Panic.*[123] For an academic work, it arrived with much fanfare. The Hollywood gossip-monger Louella Parsons even wrote about it in her column, putting "Hadly" Cantril right alongside such Hollywood royalty as Vivien Leigh and Tyrone Power.[124] Advertisements called the book a "mystery-adventure story of the American people," and noted that it contained a complete transcript of *War of the Worlds.*[125] This would have been a major selling point, since so few people had heard the broadcast and recordings would not be widely available for decades. But readers who picked it up expecting a thriller would have been sorely disappointed. Even *The New York Times* found its prose almost incomprehensible. Still, their reviewer could not help regarding the book with "awe and admiration."[126] It all sounded so scientific that few bothered to question Cantril's methods or findings. Most took the book's description of a nationwide mass panic at face value.

The Invasion from Mars is designed to give readers this false impression. Before getting into any data about who heard the broadcast and how many of them believed, it presents fourteen stories "selected almost at random" from Herzog's interviews and the Mercury's letters.[127] All are extreme cases of fright—such as a college student who sped to Poughkeepsie, driving like a maniac, to save his girlfriend from the Martians, and "an ardent Catholic" who planned to seal her windows with cement before the black smoke got her.[128] In her comments on an earlier draft, Gaudet had warned Cantril against exaggerating the panic this way. "I get the impression that there is an over-emphasis of panic-stricken cases in this chapter," she wrote. "While they are undoubtedly the most interesting, they present only the more spectacular part of the setting."[129] By the time readers get to Cantril's questionable estimate of the size of the panic, this section has already led them to believe that America was drowning in mindless terror on the night the Martians landed.[130]

In fact, the idea that all these listeners fell for a Martian invasion does not agree with the data Herzog and Gaudet collected. Cantril's working draft of *The Invasion from Mars* includes a table, not in the published version, showing what the listeners they interviewed believed the broadcast to be about. Only thirty-five understood the show to be about Martians. The vast majority (seventy-three) thought it was about a foreign invasion, a natural catastrophe, or some other earthly disaster.[131] The trend Herzog noted in her preliminary interviews proved consistent: only about a third of these listeners believed that the fake news described a supernatural event; most gave it a natural explanation. *War of the Worlds* did not have the power to engender widespread belief in the impossible that many assumed it did.

As several scholars have noted, this finding fundamentally challenged the way media effects were understood at that time. If the "magic bullet" theory was correct, and the media could inject messages directly into people's minds, then a great majority of frightened listeners should have reacted to the fake news in much the same fashion. But Herzog's research proved that they did not. Some listeners believed that the Germans had invaded, some listeners "checked up" on the broadcast successfully, some looked out the window and saw evidence that the world was coming to an end. Their reactions were all different, based on individual attitudes and circumstance.[132]

Cantril understood this to mean that each listener filtered media messages through his or her own "frames of reference." A religious frame of reference, he argued, might lead someone to misinterpret the broadcast, whereas a listener familiar with other science-fiction stories would be able to place the show properly. "Critical ability," then, became the ability to know which frame of reference to deploy in a given situation.[133] Cantril explored this idea further in his next book, *The Psychology of Social Movements*. He noted that because individual frames of reference differed from person to person, "propaganda is not uniformly the all-powerful weapon that some people assume." Propagandists could not hypnotize everyone with the same content; instead, they would have to appeal to different people in different ways.[134]

Later research supported this idea. Following publication of *The Invasion from Mars*, Lazarsfeld began a study of the 1940 presidential election with Bernard Berelson and Hazel Gaudet. Their conclusions, first published in 1944 as *The People's Choice*, showed that the media had a very limited effect on voters. Radio and newspapers could reinforce the beliefs people already held and motivate them to cast a ballot, but rarely could they get them to change their minds. The researchers were surprised to find that interpersonal communication had a much greater impact on people's decision-making than the media did alone. Lazarsfeld called this the "two-step flow of communication." Certain people, whom Lazarsfeld called "opinion leaders," paid attention to the media and passed what they heard on to less informed others. But they only did so when the messages reaffirmed their existing beliefs. "In the last analysis," Lazarsfeld, Berelson, and Gaudet wrote, "more than anything else people can move other people." This, they concluded, was "a hopeful aspect in the serious social problem of propaganda." It suggested that the mass media could not convert an entire nation into rejecting their belief in democracy or anything else. Instead, they could only reinforce what people already believed.[135]

The fright caused by *War of the Worlds* played out somewhat along the lines of Lazarsfeld's "two-step flow." People who feared a German attack, or had heard about meteors falling elsewhere in the country, or expected a Biblical apocalypse, were ready to believe in a catastrophe. The broadcast seemed to confirm their fears. Often, these listeners tried to warn others or get family, friends, and neighbors to tune in, passing on their own interpretation of the fake news. This left frightened listeners with widely varied notions of what the show was about. And as the fake news became further and further removed from its source, it became more and more believable. Cantril's focus on making the individual impervious to persuasion had blinded him to the importance of personal communication.

Lazarsfeld remained deeply dissatisfied with *The Invasion from Mars*, and not just because of its methodological flaws. He strongly felt that Cantril had not properly credited Herta Herzog's contributions to the study.[136] For decades, even after he and Herzog divorced and Herzog remarried, Lazarsfeld consistently credited her as the driving force behind *The Invasion from Mars*.[137] As late as 1975, Lazarsfeld wrote to a graduate student that his relationship with Cantril had collapsed entirely because of *War of the Worlds*. "My justified complaint," he wrote, "was that [Cantril] forced me to make him co-author of the *Invasion from Mars* while he had practically nothing to do with it."[138]

These and other "internal difficulties," as Lazarsfeld later described them, made it impossible for him to remain at Princeton. The next time the Rockefeller Foundation renewed the Radio Project's grant, he moved it to Columbia University, with Stanton but without Cantril.[139] Cantril founded his own research center at Princeton, the Office of Public Opinion Research, and never worked on radio again. For the rest of their lives, he and Lazarsfeld had few kind words to say about each other, and they carried on their research in two very different directions.[140] Cantril's overriding concern with the future of democracy drew him into public policy. Lazarsfeld, meanwhile, continued to explore the influence of media and advertising on decision making. By building on their discoveries in the Princeton Radio Project, both scholars would profoundly shape American culture and politics.

In the 1940s, Cantril became a passionate advocate for the science of opinion polling, at a time when few academics took it seriously. Not long after he published *The Invasion from Mars*, Cantril gave a short report on polling data to a contact at the White House, who passed it on to Franklin Roosevelt. The President immediately saw promise and became the first occupant of his office to benefit from this new science. During World War II, Cantril regularly provided FDR with polling data, allowing him to track public opinion almost in real time. More than once, Cantril used these data to suggest ways in which Roosevelt might alter his public statements to make them more appealing to voters and to Congress. After the war, he continued to work with the White House in using public-opinion polls to help shape American foreign policy.[141]

Lazarsfeld, meanwhile, built the Radio Project into a much larger organization—the Bureau for Applied Social Research—that carried on successfully for years. He continued to rely on private business for research funds, devising many studies into people's buying habits and preferences. As Susan Douglas has observed, Lazarsfeld helped create the idea of the mass audience and also to monetize it, turning attention into a salable commodity. Even today, the products we buy and the media we consume are all tested with the research techniques that Lazarsfeld and his students invented.[142] Herta Herzog took this one step further. She left Columbia in 1943 to work for the advertising agency McCann Erickson. There she put the tools and techniques developed in the Radio Project—such as the focus group (which she helped invent) and the Lazarsfeld-Stanton Program Analyzer—directly to use in commercial market research.[143]

Cantril's and Lazarsfeld's influence remains strongly felt in the modern political sphere. Campaigns now play out more as marketing experiments than exercises in democracy. Massive amounts of money are raised for television advertisements calculated to enrage or inspire potential voters. Politicians keep a close eye on the latest opinion polls, as Cantril first taught FDR, shaping their messages to appeal to as many voters as possible. Candidates are reduced to talking points, scripted in advance and tested in the kinds of focus groups that Lazarsfeld and Herzog developed. Some broadcasters employ focus groups of their own on the air, having undecided voters grade the candidates in real time with a modern variant of the Program Analyzer invented by Lazarsfeld and Frank Stanton.[144]

Each of these developments is based on a fundamental truth first discovered in the Radio Project's *War of the Worlds* study. Audiences do not accept media messages instinctually and unquestioningly. To appeal to voters or consumers, one has to shape one's message to fit the audience's attitudes, opinions, and beliefs. And yet this important discovery is not the lasting legacy of *The Invasion from Mars*. The book remains much more famous for its vivid, classist, and fundamentally inaccurate description of a nationwide panic. As the scholar Michael Socolow has noted, Cantril obscured the key findings of his study by focusing on extreme cases of fright. He made the panic seem larger than it really was, and therefore made the media seem more powerful and persuasive than they really are. The stories of panic in *The Invasion from Mars* imply that audiences will believe anything, even when the study's data prove that they will not.[145]

Those stories of panic remain widely influential. Even John Houseman and Howard Koch drew liberally from them in writing their own accounts of the event.[146] Welles, too, came to appreciate how Cantril's study backed up the myth of the "panic broadcast." He referenced the book when he appeared on the BBC in 1955, telling a string of exaggerated anecdotes about *War of the Worlds*. "Some of [these stories] may seem hard to believe," he said, "but they're all verified, and you'll find them in a very scholarly book Princeton University got out on the subject of mass hysteria."[147] Of course, none of the stories he told are actually in *The Invasion from Mars*, but that hardly mattered. They seemed academically authenticated, and Welles spoke so convincingly that they simply had to be true.

In a sense, readers accepted the portrait of mass panic presented in *The Invasion from Mars* for the same reason that some listeners believed in the broadcast itself. *War of the Worlds* sounded convincing because it relied on trusted figures of authority—like Welles's Princeton professor. But, as the historian Benjamin Alpers has noted, almost everything these experts say is wrong.[148] Professor Pierson is confident there is no life on Mars—up until the first Martian reveals itself. Captain Lansing tells listeners they have absolutely nothing to worry about—right before the Martians decimate the State Militia. The secretary of the interior assures listeners that the military will keep the invaders contained—even as the Martians approach New York City. Each underestimates the Martians because he overestimates his own knowledge. Within their spheres, they think they know everything. And when an unprecedented situation presents itself, they try to make it fit with what they already know.

Cantril made the same mistake. Like everyone else, he saw the panic he wanted to see. Instead of following the data, he twisted them to fit his own ideas. And, like much of the fake news surrounding *War of the Worlds*, his book remains influential because it sounds authoritative—whether or not it actually is.

10

"The Horror Man"

There is one thing certain . . . Your future is a brilliant one.

—Margaret C. Brockmeyer of Baltimore
to Orson Welles, October 31, 1938[1]

Less than two weeks before *The Invasion from Mars* was set to go on sale, Hadley Cantril received a sternly worded letter from Orson Welles. The Princeton University Press had sent Welles an advance copy of the book, in hopes that he might write a blurb for its dust jacket. Welles said that he would be happy to, if not for one thing. The study, he wrote, "in its present form contains an error so grave, and in my opinion so detrimental to my own reputation that I cannot in all fairness speak well of it until some reparation is made." He referred to three mentions in the text of Howard Koch as the writer of *War of the Worlds*.[2]

Welles explained that the show had been "a collaboration of the best sort," benefitting from the talents of John Houseman, Paul Stewart, Bernard Herrmann, and others in the Mercury Theatre. "To credit the broadcast version to [Koch] with the implication that its conception as well as its execution was his is a gross misstatement of fact," Welles wrote, "and one which I am sure you will not care to tolerate in an otherwise careful and accurate account."[3] Four days before the book's release, Cantril sent Welles a suggested change in the credit line for future printings:

SCRIPT IDEA AND DEVELOPMENT BY ORSON WELLES ASSISTED BY JOHN HOUSEMAN AND MERCURY THEATER [*sic*] STAFF AND WRITTEN BY HOWARD KOCH UNDER DIRECTION OF MR WELLES[4]

If Welles had really wanted to acknowledge his collaborators, this should have satisfied him. But it didn't. Within hours, he sent Cantril a desperate and almost incoherent telegram, claiming that the byline would harm his "PROFESSIONAL PRESTIGE AND POSITION IN THE THEATRE WORLD."[5] Welles didn't want to spread credit around; he just wanted Koch's name out of the book entirely.

As Welles's biographer Simon Callow has observed, there is more in Welles's response than simple egomania.[6] By the spring of 1940, Welles had just about worn out his welcome in Hollywood. Rumors swirled that this inexperienced kid would never manage to make a movie, and would thus let his unprecedented contract go totally to waste. The first two films he proposed to RKO—an adaptation of Joseph Conrad's *Heart of Darkness*, and a thriller called *The Smiler with a Knife*—both withered in preproduction. At the time of his flap with Cantril, Welles had only just begun work on his latest film idea: the life story of a newspaper tycoon, tentatively titled *American* (and later retitled *Citizen Kane*). Whether it, too, would fall by the wayside remained anyone's guess.[7]

Welles was still finding his way, experimenting as he had in the Mercury, but on a much costlier canvas. And once again, his company was dangerously close to insolvency. When Houseman relayed this information to Welles, at a meeting in a Beverly Hills restaurant, the long-simmering tension between them finally exploded. Houseman later wrote that he deliberately provoked Welles into the much-needed confrontation. Welles, for his part, later claimed that he engineered the blowup in order to get Houseman off his payroll. But the facts of what happened are not in dispute. Welles flew into a rage, accusing Houseman of stealing his money. As Houseman started to leave, Welles threw flaming plate-heaters at him, setting fire to a curtain. The next day, without another word to Welles, Houseman began driving back to New York City. In time, Welles would woo him back to help script *Citizen Kane*, and they produced one more play together in New York. But before too long, they drifted apart for good.[8]

Houseman wrote to a friend the day after the blowup that he worried Welles's sudden fame would prove the death of him as an artist. The broadcast had made Welles nearly as famous as the President of the United States, but he had not had time to earn his notoriety; his success outstripped his accomplishments.[9] This left Welles in a dangerous position, with his stage ventures a distant memory and his future in film uncertain.

The panic story had thrown him into national prominence as a do-it-all genius—actor, writer, producer, director—and catapulted him to Hollywood. His incredible deal with RKO depended entirely on *War of the Worlds*. Without it, in the eyes of the nation he was nothing. That is why he reacted so strongly to the prospect of crediting Howard Koch in *The Invasion from Mars*. Doing so, he imagined, would paint him as a fraud, destroying his wunderkind persona and robbing him of his only sizable accomplishment. "This is not vanity," Callow wrote; "it is terror."[10]

The Invasion from Mars went on sale as planned on April 10, over Welles's protests.[11] Cantril wrote to Welles the next day, explaining that because Koch could provide ample evidence that he had done "the actual writing" on *War of the Worlds*, there was "no other alternative than to acknowledge him as writer but not creator."[12] At the request of Welles's lawyers, Koch had even penned an erratum slip to be included with the first printing, reminding readers that Welles was the director, producer, star, and originator of the broadcast. "In a very proper sense it is Mr. Welles' achievement," Koch wrote, "to which my only contribution was the writing of the play in accordance with his general conception."[13] This was a gracious gesture, because Koch had the law on his side. Houseman had hired him with the promise that Koch would retain the rights to every radio script he wrote for the Mercury, as compensation for drawing such a low weekly salary. At the time, that might have seemed a raw deal, since there was hardly any market for used radio plays.[14] But that left Koch well within his rights, both moral and legal, to claim credit in *The Invasion from Mars*, and left Welles with nothing to stand on.

Eventually, Welles's lawyers and publicist convinced him that taking legal action against the book would be a mistake. For one thing, it was an academic work, essentially a textbook, and Welles could expect to reap little financial benefit from it. For another, as Cantril had suggested in his last letter to Welles, *The Invasion from Mars* could only enhance Welles's reputation.[15] Every article and review mentioned Welles; few, if any, mentioned Koch.[16] Even the ads referred to "the Complete Broadcast Script of the famous Orson Welles broadcast."[17] All this recognition convinced Welles that Koch's erratum slip was essentially superfluous. "The fact that I was the creator and producer, in every full sense of the word[,] of this broadcast was known to the world," he said several years later. "I was already being called 'Orson Welles, the Man from Mars.'"[18]

But Welles remained a bit ambivalent about *War of the Worlds*, keeping it somewhat at arm's length. From the get-go, RKO executives had wanted his first film to be some version of *War of the Worlds*—a surefire hit if ever there was one. But RKO president George Schaefer did not press the issue, understanding that Welles feared being typecast as "the horror man."[19] Just as in the Mercury Theatre days, Welles refused to cash in on sudden success. As an artist, he had to experiment and try new things; he hated to repeat himself. But he also passed up perhaps his only chance at a Hollywood hit, one that might have smoothed out his later difficulties in the industry.

Less than a week after filming wrapped on *Citizen Kane*, Welles traveled to San Antonio, Texas, for a speaking engagement. It just so happened that the man behind the Martians, H. G. Wells, was in the same city at the same time. The two had never met, but the local radio station KTSA brought them together for an on-air interview on October 28, 1940, just shy of the two-year anniversary of the *War of the Worlds* broadcast. The elder Wells's annoyance had apparently been forgotten; he and Welles even discussed plans to collaborate on "another horror thriller" for the radio, which unfortunately never happened.[20] Both men seemed more inclined to talk about theater and the movies than *War of the Worlds*. But the Martians had brought them together, and so there was no getting around it.[21]

"Are you sure there was such a panic in America or wasn't it your Halloween fun?" H. G. Wells asked playfully, early in the interview.

Equally jolly, the younger Welles responded, "I think that's the nicest thing that a man from England could possibly say about the men from Mars."

After some discussion of Nazi Germany's reaction to the broadcast, Wells and Welles seemed ready to laugh the whole thing off and move on. But the interviewer, Charles C. Shaw, took the panic more seriously. "Well, there was some excitement caused," he said. "I really can't belittle the amount that was caused, but I think that the people got over it very quickly, don't you . . . ?"

"What kind of excitement?" Orson Welles interjected. "Mr. H. G. Wells wants to know if the excitement wasn't the same kind of excitement that we extract from a practical joke in which somebody puts a sheet over his head and says 'Boo!' I don't think anybody believes that that individual is a ghost, but we do scream and yell and rush down the hall, and that's just about what happened."[22]

With the whole incident relatively fresh in the public mind, Welles had good reasons not to exaggerate the fright he had caused. One of his associates claimed that as late as 1944, a man in Kansas City attacked Welles, screaming that he wanted to kill him because his wife had committed suicide over the broadcast.[23] As with a lot of Orson Welles stories, there is good reason to doubt this one—if the man's wife had really killed herself because of the show, she almost certainly would have made the papers. But CBS did spend "several thousand dollars settling suits" raised by War of the Worlds, and one Mercury associate wrote to Hadley Cantril in late 1939 that "there [were] still three actions unsettled" in California alone.[24] Joking publicly about the broadcast, even two years after the fact, would not have been wise. Besides, Welles did not want War of the Worlds to define him forever. He had other things to do.

Welles's eventual first film, Citizen Kane, drew greatly upon his radio work. Many critics have praised its uniquely rich sound design, and several have compared it to the Mercury radio shows.[25] It also blurred the line between fact and fiction in much the same way as War of the Worlds. Drawing upon his memories of The March of Time, Welles used a lengthy fake newsreel early in the film to introduce audiences to his protagonist. This sequence ("News on the March") is a deliberate parody of the March of Time film series, with Welles's associate William Alland providing a good impression of the "Voice of Time" narration. To make it all look real, Welles used many tricks—a shaky handheld camera, a mismatched soundtrack, intentionally scratched-up film—that are the visual equivalents of the dead air and overlapping dialogue that worked so well in War of the Worlds.[26] But this time around, no one objected to Welles's use of fake news. It was his portrait of the protagonist, a tyrannical media baron patterned after William Randolph Hearst, that proved realistic enough to get him in trouble.

Despite a concerted effort from Hearst to block or even destroy the film, RKO released Citizen Kane on May 1, 1941—the week of Welles's twenty-sixth birthday. Like its director, Kane defied simple categorization. Its complex, nonlinear narrative challenges viewers, forcing them to decide for themselves what the film is about.[27] Welles would not talk down to his audience; he still believed what he had said at the outset of the Mercury radio show, that the mass public is smarter and more discerning than most people give it credit for. Filmmakers, he believed, had a duty to raise their audience's artistic tastes, not pander to the lowest common denominator.[28] But he soon discovered that innovation was not a recipe for box office success.

RKO promoted *Kane* by focusing on Welles's famed multifaceted genius. The souvenir program at the premiere made sure to remind readers that Welles had "scared the pants off the country" in 1938, as if anyone could forget.[29] But the studio seemed unsure how to market the actual content of the film, because it did not fit the traditional Hollywood mold. The tagline they came up with ("IT'S TERRIFIC!") is about as bland and nondescriptive as can be imagined. Eventually, they tried to sell it as a love story—"How much love can you buy for $60,000,000?" ran one ad—but by then it was too late.[30] Many theaters across the country refused to show the film, mostly in fear of Hearst but also because they believed that it was too complex for the average filmgoer.[31] "It may be a classic," the owner of one North Dakota movie theater warned at the time, "but it's plum 'nuts' to your show-going public."[32] Reviews were terrific—even then, some critics called it the greatest film ever made—but audiences stayed away. Many movie houses that showed *Kane* lost money.[33] The conventional wisdom held; Welles, it seemed, had once again overestimated the intelligence of the masses, to the tune of a $150,000 loss for RKO.[34]

Welles doubled down with his next film, an adaptation of Booth Tarkington's novel *The Magnificent Ambersons*. It told the dark and depressing story of a nineteenth-century midwestern family in decline, as their genteel way of life gives way to the grim, industrial present—not at all what Americans wanted to see at the outset of World War II.[35] Before its release, RKO tested the picture on an audience in Pomona, California; they routinely held such test screenings to see how films might fare nationally. First they screened an upbeat, patriotic musical called *The Fleet's In* (which the audience loved), and then *Ambersons*.[36] Joseph Cotten, who acted in the film and attended that screening, later wrote to Welles that when the words "a Mercury Production by Orson Welles" appeared on-screen, "there was a wonderful murmur of happy anticipation . . . And the first sound of your voice was greeted with applause."[37] Much of this goodwill has to be the result of Welles's radio work; over three years later, Americans still thought of him mainly as the "man from Mars." But then the film began, and the audience realized that it wasn't what they had come to expect from Orson Welles. The mood in the theater, by all accounts, was grim. RKO president Schaefer later wrote that sitting through that screening felt "just like getting one sock in the jaw after another for over two hours."[38]

The comment cards from that audience echo the cultural friction of the *War of the Worlds* letters, though in this case the balance fell against Welles. The fifty-three cards favorable to *Ambersons* praised the film's artistry, but many admitted they thought that average audiences would not appreciate it. "The picture was a masterpiece with perfect photography, settings and acting," read one. "It seemed too deep for the average stupid person." On the other hand, the seventy-two negative responses bluntly dismissed the film as too dark, depressing, and artistic. "I did not like it," read one. "I could not understand it." Another called it "as bad if not worse than *Citizen Kane*."[39]

Later researchers have suggested that Schaefer exaggerated the negative response in Pomona, or that this was not a typical crowd. Other preview audiences, at least, were less hostile to the film.[40] But RKO had already paid a steep price for misjudging their audience, and they were not about to make the same mistake twice. Without Welles's input, the studio drastically recut *Ambersons*, then shot a slapdash happy ending in a vain attempt to make it a crowd-pleaser. Even then, it failed to make money.[41] Schaefer, who was about to lose his job over hiring Welles, urged the young director to turn his talents in another, more profitable direction. "Orson Welles has got to do something commercial," he wrote after the Pomona preview. "We have got to get away from 'arty' pictures and get back to earth. Educating the people is expensive, and your next picture must be made for the box-office."[42]

Perhaps Schaefer should have said "back to Mars," because *War of the Worlds* remained the basis for Welles's celebrity. "The chief victim of the panic is Welles himself," wrote *The Saturday Evening Post* in 1940. "He is branded for life as the Mars man."[43] Audiences loved it when he did anything even vaguely reminiscent of the Martian broadcast—like *The Hitch-Hiker*, a radio play he starred in several times in the 1940s. Written by Lucille Fletcher, Bernard Herrmann's wife, it told of a man haunted by a spectral tramp as he drives cross-country. This ghostly little tale, Welles told listeners when it re-aired in 1942, was just what people had come to think of as "a real Orson Welles story."[44] And though he claimed not to know what that meant, his audience would have certainly gotten the joke. Quite by accident, his name had become synonymous with shock and horror. As one Mercury employee reminded him in 1945, Americans thought of Welles first and foremost as "the fantastic Mars genius," and there was little he could do to change that.[45] Nor, indeed, would he want to, because it was becoming harder and harder for him to get films made.

The commercial failure of Kane and Ambersons paled in comparison with the catastrophe surrounding Welles's third film for RKO: a quasi-documentary about Pan-American culture titled It's All True. The federal government had asked Welles to serve as a goodwill ambassador between the peoples of North and South America as part of FDR's Good Neighbor Policy. Since asthma and flat feet kept Welles off the front lines, making a film in Brazil would be his contribution to the war effort. But in order to shoot Rio de Janeiro's famed Carnival, Welles had to leave Hollywood before Ambersons was finished. This allowed RKO to bastardize the film in his absence. Once in Brazil, he spent much more time and money than the studio would have liked, and the footage he captured proved too avant-garde—and full of too many black faces—for RKO's tastes. Even worse, one of the film's subjects, a Brazilian national hero, drowned during the shoot, as he prepared to restage for Welles's cameras the feat that had made him famous. The New York Times carried news of his death on page 1.[46]

RKO, now under new management, had had just about enough of their costly boy genius. When Welles returned to America, they shelved It's All True without release. Some of the film, according to the Welles scholar Catherine Benamou, was repurposed as stock footage in an episode of The March of Time. Other portions of it were deliberately dumped in the Pacific Ocean. The rest would never be seen in Welles's lifetime, despite his repeated attempts to buy the film back and finish it himself.[47] All he had earned from his South American misadventure was a false reputation for unreliability that would follow him for the rest of his life. Soon it became a self-fulfilling prophecy. Studios and investors grew reluctant to fund his projects, because they feared he would run out on them again at the last minute, as he had done on Ambersons. He spent decades wandering the world, scrounging up money to piece together films however he could. And whenever an investor backed out or a deal fell through, "Crazy Welles" got the blame.[48]

Welles's youthful accomplishments—chiefly War of the Worlds and Citizen Kane—became his only untainted successes. And after its meager initial release, *Kane* essentially dropped out of sight; it would not be re-discovered until the mid-1950s, thanks to television and postwar European critics.[49] That left *War of the Worlds*. As Welles's fortunes declined in the mid- to late 1940s, his attitude toward the broadcast—and associating himself with it—appeared to have changed. He no longer had any reason to downplay the panic or disavow the Red Planet. Like his acting talents, his "man from Mars" persona became a marketable commodity, a way of making money that could fund his film projects. And so he began to give the people what they wanted.

In 1949, as he struggled to bring Shakespeare's *Othello* to the screen, Welles lent his name to a paperback collection of sci-fi tales called *Invasion from Mars: Interplanetary Stories*. It included Koch's script for *War of the Worlds* and nine short stories from such authors as Robert A. Heinlein, Ray Bradbury, and Isaac Asimov. Whether Welles actually selected the stories himself, or merely cashed a much-needed check, cannot be known for sure.[50] But his introduction—titled "Can a Martian Help It If He's Colored Green?"—does carry the faint impression of his personality. It singles out with particular delight a story by Anthony Boucher, about insectile Martians who land on Earth while searching the solar system for intelligent life. When the first human they meet realizes where they're from, he blurts out what the Martians are sure is "the invocation of a potent deity." In fact, it's the name "ORSON WELLES!"[51]

Around this time, Welles also appeared as a character in a *Superman* comic book inspired by *War of the Worlds*. In the story, he accidentally stumbles onto a rocket ship that takes him to Mars, where he finds fascist Martians preparing to invade Earth. He radios a warning back home, but of course no one believes him—except for Superman. The comic was meant to promote *Black Magic*, one of the many mediocre movies that Welles appeared in to pay for his own films. DC Comics only harked back to *War of the Worlds* because that's what Welles was best known for, even though most of their readers were too young ever to have heard it.[52]

As with the short-story collection, if Welles profited at all from the *Superman* comic he did so with minimal effort. These were disposable pieces of entertainment, quick cash easily forgotten, or so he would have assumed. But by 1955, Welles had warmed to *War of the Worlds* enough to include it in his own, more serious work. That year, he made a six-part TV series for the BBC titled *Orson Welles' Sketch Book*. Each episode featured Welles in close-up, talking about a topic such as theater or bullfighting for fifteen minutes at a time. The only cutaways were to his sketchpad, where he occasionally drew what he happened to be talking about. The show depended entirely on Welles's skill as a raconteur. He called it "a way to satisfy my predilection for telling stories," and he often drew upon his own experiences. On May 21, he devoted the penultimate episode to *War of the Worlds*.[53]

Looking directly into the camera like the most honest man in the world, Welles charmingly told tale after tale of people panicking because of his broadcast. He spoke of navy sailors who had their shore leave cut short so they could fight the Martians, of Red Cross workers who spent weeks trying to convince people in South Dakota that the show was fake, and of his friend the famous actor John Barrymore, who heard of the invasion and released all his beloved Great Dane dogs, saying, "Fend for yourselves!" Alternating between contrition and mirth, Welles repeatedly asked his viewers to trust him—a sure sign that he was pulling their legs. His earlier reluctance to exaggerate the panic had entirely disappeared. Now he milked it for all it was worth.[54]

Welles also used the show to claim, probably for the first time, that there had been a grand design behind *War of the Worlds*. As he explained it to viewers:

> We weren't as innocent as we meant to be, when we did the Martian broadcast. We were fed up with the way in which everything that came over this new magic box, the radio, was being swallowed. People, you know, do suspect what they read in the newspapers and what people tell them, but when the radio came, and I suppose now television, anything that came through that new machine was believed. So in a way our broadcast was an assault on the credibility of that machine; we wanted people to understand that they shouldn't take any opinion pre-digested, and they shouldn't swallow everything that came through the tap, whether it was radio or not.[55]

Of course, this is another Wellesian embellishment. The audience response to *War of the Worlds* had been a fortuitous accident, one that nobody expected. But Welles could hardly admit that the most famous part of his career, the thing that had sent him to Hollywood, had been a magnificent fluke. Claiming otherwise helped him live up to his fading reputation as a boy genius, the youthful promise he had so far failed to fulfill.

He had, after all, just turned forty, and recently seen yet another of his films, *Mr. Arkadin*, taken away from him to be thoroughly dismantled.[56] His fleeting reference to people's believing everything they see on television seems almost like a wink at his viewers, a reminder that they should take everything they see on TV with a grain of salt—including his own show.

The *Sketch Book* episode set the tone for how Welles talked about *War of the Worlds* for the rest of his life. In the many interviews and talk-show appearances that filled his later years, he reused some of the anecdotes from it, the story about John Barrymore's dogs being a particular favorite.[57] He also liked to point out that not long after his broadcast, the world had become obsessed with flying saucers, and he hinted that he was responsible for those, too.[58] He always spoke of *War of the Worlds* with a knowing glint in his eye, as if he had meant all along to teach "the lunatic fringe" a thing or two about skepticism.[59] The whole thing had been a laugh, he claimed, a great joke, and not a terrifying moment that could have ruined him.[60] All the while, he built up his personal myth, cementing his reputation as a trickster extraordinaire. Houseman and Koch added their own embellishments, but no one gilded the lily like Welles. *War of the Worlds* became both a testament to his genius and a reminder of how far he had fallen. And as it passed into legend, the gap between Welles the youthful boy wonder and Welles the aging and struggling filmmaker grew ever greater.

But, however much Welles's reputation came to depend on the broadcast, it remained, like all of his films, the property of others. In 1957, CBS aired a docudrama about the panic titled *The Night America Trembled*. Scenes set inside Studio One, with actors reading lines from Koch's script, were intercut with scenes of listeners terrorized by the show. CBS had reached out to Welles months before it aired, offering him a chance to appear in the film. Welles, believing they could not produce the show without his permission, insisted that CBS give him the opportunity to write and direct it as well. But the network already had Koch's permission to use excerpts from the broadcast, and so Welles's approval was not required. They went ahead with *The Night America Trembled* after deleting all mentions of Welles's name from its script.[61]

In response, Welles filed suit against the network, claiming $375,000 in damages for the unauthorized use of his broadcast. His lawyers argued that because Welles had come up with the fake news idea for *War of the Worlds*, he deserved recognition as its rightful co-author. But the court disagreed—finding, in part, that by allowing its script to be published under Koch's name in *The Invasion from Mars*, Welles "in April 1940 abandoned whatever rights he may have had in said script."[62] When the broadcast debuted on vinyl in 1968, Howard Koch collected all royalties. Welles, perpetually short of cash, got nothing.[63]

By bringing Welles to sudden prominence, *War of the Worlds* helped launch several brilliant careers. At Warner Brothers, Koch wrote such classic films as *Sergeant York* and *The Sea Hawk*. He won an Oscar in 1942 for co-writing *Casablanca*, before being blacklisted in the 1950s.[64] Houseman became a successful producer in film and television—even making, in 1953, his own big-budget version of Shakespeare's *Caesar*, much to Welles's chagrin.[65] Richard Wilson and William Alland, both Welles collaborators with roles in the broadcast, also went on to successful careers behind the camera. Among other credits, Wilson directed 1959's *Al Capone*, and Alland produced *The Creature from the Black Lagoon*. Kenny Delmar, the voice of Welles's "Secretary of the Interior," became famous in the 1940s for playing the blustery southern senator Beauregard Claghorn on Fred Allen's radio show.[66] The character proved so popular that it inspired an even more famous Looney Tunes parody: the loud-mouthed rooster Foghorn Leghorn. But Bernard Herrmann, who entered the movie business by writing music for *Citizen Kane*, outdid them all. He went on to become one of the industry's most successful and influential composers, scoring many of Alfred Hitchcock's best-known films, as well as Martin Scorsese's *Taxi Driver*. Then there were the Mercury actors—like Joseph Cotten, Agnes Moorehead, and Everett Sloane—who did not have roles in the broadcast but made it big in Hollywood after debuting in *Citizen Kane*.

In time, these artists' connections and contributions to the broadcast would be largely forgotten. Few today would associate Foghorn Leghorn or the shrieking violins of *Psycho*'s shower scene with the Martian invasion of 1938. But everybody knows the twenty-three-year-old enfant terrible at the center of the storm, thanks in part to his own embellishments. As late as the 1970s, according to his biographer David Thomson, even many film students thought of Welles mainly as the man behind *War of the Worlds*, and not as the director of *Citizen Kane*.[67] Welles may have shunned the broadcast in his youth to avoid being defined as "the horror man," but he came to prefer that reputation to the one of failure that threatened to consume him in old age. In playing it up, he lent further credence to the panic story born on the front pages of American newspapers in 1938 and legitimized in *The Invasion from Mars* in 1940.

Welles liked to joke, in later years, that the people who copied his broadcast in other countries all wound up in jail, whereas he got away with a Hollywood contract.[68] But, in a sense, *War of the Worlds* landed him in his own private prison. Nothing he ever did made a greater splash than that broadcast, and he remained locked in competition with his younger, more successful self until the day he died. He embellished the story to add to his own legend, but that only made it harder to catch up with himself. Welles needn't have worried, back in 1940, that mentioning Koch in *The Invasion from Mars* would somehow rob him of credit for the broadcast. On the contrary, no one would ever let him forget it.

The notoriety of Welles's *War of the Worlds* inspired a host of imitators.[69] They rarely wound up in jail, as Welles claimed, but in at least two cases their work had fatal consequences. The first remake occurred in Chile on November 12, 1944. It was the brainchild of an American expat named William Steele who had written for Welles's own *The Shadow*. Steele and another writer, Raúl Zenteno, rewrote Koch's script for the Cooperativa Vitalicia radio network in Santiago, moving the story to a Chilean setting. Instead of landing in Grover's Mill, Steele and Zenteno's Martians arrived in the small town of Puente Alto, fifteen miles outside the city.[70] In order to prevent a panic, the network heavily promoted the show, placing ads in local newspapers and airing frequent announcements in the days before the broadcast.[71] But some listeners still missed all these warnings and believed what they heard, and this should not be surprising. World War II had just entered its fifth year, with no end in sight. Chile had remained neutral so far, but, as the researcher John Gosling has noted, both the Allies and the Axis were actively working to win them over.[72] With the entire world at war, radio reports of a sudden invasion in Chile would not have been hard to believe.

The public reaction played out much as it had in 1938. Newspaper offices found themselves besieged with telephone calls. Press reports describe agitated crowds in the streets of Santiago, suggesting that once again news of the "invasion" spread quickly by word of mouth.[73] The story of a Chilean provincial governor who put the military on alert may be apocryphal, but in the climate of the times it seems far from impossible.[74] As before, listeners apparently found the use of real place-names and government institutions most convincing.[75] And if 1938 is any indication, much of the audience probably did not realize that the show was about aliens. But the effects of the Chilean remake exceeded those of the original in one respect. In the city of Valparaíso, sixty-five miles away from Santiago, an electric worker named José Villarroel died of a heart attack while listening to the show. His is the first death directly tied to a *War of the Worlds* broadcast, though it would not be the last.[76]

A young Chilean actor named Alfredo Vergara Morales took note of the uproar surrounding Steele and Zenteno's broadcast.[77] The press roundly criticized the network, and the authorities announced plans to take "drastic measures" against the station. But these threats were never carried out, and the network escaped punishment.[78] This lack of official censure apparently convinced Morales that it would be safe to remake *War of the Worlds* again, five years later.

At the time, Morales lived in Quito, the capital of Ecuador, under the stage name "Eduardo Alcaraz." Quito was then a small city, with about 175,000 people, and was known for its peaceful disposition.[79] Its oldest and most respected newspaper, *El Comercio*, shared a building in the center of town with its primary radio station, Radio Quito.[80] Alcaraz worked as the station's program director. In early 1949, he showed a copy of Steele and Zenteno's script to the station manager, Nicolas Mantilla, and suggested that they remake it. Mantilla liked the idea and brought it to Leonardo Páez, a well-known performer and songwriter who served as Radio Quito's artistic director. Páez agreed to help produce the show and to appear in it as himself.[81]

The Ecuadorian *War of the Worlds* aired over Radio Quito at 9:00 p.m. on Saturday, February 12, 1949. It closely followed the basic story and fake news format of the earlier broadcast, with Páez interrupting a musical program to announce that Martians had landed in the nearby town of Cotocollao. From there, the Martians killed Páez, attacked an air base, and gassed several nearby towns before overwhelming Quito itself.[82] Apart from localizing the story, Páez and Alcaraz took several steps to heighten their show's realism. They had actors impersonate three officials: a government minister, the mayor of Quito, and a priest, who asked for divine mercy as church bells sounded an alarm.[83] They also used two of Ecuador's most popular musicians, Potolo Valencia and Gonzalo

Benítez, for the musical numbers at the start of the show. Valencia and Benítez usually only performed on Mondays, Wednesdays, and Fridays; their appearance on a Saturday night was unusual enough to attract many listeners.[84] Most crucially, Páez and Alcaraz did not begin their show with an announcement that it was fiction, nor, apparently, did they plan any interruptions until the end.[85] Instead, local newspapers promoted the show with cryptic ads asking "What will happen on February 12?" and fake news stories about flying saucers in the area.[86] This strongly suggests that someone—probably Alcaraz—meant to cause a sensation by deliberately misleading listeners, though no one had any idea how far it would go.

Radio Quito's fake invasion touched a very sensitive nerve for many listeners. In 1941, Peru had invaded southern Ecuador, starting a war that Ecuador ultimately lost.[87] Now some Quiteños listening to the show believed that Peru had invaded again; others thought they were under attack from the Soviet Union.[88] People began running about in the streets, going to friends and neighbors to spread the news. This activity further convinced many that something serious was up.[89] The local police even sent a squad to Cotocollao to investigate what they believed to be the source of the broadcast.[90] Calls poured into the offices of Radio Quito from people wanting to know if the invasion was real, and someone at the station decided to break into the broadcast with a disclaimer immediately.[91] But by that point, it was already too late.[92]

A crowd began to gather outside the building that housed Radio Quito and *El Comercio*. Most sources assume that these were people angered at being deceived, marching on the station to exact vengeance.[93] But a United Press correspondent on the scene that night reported that the crowd gave "shouts of protest when it was discovered the program was fiction." In other words, they only found out that the invasion was fake after they arrived at the building. Also, some in the crowd came from far afield; the UP reporter described "groups arriving from neighboring towns in cars and buses."[94] They were heading *into* the city, not fleeing before the imaginary invaders. It seems likely that, as happened during every other radio hoax, these were people trying to verify the reports or rumors that they had heard. Perhaps they did not have access to a telephone, or they tried to call the station and found its switchboards jammed. Quito, after all, was a small city with one major radio station in the same building as its primary newspaper. One would expect people searching for information to converge at that spot. And only after they discovered that it was all fake, that they had been tricked, did the crowd turn into a mob.

About a hundred radio-station and newspaper employees were inside the building when people in the streets began throwing rocks and screaming, "Death to the radio."[95] Some employees fled out the back, and others ran upstairs to call the police.[96] But when four officers arrived on the scene, the mob attacked them, beating one senseless. The rest called for reinforcements, but none could get there quickly, because the other squad had been sent to Cotocollao.[97] Meanwhile, the mob laid siege to the building, beating against the locked doors and breaking windows to gain access. Once inside, they looted typewriters and other valuable equipment and smashed *El Comercio*'s printing presses.[98] Finally, some members of the mob used gasoline and flaming wads of paper to set fire to the building. Fueled by the ink, paper, and printing apparatus of *El Comercio*, the flames spread rapidly, engulfing the entire ground floor.[99]

As the smoke rose to the upper floors, those still inside began frantically searching for an escape route. Gonzalo Benítez, one of the musicians who had kicked off the fatal broadcast, fled out a skylight in the men's room.[100] Others tried to form "a human chain" to the roofs of other buildings. But it soon broke apart, dropping them into the streets below. Trapped by the flames, some had no choice but to leap from third-story windows.[101] One of them—the station manager, Nicolas Mantilla—died when he hit the ground.[102] Páez clambered onto the roofs of nearby buildings and eventually made it to the street.[103] Alcaraz also made it out alive, though the press did not record how.[104]

Back inside, the disc jockey, Luis Beltrán, stayed by the microphone, calling for help as flames consumed the building.[105] When firefighters arrived, the mob blocked their way, knocking over fire hydrants to prevent them from extinguishing the blaze.[106] One man in the square that night recalled hearing Beltrán's voice pleading with the crowd to make way for the firefighters.[107] Surrounded by flames, Beltrán finally had no choice but to abandon the studio. He ran to a window and leapt, grabbing the railing of a second-story balcony as he fell. The red-hot metal seared his hand, taking the skin off his palm, and he dropped into the street—right in the middle of the mob. But as his daughter later told NPR's

Radiolab, the crowd took pity on Beltrán's burned, broken, and unconscious body. Someone took him to a nearby hospital, where he made a full recovery.[108]

By now, the fire had completely consumed the *Comercio* building and spread to neighboring structures.[109] More police arrived, using tear gas and military tanks to disperse the mob so the firefighters could reach the flames.[110] They battled the blaze until 3:00 a.m., managing to save the surrounding structures but not the *Comercio* building.[111] The next day, only its front wall remained standing. The authorities found about twenty corpses in its wreckage, and another fifteen people were injured in the violence that night.[112] The press later estimated that the riot caused about $350,000 in damage, leaving the operations of Radio Quito and *El Comercio* in ruins.[113]

The Ecuadorian minister of defense, Manuel Diaz Granados, began an immediate investigation, rounding up fifteen Radio Quito employees for questioning. The surviving heads of the station told police that Páez and Alcaraz had kept the show a secret from them, putting it on the air without their knowledge.[114] Indictments were drawn up against the two men, and police combed the city for any sign of them.[115] Páez could not be found, but Alcaraz was quickly arrested. And, once in custody, he blamed his absent partner for everything. Páez, Alcaraz claimed, had enjoyed throwing Quito into chaos, doing everything he could to fool as many people as possible.[116] Apparently, Alcaraz failed to mention that the show had been his idea in the first place. But with Páez missing and Mantilla, the station manager, dead, there was no one left to contradict him. He escaped punishment and moved to Mexico, where he went on to become a successful actor in film and television.[117]

Alcaraz left Páez holding much of the blame, but police still had no idea where he was. Legend has it that he disappeared on the night of the broadcast, never to be seen in Ecuador again. But his daughter, Ximena Páez, later told the researcher John Gosling that Páez returned to Quito several months later, after hiding out in a farm seventy miles away until the heat had died down. He brought with him documents proving that Radio Quito's management had known about the show in advance, and that Alcaraz had blamed him unfairly for its effects. The police exonerated him of any responsibility for the riot, and he lived out his days in Venezuela, returning to Quito in 1985 to receive the key to the city.[118]

The Ecuadorian *War of the Worlds* made the front page of *The New*

York Times and many other papers. The worst fears of Welles and others in the hectic hours after the 1938 broadcast had finally come true, almost three thousand miles away. *The Washington Post* described Welles as "conscience-stricken"; he said he had never imagined that the original show "would have such repercussions."[119] And, once again, the trade journal *Broadcasting* cited the incident as proof that radio "cannot be tampered with by government," because it showed how the medium could be used to spread fear. Commercial broadcasters, they wrote, could be depended on to treat their licenses as "a public trust."[120] Ecuadorian officials disagreed. Just days after the riot, they announced that they were creating a new governmental office to monitor all radio scripts before they aired, much as Senator Herring had suggested in 1938.[121]

Even these dire repercussions were not enough to stop others from trying their own versions of the Martian broadcast. Station WKBW in Buffalo, New York, became the first American station to remake *War of the Worlds*, on October 31, 1968. The program director, Jefferson Kaye, thoroughly modernized the story, mixing false reports of the Martian attack in with real news of the Vietnam War and current pop songs like the Beatles' "Hey Jude." The station's real correspondents performed under their own names, ad-libbing their descriptions of the invasion. The engineer Dan Kriegler's sound design added another layer of realism, mixing recorded sound effects with the authentic crackle of mobile broadcast units. This improvised dialogue and delicately woven sound surpasses, in many ways, the realism of the 1938 original.[122]

WKBW widely promoted the program ahead of time, and interrupted the broadcast every twelve minutes for commercial breaks.[123] But radio listening had changed dramatically since 1938. The medium had gone from the nation's primary source for news and entertainment to background noise at home or in a car, and hardly anyone paid attention to the commercials. As soon as the show started to heat up, frightened listeners began calling the station to find out if it was real. Kaye found this alarming enough to interrupt the program with a disclaimer.[124] But *Broadcasting* reported that WKBW only received about two hundred calls, along with "numerous" inquiries to police and newspaper offices— hardly a mass panic.[125] It seems that most listeners appreciated the show as a finely crafted radio drama, and it ran again in 1971 and 1975 without incident.[126]

Inspired by WKBW's success, station WPRO in Providence, Rhode

Island, aired a very similar adaptation of *War of the Worlds* on October 30, 1974. The station had a smaller listening area, and the show generated fewer calls than the 1968 broadcast. But enough frightened listeners complained to the FCC so that the commission opened a formal inquiry into the show. As the legal scholar Justin Levine has observed, the FCC, motivated by the quiz-show scandals and by lingering memories of Orson Welles, had tightened restrictions on airing misleading content in the 1960s. After reviewing WPRO's show, they found the station in violation of a 1966 notice banning "Contests and Promotions Which Adversely Affect the Public Interest." This meant a formal rebuke, but little chance of punishment; because no real damage had been done, the station would get to keep its license. Yet, as Levine has noted, this marked the first time that the FCC ever officially reprimanded a station for airing a *War of the Worlds*–style program.[127]

Although Welles's broadcast remained as famous as ever, some listeners, at least, kept falling for the same alien-invasion story over and over again.[128] This speaks less to the brilliance of the story, or the gullibility of audiences, than it does to radio's lack of visuals. Because listeners have to form their own mental pictures based on what they hear, they can more easily be misled. It's not so much that picturing the Martians in one's head makes them easier to believe in as it is that people see the Martians they are ready to see. Just as they did in 1938, half-heard radio reports of an alien attack can still easily transform in a listener's mind into news of a natural disaster, a foreign invasion, or some other catastrophe—no matter how many times the show mentions the Red Planet.

The same cannot be said for television. As Hadley Cantril and others have observed, radio requires people to use their own imaginations, whereas TV does not.[129] Viewers are not invited to add their own elements; they must accept only what they see. And seeing, in this case, is not necessarily believing. "It is easy to trick the ear by sleight of sound," wrote one *New York Times* columnist after Welles's *War of the Worlds*, but the eye is more discerning.[130] Bad special effects, jumps in space and time, and disclaimers are all easier to see than they are to hear. Most important, TV viewers cannot mistake fake news about aliens for reports of a real-life catastrophe in the same way radio listeners did time and again. *Seeing* the invaders fixes them in the mind; they cannot easily morph into something more believable.

Even when the fake news in question is not at all far-fetched, TV viewers remain harder to hoax than radio listeners. In 1983, NBC aired *Special Bulletin*, a TV movie about a terrorist attack on Charleston, South Carolina. The film mimicked a breaking-news broadcast so perfectly that the president of NBC News worried that it might mislead audiences, but his concerns proved unfounded. *Special Bulletin* did provoke a couple of thousand phone calls to TV stations nationwide, but most were from viewers complaining that the show was too frightening and might inspire real terrorists. Only a relative handful wanted to know if it was real.[131] Police in Charleston reported an influx of calls, but mostly from reporters asking how many frightened viewers had called them. The answer was: very few.[132]

Eleven years later, on October 30, 1994, CBS marked the fifty-sixth anniversary of *War of the Worlds* with another fake news telemovie, *Without Warning*. Loosely inspired by Welles's broadcast, it featured real journalists playing themselves during an alien attack.[133] The show's realism prompted one media columnist to suggest that CBS intended to trick their viewers, in hopes of boosting their ratings with a little controversy.[134] But few people tuned in, and hardly any believed. *Without Warning* was the lowest-rated show on CBS that night, and the network only received about 250 to 300 calls about it in total. Most, according to *The New York Times*, came from people who were not frightened but considered the show "either irresponsible or just plain bad."[135] A CBS spokesman also said that more reporters called the news department, wanting to know if they were swamped with calls, than frightened viewers did.[136]

The realism of *Special Bulletin* and *Without Warning* may have failed to frighten many people, but that does not mean American audiences were any less gullible in the eighties and nineties than they were in the thirties. They had certainly become more media-savvy, but the media they consumed failed to excite their imaginations in the way radio did decades earlier. Brilliant writing, acting, and effects can only go so far. Welles's *War of the Worlds* and its many remakes fired something in listeners' minds, making them unconscious collaborators in crafting a fictional world. Audiences saw something powerful in their mind's eye, whether they believed in the Martians or not. Television—or, indeed, any visual medium—can never have the same effect. If radio is the "theater of the imagination," then *War of the Worlds* was its defining moment.

Welles showed how television would have ruined *War of the Worlds* in his 1975 film *F for Fake*, a brisk pseudo-documentary that erases the line between truth and fiction. Over scenes from the 1956 B-movie *Earth vs. the Flying Saucers*, Welles plays a re-creation of the Martian broadcast, with different dialogue from what was used in the original show. Perhaps he meant to further the film's themes of fakery and illusion by faking his own broadcast, or perhaps he simply did it to avoid having to pay royalties to Howard Koch. Either way, the faked lines only add to the hokeyness of the visuals, proving Welles's point that people believed in the broadcast merely because they could not see it. "TV would have shown us up," he says in narration. "Half the population got the screaming jeebies just because they couldn't see how silly it all would have looked."[137]

F for Fake also features brief cameos from some former Mercurians: Paul Stewart, Richard Wilson, and Joseph Cotten. Houseman is conspicuously absent. He and Welles had barely seen each other since they drifted apart in 1941. They had met at least once, in a London nightclub in 1955, but it did not end well. Houseman, of course, claimed that Welles had lost his temper, and Welles, of course, claimed that Houseman had deliberately nettled him.[138] Their relationship passed the point of no return in 1972, when Houseman published *Run-Through*, the first volume of his memoirs. His account of their Mercury Theatre days is thrilling, perceptive, and affectionate; more than one observer has found the book full of love for Welles.[139] But Houseman also claimed, despite much evidence to the contrary, that Welles did not deserve his writing credit on *Citizen Kane*. This, perhaps more than anything else, confirmed Welles in the belief that Houseman hated him and sought to destroy his reputation out of jealousy.[140]

Whereas Welles had been precocious, Houseman was a late bloomer in almost every respect. He began an acting career at age seventy-one by playing the crusty Harvard law professor Charles Kingsfield in 1973's *The Paper Chase*. The part earned him an Academy Award and led to a string of patrician roles in film and television, even a *Paper Chase* TV series.[141] Suddenly Houseman was a celebrity, while Welles's financial struggles continued.[142] Welles resented, too, Houseman's directing a revival of *The Cradle Will Rock* in New York in 1983. The show mimicked the spare style of their 1937 production, which, Welles now claimed to friends, Houseman had had little to do with.[143] The two men had met one last time, in the mid-1970s, for a staged reunion on *The Merv Griffin Show*, where they hugged and danced about the studio like old friends.[144] But, privately, Welles still saw Houseman as his Iago—"a jealous son of a bitch."[145]

In 1984, the film producer Michael Fitzgerald showed Welles a screenplay he had commissioned about the story behind the 1937 production of *The Cradle Will Rock*. He sought Welles's approval to make it into a movie, and eventually offered him the chance to direct. At first, Welles demurred. It had been a decade since the release of *F for Fake*, and he did not want his Hollywood comeback to be a film about himself. "I cannot, in my old age, live off pieces of my youth," he told the film director Henry Jaglom. But Fitzgerald said he had four million dollars lined up, and he promised Welles the right to final cut—something Welles had not had on a major motion picture since *Citizen Kane*. It would also be a chance to refute Houseman by presenting his own version of events. There was no way he could say no. That summer, he began rewriting the screenplay, with filming set to begin that winter.[146]

Welles found researching and writing about his own life a strange experience. He told several friends at the time that he didn't really recognize his younger self.[147] His script is both rousingly comedic and painfully nostalgic—a wistful look back at a life lived too fast. Welles even wove in his radio work, with scenes of him racing across the city by ambulance to appear in *The Shadow* and *The March of Time*. He readily admitted that this was an idealized version of events, but he didn't set out to settle any scores. As the Welles scholar Jonathan Rosenbaum has noted, Welles handled his real-life characters kindly, particularly his ex-wife, Virginia Nicolson. He even treated Houseman with fairness. If the script takes anyone down a peg, it's the author himself and the myth that has grown up around him.[148]

Early on, Houseman's character describes Welles as the "Mephistophilis [sic] to his own Faust," hinting at the costs of his rapid rise: "In Dublin, when he started in the theatre he was just sixteen and claiming to be what he is now—twenty-two. In effect, this was a pact with Hell; he sold his youth for grown-up glory." At the end of the script, as the cast triumphantly performs *Cradle* in the aisles, Welles stands outside the theater with his wife, talking about their future. She urges him to use his newfound fame to break into the movie business, while he toys with the idea of going into politics. "After tonight you've got this town in the palm of your hand," she says. "Good time to quit," Welles replies.[149]

Factually, this conversation is a bit premature: it anticipates Welles's fame following *War of the Worlds* and his political activities in the 1940s. But Welles condensed these facts to get at a deeper truth about himself. In his later years, he came to believe that going into filmmaking had been "essentially a mistake," because it doomed him to a life spent searching for money to make movies. "I would have been more successful if I'd left movies immediately, stayed in the theatre, gone into politics, written, anything," he told a BBC interviewer in 1982.[150] Welles's screenplay for *The Cradle Will Rock* is so exuberant, and so sad, because it captures the moment in his youth when his prospects seemed truly limitless, before he went to Hollywood—and before *War of the Worlds*.

Despite his earlier misgivings about the project, Welles finished the script with great enthusiasm, calling it "the best thing I've ever written."[151] He spent the fall of 1984 casting the film and scouting locations. For cost reasons, much of the shooting would take place in Italy, but Welles also planned to film exteriors in New York.[152] He remarked to his old schoolmaster and close friend, Roger Hill, that the city had changed so much that he barely knew it anymore.[153] A schedule was drawn up, and sets were built. And then, about three weeks before production was slated to begin, Welles learned that the funding had fallen through. *The Cradle Will Rock* would not be happening.[154] "I have a wonderful cast," he told Hill the next day. "I have everything. Except the money."[155] But he remained optimistic. He continued to search for money to make *Cradle* and for ways to complete his other film projects, including his Hollywood satire *The Other Side of the Wind* and an adaptation of Shakespeare's *King Lear.*[156] He was sitting at his typewriter, working on yet another unfinished screenplay, when a massive heart attack killed him in the early-morning hours of October 10, 1985. He was seventy years old.[157]

Houseman, thirteen years Welles's senior, survived him by three. Like Welles, he had lived to see *The March of Time*'s "journalism and *showmanship*" begin to take over the news business. In 1980, the first twenty-four-hour news network, CNN, debuted on cable television. It brought with it a new kind of visual style, full of images, graphics, and live feeds. Network news shows and TV newsmagazines responded by upping their own level of flash and glitz. This "extreme self-consciousness of style," writes the media scholar John Caldwell, came to define 1980s TV. Caldwell called it "televisuality."[158] Broadcast journalism was becoming less and less about issues and facts, and more and more about entertainment.

"Radio is a much better news medium than television," Houseman said in 1988. "In television you waste an awful lot of time with those ridiculous little images, maps and drawings. It's insane."[159] And it would only get worse in the years to come.

Houseman also lived long enough to see his youthful exploits with Welles and the Mercury turn first into legend, then into kitsch. On October 28, 1988, two days before the fiftieth anniversary of *War of the Worlds*, the Museum of Broadcasting in New York City opened a special exhibit on Welles's radio work.[160] Fifty-five miles to the south, Grover's Mill, New Jersey, pulled out all the stops with a three-day anniversary festival featuring an art show, a NASA panel on exploring Mars, and a "Martian Panic 10K Run." Howard Koch and Richard Wilson were on hand for the dedication of a fifteen-thousand-dollar bronze monument to the broadcast, installed at the "Martian Landing Site," near the millpond. Reporters from all over the world descended on the town, re-creating the media circus of fifty years before. All this activity left some locals bewildered. "It doesn't make sense," said one resident who could still remember the night the Martians landed. "Never has. Never will." Another remarked: "I have to wonder why people still come so far to find a place where something that was supposed to happen didn't happen."[161]

But John Houseman, eighty-six years old and suffering from spinal cancer, was too ill to attend. He died in his California home on Halloween, October 31, 1988—fifty years and one day after the infamous "panic broadcast."[162]

Conclusion

What would you of done if television was in all homes? Your mind would think of a good scheme to see in television, I know that.

                —Esther Langman (age thirteen) of St. Paul, Minnesota,
                                    to Orson Welles, October 31, 1938[1]

The rise of the radio had much in common with the advent of the Internet. Both technologies began in the basements of hobbyists and tinkerers, then saw a sudden explosion of popularity as creators learned how to appeal to a mass audience. And in both cases, this led to a somewhat chaotic state of affairs. In the 1920s, hundreds of radio stations filled the American airwaves. Listeners could pick up music, news, drama, or sermons; they could even take courses at a wireless university. But stations constantly competed for the same frequencies, and listeners often had to battle interference. The establishment of the Federal Radio Commission (later the FCC) and the major broadcast networks, however, brought this chaos to an end, allowing a few programs to be heard from coast to coast for the first time. For a brief period, this allowed radio to reach new heights as a medium of art and information.[2]

In the 1930s, several factors came together to create a "golden age." Radio sets became more and more common, until virtually every American had access to one. The FCC, by stringently enforcing its public interest requirement, opened the airwaves to a diverse array of programming, and the networks made it possible for a show like *The Mercury Theatre on the Air*, even with its relatively small audience, to reach listeners all over the country. Broadcasters offered something for everyone, instead of appealing to the lowest common denominator. Listeners, too, were remarkably active; by writing fan mail to radio stations, they achieved some measure of control over what was aired.[3]

As several scholars have argued, broadcasters in the 1930s encouraged this kind of audience response. Still figuring out how to appeal to the mass public, they solicited fan mail and other input from listeners to help craft successful programming. Radio was never the two-way medium that many Americans wanted it to be; their influence over it had very serious limitations. Nevertheless, that influence existed, and it did shape American broadcasting in the 1930s.[4] But it also did not last very long. As broadcasters got better and better at predicting audience tastes, thanks to the work of market researchers like Paul Lazarsfeld and Herta Herzog, they no longer needed to ask listeners what they wanted to hear. By the 1940s, listener letters had lost the clout they carried a decade earlier.[5]

Orson Welles and his Mercury Theatre came along at just the right time. Ten years before *War of the Worlds*, the mass audience was only just coming into existence. Welles could never have reached a truly nationwide listenership, even a limited one. Ten years after *War of the Worlds*, the Mercury Theatre could never have found a home on any of the major networks. By the end of the 1940s, in part because of the *War of the Worlds* controversy itself, sponsors controlled the airwaves, and they only wanted programs with broad appeal. The "sustaining shows" of the previous decade were largely a thing of the past, and radio's days as an experimental medium were over.[6]

But the 1930s saw a unique balancing act involving the networks, the FCC, and listeners themselves. Everyone agreed, at least in principle, that the airwaves belonged to the people, and that broadcasters had a duty to their audiences, not just their sponsors. If they failed in that duty, they could expect a truckload of angry letters and possibly an official reprimand. With the public interest as their governing philosophy, broadcasters opened American airwaves like never before or since. This led to a veritable renaissance, an outpouring of on-air creativity that, as the historian Erik Barnouw has observed, reached its peak with *War of the Worlds*.[7]

In many respects, today's Internet recalls this phase of radio's history, but everything is magnified. There are more users, more producers, and exponentially more choices than there ever were in the early days of broadcasting. At the same time, certain platforms allow exceptional content to rise above the noise and find an audience. Like the major broadcast networks, companies have monetized the new means of communication, and often turned quite a profit in doing so. The key difference is that the threshold for reaching a mass audience is much lower than it was eight decades ago. If Orson Welles were just starting out today, he wouldn't need CBS to become a star. He might use YouTube and Twitter to similar effect, much more cheaply and quickly. Individuals can use these platforms to reach the mass public, but the system only works because everyone has access.

The Internet has unleashed the active audience that tried so hard to make itself heard during radio's golden age. Fan mail has given way to instantaneous online communication. Content providers, like their forebears in broadcasting, encourage input from the public and pay at least some attention to what it has to say. In many ways, the line between user and creator seems to be disappearing. Much like radio in the 1930s, these developments promise to democratize our media, making those who entertain and inform us more receptive to the will of their audience. But they also intensify some of the problems that Americans struggled with at the dawn of mass communication—the hazards that Welles's broadcast brought to the fore.

According to popular legend, *War of the Worlds* sent multitudes fleeing from their homes because of their complete and total trust in the radio. But the letters sent to the Mercury and the FCC prove that that's not at all what happened. The vast majority of listeners understood the broadcast correctly, and those few who were frightened did not passively accept what came to them over the airwaves. They often tried to verify the information in any way they could, and most of them subconsciously changed the Martians into something more credible. The "panic," as many newspapers defined it, only began when some listeners passed the fake news on to unsuspecting others, spreading their fear and confusion. This behavior was not the mass headlong flight from reality that the word "panic" implies. Instead, as the scholars Joy Elizabeth Hayes and Kathleen Battles have observed, it was a complex series of interactions, as listeners tried to make sense of their experiences by communicating with one another and with the radio itself.[8]

In the age of the Internet, media producers and consumers are much more tightly connected, accelerating and amplifying this communication. In such an environment, the kinds of rumors that *War of the Worlds* created can get out of hand very quickly. Anyone can say whatever he or she wants online and watch a claim, true or not, ricochet around the world faster than a bolt of lightning.[9] Those claims have added credibility because, despite the rise of streaming video, much communication on the Internet is still text-based. Like the disembodied voice of the radio, text presents an incomplete picture, inviting the reader to enhance the story with his or her own imagination.[10] At only 140 characters, a tweet is even more compact than a radio news bulletin, and it is even more easily shared. In 1938, listeners had to pick up a phone or run next door to spread news of the Martian invasion. Now they could satisfy that impulse with a single click.[11]

The Mexican port city of Veracruz discovered this in August 2011, during a period of brutal drug violence. As reported by the BBC, residents there had come to depend upon social media for real-time information. They would check sites like Twitter and Facebook before leaving their homes in order to learn which areas were unsafe. On August 25, two people from Veracruz, Maria de Jesus Bravo Pagola and Gilberto Martinez Vera, allegedly posted false reports of violent episodes in their city. The messages described drug gangs kidnapping children from one school while helicopters fired on another during recess. None of it was true, but with all they had so far experienced, residents had little reason to doubt it. Authorities reported twenty-six car crashes as parents rushed to pick their children up from school, and phone lines "totally collapsed" as people tried to spread the word. One official claimed that the posts caused more hysteria than Welles's *War of the Worlds*.[12]

Pagola and Martinez Vera were arrested and accused of "terrorism and sabotage," charges that carried up to thirty years in prison. But many observers criticized the authorities for equating false tweets with "terrorism." Thousands protested the charges on social media; Amnesty International called the arrests a violation of "justice and freedom of expression." Eventually, the charges were dropped, after the state passed a new law making it a crime to spread misinformation. Throughout, Pagola and Martinez Vera maintained that they had not made anything up, but had only passed on reports already circulating on social media.[13] In other words, they acted like many misinformed listeners in 1938, spreading word of a false yet plausible catastrophe. But, unlike those listeners, they used the same means to pass on the misinformation that they'd used to receive it. In no time at all, they were able to reach a much wider audience than any individual could have done on the night the Martians landed.

The Veracruz "Twitter panic" is only the most extreme example of a very common phenomenon. False reports are mistakenly spread through social media all the time, creating varying degrees of fear and confusion.[14] Some Web sites have even capitalized on this by writing fake news stories with provocative headlines, designed to be shared on social media. This "clickbait," as it's called, can generate a small fortune in ad revenue by exploiting gullibility.[15] But other false alarms can have more serious consequences.

In April 2013, automated trading programs reacted to a false tweet about a bombing attack on the White House by immediately dumping stocks. Within two minutes, the Dow had dropped 145 points, wiping two hundred billion dollars from the stock market. But this time, gullible computers were to blame, not gullible people. The trading software had reacted automatically to key words in the tweet, selling stocks before anyone knew what had happened. Technology had amplified a very human impulse, the need to spread the word, and accelerated it far beyond the speed of thought.[16]

There is, however, a silver lining. The same technology that spread the false report also made it possible to verify the story in almost no time at all. After the tweet proved false, the Dow rebounded in minutes, and little permanent damage was done.[17] Listeners in 1938 had to call police or newspaper offices to find out if what they heard over the radio was true. Today one could investigate similar rumors simply by pulling up Google on a smartphone. We have more information, good and bad, at our fingertips than ever before, but it is up to us to make sense of it.

After *War of the Worlds*, Americans also faced the question of how to protect themselves from misinformation and propaganda. Many frightened listeners felt that the government should prevent broadcasters from deceiving their audiences. In their letters, a few advocated federal censorship as the means to this end. But a majority of Americans, concerned about the rise of fascism abroad, believed that censorship would do more harm than good. The only way democracy could survive in the age of mass media, they argued, was in an informed and actively skeptical public. As one Pennsylvania woman put it in a letter to the FCC:

> If it be claimed that anything coming over the radio must be like Gospel to everyone, there are at least two staunch supporters of this view—one named Hitler and one named Mussolini. And, of course, many

candidates for public office will support this view. Most of them use radio for their campaigns nowadays . . . What we need is education, not prohibitions, and I believe this broadcast will prove to have been beneficial in that it will, for a time at least, make people a little more careful of the source and nature of their information.[18]

This seems to be the lesson that most people took away from the broadcast. Instead of choosing to restrict access to information, they believed it should be up to the people to regulate themselves, to question everything they heard before letting fear get the best of them. Listeners were required to engage actively with what they heard.

Yet few Americans applied this skepticism to the story of the panic itself. The idea that millions had fallen for a hoax was its own kind of fake news—a newspaper exaggeration born of haste and misunderstanding. And it inspired a much larger panic, over fears of the media's influence on society, that helped upset the delicate balance allowing shows like *The Mercury Theatre on the Air* to exist in the first place. By falsely inflating radio's persuasive power, the panic story seemed to back up the argument that any government involvement in broadcasting would inevitably lead to censorship and tyranny. This weakened the FCC and gave broadcasters and sponsors greater control over what went on the air. The industry, in turn, fearful of further controversies that might drive listeners away, retreated from the inventiveness and creativity that had defined radio's golden age.

The FCC was far from perfect, but its strong enforcement of the public interest requirement in the 1930s played a crucial role in keeping the airwaves open to many different kinds of programs, even those that were unprofitable. Listeners, after all, were not the networks' primary customers. The "American system" of radio existed to help companies push products; audience attention was the commodity that broadcasters sold to advertisers. It was in the industry's best interests to maximize the size of its audiences, and this commercial imperative led broadcasters to produce a surfeit of variety shows, melodramas, and soap operas that were broadly appealing and inoffensive. But the public interest ethos helped ensure that a protected space existed for artistic or informational shows that could not compete in the ratings, and American culture was better off because of it.

Nowhere is the need for such a protected space clearer than in news broadcasting. When news is forced to compete for ratings, journalism all too easily gives way to sensationalism. An alarming but fundamentally inaccurate news report, or commentary from a charismatic but misleading pundit, might be expected to grab a much larger audience than a sober discussion of the issues at play. This can lead to a dangerous form of fake news with long-lasting repercussions. Newspapers in 1938 exaggerated and misinterpreted the *War of the Worlds* panic in part to attract readers with alarming headlines. Those headlines sold a lot of papers, but they also inspired false fears and half-truths that are still very much with us over seventy-five years later.

In 1949, the FCC took action to keep news broadcasters from misleading the public in a similar way. It ruled that station owners were required to "devote a reasonable percentage of their broadcasting time to the discussion of public issues of interest in the community" and to give all sides a fair hearing in those discussions.[19] This ruling came to be called the "Fairness Doctrine." It was based on the idea that the people—not broadcasters, sponsors, or the government—owned the airwaves, and that the public had a right to be informed. "No discussion of the issues involved in any controversy," wrote the commissioners, "can be fair or in the public interest where such discussion must take place in a climate of false or misleading information concerning the basic facts of the controversy."[20]

The Fairness Doctrine lasted almost forty years, until the FCC unanimously voted to do away with it in 1987.[21] This gave broadcasters the freedom to tailor news content toward certain demographics, in order to maximize their ratings and appeal to advertisers. Instead of keeping everyone informed on the same topics, each audience would get its own information, slanted to reaffirm what it already believes. As a result, on too many issues Americans can no longer agree on which facts are really facts, on which news is true and which is fake. All the while, televised news has increasingly come to resemble *The March of Time*'s "fakery in allegiance to the truth"—news content repackaged as entertainment. Too often, stories are crafted first and foremost to grab viewers, rather than to inform.

And yet the erasure of the line between news and entertainment has also allowed new forms of journalism to emerge, twisting the news in an ironic or satirical way. As the scholar Geoffrey Baym has argued, this has the effect of making viewers think critically about current events.

Audiences have to decipher the satire, and this gets them actively engaged in the content. By being up front with their fakery, and refusing to hide behind a curtain of objectivity, these shows earn the trust of their viewers.[22] The novelist Robert Anton Wilson once said that Welles's *F for Fake*, unlike most documentaries, acknowledges the fakery inherent in all nonfiction films. "A documentary that admits it's lying is honest," Wilson said; "a documentary that pretends to be honest is lying."[23] Much the same could be said of modern journalism, of news both real and fake.

Jon Stewart and Stephen Colbert, hosts of the satirical newscasts *The Daily Show with Jon Stewart* and *The Colbert Report*, redefined "fake news" in the first decade of the twenty-first century. Instead of making fiction sound like fact, they covered real news in an ironic way. Frequently, they satirized the news media themselves for failing to live up to their status as the Fourth Estate. Colbert even assumed the character of an ignorant TV pundit, spouting rhetoric he did not believe in order to poke fun at conservative views. His work, like Stewart's, brought "fakery in allegiance to the truth" full-circle. Their mixture of comedy and current events kept viewers better informed than many conventional news shows did.[24]

On October 30, 2010—seventy-two years to the day after *War of the Worlds*—Stewart and Colbert hosted a massive "Rally to Restore Sanity and/or Fear" on the National Mall in Washington, D.C. Stewart announced the event as "a clarion call for rationality," a plea for proof that Americans are more reasonable than the people they watch on TV.[25] In a series of comedy sketches and musical numbers, Stewart and Colbert satirized the news media's penchant for stirring up false fears and baseless conflicts. "The press can hold its magnifying glass up to our problems, bringing them into focus, illuminating issues heretofore unseen," Stewart said at the end of the event. "Or they can use that magnifying glass to light ants on fire, and then perhaps host a week of shows on the sudden, unexpected, dangerous flaming ant epidemic." This focus on fear, he argued, had needlessly divided the country, making it difficult to find solutions to the day's most pressing problems.[26]

Stewart's message, and his frustration, struck a chord with viewers. More than two hundred thousand people attended the Rally to Restore Sanity.[27] They completely booked up area hotels, overloaded D.C.'s transit system, and jammed local roadways.[28] When they met on the National Mall, the crowd stretched, one commentator noted, "from almost in front of the Capitol to the Washington Monument."[29] And more than a thousand spontaneous "satellite meetings" were also held all over the world, so people unable to come to D.C. could still take part.[30] It was almost certainly the biggest fake news event since *War of the Worlds*, and, like Welles's broadcast, it led to an outpouring of dissatisfaction with the state of the country and the media. Many listeners in 1938 wrote letters, both in praise and in protest of Welles, in order to assert some control over the radio. The rally's attendees seemed motivated by a similar impulse: they wanted more from the mainstream media than they were currently getting. As one handmade sign put it: "It's a sad day when our politicians are comical, and I have to take our comedians *SERIOUSLY!*"[31]

The Rally to Restore Sanity failed to effect much change, because broadcast media are no longer as responsive to the general public as they once were. Over seventy-five years after *War of the Worlds*, broadcasters have replaced print journalists as the establishment, and the Internet has taken radio's place as the upstart. But the rally demonstrated the kind of active engagement that is needed in order to keep the Internet from treading the same path as its predecessor. Like radio in the 1930s, the Internet remains in flux, but users have a greater ability to shape its destiny than radio listeners ever did. The idea of the open Internet, that all online content should be treated equally, holds providers accountable to the public interest. If users give that power up, as Americans did in the early days of radio, then the Internet will inevitably become another medium that speaks *to* the people, instead of *for* the people.

War of the Worlds remains an important symbol of the mass media's power. The panic story can still serve as a reminder to treat all information critically, to avoid jumping to conclusions and getting carried away by fear. But the American response to that story in 1938 shows that the public must remain vigilant, in order to ensure that the media act in their best interests. The broadcast may have been fake news, but its story carries a great deal of truth.

A Note on Sources

This is the first book to bring together all of the surviving listener letters from the *War of the Worlds* broadcast. These nearly two thousand pieces of mail are spread over four archival collections in three separate facilities and as many states. Because no general accounting of these materials exists, I have had to invent my own system for cataloguing and analyzing them. Those seeking to explore the broadcast further might appreciate a word of explanation for how I came up with the percentages and other figures used in the text.

Over the course of this project, I went through each set of letters twice. I first set out to determine how many letters supported Welles and his broadcast, and how many criticized them. But I soon discovered that some letters gave no opinion on either, or expressed contradictory feelings that made it difficult to place them one way or the other. So I broke the letters down into four separate categories: pro-Welles, anti-Welles, neutral, and ambivalent. These judgments are somewhat subjective, and a different researcher might come up with slightly different totals for each category. But I do not believe the difference would be statistically significant. The vast majority of letters take a very clear stand either for Welles or against him; the neutral and ambivalent letters make up less than 10 percent of the total.

The National Archives II facility in College Park, Maryland, holds 625 letters received by the Federal Communications Commission regarding the broadcast. They include letters sent to other federal agencies that were forwarded to the FCC for review. A handful of people sent similar letters, often identical copies, to more than one agency, and so they are represented more than once in the collection. The FCC counted each letter individually, resulting in their total of 625. But when the letters are substantially similar, I've elected not to count them twice.[1] Therefore, the calculations in this text are based on a total of 619 letters. These letters appear to be kept in the order in which the FCC received them, and they are roughly separated into pro- and anti-Welles folders. Most take the form of official protests, so judging their stance on Welles is not difficult. This collection holds no ambivalent letters, and the few neutral letters are mostly requests that the broadcast be repeated. By my calculations, there are 244 pro-Welles letters (39 percent), 353 anti-Welles letters (57 percent), and 22 neutral letters (4 percent).

The Mercury letters require a bit more explanation. Following the broadcast, Richard

Baer—the young Princeton grad with dreams of becoming an actor, whom Houseman hired for a song—gathered and read all the mail the Mercury Theatre received about the show.[2] He apparently sorted them alphabetically by state, and then alphabetically by city, probably in order to get a sense of the size and location of the Mercury's audience.[3] He or someone else also left penciled notes on some letters, like a "P" for praise or "Sc" for a request for the broadcast's script. The following year, the Mercury shared some of these letters with Hadley Cantril and the Princeton Radio Research Project, as part of the research for *The Invasion from Mars*.[4] Then the letters returned to the files of Mercury Productions and fell under the care of Richard Wilson, Welles's producing partner.

In the words of the radio historian Michael Ogden, Wilson "was the self-appointed 'saver' of the Mercury Theatre." He took it upon himself to preserve whatever documents from Welles's career that he could.[5] All Welles aficionados owe Wilson a tremendous debt, because the records he saved continue to shed light on Welles's creative process, and to disprove many of the unkind myths that have sprung up around him. Following the collapse of Mercury Productions in the 1940s, these materials probably would have been lost had not Wilson paid to keep them in a storage facility. Eventually, he moved them to his garage in Santa Monica, and Wilson and Welles sold a large portion to the Lilly Library at Indiana University in the 1970s.[6] The rest, including most of the *War of the Worlds* letters, stayed at Wilson's home until his death in 1991. Fourteen years later, his son donated the remaining materials to the University of Michigan, in Ann Arbor, because Wilson had previously worked with a professor there, the Welles scholar Catherine L. Benamou.

The vast majority of the *War of the Worlds* letters received by the Mercury (1,344) are part of the Richard Wilson-Orson Welles Papers at the University of Michigan. Another two were among the papers Welles owned at his death, and were donated to the University of Michigan by his companion, Oja Kodar, at the same time as the Wilson materials. It's not known why Welles kept these two letters in particular. One of them, from a judge in South Carolina, denounces him so floridly that it must have caught his fancy. Someone at the Mercury typed up several copies, presumably so it could be passed around the office.[7] Another ten *War of the Worlds* letters are preserved among the materials that Wilson and Welles sold to the Lilly Library in the 1970s. Most of these are carbon copies of letters sent to the FCC, all in Welles's favor, and two are copies of letters sent to Walter Winchell.[8] It remains unclear why these few letters wound up at the Lilly, while the rest ended up at the University of Michigan. Perhaps they were set aside at the time as evidence for Welles's defense, because the copies of the FCC letters are some of the most eloquent in that collection. Taken together, these three archival collections yield a total of 1,355 Mercury letters, 1,094 pro-Welles (81 percent), 115 anti-Welles (8 percent), 38 ambivalent (3 percent), and 108 neutral (8 percent).

Combined, the Mercury and FCC collections contain 1,974 letters. Men appear to have written to the FCC in greater numbers, and slightly more of the Mercury letters were written by women.[9] Jeanette Sayre, a member of the Princeton Radio Research Project who made a study of listener letters in 1939, noted that most radio shows received far more letters from women than men, often as many as five to one.[10] That both collections seem fairly evenly divided along gender lines suggests that they are slightly more representative than most radio fan mail. They also appear more economically and geographically diverse than most listener letters. Hadley Cantril and Gordon Allport noted in 1935 that the writers of radio fan mail tended to reside "in the lower economic classes and in nonurban areas."[11] But both collections contain many letters from doctors, lawyers, and other professionals, as well as people from most of the country's major cities, particularly in New York and New Jersey.[12] This suggests that the *War of the Worlds* letters better represent the country than most radio fan mail—reflecting, perhaps, the unusual nature of the broadcast in question.

Table 1 shows the point of origin for the letters in both collections. The regions are based on the divisions used by the U.S. Census Bureau. Hadley Cantril used the same divisions in *The Invasion from Mars* to report the geographical distribution of the broadcast's audience.[13] As might be expected, more listeners from New York, New Jersey, and to a lesser extent Pennsylvania wrote than from any other states. Letters from those three states alone make up about 43 percent of the Mercury collection and 36 percent of the FCC collection.[14] However, the number of letters from New England is surprisingly high, since no major stations in that region carried *War of the Worlds*.[15]

TABLE 1			
	Mercury	FCC	Total
New England*	77	37	114
Middle Atlantic†	588	223	811
East North Central‡	204	81	285
West North Central§	68	36	104
South Atlantic**	129	98	227
South Central††	69	41	110
Mountain‡‡	21	17	38
Pacific§§	87	63	150
No Location	76	21	97
International***	36	2	38
Total	1,355	619	1,974

   * Maine, Vermont, New Hampshire, Massachusetts, Connecticut, Rhode Island.
   † New York, New Jersey, Pennsylvania.
   ‡ Michigan, Wisconsin, Indiana, Illinois, Ohio.
   § Iowa, Minnesota, Missouri, North Dakota, South Dakota, Nebraska, Kansas.
  ** District of Columbia, Delaware, Maryland, West Virginia, Virginia, North Carolina, South Carolina, Georgia, Florida.
  †† Kentucky, Tennessee, Mississippi, Alabama, Arkansas, Oklahoma, Texas, Louisiana.
  ‡‡ Montana, Idaho, Wyoming, Nevada, Utah, Colorado, Arizona, New Mexico.
  §§ Washington, Oregon, California.
*** Primarily Canada, with one letter each from Bermuda, Great Britain, and Chile.

After organizing the letters by their stance on the broadcast and by their geography, I went through them again, looking for evidence of fright or panic. "Frightened" listeners, as I defined them, were people who believed the broadcast to be true but gave no indication that they did anything besides listen to the show. "Panicked" people, on the other hand, actually took some action in response to the broadcast, such as trying to flee their homes. Listeners who believed briefly, but quickly figured out that the show was fiction,

TABLE 2

	MERCURY					FCC				BOTH
	Pro-Welles	Anti-Welles	Ambivalent	Neutral	Total	Pro-Welles	Anti-Welles	Neutral	Total	Total
Not Frightened	870	18	0	69	957	222	87	12	321	1,278
Not Frightened but Saw People Who Were	25	5	1	1	32	2	10	0	12	44
Not Frightened but Saw Panic	6	0	0	0	6	0	2	0	2	8
Momentarily Believed	46	0	0	1	47	5	5	0	10	57
Frightened	71	71	22	6	170	3	225	2	230	400
Told by Someone Else and Frightened	5	6	3	0	14	0	9	0	9	23
Frightened and Saw Panic	5	7	3	0	15	0	8	0	8	23
Panicked	4	3	7	3	17	1	3	0	4	21
Panicked and Saw Panic	1	2	2	0	5	0	3	0	3	8
Did Not Hear Broadcast and Not Frightened	58	2	0	28	88	11	0	8	19	107
Did Not Hear Broadcast and Saw Panic	3	1	0	0	4	0	1	0	1	5
Total	1,094	115	38	108	1,355	244	353	22	619	1,974
Total Untouched by Fright or Panic	974	20	0	98	1092	238	92	20	350	1,442
Total with Evidence of Fright or Panic	120	95	38	10	263	6	261	2	269	532
Total	1,094	115	38	108	1,355	244	353	22	619	1,974

are classified as "momentarily believed." I adhered to these categories very strictly, and only included as "frightened" or "panicked" letters whose writers gave specific evidence for either category. Letters that expressed anger about the broadcast but did not specifically state that the writer believed in it or saw anyone who did, were classified as "not frightened." My results, therefore, most likely underrepresent the number of listeners truly frightened by the broadcast, but probably only slightly. In general, listeners went into their experiences in great detail, in order to justify why they reacted in the way that they did. And as Table 2 shows, the vast majority of the letters, nearly three-quarters, show no evidence of fright or panic.

As far as is known, these are the only listener letters regarding *War of the Worlds* still in existence. Newspaper accounts and other sources state that CBS received many letters regarding the show, as did the network affiliate (WABC) that produced the program and many other stations, but these apparently have not survived. In *The Invasion from Mars*, Hadley Cantril gives the number of letters sent to WABC, the Mercury, and the FCC, as well as the percentages of each that were pro- and anti-Welles, but his totals do not agree with the letters that currently exist.[16] His total for the FCC (644) is probably in error, because contemporary information from the FCC supports the lower figure of 625.[17] Regardless, the difference is slight. Cantril's total for the Mercury, on the other hand, is off by nearly a hundred, 1,450 instead of 1,355. This may be another mistake, or it may indicate that some Mercury letters are still missing, or both. It seems unlikely that the missing letters are the ones that the Mercury sent to Cantril, because Cantril appears to have returned them after completing his study.[18] Another possibility is that the Mercury forwarded the more litigious letters to CBS's legal department. A handful of Mercury letters do threaten lawsuits or ask for some kind of remuneration, but not nearly as many as might be expected. However, those letters would almost certainly be overwhelmingly anti-Welles, and Cantril's percentage of anti-Welles Mercury letters (9 percent) is very close to my own finding (8 percent).[19]

I have made every effort to track down all known primary sources regarding the broadcast. But if these missing letters do exist, then I hope to include them, along with any other undiscovered documents, in a future edition of this book.

The Events That Stopped Our Lives . . . from the Hindenburg Explosion to the Attacks of September 11, 3rd ed. (Naperville, Ill.: Sourcebooks, Inc., 2002), pp. 2–3.

33. Tate, "WLS Scoops the World," pp. 14–15. Archbold and Marschall, *Hindenburg*, p. 180. Mooney, *Hindenburg*, p. 232. Garner, *We Interrupt*, p. 2. Miller, *Emergency Broadcasting*, pp. 58–59, 69. Brown, *Manipulating the Ether*, p. 141.

34. Tate, "WLS Scoops the World," pp. 14–15. Archbold and Marschall, *Hindenburg*, pp. 183–93. Mooney, *Hindenburg*, pp. 237–52. Brown, *Manipulating the Ether*, pp. 141–42. Garner, *We Interrupt*, p. 3.

35. The full recording is available at "Hindenburg Disaster: Herb Morrison Reporting," *Radio Days*, www.otr.com/hindenburg.shtml (accessed May 21, 2014).

36. Tate, "WLS Scoops the World," pp. 14–15. Bruce Robertson, "Radio Gives Fast Zeppelin Coverage," *Broadcasting*, May 15, 1937, p. 14. Brown, *Manipulating the Ether*, pp. 142–43. Garner, *We Interrupt*, p. 3.

37. Tate, "WLS Scoops the World," pp. 14–15.

38. Ibid., pp. 14–15. Barnouw, *Golden Web*, p. 109 n. 2.

39. Archbold and Marschall, *Hindenburg*, p. 193. Brown, *Manipulating the Ether*, pp. 141–42.

40. Barnouw, *Tower in Babel*, p. 277.

41. A Gallup poll taken in 1937 found that 4 percent of radio listeners cited *The March of Time* as their favorite radio program. Another 4 percent mentioned "News Broadcasts" in general. The next-most-popular news program, that of commentator Lowell Thomas, was only mentioned by 2 percent of respondents. According to this poll, *The March of Time* was just as popular as such radio stalwarts as *Amos 'n' Andy* and *Lum and Abner*, and significantly more so than such popular programs as *The Lux Radio Theatre* (2 percent), *Gangbusters* (2 percent), and the musician Rudy Vallee (2 percent). (Mildred Strunk and Hadley Cantril, eds., *Public Opinion: 1935–1946* [Princeton: Princeton University Press, 1951], p. 716.) See also Herbert I. Diamond, "The March of Time," *Radio News*, May 1938, p. 20; Barnouw, *Tower in Babel*, pp. 277–78; Barnouw, *Golden Web*, p. 109; Brown, *Manipulating the Ether*, pp. 150–52; Douglas, *Listening In*, p. 166; White, *News on the Air*, p. 249.

42. Diamond, "March of Time," p. 21. John Dunning, *On the Air: The Encyclopedia of Old-Time Radio* (New York: Oxford University Press, 1998), pp. 434–36.

43. Quoted in Barnouw, *Tower in Babel*, p. 277. See also Robert T. Elson, *Time Inc.: The Intimate History of a Publishing Enterprise, 1923–1941*, ed. Duncan Norton-Taylor (New York: Atheneum, 1968), p. 178.

44. Barnouw, *Tower in Babel*, p. 278. Dunning, *On the Air*, p. 435. Elson, *Time Inc.*, pp. 175–77. Raymond Fielding, *The March of Time, 1935–1951* (New York: Oxford University Press, 1978), pp. 7–10.

45. Dunning, *On the Air*, p. 435.

46. Quoted in Elson, *Time Inc.*, p. 177. See also Fielding, *March of Time*, pp. 8–9.

47. Quoted in Fielding, *March of Time*, p. 9.

48. Elson, *Time Inc.*, pp. 177–79. Fielding, *March of Time*, pp. 10–11.

49. Elson, *Time Inc.*, pp. 178–79.

50. Tom Everitt, "Time Marches On," *Radio Guide*, March 25, 1933, pp. 12–13. Hally Pomeroy, "Time Marches On," *Radio Guide*, July 18, 1936, pp. 20–21. Diamond, "March of Time," pp. 20–21. Barnouw, *Tower in Babel*, pp. 277–78. Brown, *Manipulating the Ether*, pp. 150–52. Dunning, *On the Air*, pp. 435–37. Elson, *Time Inc.*, pp. 179–81. Fielding, *March of Time*, pp. 14–18. White, *News on the Air*, pp. 254, 256–64.

51. Quoted in Elson, *Time Inc.*, p. 237.

52. See Neil Verma, *Theater of the Mind: Imagination, Aesthetics, and American Radio Drama* (Chicago: University of Chicago Press, 2012), pp. 66–68; White, *News on the Air*, pp. 250–53.

53. Cantril and Allport, *Psychology of Radio*, p. 71.
54. Brown, *Manipulating the Ether*, p. 151. Elson, *Time Inc.*, pp. 178–79. Fielding, *March of Time*, pp. 10–11, 17–18, 102–104.
55. Quoted in Elson, *Time Inc.*, p. 179.
56. "Letters," *Time*, March 23, 1931, p. 4. "Letters," *Time*, April 6, 1931, p. 4. "Letters," *Time*, June 8, 1931, pp. 8, 12. "Letters: Ghandi's [sic] Watch Pocket," *Time*, Nov. 2, 1931, p. 2. "Letters," *Time*, Nov. 23, 1931, p. 4. Elson, *Time Inc.*, p. 182.
57. Jack Banner, "The Pause in the Flight of Time," *Radio Guide*, March 30, 1935, p. 5. See also Barnouw, *Tower in Babel*, p. 278. Elson, *Time Inc.*, p. 178. Dunning, *On the Air*, pp. 435–37. "Letters," *Time*, Jan. 23, 1933, pp. 4, 6.
58. "Theater: Air Drama," *Time*, Dec. 7, 1931, p. 44.
59. Elson, *Time Inc.*, pp. 182–83. Fielding, *March of Time*, pp. 18–19.
60. "Art: The March of Time," *Time*, Feb. 29, 1932, pp. 24–25. See also Elson, *Time Inc.*, p. 183. Fielding, *March of Time*, p. 19.
61. Cantril and Allport, *Psychology of Radio*, pp. 36–47, 65–68, 73–84.
62. Barnouw, *Golden Web*, pp. 22–27. Goodman, *Radio's Civic Ambition*, pp. 3–6.
63. Goodman, *Radio's Civic Ambition*, pp. 3–64. See also Cantril and Allport, *Psychology of Radio*, p. 41; Leonard Maltin, *The Great American Broadcast: A Celebration of Radio's Golden Age* (New York: Dutton, 1997), pp. 160–61; Simon Callow, *Orson Welles: The Road to Xanadu* (New York: Viking, 1995), pp. 370–72.
64. Cantril and Allport, *Psychology of Radio*, pp. 41, 73–78.
65. "The Press: Question of Responsibility," *Time*, Feb. 29, 1932, p. 32.
66. "Press: Time Marches Back," *Time*, June 13, 1932, p. 48. Elson, *Time Inc.*, pp. 183–84. Fielding, *March of Time*, p. 19.
67. Diamond, "March of Time," p. 81. Elson, *Time Inc.*, p. 184. Fielding, *March of Time*, p. 19.
68. Dunning, *On the Air*, p. 434.
69. Pomeroy, "Time Marches On," pp. 21, 42. Diamond, "March of Time," pp. 21, 81. Barnouw, *Tower in Babel*, pp. 277–78. Elson, *Time Inc.*, p. 180. Fielding, *March of Time*, pp. 12–15. Dunning, *On the Air*, pp. 435–37.
70. Frederic William Wile, Jr., "Ghost Voices of the White House," *Radio Guide*, Dec. 16, 1933, p. 5. See also "Letters," *Time*, Feb. 13, 1933, pp. 4, 6; Dunning, *On the Air*, p. 435.
71. Elson, *Time Inc.*, p. 184. Lenthall, *Radio's America*, p. 89.
72. "Letters," *Time*, Jan. 22, 1934, pp. 2, 4. Elson, *Time Inc.*, pp. 184–85.
73. "Letters," *Time*, Jan. 29, 1934, pp. 4, 6.
74. Dunning, *On the Air*, p. 436. Elson, *Time Inc.*, p. 185. Fielding, *March of Time*, p. 18. Harry M. Geduld, "Welles or Wells?—A Matter of Adaptation," in *Perspectives on Orson Welles*, ed. Morris Beja (New York: G. K. Hall, 1995), pp. 262–63.
75. Franklin Mitchell, Jack Kessler, and Eric Howlett, *35 Eventful Years: 1922–1957* (Detroit: WJR, 1957), vinyl record XTV 26363, side 2. See also Katharine Seymour and John T. W. Martin, *Practical Radio Writing: The Technique of Writing for Broadcasting Simply and Thoroughly Explained* (London: Longmans, Green, 1938), p. 196; Maltin, *Great American Broadcast*, p. 215; Verma, *Theater of the Mind*, p. 66; White, *News on the Air*, pp. 249–50, 264–97.
76. Brown, *Manipulating the Ether*, p. 152.
77. "Radio Skit Causes an Earhart Mix-Up," *New York Times*, July 10, 1937, p. 7. See also Brown, *Manipulating the Ether*, p. 200.
78. Barnouw, *Golden Web*, pp. 51–52. Chase, *Sound and Fury*, pp. 232–33.
79. See Barnouw, *Tower in Babel*, pp. 277–78; Brown, *Manipulating the Ether*, pp. 150–52; Dunning, *On the Air*, pp. 434–37; Elson, *Time Inc.*, pp. 175–85; Fielding, *March of Time*, pp. 8–19.
80. See Brown, *Manipulating the Ether*, pp. 152, 256.
81. *Crisis: A Report from the Columbia Broadcasting System* (New York: CBS, 1938), p. 5.

82. Barnouw, *Golden Web*, p. 79. Chase, *Sound and Fury*, pp. 153–54, 156–57. *Crisis*, pp. 5–8.

83. Brown, *Manipulating the Ether*, p. 161. *Crisis*, p. 2.

84. Brown, *Manipulating the Ether*, p. 167. For a timetable of CBS's news broadcasts during the Czech crisis, see *Crisis*, pp. 164–73.

85. Margaret Reid to the FCC, Nov. 1, 1938, box 238, NARA. Hadley Cantril with Hazel Gaudet and Herta Herzog, *The Invasion from Mars: A Study in the Psychology of Panic* (New York: Harper & Row, 1966), pp. 159–61.

86. Cherie Burns, *The Great Hurricane: 1938* (New York: Atlantic Monthly Press, 2005), pp. 52–54, 77–78, 156–57, 165–66, 169–171, 200, 204–206, 209.

87. Robert W. [unclear] to the Federal Radio Commission [sic], Oct. 31, 1938, box 238, NARA. See also Mrs. G. Nesbith to the Federal Radio Commission [sic], Nov. 1, 1938; Gordon G. Macintosh to the FCC, Nov. 5, 1938; Loretta Place to Franklin D. Roosevelt, Oct. 30, 1938, all box 238, NARA; Harold Greenhalgh to Orson Welles, Oct. 30, 1938, box 24, "New York (state)" folder 1 (36/54), Wilson-Welles Papers.

88. Burns, *Great Hurricane*, p. 213.

89. *Crisis*, p. 144.

90. Barnouw, *Golden Web*, p. 80.

91. Brown, *Manipulating the Ether*, pp. 168–69. Douglas, *Listening In*, pp. 161–62.

92. Barnouw, *Golden Web*, pp. 80–83. Brown, *Manipulating the Ether*, p. 171. Chase, *Sound and Fury*, pp. 172–74. *Crisis*, pp. 2–3. Fang, *Commentators!*, p. 34. White, *News on the Air*, pp. 46–47.

93. *Crisis*, pp. 158, 162.

2. Winged Mercury

1. Eleanor B. Craig to Orson Welles, Nov. 1, 1938, box 24, "New York, NYC & boroughs" folder 2 (34/54), Wilson-Welles Papers.

2. John Houseman, *Run-Through: A Memoir* (New York: Simon & Schuster, 1972), pp. 144–45.

3. Houseman, *Run-Through*, pp. 15, 63–145.

4. Jonathan Rosenbaum, "Welles' Career: A Chronology," in Orson Welles and Peter Bogdanovich, *This Is Orson Welles*, ed. Jonathan Rosenbaum (New York: Da Capo Press, 1998), p. 326.

5. Alva Johnston and Fred Smith, "How to Raise a Child: The Education of Orson Welles, Who Didn't Need It," *Saturday Evening Post*, vol. 212, no. 30 (Jan. 20, 1940), p. 9.

6. Quoted in Barbara Leaming, *Orson Welles: A Biography* (New York: Viking, 1985), p. 8.

7. Simon Callow, *Orson Welles: The Road to Xanadu* (New York: Viking, 1995), pp. 21–22.

8. Rosenbaum, "Welles' Career," p. 327.

9. Paul Heyer, *The Medium and the Magician: Orson Welles, the Radio Years, 1934–1952* (Lanham, Md: Rowman & Littlefield, 2005), p. 7. Todd Tarbox, *Orson Welles and Roger Hill: A Friendship in Three Acts* (Albany, Ga.: BearManor Media, 2013), p. 270.

10. Hugh Curran, "Chicago Boy Makes Hit as Irish Actor," *Chicago Daily Tribune*, Nov. 29, 1931, p. C16.

11. Callow, *Road to Xanadu*, pp. 151–54, 185–90.

12. Houseman, *Run-Through*, pp. 147–52.

13. Ibid., pp. 152–65. Frank Brady, *Citizen Welles: A Biography of Orson Welles* (New York: Scribner, 1989), pp. 69–70. Callow, *Road to Xanadu*, pp. 200–204.

14. Brady, *Citizen Welles*, pp. 70–71. Callow, *Road to Xanadu*, pp. 200, 204–205.

15. Brady, *Citizen Welles*, pp. 70–71. Leaming, *Orson Welles*, p. 93.

16. "Life . . . on the Air!," *Life*, July 11, 1938, p. 65. Brady, *Citizen Welles*, pp. 74–75. Welles and Bogdanovich, *This Is Orson Welles*, p. 75. Francis Chase, Jr., *Sound and Fury: An Informal History of Broadcasting* (New York: Harper & Brothers, 1942), p. 203.

17. Welles and Bogdanovich, *This Is Orson Welles*, p. 74. Rosenbaum, "Welles' Career," p. 340.

18. Callow, *Road to Xanadu*, p. 205. Leaming, *Orson Welles*, pp. 93, 120–21. Welles and Bogdanovich, *This Is Orson Welles*, pp. 10–11.

19. Houseman, *Run-Through*, pp. 361–62. Richard Barr, interviewed by Frank Beacham, p. 6, box 14, "*Theatre of the Imagination* (1988). Interviews [transcripts]. 1988" folder, Wilson-Welles Papers. Leonard Maltin, *The Great American Broadcast: A Celebration of Radio's Golden Age* (New York: Dutton, 1997), pp. 216, 226.

20. Michael Hiltzik, *The New Deal: A Modern History* (New York: Free Press, 2011), pp. 285–95. Houseman, *Run-Through*, pp. 173–74. Robert S. McElvaine, *The Great Depression: America, 1929–1941* (New York: Three Rivers Press, 1993), pp. 264–72.

21. Callow, *Road to Xanadu*, pp. 216–19. Hiltzik, *New Deal*, pp. 294–98. Houseman, *Run-Through*, pp. 174–75. McElvaine, *Great Depression*, pp. 272–74.

22. Callow, *Road to Xanadu*, pp. 219–22. Hiltzik, *New Deal*, pp. 298–99. Houseman, *Run-Through*, pp. 175–85. McElvaine, *Great Depression*, pp. 272–73.

23. Hiltzik, *New Deal*, pp. 290, 298–99. Houseman, *Run-Through*, pp. 172, 175, 181, 185–86.

24. Houseman, *Run-Through*, pp. 185–86, 189–97. Leaming, *Orson Welles*, pp. 102–104.

25. Houseman, *Run-Through*, pp. 198–200.

26. Ibid., pp. 200–202. Brady, *Citizen Welles*, pp. 88–90. Callow, *Road to Xanadu*, pp. 236–43.

27. Houseman, *Run-Through*, pp. 206–209.

28. Houseman, *Run-Through*, pp. 231–41. Callow, *Road to Xanadu*, pp. 266–82. Charles Higham, *Orson Welles: The Rise and Fall of an American Genius* (New York: St. Martin's, 1985), pp. 90–91. Welles described the effects behind his *Faustus* in his unproduced autobiographical screenplay *The Cradle Will Rock*, written shortly before his death (Orson Welles, *The Cradle Will Rock: An Original Screenplay* [Santa Barbara: Santa Teresa Press, 1994], pp. 18–20).

29. Quoted in Callow, *Road to Xanadu*, p. 272.

30. Ibid., pp. 284–85. Welles and Bogdanovich, *This Is Orson Welles*, pp. 12–13.

31. Leaming, *Orson Welles*, p. 121. Welles and Bogdanovich, *This Is Orson Welles*, p. 11. Orson Welles, interviewed by Leslie Megahey, in *The Orson Welles Story*, BBC, 1982, in *Orson Welles: Interviews*, ed. Mark W. Estrin (Jackson: University Press of Mississippi, 2002), p. 181. Geraldine Fitzgerald interview, Feb. 24, 1988, p. 5, box 14, "*Theatre of the Imagination* (1988). Interviews [transcripts]. 1988" folder, Wilson-Welles Papers.

32. Callow, *Road to Xanadu*, p. 283. Higham, *Orson Welles*, pp. 90–91. Leaming, *Orson Welles*, pp. 120–21.

33. Heyer, *Medium and Magician*, pp. 25–29. Anthony Tollin, "Spotlight on the Shadow: 'On the Air,'" in *The Shadow #4: "The Murder Master" & "The Hydra"* (Encinitas, Calif.: Nostalgia Ventures, 2007), pp. 62–65.

34. Orson Welles to Virginia Welles, n.d., box 1, "Correspondence. Orson Welles to Virginia Nicolson, 1937–1939. (3 of 7)" folder, Welles-Feder Collection. Welles and Bogdanovich, *This Is Orson Welles*, p. 11.

35. Brady, *Citizen Welles*, p. 78. Callow, *Road to Xanadu*, p. 321. Leaming, *Orson Welles*, p. 153. Heyer, *Medium and Magician*, p. 27. Welles and Bogdanovich, *This Is Orson Welles*, p. 11. "The White Legion," *The Shadow*, Mutual Broadcasting System (New York: WOR, March 20, 1938), in *The Story of The Shadow* (Radio Spirits, 1985), CD, disc 3.

36. May Greene to Orson Welles, Nov. 3, 1938, box 24, "Pennsylvania" folder 1 (42/54), Wilson-Welles Papers.

37. Houseman, *Run-Through*, p. 362. Callow, *Road to Xanadu*, pp. 204–205, 373–74, 378–79.

38. William Alland, interviewed by Frank Beacham, April 12, 1988, p. 3, box 14, "*Theatre of the Imagination* (1988). Interviews [transcripts]. 1988" folder, Wilson-Welles Papers.

39. Barnouw, *Golden Web*, pp. 65–66. John Dunning, *On the Air: The Encyclopedia of Old-Time Radio* (New York: Oxford University Press, 1998), pp. 169–71. Heyer, *Medium and Magician*, p. 32.

40. Dunning, *On the Air*, p. 171. Rosenbaum, "Welles' Career," pp. 332, 337.

41. Houseman, *Run-Through*, pp. 365–66. Rosenbaum, "Welles' Career," p. 332.
42. Barnouw, *Golden Web*, pp. 66–69. Brady, *Citizen Welles*, pp. 106–109. Dunning, *On the Air*, pp. 170–71. Bruce Lenthall, *Radio's America: The Great Depression and the Rise of Modern Mass Culture* (Chicago: University of Chicago Press, 2007), pp. 180–81. Heyer, *Medium and Magician*, pp. 29–32. Neil Verma, *Theater of the Mind: Imagination, Aesthetics, and American Radio Drama* (Chicago: University of Chicago Press, 2012), pp. 17–21.
43. Heyer, *Medium and Magician*, pp. 30–31.
44. Lenthall, *Radio's America*, p. 180.
45. Harry M. Geduld, "Welles or Wells?—A Matter of Adaptation," in *Perspectives on Orson Welles*, ed. Morris Beja (New York: G. K. Hall, 1995), p. 261.
46. Houseman, *Run-Through*, pp. 245–50.
47. Houseman, *Run-Through*, pp. 248–56. Callow, *Road to Xanadu*, pp. 293–95. Hiltzik, *New Deal*, pp. 302–304.
48. Quoted in Leaming, *Orson Welles*, p. 135.
49. "Steel Strike Opera Is Put Off by WPA," *New York Times*, June 17, 1937, pp. 1, 4. Houseman, *Run-Through*, pp. 264–74. Callow, *Road to Xanadu*, pp. 296–98.
50. Quoted in Brady, *Citizen Welles*, p. 116.
51. "Steel Strike Opera," pp. 1, 4. Houseman, *Run-Through*, pp. 274–79. Callow, *Road to Xanadu*, pp. 301–302.
52. Welles told both Peter Bogdanovich and Barbara Leaming that he had once played himself in an episode of *The March of Time*, but he gave different accounts of the event to each. He claimed to Bogdanovich that the episode in question had covered his "Voodoo *Macbeth*" (Welles and Bogdanovich, *This Is Orson Welles*, p. 74). He told Leaming that the show had been about *The Cradle Will Rock* (*Orson Welles*, p. 513). It's doubtful that Welles played himself on *The March of Time* more than once, and the version he told to Leaming seems most probable. *Macbeth* occurred before Welles became a regular on *The March of Time* (see Rosenbaum, "Welles' Career," pp. 334–40), and *Cradle* was a much bigger news event.
53. Callow, *Road to Xanadu*, p. 304. Heyer, *Medium and Magician*, pp. 34–35. Verma, *Theater of the Mind*, p. 60.
54. Callow, *Road to Xanadu*, pp. 304–306. Heyer, *Medium and Magician*, pp. 34–37. Interview with Richard Wilson, in *Theatre of the Imagination: The Mercury Company Remembers*, audio documentary written and produced by Frank Beacham, narrated by Leonard Maltin (Santa Monica: Voyager Company, 1988), in *Theatre of the Imagination: Radio Stories by Orson Welles and the Mercury Theatre* laserdisc, side 2, analog track 2, chap. 14. Additional material from William Alland, interviewed by Frank Beacham, April 12, 1988, p. 6, box 14, "*Theatre of the Imagination* (1988). Interviews [transcripts]. 1988" folder, Wilson-Welles Papers. John Gosling, *Waging the War of the Worlds: A History of the 1938 Radio Broadcast and Resulting Panic* (Jefferson, N.C.: McFarland, 2009), p. 41.
55. Houseman, *Run-Through*, pp. 280–87. Callow, *Road to Xanadu*, pp. 306–308.
56. Orson Welles and John Houseman, "Plan for a New Theatre," *New York Times*, Aug. 29, 1937, sect. 10, p. 1.
57. Houseman, *Run-Through*, pp. 286–313.
58. Ibid., pp. 309–13.
59. Brooks Atkinson, "The Play," *New York Times*, Nov. 12, 1937, p. 26.
60. Richard Watts, Jr., "The Theaters," *New York Herald Tribune*, Nov. 12, 1937, p. 22.
61. Houseman, *Run-Through*, pp. 315–21; quote on p. 321.
62. "The Theatre: Marvelous Boy," *Time*, May 9, 1938, p. 34.
63. Houseman, *Run-Through*, pp. 354–55, 359–60. Callow, *Road to Xanadu*, pp. 370–72.
64. "Orson Welles, Mercury Theater [sic] to Present Nine 1-Hour CBS Broadcasts," Columbia Broadcasting System press release (New York, N.Y., June 8, 1938), box 7, folder 22,

Welles mss. Houseman (*Run-Through*, pp. 360-61) reports that Welles accepted CBS's offer less than two weeks before their debut. But here, as perhaps elsewhere, he embroidered the facts.

65. Quoted in Richard B. O'Brien, "'The Shadow' Talks," *New York Times*, Aug. 14, 1938, p. 136.
66. Chase, *Sound and Fury*, p. 204.
67. See Callow, *Road to Xanadu*, pp. 372-73.
68. Brady, *Citizen Welles*, pp. 138-39. Houseman (*Run-Through*, pp. 362-63) claims this change occurred just three days before airtime, and describes a seventeen-hour writing session at Reuben's Restaurant where he and Welles slapped a script together. As thrilling as this story is, it seems highly unlikely. For one thing, CBS announced the switch in a press release about a week before the show aired ("'Dracula' to Inaugurate Orson Welles's 'First Person Singular' Series," Columbia Broadcasting System press release [New York, July 5, 1938], box 7, folder 22, Welles mss.) For another, it seems that Welles had been planning to use *Dracula* as the second *First Person Singular* broadcast for some time (see "Me, Myself and I," *Radio Guide*, July 16, 1938, p. 3). This suggests that they were not as unprepared as Houseman implies. Finally, in the recorded interviews that would make up the book *This Is Orson Welles*, Welles talked extensively with Peter Bogdanovich about *Dracula* (the novel, the stage play, and the Mercury radio show) but never alluded to the marathon writing session (Orson Welles, interviewed by Peter Bogdanovich, in *This Is Orson Welles* [New York: Harper Audio, 1992], tape 4, side 7; see also Welles and Bogdanovich, *This Is Orson Welles*, pp. 13-14). Houseman's (sometimes unreliable) memoir is the only source for this anecdote.
69. Callow, *Road to Xanadu*, pp. 377-80. Heyer, *Medium and Magician*, pp. 53-57. Verma, *Theater of the Mind*, p. 60.
70. Welles and Bogdanovich, *This Is Orson Welles*, p. 13. See Edward J. Gelbuth to Orson Welles, Nov. 1, 1938, box 24, "No Location" folder; Hume V. Stephani to Orson Welles, Nov. 4, 1938, box 24, "No Location" folder; John M. Loving to Orson Wells [sic], Nov. 3, 1938, box 24, "Texas" folder (48/54), all Wilson-Welles Papers.
71. Tim Price to Orson Welles, Oct. 31, 1938, box 24, "Oregon" folder (41/54), Wilson-Welles Papers.
72. John Houseman, interviewed by Leonard Maltin, April 22, 1988, p. 4, box 14, "Theatre of the Imagination (1988). Interviews [transcripts]. 1988" folder, Wilson-Welles Papers. See also William Alland, interviewed by Frank Beacham, April 12, 1988, p. 7, box 14, "Theatre of the Imagination (1988). Interviews [transcripts]. 1988" folder, Wilson-Welles Papers.
73. Houseman, *Run-Through*, pp. 368-69, 390-93. Callow, *Road to Xanadu*, pp. 376-77. Interview with John Houseman, in *Theatre of the Imagination: The Mercury Company Remembers*, audio documentary written and produced by Frank Beacham, narrated by Leonard Maltin (Santa Monica: Voyager Company, 1988), in *Theatre of the Imagination: Radio Stories by Orson Welles and the Mercury Theatre* laserdisc, side 2, analog track 2, chap. 14.
74. Maltin, *Great American Broadcast*, pp. 82-83.
75. Houseman, *Run-Through*, pp. 369, 391-92. Callow, *Road to Xanadu*, p. 377.
76. Houseman, *Run-Through*, pp. 369-71. William Alland, interviewed by Frank Beacham, April 12, 1988, page 6, box 14, "Theatre of the Imagination (1988). Interviews [transcripts]. 1988" folder, Wilson-Welles Papers.
77. Houseman, *Run-Through*, p. 371. Interview with John Houseman, in *Theatre of the Imagination: The Mercury Company Remembers*, audio documentary written and produced by Frank Beacham, narrated by Leonard Maltin (Santa Monica: Voyager Company, 1988), in *Theatre of the Imagination: Radio Stories by Orson Welles and the Mercury Theatre* laserdisc, side 2, analog track 2, chap. 14.

78. Callow, *Road to Xanadu*, pp. 387–88. Houseman (*Run-Through*, pp. 370–71) relates a similar anecdote about adding an extended speech to the Mercury's broadcast of *The Man Who Was Thursday* because it ran sixteen minutes short, but he either misremembered the *Treasure Island* incident or embroidered the facts again. Surviving recordings of *The Man Who Was Thursday* do not include the speech Houseman described.

79. Houseman, *Run-Through*, p. 390.

80. Ibid., pp. 369, 390–94. Callow, *Road to Xanadu*, pp. 376–77.

81. Houseman, *Run-Through*, pp. 356–59, 372–74. Brady, *Citizen Welles*, pp. 144–50. Callow, *Road to Xanadu*, pp. 383–85. For decades, the film segments of *Too Much Johnson* were thought lost in a fire in Welles's Spanish home. But they were rediscovered in Italy in 2008. Restored to near perfection by George Eastman House of Rochester, New York, the film portions of *Too Much Johnson* made their long-delayed debut in October 2013, seventy-five years after they were shot. See Dave Kehr, "Early Film by Orson Welles Is Rediscovered," *New York Times*, Aug. 7, 2013, www.nytimes.com/2013/08/11/movies/early-film-by-orson-welles-is-rediscovered.html (accessed Feb. 18, 2014).

82. Houseman, *Run-Through*, pp. 375–78. Brady, *Citizen Welles*, pp. 150–51. Callow, *Road to Xanadu*, pp. 386–87.

83. Callow, *Road to Xanadu*, p. 389. Welles, interviewed by Bogdanovich, in *This Is Orson Welles*, tape 4, side 7.

84. Houseman, *Run-Through*, pp. 370–71. Callow, *Road to Xanadu*, pp. 387–89.

85. Susan J. Douglas, *Listening In: Radio and the American Imagination* (Minneapolis: University of Minnesota Press, 2004), pp. 119–20. Gosling, *Waging the War*, pp. 70–71.

86. Leaming, *Orson Welles*, p. 159. Callow, *Road to Xanadu*, pp. 371–72.

87. Brady, *Citizen Welles*, p. 161.

88. Clementine Wein to Orson Wells [*sic*], Nov. 6, 1938, box 23, "Illinois" folder (12/54), Wilson-Welles Papers.

89. Margaret Morris to Orson Welles, Nov. 18, 1938, box 23, "Illinois" folder (12/54), Wilson-Welles Papers.

90. "turgid": George Coulouris, quoted in Callow, *Road to Xanadu*, p. 391. "a piece of shit": Martin Gabel, quoted in Leaming, *Orson Welles*, p. 157.

91. Houseman, *Run-Through*, pp. 378–88.

92. John Houseman, introduction to Howard Koch, *As Time Goes By: Memoirs of a Writer* (New York: Harcourt Brace Jovanovich, 1979), pp. xi–xiii. John Houseman, interviewed by Leonard Maltin, April 22, 1988, pp. 2–3, box 14, "Theatre of the Imagination (1988). Interviews [transcripts]. 1988" folder, Wilson-Welles Papers. Howard Koch deposition, June 7, 1960, in Transcript of Record, *Orson Welles v. Columbia Broadcasting System, Inc., et al.*, U.S. Court of Appeals, 9th Circuit, Vol. 3264, No. 17518 (1962), pp. 252, 256, 269–70.

93. Howard Koch, *The Panic Broadcast: Portrait of an Event* (Boston: Little, Brown, 1970), pp. 12–13. Houseman, introduction to Koch, *As Time Goes By*, p. xiii. Houseman, *Run-Through*, p. 390.

94. Howard Koch, "Orson Welles—Some Reminiscences," in *Orson Welles on the Air: The Radio Years* (New York: Museum of Broadcasting, 1988), p. 29. Houseman, introduction to Koch, *As Time Goes By*, p. xiii.

95. Orson Welles deposition, July 8, 1960, in Transcript of Record, *Orson Welles v. CBS*, pp. 67, 69–73, quoted on 70–71. Houseman, *Run-Through*, 392. For Stewart's role in the Mercury broadcasts, see Callow, *Road to Xanadu*, 376–77; Welles, interviewed by Bogdanovich, *This Is Orson Welles*, tape 4, side 7. There has been some debate over the source of the news bulletin conceit for *War of the Worlds*. Callow (*Road to Xanadu*, pp. 398–99) and David Thomson (*Rosebud: The Story of Orson Welles* [New York: Vintage Books,

1996], p. 100) wrongly credit Houseman with the newscast style; Higham (*Orson Welles*, p. 124) gives credit to Koch; and Gosling (*Waging the War*, p. 33) sees "no consensus" in determining its source. But Houseman and Koch both publicly gave credit to Welles for the fake news idea, and the concept is entirely consistent with Welles's creative modus operandi before and after the broadcast. There should, therefore, be no doubt that Welles decided to do *War of the Worlds* as a series of fake news bulletins, but was not otherwise involved until the day of the broadcast itself. See Houseman, introduction to Koch, *As Time Goes By*, p. xiii; Koch, *As Time Goes By*, p. 3; Howard Koch, interviewed by Joe Bevilacqua, in *We Take You Now to Grover's Mill: The Making of the War of the Worlds Broadcast* (Napanoch, N.Y.: Waterlogg Productions, 2011); Howard Koch to C. A. Wilson, June 25, 1975, box 6, folder 6-4, Howard E. Koch Papers, Wisconsin Historical Society, Madison, Wisc.

96. Houseman, *Run-Through*, pp. 392–93. Koch deposition, in Transcript of Record, *Welles v. CBS*, p. 165. See also Houseman, interviewed by Bevilacqua, in *We Take You Now to Grover's Mill*.

97. Houseman, *Run-Through*, pp. 392–93. Koch, "Orson Welles—Some Reminiscences," p. 29.

98. Houseman, *Run-Through*, p. 393.

99. Ibid.

100. John Houseman, "The Men from Mars," *Harper's Magazine*, Dec. 1948, p. 76.

101. Houseman, *Run-Through*, p. 393.

102. Koch, *Panic Broadcast*, p. 13.

103. Houseman, *Run-Through*, p. 393.

3. Martians of the Mind's Eye

1. Abner I. Weisman to Orson Welles, Oct. 31, 1938, box 24, "New York, NYC & boroughs" folder 2 (34/54), Wilson-Welles Papers.

2. H. G. Wells, *Experiment in Autobiography: Discoveries and Conclusions of a Very Ordinary Brain (Since 1866)* (New York: Macmillan, 1934), pp. 457–58. David Y. Hughes and Harry M. Geduld, eds., *A Critical Edition of The War of the Worlds: H. G. Wells's Scientific Romance* (Bloomington: Indiana University Press, 1993), p. 1.

3. John R. Hammond, *H. G. Wells's The Time Machine: A Reference Guide* (Westport, Conn.: Greenwood, 2004), p. 48.

4. John Gosling, *Waging the War of the Worlds: A History of the 1938 Radio Broadcast and Resulting Panic* (Jefferson, N.C.: McFarland, 2009), pp. 13–14. Brian Holmsten and Alex Lubertozzi, eds., *The War of the Worlds: Mars' Invasion of Earth, Inciting Panic and Inspiring Terror from H. G. Wells to Orson Welles and Beyond* (Naperville, Ill.: Sourcebooks, 2001), p. 102. Eric S. Rabkin, *Mars: A Tour of the Human Imagination* (Westport, Conn.: Praeger, 2005), p. 105. For the political dimensions of *War of the Worlds*, see Leon Stover, introduction to H. G. Wells, *The War of the Worlds: A Critical Text of the 1898 London First Edition, with an Introduction, Illustrations and Appendices*, ed. Leon Stover (Jefferson, N.C.: McFarland, 2001), pp. 1–46.

5. Gosling, *Waging the War*, p. 13. Wells, *The War of the Worlds: Critical Text*, pp. 55–56. Hughes and Geduld, p. 198, n. 16. See also David Goodman: *Radio's Civic Ambition: American Broadcasting and Democracy in the 1930s* (Oxford: Oxford University Press, 2011), p. 253.

6. Quoted in Hughes and Geduld, p. 1.

7. Ibid., p. 1. On anticolonialism in *War of the Worlds*, see Harry M. Geduld, "Welles or Wells?—A Matter of Adaptation," in *Perspectives on Orson Welles*, ed. Morris Beja (New York: G. K. Hall, 1995), p. 268; Gosling, *Waging the War*, pp. 13–14; Holmsten and Lubertozzi, eds., *War of the Worlds*, p. 78; Rabkin, *Mars*, pp. 108–109, note.

8. Wells, *War of the Worlds: Critical Text*, p. 49.

9. H. G. Wells, "Preface to the Atlantic Edition (1924)," in *War of the Worlds: Critical Text*, p. 284.

10. See Wells, *War of the Worlds: Critical Text*, p. 191, n. 137.

11. See ibid., pp. 57-58, 61, 67, 86, 134-35, 191, 247. The article Wells wrote himself (referenced at ibid., p. 191), which prefigures his description of the Martians' anatomy, is reprinted as appendix I of Stover's critical text of *The War of the Worlds* (H. G. Wells, "The Man of the Year Million," in ibid., pp. 257-63).

12. Holmsten and Lubertozzi, eds., *War of the Worlds*, p. 104. Quote is from Wells, *Experiment in Autobiography*, p. 458.

13. Gosling, *Waging the War*, pp. 14-15.

14. Wells, "Preface to Atlantic Edition (1924)," p. 284.

15. Gosling, *Waging the War*, pp. 7-8. Rabkin, *Mars*, pp. 83-85.

16. Gosling, *Waging the War*, pp. 8-9. Rabkin, *Mars*, p. 93.

17. Gosling, *Waging the War*, p. 9. Rabkin, *Mars*, pp. 96-103.

18. Gosling, *Waging the War*, p. 9. Rabkin, *Mars*, pp. 94-95.

19. See Wells, *War of the Worlds: Critical Text*, p. 54.

20. Gosling, *Waging the War*, p. 33.

21. H. Gordon Garbedian, "Mars Poses Its Riddle of Life," *New York Times*, Dec. 9, 1928, p. SM1. See also Waldemar Kaempffert, "Life on Other Planets? Science Still Asks," *New York Times*, July 31, 1938, p. 102; Charles Sweeney, Jr., to Orson Welles, Oct. 31, 1938, box 23, "Delaware" folder (7/54); Anonymous to Orson Welles, Nov. 2, 1938, box 24, "Rhode Island" folder (44/54); H. E. Sanders to Orson Welles, Nov. 11, 1938, box 23, "Kentucky" folder (16/54), all Wilson-Welles Papers; Lillian M. Davenport to Frank R. McNinch, Nov. 2, 1938, box 237, NARA.

22. Howard Koch, *The Panic Broadcast: Portrait of an Event* (Boston: Little, Brown, 1970), p. 13.

23. Raymond Fischer to WABC, Oct. 30, 1938, box 24, "New Jersey" folder 2 (30/54), Wilson-Welles Papers.

24. See Koch, *Panic Broadcast*, p. 15.

25. John Houseman, *Run-Through: A Memoir* (New York: Simon & Schuster, 1972), p. 393. See also John Houseman, interviewed by Leonard Maltin, April 22, 1988, p. 5, box 14, "*Theatre of the Imagination* (1988). Interviews [transcripts]. 1988" folder, Wilson-Welles Papers.

26. Howard Koch deposition, June 7, 1960, in Transcript of Record, *Orson Welles v. Columbia Broadcasting System, Inc., et al.*, U.S. Court of Appeals, 9th Circuit, Vol. 3264, No. 17518 (1962), pp. 147-51, 165-66. Howard Koch to Nicholas Meyer, March 5, 1975, and Howard Koch to C. A. Wilson, June 25, 1975, box 6, folder 6-4, both in Howard E. Koch Papers, Wisconsin Historical Society, Madison, Wisc. See also John Houseman and Howard Koch, interviewed by Joe Bevilacqua, in *We Take You Now to Grover's Mill: The Making of the War of the Worlds Broadcast* (Napanoch, N.Y.: Waterlogg Productions, 2011). For examples of Koch's original manuscript pages of the *War of the Worlds* script, see "*Invasion from Mars* radio broadcast: Working script with original msc. Pages, 1938," box 1, folder 1-3, Howard E. Koch Papers, Wisconsin Historical Society, Madison, Wisc.

27. Koch, *Panic Broadcast*, pp. 12, 15.

28. Houseman, *Run-Through*, p. 393.

29. Koch donated two drafts of the broadcast's script to the University of Wisconsin, Madison, in 1964, which he described in an accompanying letter as "a work script of the radio play" and "a final script as it was broadcast." These are now preserved at the Wisconsin Historical Society in Madison. Although it is impossible to say for sure, it seems likely that the "working script," or one very much like it, was the draft recorded

at the Mercury's Thursday rehearsal. It follows the Wells novel even more closely than the broadcast version, with a couple of scenes, in which Pierson meets the deranged curate and witnesses the Martians feeding on humans, that were cut from the final version ("Working script," pp. 31–36). Howard Koch to David M. Knauf, Jan. 5, 1964, box 1, folder 1-1, Howard E. Koch Papers, Wisconsin Historical Society, Madison. Howard Koch, "*Invasion from Mars* radio broadcast: Final script, 1938, Oct. 30," folder 1-2, and "Working script," box 1, folder 1-3, both in Howard E. Koch Papers, Wisconsin Historical Society, Madison, Wisc.

30. See John Houseman, interviewed by Leonard Maltin, April 22, 1988, p. 5, box 14, "*Theatre of the Imagination* (1988). Interviews [transcripts]. 1988" folder, Wilson-Welles Papers; Houseman and Koch, interviewed by Bevilacqua, in *We Take You Now to Grover's Mill*.

31. Simon Callow, *Orson Welles: The Road to Xanadu* (New York: Viking, 1995), pp. 222–23, 380, 389–90.

32. See Holmsten and Lubertozzi, eds., *War of the Worlds*, p. 21.

33. Quoted in Frank Brady, *Citizen Welles: A Biography of Orson Welles* (New York: Scribner, 1989), p. 143.

34. Ibid., pp. 159–60. Houseman, *Run-Through*, p. 392. Joseph Bulgatz, *Ponzi Schemes, Invaders from Mars & More Extraordinary Popular Delusions and the Madness of Crowds* (New York: Harmony Books, 1992), p. 127. Paul Heyer, *The Medium and the Magician: Orson Welles, the Radio Years, 1934–1952* (Lanham, Md.: Rowman & Littlefield, 2005), pp. 66–67.

35. See Welles's comments in Orson Welles, interviewed by Edward R. Murrow, *Person to Person*, CBS, Nov. 25, 1955, Paley Center Collection for Colleges, catalog ID T86:1589; Orson Welles, interviewed by Leslie Megahey, *The Orson Welles Story*, BBC, 1982, in *Orson Welles: Interviews*, ed. Mark W. Estrin (Jackson: University Press of Mississippi, 2002), p. 181. See also Brady, *Citizen Welles*, pp. 164–66; Robert J. Brown, *Manipulating the Ether: The Power of Broadcast Radio in Thirties America*, (Jefferson, N.C.: McFarland, 1998) pp. 224–27. Gosling, *Waging the War*, pp. 78–85; Holmsten and Lubertozzi, eds., *War of the Worlds*, pp. 20–22.

36. See John Houseman, "The Men from Mars," *Harper's Magazine*, Dec. 1948, p. 74; David A. Crespy, *Richard Barr: The Playwright's Producer* (Carbondale: Southern Illinois University Press, 2013), p. 16; Richard Barr, interviewed by Frank Beacham, p. 2, box 14, "*Theatre of the Imagination* (1988). Interviews [transcripts]. 1988" folder, Wilson-Welles Papers; Koch, *Panic Broadcast*, pp. 11–16, 24; William Alland, interviewed in *The Battle Over Citizen Kane* (1996), *American Experience* (WGBH Boston), *Citizen Kane* DVD, disc 2, directed by Michael Epstein and Thomas Lennon (Atlanta: Turner Home Entertainment, 2001); Edward Oxford, "Night of the Martians," *American History Illustrated*, vol. 23, no. 6 (Oct. 1988), p. 48; Gosling, *Waging the War*, p. 84.

37. John Houseman, interviewed by Leonard Maltin, April 22, 1988, p. 9, box 14, "*Theatre of the Imagination* (1988). Interviews [transcripts]. 1988" folder, Wilson-Welles Papers. For probably the earliest instance of this claim, see Barbara Leaming, *Orson Welles: A Biography* (New York: Viking, 1985), p. 159. See also *The Battle Over Citizen Kane* (1996).

38. See Geduld, "Welles or Wells?," pp. 262–65.

39. "The Death Triangle," *The Shadow*, Mutual Broadcasting System (New York: WOR, Dec. 12, 1937), CD (Radio Spirits). Anthony Tollin, "A Chronology of 'The Shadow' Radio Broadcasts," in *The Shadow Scrapbook*, ed. Walter B. Gibson (New York: Harcourt Brace Jovanovich, 1979), p. 84. Heyer, *Medium and Magician*, p. 28.

40. Ralph Rogers, *Dos and Don'ts of Radio Writing*, quoted in Geduld, "Welles or Wells?," p. 262.

41. Brady, *Citizen Welles*, p. 165. Callow, *Road to Xanadu*, p. 400. Gosling, *Waging the War*, p. 37. Heyer, *Medium and Magician*, pp. 90–91.

42. Archibald MacLeish, *Three Short Plays* (New York: Dramatists Play Service, 1961), p. 39. Bruce Lenthall, *Radio's America: The Great Depression and the Rise of Modern Mass Culture* (Chicago: University of Chicago Press, 2007), p. 197.

43. Brady, *Citizen Welles*, p. 165.

44. This photograph is reproduced in Irving Settel, *A Pictorial History of Radio* (New York: Grosset & Dunlap, 1967), p. 102. Another photograph from the same session, featuring Welles, Robson, and MacLeish, is printed in Todd Tarbox, *Orson Welles and Roger Hill: A Friendship in Three Acts* (Albany, Ga.: BearManor Media, 2013), p. 54, but the author incorrectly identifies it as from a rehearsal of *The Fall of the City* in 1937. Robson directed *Air Raid*, but Irving Reis directed *The Fall of the City*.

45. In the interview with Bogdanovich, Welles got the date of this broadcast wrong, but the reference is clear (Orson Welles, interviewed by Peter Bogdanovich, *This Is Orson Welles* [New York: Harper Audio, 1992], tape 4, side 7).

46. John Houseman, interviewed by Leonard Maltin, April 22, 1988, p. 9, box 14, "Theatre of the Imagination (1988). Interviews [transcripts]. 1988" folder, Wilson-Welles Papers. Gosling (*Waging the War*, pp. 81–82) establishes that neither Welles nor Houseman could have heard this broadcast firsthand, but Houseman makes clear in his interview with Maltin that he recalled newspaper coverage of it. Welles, too, could have seen news articles about it in the American press, and its script had been published in 1928. (See Ronald A. Knox, *Essays in Satire* [London: Sheed & Ward, 1928], pp. 279–87.) Indeed, the broadcast appears to have been somewhat well known in the United States in 1938. Several newspapers referred to it in the aftermath of *War of the Worlds*, and *The Daily Princetonian* even described it as "famous" (See Ariel, "Armchair Audience: Disturbance on Mars," *Daily Princetonian*, Nov. 1, 1938, p. 2).

47. Milton Walsh, *Ronald Knox as Apologist: Wit, Laughter and the Popish Creed* (San Francisco: Ignatius Press, 2007), pp. 39–40. Paul Slade, "Holy Terror: The First Great Radio Hoax," www.planetslade.com/ronald-knox.html (accessed Feb. 12, 2013). Robert Speaight, *Ronald Knox: The Writer* (New York: Sheed & Ward, 1965), p. 107. David Rooney, *The Wine of Certitude: A Literary Biography of Ronald Knox* (San Francisco: Ignatius Press, 2009), pp. 181, 192–99, 207. Evelyn Waugh, *The Life of the Right Reverend Ronald Knox, Fellow of Trinity College, Oxford, and Protonotary Apostolic to His Holiness Pope Pius XII* (Bungay, Suffolk: Chapman & Hall, 1959), pp. 187–89 (on Sherlock Holmes, see p. 122).

48. Ronald Knox, *Broadcast Minds* (London: Sheed & Ward, 1932), pp. 5–19 (quote on p. 10). Rooney, *Wine of Certitude*, pp. 113–14. Slade, "Holy Terror."

49. Slade, "Holy Terror."

50. David Pat Walker, *The BBC in Scotland: The First Fifty Years* (Cornwall: MPG Books Ltd., 2011), p. 54. Waugh, *Life of Knox*, p. 189.

51. "Wireless Scare: Burlesque News Believed," *Manchester Guardian*, Jan. 18, 1926, p. 7. "Broadcasting: The Programmes," *The Times*, Jan. 16, 1926, p. 4.

52. No recording of the broadcast exists, but its script is reprinted in Knox, *Essays in Satire*, pp. 279–87.

53. "Father Knox's Saturday Night: 'The Revolution of 1926,'" *Manchester Guardian*, Jan. 19, 1926, p. 5. See also Knox, *Essays in Satire*, pp. 280–84.

54. "Father Knox's Saturday Night," p. 5. See also Knox, *Essays in Satire*, p. 285.

55. "Wireless Scare," p. 7.

56. "Father Knox's Saturday Night," p. 5. See also Knox, *Essays in Satire*, pp. 285–86.

57. "Father Knox's Saturday Night," p. 5. See also Knox, *Essays in Satire*, p. 287.

58. See "Broadcasting: The Programmes," p. 4; Joanna Bourke, *Fear: A Cultural History* (Emeryville, Calif.: Shoemaker & Hoard, 2005), p. 170.

59. Waugh, *Life of Knox*, p. 191. Bourke, *Fear*, p. 170.

60. Bourke, *Fear*, pp. 171–72. Slade, "Holy Terror."
61. Quoted in Slade, "Holy Terror."
62. "Father Knox's Wireless Talk: An Imaginary Revolution Explained," *The Times*, Jan. 18, 1926, p. 6. "Broadcast in 1926 Showed English Get Panicky, Too," *Baltimore Sun*, Nov. 1, 1938, p. 6. Bourke, *Fear*, pp. 170–71.
63. Quoted in "Wireless Scare," p. 7.
64. See Robert E. Bartholomew and Benjamin Radford, *The Martians Have Landed!: A History of Media-Driven Panics and Hoaxes* (Jefferson, N.C.: McFarland, 2012), pp. 13–15; Bourke, *Fear*, pp. 168–70; Hadley Cantril with Hazel Gaudet and Herta Herzog, *The Invasion from Mars: A Study in the Psychology of Panic* (New York: Harper & Row, 1966), pp. xvii–xxviii; Holmsten and Lubertozzi, eds., *War of the Worlds*, pp. 20–21; Slade, "Holy Terror."
65. Ernest Marshall, "Hoaxes and Politics Fail to Win Britain," *New York Times*, Jan. 24, 1926, p. E1. "Broadcast in 1926," p. 6.
66. Waugh, *Life of Knox*, p. 190. Bourke, *Fear*, p. 171.
67. Quoted in Bourke, *Fear*, p. 173. See also Bartholomew and Radford, *Martians*, p. 14. Walker, *BBC in Scotland*, p. 55.
68. Quoted in Bourke, *Fear*, p. 176.
69. Ibid., pp. 172–75. Slade, "Holy Terror." Bartholomew and Radford, *Martians*, pp. 13–14.
70. Margaret Morris, *The British General Strike 1926*, General Series Pamphlet No. 82 (London: Historical Association, 1973), pp. 5–9. Bartholomew and Radford, *Martians*, p. 13; Gosling, *Waging the War*, p. 81; Walker, *BBC in Scotland*, pp. 55–56.
71. See Bourke, *Fear*, pp. 176–78; Slade, "Holy Terror"; Walker, *BBC in Scotland*, p. 55.
72. Quoted in Slade, "Holy Terror." See also Walker, *BBC in Scotland*, p. 55.
73. Bourke, *Fear*, p. 177.
74. "Father Knox's Wireless Talk," p. 6. "Broadcast in 1926," p. 6. Slade, "Holy Terror."
75. "Topics of the Times," *New York Times*, Jan. 19, 1926, p. 26.
76. Slade, "Holy Terror."
77. Both quoted in Bourke, *Fear*, p. 176.
78. Raymond Snoddy, "Show That Sparked a Riot," *BBC NewsWatch*, June 13, 2005, http://news.bbc.co.uk/newswatch/ifs/hi/newsid_4080000/newsid_4081000/4081060.stm (accessed Jan. 30, 2014). Slade, "Holy Terror." See also Walker, *BBC in Scotland*, p. 55.
79. Slade, "Holy Terror."
80. Walker, *BBC in Scotland*, p. 55.
81. Snoddy, "Sparked a Riot." Slade, "Holy Terror."
82. Waugh, *Life of Knox*, p. 192.
83. Kate Lacey, "Assassination, Insurrection and Alien Invasion: Interwar Wireless Scares in Cross-National Comparison," in *War of the Worlds to Social Media: Mediated Communication in Times of Crisis*, ed. Joy Elizabeth Hayes, Kathleen Battles, and Wendy Hilton-Morrow (New York: Peter Lang, 2013), pp. 57–58, 64–65.
84. "'Contretemps' of a Berlin Broadcast," *The Times*, Sept. 27, 1930, p. 9.
85. Lacey, "Assassination," pp. 57–67.
86. Ibid., pp. 67–71.
87. The sound quality in the clip is poor, and the reporter claims that the show aired in Vienna, but it seems almost certain that he is referring to *Der Minister ist ermordet!* (The Digital Implosion, "George Orson Welles Apologizes for the War of the Worlds Broadcast [October 31 1938]," 7:06, YouTube, http://youtu.be/uuEGiruAFSw [accessed May 17, 2014].)
88. Because the "Working script" preserved among the Koch papers at the Wisconsin Historical Society is clearly the earliest of the known drafts, it seems likely that it or something very much like it was the script rehearsed that Thursday. Later versions of the script seem to reflect the changes Houseman describes in *Run-Through* (p. 393) follow-

ing the Thursday rehearsal. Fifty years later, Richard Baer (who had by then changed his name to "Barr") claimed in an interview that the script they rehearsed that Thursday was set in England and not Princeton, though he admitted that his memory was "not perfect" (Richard Barr, interviewed by Frank Beacham, p. 2, box 14, *Theatre of the Imagination* [1988]. Interviews [transcripts]. 1988" folder, Wilson-Welles Papers). However, other sources make clear that Welles intended to modernize and Americanize *War of the Worlds* from the beginning. It seems likely that Barr misremembered the changes evident in Koch's preserved drafts.

89. Richard Barr, interviewed by Frank Beacham, p. 2, box 14, *Theatre of the Imagination* (1988). Interviews [transcripts]. 1988" folder, Wilson-Welles Papers. Welles, interviewed by Bogdanovich, in *This Is Orson Welles*, tape 4, side 7.

90. Callow, *Road to Xanadu*, pp. 376–77.

91. Houseman, *Run-Through*, pp. 390–93.

92. Crespy, *Richard Barr*, pp. 13–15.

93. Richard Barr, interviewed by Frank Beacham, p. 2, box 14, *Theatre of the Imagination* (1988). Interviews [transcripts]. 1988" folder, Wilson-Welles Papers. Welles, interviewed by Bogdanovich, in *This Is Orson Welles*, tape 4, side 7.

94. Crespy, *Richard Barr*, p. 15.

95. Houseman, *Run-Through*, p. 393.

96. The final version of the broadcast contains an exchange between ham-radio operators that the scholar Harry M. Geduld has convincingly argued was lifted from an earlier episode of *The March of Time* (Geduld, "Welles or Wells?," pp. 263–64). Geduld argues that Welles suggested the change, but, given his lack of involvement with the broadcast at this stage, it seems unlikely. Paul Stewart may be the more likely source, because he was also a *March of Time* veteran (see Raymond Fielding, *The March of Time, 1935–1951* [New York: Oxford University Press, 1978], p. 13). Overall, Geduld uses the ham-radio exchange, and other evidence from the broadcast, to argue that it reflects Welles's authorship and not Koch's (see Geduld, "Welles or Wells?," pp. 265–67). He does not, however, cite the script drafts preserved at the Wisconsin Historical Society, and they do not support some of his contentions. For example, Geduld argues that the scene between Pierson and the Stranger, which reveals the Stranger's megalomaniacal, pseudo-fascist desires, reflects Welles's political beliefs and, therefore, his authorship (pp. 270–71). But that exchange is in both Koch's "Working script" (pp. 37–44) and "Final script" (pp. 35–40) virtually unchanged, suggesting that it came from Koch and not Welles. *War of the Worlds* was, first and foremost, a collaborative effort, and so its "authorship" cannot be ascribed solely to Welles or to anyone else.

97. Houseman, *Run-Through*, p. 393. Houseman implies that he, Stewart, Koch, and Froelich all worked together on the script in Welles's hotel suite. But in letters written to the filmmakers of *The Night That Panicked America*, Koch states that he never worked directly with Stewart during that entire week. In fact, he never left his apartment. (Howard Koch to Nicholas Meyer, March 5, 1975, and Howard Koch to C. A. Wilson, June 25, 1975, box 6, folder 6-4, Howard E. Koch Papers, Wisconsin Historical Society, Madison.) Koch later described Houseman as the one running pages back and forth from his apartment to the studio (Koch, interviewed by Bevilacqua, in *We Take You Now to Grover's Mill*). It seems likely that, in his account, Houseman conflated different work sessions at different locations into one in Welles's hotel suite.

98. Koch significantly shortened the second half of the script by removing a scene from the Wells novel in which the narrator encounters an insane clergyman. See Koch, "Working script," pp. 30–36; Koch, "Final script," pp. 34–35.

99. The first half of Koch's "Working script" contained a brief sequence of vignettes describing the spread of the Martians' black smoke, which does not appear in the final broadcast. As originally written, the script faded from a transmission from army gunners

in the Watchung Mountains to a scene inside a church and then a street scene, as each location is overrun with poison gas (Koch, "Working script," pp. 25–26). In place of this sequence, Koch wrote a brief exchange between ham-radio operators (cited above), conveying the same information without breaking the news-broadcast fiction (Koch, "Final script," p. 27). Koch also deleted a brief bit of dialogue between the reporter Carl Phillips and Professor Pierson, supposedly occurring after the microphones had been turned off and listeners could no longer hear them, in order not to break the fake news conceit (Koch, "Working script," p. 7; Koch, "Final script," p. 7).

100. Koch, "Working script," p. 16. See also Koch, "Working script," pp. 13, 27; Koch, "Final script," p. 29.

101. Houseman, *Run-Through*, pp. 400–401.

102. Brady, *Citizen Welles*, p. 167. Gosling, *Waging the War*, pp. 37–39.

103. Brady, *Citizen Welles*, p. 167.

104. See Welles, interviewed by Bogdanovich, in *This Is Orson Welles*, tape 4, side 7.

105. Orson Welles to Hadley Cantril, March 26, 1940, Correspondence box 1, "1940. Mar." folder, Welles mss.

106. John Houseman, interviewed by Leonard Maltin, April 22, 1988, p. 5, box 14, "*Theatre of the Imagination* (1988). Interviews [transcripts]. 1988" folder, Wilson-Welles Papers. Houseman, interviewed by Bevilacqua, in *We Take You Now to Grover's Mill*.

107. Brady, *Citizen Welles*, p. 163. Koch, "Working script," p. 43. Koch, "Final script," p. 39.

108. Houseman, *Run-Through*, p. 399.

109. Ben Gross, *I Looked and Listened: Informal Recollections of Radio and TV* (New York: Random House, 1954), p. 197.

110. Houseman, "Men From Mars," p. 76. Houseman, *Run-Through*, pp. 393–94. Orson Welles to Hadley Cantril, March 26, 1940, Correspondence box 1, "1940. Mar." folder, Welles mss.

111. Orson Welles deposition, July 8, 1960, in Transcript of Record, *Orson Welles v. CBS*, pp. 69–73. Welles, interviewed by Bogdanovich, in *This Is Orson Welles*, tape 4, side 7. Joseph McBride, *What Ever Happened to Orson Welles?: A Portrait of an Independent Career* (Lexington: University Press of Kentucky, 2006), p. 195.

112. Alan Gallop, *The Martians Are Coming!: The True Story of Orson Welles' 1938 Panic Broadcast* (Gloucestershire: Amberley Publishing, 2011), p. 53. Hally Pomeroy, "Time Marches On," *Radio Guide*, July 18, 1936, p. 42. Fielding, *March of Time*, p. 12. Leonard Maltin, *The Great American Broadcast: A Celebration of Radio's Golden Age* (New York: Dutton, 1997), pp. 89–91.

113. Gosling, *Waging the War*, p. 40. Gallop, *Martians*, p. 53.

114. Quoted in Maltin, *Great American Broadcast*, p. 92.

115. Alva Johnston and Fred Smith, "How to Raise a Child: The Disturbing Life—to Date—of Orson Welles," *Saturday Evening Post*, Feb. 3, 1930, pp. 27, 38. Johnston and Smith state that Welles heard these comments before listening to the acetate recording of the rehearsal, but it seems very likely that this is the same phone call that Houseman (*Run-Through*, p. 394) describes as occurring after the tech rehearsal. For one thing, Welles was so busy with *Danton's Death* that he seems not to have been interested in *War of the Worlds* before hearing the acetate recording. For another, so few people participated in the recorded rehearsal that it seems unlikely a "technician," as Johnston and Smith describe him, would have been involved.

116. See Houseman, *Run-Through*, p. 239.

117. Ibid., p. 390.

118. Steven C. Smith, *A Heart at Fire's Center: The Life and Music of Bernard Herrmann* (Berkeley: University of California Press, 2002), p. 66.

119. For the layout of Studio One during the Mercury Theatre broadcasts, see the photographs printed, among other places, in Holmsten and Lubertozzi, eds., *War of the*

Worlds, pp. 20, 32; Koch, *Panic Broadcast*, pp. 34–35; *Orson Welles on the Air: The Radio Years* (New York: Museum of Broadcasting, 1988), p. 15.

120. Callow, *Road to Xanadu*, p. 377. Crespy, *Richard Barr*, p. 17.
121. Quoted in Crespy, *Richard Barr*, p. 16. See also Callow, *Road to Xanadu*, p. 400.
122. Gallop, *Martians*, p. 57.
123. Houseman, *Run-Through*, p. 391. See also Crespy, *Richard Barr*, p. 16.
124. Alland, interviewed in *Battle Over Citizen Kane* (1996). Welles, interviewed by Bog-danovich, in *This Is Orson Welles*, tape 4, side 7.
125. Houseman, interviewed by Bevilacqua, in *We Take You Now to Grover's Mill*.
126. Houseman, *Run-Through*, pp. 400–402.
127. Neil Verma, *Theater of the Imagination* (Chicago: University of Chicago Press, 2012), pp. 66–72.
128. Koch, "Working script," pp. 21–22. The final script does, however, have a large white space where that speech would have been, possibly suggesting the intent to reinstate it (Koch, "Final script," p. 24).
129. Brown, *Manipulating the Ether*, pp. 230–31. Houseman, *Run-Through*, p. 402. Field-ing, *March of Time*, p. 13.
130. See "Roosevelt Mimic Is Cut Off the Air," *New York Times*, April 11, 1937, p. 52.
131. Holmsten and Lubertozzi, eds., *War of the Worlds*, p. 20.
132. Quoted in Maltin, *Great American Broadcast*, p. 81.
133. Houseman, *Run-Through*, p. 398.
134. See script pages reproduced in Gallop, *Martians*, pp. 156–57. See also Houseman, *Run-Through*, p. 391.
135. Houseman, *Run-Through*, p. 391.
136. Ibid., p. 394. Gallop, *Martians*, pp. 153–57.

4. "Yours in Terror"

1. Chapter title is from Ann Simpson to Orson Welles, Oct. 30, 1938, box 24, "Pennsyl-vania" folder 2 (42/54), Wilson-Welles Papers. Epigraph is from Henry Clark to Orsen [*sic*] Welles, Oct. 30, 1938, box 24, "NYC & boroughs" folder 1 (33/54), Wilson-Welles Papers.
2. James G. Cooper to the Mercury Theater [*sic*], n.d., box 23, "Maine" folder (18/54); Robert C. Murphy to the Mercury Theatre, Oct. 31, 1938, box 24, "Oregon" folder (41/54); J. V. Yaukey to Orson Welles, Nov. 1, 1938, box 24, "South Dakota" folder (46/54); John M. Loving to Orson Wells [*sic*], Nov. 3, 1938, box 24, "Texas" folder (48/54), all Wilson-Welles Papers. See also "Canada" folder, box 24, Wilson-Welles Papers. A copy of the Yaukey letter is also in box 237, NARA.
3. Jim Harmon, *The Great Radio Heroes*, rev. ed. (Jefferson, N.C.: McFarland, 2001), p. 162.
4. John Houseman, *Run-Through: A Memoir* (New York: Simon & Schuster, 1972), pp. 364–65.
5. Theodor W. Adorno, *The Culture Industry: Selected Essays on Mass Culture* (London: Routledge, 1991), p. 145. See also David Goodman, *Radio's Civic Ambition: American Broadcasting and Democracy in the 1930s* (Oxford: Oxford University Press, 2011), p. 258.
6. See Richard B. O'Brien, "'The Shadow' Talks," *New York Times*, Aug. 14, 1938, p. 136.
7. Christine Haycock and family to Orson Welles, Nov. 11, 1938, box 24, "New Jersey" folder 2 (30/54), Wilson-Welles Papers. See also Elena Tomlinson to Orson Welles, Nov. 1, 1938, box 23, "District of Columbia" folder (8/54), Wilson-Welles Papers.
8. Herbert J. Gans, *Popular Culture & High Culture: An Analysis and Evaluation of Taste* (New York: Basic Books, 1999), pp. 106–10. See also Goodman, *Radio's Civic Ambi-tion*, p. 272.

9. Mr. and Mrs. David Ressler to Orson Welles, Oct. 31, 1938, box 24, "New York, NYC & boroughs" folder 2 (34/54), Wilson-Welles Papers. See also David W. Sallume to Frank McNinch, Oct. 31, 1938; Mark Pheifer to Frank McNinch, Nov. 1, 1938, both box 237, NARA.

10. See Howard S. Bradley to Orson Welles, Nov. 5, 1938, box 24, "Canada" folder; George Reynolds to the Mercury Theater [sic], Oct. 31, 1938, box 24, "New York (state)" folder 2 (37/54); C. H. Spratly to Orson Wells [sic], Nov. 1, 1938, box 24, "New York (state)" folder 2 (37/54); Mrs. Ethel M. Cannon to CBS, Nov. 2, 1938, box 24, "New York (state)" folder 2 (37/54); and Skulda Banér to the Federal Communications Bureau, n.d., box 24, "Wisconsin" folder (54/54), all Wilson-Welles Papers. A copy of the Banér letter is also in box 237, NARA.

11. See Harriet M. Bergstrom to Orson Welles, Nov. 1, 1938, box 23, "Minnesota" folder (22/54); Janet Roughton to Orson Welles, Nov. 3, 1938, box 24, "New York, NYC & boroughs" folder 2 (34/54); Florence and Lillian Schalow to Orson Welles, Nov. 4, 1938, box 24, "New York, NYC & boroughs" folder 2 (34/54); Anonymous to W. B. Lewis, Nov. 1, 1938, box 24, "No Location" folder; W. J. Crehan, Frances Crehan, "and friends" to Orson Welles, Nov. 2, 1938, box 24, "No Location" folder; Hume V. Stephani to Orson Welles, Nov. 4, 1938, box 24, "No Location" folder; Betty Riegler to Orson Welles, Nov. 5, 1938, box 24, "No Location" folder; Theodore Huston to Orson Welles, Nov. 1, 1938, box 24, "Pennsylvania" folder 1 (42/54), all Wilson-Welles Papers. For people in rural areas, see Genevieve E. Myers and Harry R. Wailling to Orson Welles, Nov. 3, 1938, box 24, "New York (state)" folder 2 (37/54); Mrs. M. B. Lewis et al. to CBS, Oct. 31, 1938, box 24, "Nebraska" folder (26/54); Mr. and Mrs. Ira S. Pearce to Orson Welles, Nov. 2, 1938, box 24, "Nevada" folder (27/54), all Wilson-Welles Papers.

12. H. Pauline Geiger to Orson Welles, Nov. 1, 1938, box 24, "New Jersey" folder 2 (30/54), Wilson-Welles Papers.

13. Helen Weinberg to Orson Wells [sic], Nov. 2, 1938, box 24, "Wisconsin" folder (54/54), Wilson-Welles Papers. See also Donald B. Deser to the FCC, Nov. 3, 1938, box 237, NARA; Elston Kent to Orson Wells [sic], Oct. 28, 1938, box 23, "Michigan" folder (21/54); Giovannia Nuccio to Orson Welles, Nov. 5, 1938, box 24, "New York (state)" folder 1 (36/54); John R. Snyder to Orson Welles, Nov. 8, 1938, box 24, "New York (state)" folder 1 (36/54); Stanley Lieher to Orson Welles, Nov. 1, 1938, box 24, "North Carolina" folder (38/54); Stena Cable to Orson Welles, Nov. 9, 1938, box 24, "North Carolina" folder (38/54); Leonard Hast to Orson Wells [sic], Oct. 31, 1938, box 24, "Pennsylvania" folder 2 (43/54), all Wilson-Welles Papers.

14. Charles Zimmerman to Orson Welles, Oct. 31, 1938, box 23, "Maryland" folder (19/54), Wilson-Welles Papers.

15. Hadley Cantril with Hazel Gaudet and Herta Herzog, The Invasion from Mars: A Study in the Psychology of Panic (New York: Harper & Row, 1966), pp. 56, 82.

16. See Mrs. Fred Hamilton to Orson Wells [sic], Oct. 31, 1938, box 24, "Canada" folder; Martha P. Gibson to Orson Welles, Nov. 5, 1938, box 24, "Ohio" folder (39/54), both Wilson-Welles Papers.

17. See Beatrice Horn to Orson Welles, n.d., box 24, "Canada" folder; Mrs. W. D. Nesbitt to Orson Welles, Oct. 31, 1938, box 23, "California" folder (4/54); Joan Knight to Orson Welles, Oct. 31, 1938, box 23, "Maryland" folder (19/54); William R. Cooper to Orson Wells [sic], Oct. 31, 1938, box 23, "Michigan" folder (21/54); Grace B. Bladget to Orson Welles, Oct. 31, 1938, box 24, "New Jersey" folder 1 (29/54); David H. Schwartz to Orson Welles, Oct. 31, 1938, box 24, "NYC & boroughs" folder 1 (33/54); Edward A. Callan to Orson Welles, Oct. 31, 1938, box 24, "New York (state)" folder 1 (36/54); Marjorie Lyndon Smith et al. to Orson Wells [sic], Oct. 31, 1938, box 24, "New York (state)" folder 1 (36/54); Arthur Van Voris to the Columbia Radio Network, Nov. 7, 1938,

box 24, "New York (state)" folder 1 (36/54); Mrs. Charles H. Earles to Orson Welles, Nov. 1, 1938, box 24, "New York (state)" folder 2 (37/54); Damon A. Turner to Orson Welles, Oct. 31, 1938, box 24, "Ohio" folder (39/54); H. E. Rieger to Orson Welles, Oct. 31, 1938, box 24, "Ohio" folder (39/54); C. S. Hoase to CBS, Oct. 31, 1938, box 24, "Wisconsin" folder (54/54); Florence Von Clare to Orson Welles, Oct. 31, 1938, box 24, "No Location" folder, all Wilson-Welles Papers.

18. Mary Jane Sears to Orson Welles, Nov. 7, 1938, box 24, "New York, NYC & boroughs" folder 2 (34/54), Wilson-Welles Papers.

19. See Mr. and Mrs. Joe McClellan to Orson Welles, Nov. 5, 1938, box 24, "Washington" folder (52/54), Wilson-Welles Papers.

20. *The Chase & Sanborn Hour*, NBC (New York, NY: WEAF, Oct. 30, 1938), in *The 60 Greatest Old-Time Radio Shows of the 20th Century*, ed. Walter Cronkite (Radio Spirits, 1999), audiocassette, tape 2, side 1.

21. See Professor L. J. Bennett to Frank R. McNinch, Oct. 31, 1938, box 237; Lynn Montross to the Communications Commission, Nov. 1, 1938, box 238, both NARA; and Mrs. J. E. Darys to Orson Welles, Nov. 3, 1938, box 23, "California" folder (4/54); Philip L. Shenk to Orson Welles, Nov. 1, 1938, box 23, "Michigan" folder (21/54), both Wilson-Welles Papers. See also "F.C.C. Inquiry Is Ordered into Radio War Play," *New York Herald Tribune*, Nov. 1, 1938, p. 19; "Charlie Saved Us," *Baltimore Sun*, Nov. 1, 1938, p. 10; Robert J. Brown, *Manipulating the Ether: The Power of Broadcast Radio in Thirties America* (Jefferson, N.C.: McFarland, 1998), p. 238.

22. Quoted in W. Joseph Campbell, *Getting It Wrong: Ten of the Greatest Misreported Stories in Journalism* (Berkeley: University of California Press, 2010), p. 200, n. 8. See also "Radio's Cruel Hoax," *Detroit News*, Oct. 31, 1938, p. 1, box 2, "Clippings and Articles, 1936–1940" folder (2 of 4), Welles-Feder Collection. Goodman, *Radio's Civic Ambition*, pp. 236–37; John Gosling, *Waging the War of the Worlds: A History of the 1938 Radio Broadcast and Resulting Panic* (Jefferson, N.C.: McFarland, 2009), p. 69.

23. Goodman, *Radio's Civic Ambition*, pp. 258–59. Orrin E. Dunlap Jr., "Message from Mars: Radio Learns That Melodrama Dressed Up as a Current Event Is Dangerous," *New York Times*, Nov. 6, 1938, p. 184. See Mrs. N. G. DeWeend to Orson Wells [sic], Oct. 31, 1938, box 23, "Michigan" folder (21/54); Nick Tsirikos to Orson Welles, Oct. 31, 1938, box 24, "New Jersey" folder 2 (30/54); F. W. Abbey to Orson Welles, Nov. 1, 1938, box 24, "New Jersey" folder 2 (30/54); Elizabeth Salk to Orson Welles, Nov. 1, 1938, box 24, "New York (state)" folder 2 (37/54), all Wilson-Welles Papers; and Mrs. Ralph E. Sanders to Frank R. McNinch, Nov. 1, 1938; Edward G. Burrows to Frank P. [sic] McNinch, Oct. 31, 1938; Robert B. MacDougall to Frank McNinch, Oct. 31, 1938, and Nov. 1, 1938, all box 237, NARA.

24. Jerome W. Stone to Orson Welles, n.d., box 23, "Arizona" folder (2/54), Wilson-Welles Papers.

25. See Goodman, *Radio's Civic Ambition*, p. 278.

26. C. R. Kennan to Frank McNinch, Oct. 31, 1938; H. Arthur Schmidt to CBS, Oct. 31, 1938, both box 238, NARA. Mrs. R. Crawford to the Mercury Theatre, Oct. 31, 1938, box 24, "Canada" folder; "An Irate Parent" to Orson Welles, Nov. 2, 1938, box 24, "No Location" folder; Bob Moore to Orson Welles, n.d., box 24, "Texas" folder (48/54); John F. Powers to Orson Wells [sic], Oct. 30, 1938, box 23, "Massachusetts" folder (20/54), all Wilson-Welles Papers. Fifteen other letters describe people who listened or tried to listen to both *War of the Worlds* and *The Chase & Sanborn Hour* that night, but who did not panic in the way the "dialitis" myth suggests. Eight came from people who landed on *War of the Worlds* after tuning out *The Chase & Sanborn Hour* but knew immediately that the invasion was not real. (L. J. Bennett to Frank R. McNinch, Oct. 31, 1938; William C. McIntire to Frank R. McNinch, Oct. 31, 1938; Harry Wright, Jr., to Frank P. [sic] McNinch, Nov. 1, 1938, all box 237, NARA. Harry Wright letter also in Correspondence

box 1, "1938. May–Dec." folder, Welles mss. Joan Knight to Orson Welles, Oct. 31, 1938, box 23, "Maryland" folder [19/54]; H. E. Huppert to Orson Welles, Oct. 31, 1938, box 24, "New York [state]" folder 2 [37/54]; Lorette DeWallt to Orson Welles, Nov. 2, 1938, box 24, "No Location" folder; Beatrice Peacock to Orson Welles, Nov. 1, 1938, box 24, "New York [state]" folder 2 [37/54]; Mr. and Mrs. Joe McClellan to Orson Welles, Nov. 5, 1938, box 24, "Washington" folder [52/54], all Wilson-Welles Papers.) Six came from frightened listeners who tuned out *The Chase & Sanborn Hour* only after being told by a neighbor or relative to listen to *War of the Worlds*. (Helen Degen to Frank P. [sic] McNinch, Oct. 31, 1938; Justine J. Roseman to Frank R. McNinch, Nov. 13, 1938, both box 238, NARA. Charles Nelson Coon to Orson Wells [sic], Nov. 1, 1938, box 24, "NYC & boroughs" folder 1 [33/54]; J. Ford to Orson Welles, Oct. 30, 1938, box 24, "Pennsylvania" folder 1 [42/54]; Alvesta C. Flanagan to Orson Welles, Oct. 30, 1938, box 24, "Pennsylvania" folder 2 [43/54]; Lillian Spear to Orson Welles, Oct. 30, 1938, box 24, "New York, NYC & boroughs" folder 3 [35/54], all Wilson-Welles Papers.) One describes three people who tried to pick up "the Nelson Eddy program" on their car radio and stumbled upon *War of the Worlds* by accident, without hearing any part of *The Chase & Sanborn Hour*. (Anonymous to the Federal Radio Commission [sic], n.d., box 238, NARA.)

27. This survey, by Hadley Cantril and the Princeton Radio Research Project, was not restricted to listeners frightened by *War of the Worlds*. Some people probably stayed listening to CBS not because they were panicked, but because they found the show interesting. But because Cantril's team focused primarily on people who believed the broadcast to be true (see Chapter 9), it is likely that they oversampled frightened listeners here as well (Cantril, *Invasion*, pp. 82–83). Cantril's phrasing in presenting these findings is misleading and has confused some (such as Simon Callow, *Orson Welles: The Road to Xanadu* [New York: Viking, 1995], pp. 401–402) into thinking his team found that 12 percent of the *Chase & Sanborn* audience drifted to *The Mercury Theatre on the Air* after the first comedy routine. But Cantril did not survey NBC's audience that night, just people known to have heard *War of the Worlds*. See Elizabeth McLeod, "The 'Nelson Eddy Tuneout' Myth" and "The Eddy Tuneout, Again," postings to oldradio.net, Sept. 19, 2000, and Aug. 6, 2001, http://jeff560.tripod.com/wotw.html (accessed Feb. 19, 2013).

28. See Gosling, *Waging the War*, pp. 70–72. The source of the "Neapolitan Love Song" mistake appears to be Frank Brady, *Citizen Welles: A Biography of Orson Welles* (New York: Scribner, 1989), pp. 169–70. See also Joseph Bulgatz, *Ponzi Schemes, Invaders from Mars & More Extraordinary Popular Delusions and the Madness of Crowds* (New York: Harmony Books, 1992), p. 137; Paul Heyer, *The Medium and the Magician: Orson Welles, the Radio Years, 1934–1952* (Lanham, Md.: Rowman & Littlefield, 2005), p. 82; Brian Holmsten and Alex Lubertozzi, eds., *The War of the Worlds: Mars' Invasion of Earth, Inciting Panic and Inspiring Terror from H. G. Wells to Orson Welles and Beyond* (Naperville, Ill.: Sourcebooks, 2001), pp. 4–5. Houseman (*Run-Through*, p. 395) blames "a new and not very popular singer" on *The Chase & Sanborn Hour*, instead of Nelson Eddy, who came on at 8:12 p.m. The reference can only be to Dorothy Lamour, but it would be inaccurate to call her unpopular in 1938. See also Alan Gallop, *The Martians Are Coming!: The True Story of Orson Welles' 1938 Panic Broadcast* (Gloucestershire: Amberley Publishing, 2011), pp. 61–62; Barbara Leaming, *Orson Welles: A Biography* (New York: Viking, 1985), p. 161; David Thomson, *Rosebud: The Story of Orson Welles* (New York: Vintage Books, 1996), p. 102.

29. Wesley Thurstin III to Orson Welles, Oct. 31, 1938, box 24, "Ohio" folder (39/54), Wilson-Welles Papers.

30. See M. Solomon to Orson Wells [sic], n.d., "Pennsylvania" folder 2 (43/54), Wilson-Welles Papers.

31. Kenneth N. Trueblood to Orson Welles, Nov. 2, 1938, box 23, "Massachusetts" folder (20/54), Wilson-Welles Papers. Robert W. [unclear] to the Federal Radio Commission [sic], Oct. 31, 1938, box 238; Gordon G. Macintosh to the FCC, Nov. 5, 1938, box 238, both NARA. See also "Worried Listeners Ask News of Globe," Boston Globe, Oct. 31, 1938, p. 10; Cantril, Invasion, p. 57. For a Texas listener with the same problem, see Rhea Johnson to the FCC, Oct. 30, 1938, box 238, NARA.

32. See Pauline Stiles to Orson Welles, Nov. 6, 1938, box 23, "California" folder (4/54); Carolyn D. Gregory to Orson Wells [sic], Oct. 30, 1938, box 24, "NYC & boroughs" folder 1 (33/54); M. H. Chaseman to Orson Welles, Oct. 31, 1938, box 24, "New York (state)" folder 1 (36/54); George Weeden to the Mercury Theater [sic], Oct. 30, 1938, box 24, "Wisconsin" (54/54); E. C. Parmenter to Orson Welles, Oct. 31, 1938, box 24, "Ohio" folder (39/54); Amis Cooper to Orson Welles, Oct. 31, 1938, box 24, "Pennsylvania" folder 1 (42/54), all Wilson-Welles Papers.

33. Mrs. A. H. McMinn to the Federal Radio Commission [sic], n.d., box 238, NARA.

34. Houseman, Run-Through, pp. 400-402.

35. Mildred Strunk and Hadley Cantril, eds., Public Opinion: 1935-1946 (Princeton: Princeton University Press, 1951), p. 717.

36. Reading: H. A. Beasley to the Federal Radio Commission [sic], Oct. 30, 1938; Louis F. Heidenrich to the FCC, Oct. 31, 1938, both box 238, NARA. Studying: Robert Keplinger to Orson Wells [sic], Oct. 30, 1938, box 23, "Kansas" folder (15/54), Wilson-Welles Papers. Doing the dishes: Florence Schelling to Orson Welles, Oct. 29 [sic], 1938, box 23, "Indiana" folder (13/54); Ingeborg Zimmer to CBS, Oct. 31, 1938, box 24, "New Jersey" folder 1 (29/54), both Wilson-Welles Papers. Putting children to bed: Harley Davis to the FCC, Oct. 31, 1938, box 238, NARA; Mrs. M. Carrcini to Orson Wells [sic], Oct. 30, 1938, box 24, "NYC & boroughs" folder 1 (33/54), Wilson-Welles Papers. See also Laura V. Smith to the FCC, Oct. 31, 1938, box 238, NARA; and Raymond Fischer to WABC, Oct. 30, 1938, box 24, "New Jersey" folder 2 (30/54); Mary D. Simmons to Orson Welles, Oct. 31, 1938, box 23, "Maine" folder (18/54), both Wilson-Welles Papers.

37. John H. Dent to the FCC, Oct. 31, 1938; Cash L. Logan to the FCC, Oct. 31, 1938; David L. Reifer to Frank W. [sic] McNinch, Oct. 31, 1938; Frank N. Percival to the United States Radio Commission [sic], Oct. 31, 1938; T. J. Stansel to Frank R. McNinch, Nov. 2, 1938, all box 238, NARA. Martin Golda to the Mercury Theatre, Oct. 30, 1938, box 24, "New Jersey" folder 1 (29/54); William Kaiser to Orson Welles, Oct. 31, 1938, box 24, "New York (state)" folder 2 (37/54), both Wilson-Welles Papers.

38. Alice Adams to Orson Welles, n.d., box 24, "No Location" folder, Wilson-Welles Papers. E. M. Moody to CBS, Oct. 31, 1938, box 238, NARA.

39. Annabelle Jackman to Frank R. McNinch, Oct. 31, 1938, box 238, NARA.

40. Hadley Cantril and Gordon Allport, The Psychology of Radio (New York: Harper & Brothers, 1935), p. 97. Cantril, Invasion, p. 80.

41. James L. Carling to Orson Welles, Oct. 31, 1938, box 23, "California" folder (4/54), Wilson-Welles Papers.

42. See Rose Libman to WABC, n.d., box 23, "Connecticut" folder (6/54); Robert C. Bust to Orson Wells [sic], Oct. 30, 1938, box 24, "Pennsylvania" folder 1 (42/54); Ingeborg Zimmer to CBS, Oct. 31, 1938, box 24, "New Jersey" folder 1 (29/54), all Wilson-Welles Papers; and Mable Clements to Frank R. McNinch, Nov. 2, 1938; Mrs. Lloyd Face to the Federal Radio Commission [sic], Oct. 31, 1938; Iva Collins to the FCC, Nov. 1, 1938; "A radio listener in Los Angeles" to the FCC, Oct. 30, 1938; Mrs. William T. Waterbury to Eleanor Roosevelt, Oct. 31, 1938; Lynn Montross to the Communications Commission, Nov. 1, 1938, all box 238, NARA.

43. Lucile McLain to Orson Welles, Oct. 30, 1938, box 24, "Oregon" folder (41/54), Wilson-Welles Papers.

44. Johanna Wilizenski to Franklin D. Roosevelt, Nov. 1, 1938, box 238, NARA.

45. See "An Irate Parent" to Orson Welles, Nov. 2, 1938, box 24, "No Location" folder, Wilson-Welles Papers; Mrs. G. M. Brown to the FCC, Nov. 1, 1938, box 237, NARA.

46. Edward A. Callan to Orson Welles, Oct. 31, 1938, box 24, "New York (state)" folder 1 (36/54), Wilson-Welles Papers.

47. Ibid.

48. E. C. Parmenter to Orson Welles, Oct. 31, 1938, box 24, "Ohio" folder (39/54), Wilson-Welles Papers.

49. Ibid.

50. See Thomas J. Rucker to the FCC, Nov. 10, 1938, box 237, NARA; Raymond Fischer to WABC, Oct. 30, 1938, box 24, "New Jersey" folder 2 (30/54), Wilson-Welles Papers.

51. Mrs. F. M. Dekker to the Federal Radio Communications Commission [sic], Oct. 31, 1938, box 238, NARA.

52. See Bendie Stein to WABC, Oct. 30, 1938, box 24, "NYC & boroughs" folder 1 (33/54); Mrs. M. Carrcini to Orson Wells [sic], Oct. 30, 1938, box 24, "NYC & boroughs" folder 1 (33/54); John King et al. to CBS, Oct. 30, 1938, box 24, "NYC & boroughs" folder 1 (33/54); Bertha E. Boughton to Orson Wells [sic], n.d., box 24, "New York (state)" folder 1 (36/54), all Wilson-Welles Papers. See also Brown, *Manipulating the Ether*, p. 209.

53. Edith B. Slack to Frank R. McNinch, Nov. 1, 1938, box 238, NARA.

54. Jean McLean to Orson Welles, Nov. 1, 1938, box 23, "Connecticut" folder (6/54), Wilson-Welles Papers.

55. William Kaiser to Orson Welles, Oct. 31, 1938, box 24, "New York (state)" folder 2 (37/54), Wilson-Welles Papers. See also Lillian Dunston to Frank R. McNinch, Nov. 3, 1938; Mryle Johnson to the FCC, Nov. 3, 1938, both box 237, NARA.

56. Mrs. F. M. Dekker to the Federal Radio Communications Commission [sic], Oct. 31, 1938, box 238, NARA. See also Elizabeth Templeman to the FCC, Oct. 30, 1938, box 238, NARA.

57. Heyer, *Medium and Magician*, p. 102.

58. Laura V. Smith to the FCC, Oct. 31, 1938, box 238, NARA. See also Gerta S. Brown to the Mercury Theater [sic], Nov. 2, 1938, box 24, "New York (state)" folder 2 (37/54), Wilson-Welles Papers.

59. Joseph E. Moore to CBS, Nov. 1, 1938, box 238, NARA.

60. Mrs. William Elliott to Frank McNinch, Oct. 31, 1938, box 238, NARA. See also Anonymous to the Federal Radio Commission [sic], n.d., box 238, NARA.

61. Frances A. Krpejs to the Mercury Theater [sic], Nov. 2, 1938, box 23, "Illinois" folder (12/54), Wilson-Welles Papers.

62. See Mrs. H. F. Noske to Harold Ickes, Oct. 31, 1938; Max H. Lipe to Frank B. [sic] McNinch, Nov. 3, 1938; Mrs. G. W. James to the Radio Commission [sic], Oct. 30, 1938; Lynn Montross to the Communications Commission [sic], Nov. 1, 1938, all box 238, NARA; and Bendie Stein to WABC, Oct. 30, 1938, box 24, "NYC & boroughs" folder 1 (33/54), Wilson-Welles Papers.

63. David Acord, "'When Mars Attacked: The War of the Worlds' Part 3—Fire in the Sky," Wellesnet, www.wellesnet.com/?p=7639 (accessed Jan. 6, 2014). See Charles Nelson Coon to Orson Wells [sic], Nov. 1, 1938, box 24, "NYC & boroughs" folder 1 (33/54); Mrs. J. R. McCalla to Orson Wells [sic], Oct. 31, 1938, box 23, "Georgia" folder (10/54), both Wilson-Welles Papers.

64. See Peter Bogdanovich, interviewed in *The Battle Over Citizen Kane* (1996), *American Experience* (WGBH Boston), *Citizen Kane* DVD, disc 2, directed by Michael Epstein and Thomas Lennon (Atlanta: Turner Home Entertainment, 2001).

65. Anna Farrell to Orson Welles, Nov. 2, 1938, box 24, "New York, NYC & boroughs" folder 2 (34/54), Wilson-Welles Papers. See also Bertha E. Boughton to Orson Wells [sic], n.d., box 24, "New York (state)" folder 1 (36/54), Wilson-Welles Papers.

66. George B. Wright to Frank R. McNinch, Nov. 1, 1938, box 237, NARA.

67. David L. Miller, *Introduction to Collective Behavior and Collective Action*, 3rd ed. (Long Grove, Ill.: Waveland Press, 2013), p. 141. Harry M. Geduld, "Welles or Wells?— A Matter of Adaptation," in *Perspectives on Orson Welles*, ed. Morris Beja (New York: G. K. Hall, 1995), p. 269.

68. See Julia M. Donnelly to the Secretary of the Interior, Oct. 30, 1938; R. V. McAron et al. to the FCC, Oct. 30, 1938; Vincent M. Earley to the Federal Radio Commission [*sic*], Oct. 30, 1938; L. C. Miller to the Federal Radio Commission [*sic*], Oct. 31, 1938; Garland B. Fletcher, Oct. 31, 1938; Neil H. Jenkins to Frank P. [*sic*] McNinch, Oct. 31, 1938; V. R. Waxweiler to Frank P. [*sic*] McNinch, Oct. 31, 1938; L. Lain to the FCC, Oct. 31, 1938; David L. Reifer to Frank W. [*sic*] McNinch, Oct. 31, 1938, all box 238, NARA; and Lucile McLain to Orson Welles, Oct. 30, 1938, box 24, "Oregon" folder (41/54); Miss K. Doyle to Orson Welles, Oct. 30, 1938, box 24, "Rhode Island" folder (44/54); "Relieved" to the Mercury Theatre, n.d., box 24, "No Location" folder; Mrs. Fred A. Raabe to the Mercury Theater [*sic*], Oct. 30, 1938, box 24, "Ohio" folder (39/54); "A TAX PAYER" to the Mercury Theatre, Oct. 30, 1938, box 24, "No Location" folder; "a nervous listener" to "W. G. Wells," Oct. 31, 1938, box 24, "New York (state)" folder 1 (35/54); Margaret M. McLean to CBS, Oct. 31, 1938, box 24, "Oklahoma" folder (40/54); F. D. Ripley to Orson Welles, Nov. 1, 1938, box 24, "West Virginia" folder (53/54); "Twenty Well Shaken Girls" to Orson Wells [*sic*], Oct. 30, 1938, box 24, "No Location" folder; Margery Sem to Orson Wells [*sic*], Oct. 30, 1938, box 24, "Washington" folder (52/54); Marie Cassara to Orson Welles, Oct. 31, 1938, box 24, "New York, NYC & boroughs" folder 3 (35/54); John F. Powers to Orson Wells [*sic*], Oct. 30, 1938, box 23, "Massachusetts" folder (20/54), all Wilson-Welles Papers.

69. Mary Reilly to Orson Welles, Oct. 30, 1938, box 24, "New York, NYC & boroughs" folder 2 (30/54), Wilson-Welles Papers.

70. "An Irate Parent" to Orson Welles, Nov. 2, 1938, box 24, "No Location" folder, Wilson-Welles Papers. See also Justine J. Roseman to Frank R. McNinch, Nov. 13, 1938, box 238, NARA.

71. See Willson Bader to "Austin" Welles, n.d., box 24, "New Jersey" folder 1 (29/54); Julia Summons to Orson Welles, Nov. 7, 1938, box 24, "New Jersey" folder 2 (30/54); Betty Scymansky to Orson Welles, Oct. 30, 1938, box 24, "New Jersey" folder 1 (29/54); Mrs. M. Garrison to the Mercury Theatre, Oct. 30, 1938, box 24, "New Jersey" folder 2 (30/54); Gladys C. Turton to Orson Welles, Oct. 30, 1938, box 24, "New Jersey" folder 2 (30/54); Martin Golda to the Mercury Theatre, Oct. 30, 1938, box 24, "New Jersey" folder 1 (29/54), all Wilson-Welles Papers; and Ruth Bogert to the Federal Radio Commission [*sic*], Oct. 30, 1938, box 238, NARA.

72. Charles Merserau to Franklin D. Roosevelt, Oct. 30, 1938, box 238, NARA.

73. In 1933, H. G. Wells published *The Shape of Things to Come*, a speculative "history of the future" chronicling world events through the year 2105. Among other things, the book predicted that another world war would break out in the year 1940, and that it would entail the widespread use of poison gas on civilian populations. By 1942, Wells wrote, gas masks would be a standard fashion accessory, and "air-raid pillars" holding "respirators and first-aid sets for possible gas victims" would be found in many cities. As Wells put it, "It was a 'gas-minded' world in the forties." (H. G. Wells, *The Shape of Things to Come* [London: Penguin Books, 2005 (orig. 1933)], pp. 58, 168–78). See also Brown, *Manipulating the Ether*, p. 215.

74. Gladys C. Turton to Orson Welles, Oct. 30, 1938, box 24, "New Jersey" folder 2 (30/54), Wilson-Welles Papers.

75. Julia M. Donnelly to the Secretary of the Interior, Oct. 30, 1938, box 238, NARA.

76. See Edouard Supubo to the Federal Radio Commission [*sic*], Oct. 31, 1938; Helen K. Matthew to F. P. [*sic*] McNinch, n.d.; J. Phillip Schaefer to the FCC, Oct. 31, 1938; Elizabeth

Templeman to the FCC, Oct. 30, 1938; Mrs. Kathryn A. Kraemer to the FCC, Oct. 30, 1938; Max Winkler to the FCC, Oct. 30, 1938; Roger E. Moore to Frank P. [sic] McNinch, Oct. 31, 1938; Mary E. Ferguson to the FCC, Oct. 31, 1938; Mrs. Amos S. Draa to CBS, Oct. 31, 1938; Mrs. A. H. McMinn to the Federal Radio Commission [sic], n.d.; S. L. Williams to the FCC, Nov. 1, 1938; Mrs. H. F. Noske to Harold Ickes, Oct. 31, 1938; Mrs. H. F. Noske to the FCC, Nov. 1, 1938; A. C. Patterson to the Radio Commission [sic], Oct. 30, 1938; Mrs. Lloyd Face to the Federal Radio Commission [sic], Oct. 31, 1938; George E. Tinkham to Frank R. McNinch, Nov. 5, 1938; Joseph E. Moore to CBS, Nov. 1, 1938; Mrs. M. W. Durham to Frank McNinch, n.d., all box 238, NARA; and Raymond Fischer to WABC, Oct. 30, 1938, box 24, "New Jersey" folder 2 (30/54), Wilson-Welles Papers. See also Cantril, *Invasion*, pp. 70–71; Goodman, *Radio's Civic Ambition*, pp. 276–77.

77. "An Irate Parent" to Orson Welles, Nov. 2, 1938, box 24, "No Location" folder, Wilson-Welles Papers.

78. See C. C. Washington to CBS, Oct. 31, 1938; Thomas Brosnan to Harold Ickes, Nov. 2, 1938, both box 238, NARA.

79. Margaret Reid to the FCC, Nov. 1, 1938, box 238, NARA.

80. See Sadie B. Quinn to the Radio Commission [sic], Oct. 31, 1938; Mary E. Ferguson to the FCC, Oct. 31, 1938, both box 238, NARA; and Anna Farrell to Orson Welles, Nov. 2, 1938, box 24, "New York, NYC & boroughs" folder 2 (34/54); Merle Jennings to WBBM, Oct. 30, 1938, box 23, "Illinois" folder (12/54), both Wilson-Welles Papers. See also "Radio War Drama Creates a Panic," *New York Times*, Oct. 31, 1938, p. 4; Brown, *Manipulating the Ether*, p. 231; Heyer, *Medium and Magician*, p. 103.

81. Mrs. H. F. Noske to Harold Ickes, Oct. 31, 1938; W. L. Myers to the Secretary of the Interior, Oct. 31, 1938; George M. Havens to the Secretary of the Interior, Oct. 31, 1938; William A. Dickson to the Secretary of the Interior, Oct. 31, 1938; Julia M. Donnelly to the Secretary of the Interior, Oct. 30, 1938; Thomas Brosnan to Harold I. Ickes, Nov. 2, 1938; H. H. Downey to the Secretary of the Interior, Oct. 31, 1938; Almena Wuerthner to the Secretary of the Interior, Oct. 31, 1938; A. G. Kennedy to Harold Ickes, Oct. 31, 1938; Warner Ogden to the Secretary of the Interior, Oct. 30, 1938, all box 238, NARA. One letter was addressed to the "Sec. of State" but was routed through the Department of the Interior before reaching the FCC (Clifford Kahllo to the Secretary of State, Oct. 30, 1938, box 238, NARA).

82. C. R. Kennan to Frank McNinch, Oct. 31, 1938, box 238, NARA. See also Mrs. Malcolm R. Stephens to the FCC, Nov. 1, 1938; Mrs. H. D. Graham to Frank R. McNinch, Nov. 1, 1938; Joseph Safran to John F. Killeen, Oct. 30, 1938, all box 238, NARA.

83. Thomas Brosnan to Harold Ickes, Nov. 2, 1938, box 238, NARA. See also Robert Triplett to the FCC, Oct. 30, 1938, box 238, NARA.

84. Number of books owned: Harley Davis to the FCC, Oct. 31, 1938, box 238, NARA. See also F. C. Adams to the FCC, Oct. 30, 1938; L. R. Demond to the Federal Radio Commission [sic], Oct. 30, 1938; Helen Markham to Frank P. [sic] McNinch, Oct. 31, 1938; Mrs. William T. Waterbury to Eleanor Roosevelt, Oct. 31, 1938; Grace K. Voeller to the FCC, Nov. 1, 1938; Mrs. H. E. Schmidtke to Frank P. [sic] McNinch, Nov. 1, 1938; Anonymous to the Federal Radio Commission [sic], n.d.; Mrs. A. Millis to the FCC, n.d., all box 238, NARA.

85. Mr. and Mrs. Fred Baker to Orton [sic] Welles, Oct. 30, 1938, box 23, "Michigan" folder (21/54), Wilson-Welles Papers.

86. Martin E. Rooney to the FCC, Oct. 30, 1938, box 238, NARA.

87. Quoted in H. G. Wells, *The War of the Worlds: A Critical Text of the 1898 London First Edition, with an Introduction, Illustrations and Appendices*, ed. Leon Stover (Jefferson, N.C.: McFarland, 2001), p. 167.

88. See Arthur William Wright to Orson Welles, Oct. 30, 1938, box 24, "New York (state)" folder 1 (36/54); A. M. McLeod to Orson Wells [sic], Oct. 31, 1938, box 24, "Canada"

folder; Cora Hardin to Orson Welles, Oct. 31, 1938, box 24, "New Jersey" folder 3 (31/54); Joseph L. Stephens to Orson Welles, Oct. 31, 1938, box 24, "Ohio" folder (39/54); Nell Moon to Orson Welles, Oct. 31, 1938, box 24, "Ohio" folder (39/54); Martha Pamplin to Orson Welles, Nov. 1, 1938, box 23, "Indiana" folder (13/54); Winona Fontaine to Orson Welles, Nov. 1, 1938, box 24, "New York (state)" folder 2 (37/54); Theodore Rand to Orson Welles, Nov. 11, 1938, box 24, "New York, NYC & boroughs" folder 3 (35/54); Mrs. W. H. Linville to Orson Welles, n.d., box 23, "Kansas" folder (15/54); Irene Gottesman to Orson Welles, n.d., box 24, "New York, NYC & boroughs" folder 3 (35/54); Lillian Swartz to H. G. Wells, n.d., box 24, "North Carolina" folder (38/54), all Wilson-Welles Papers.

89. Mabel A. Clark to Orson Wells [sic], Oct. 30, 1938, box 24, "Pennsylvania" folder 1 (42/54), Wilson-Welles Papers.

90. Florence Von Clare to Orson Welles, Oct. 31, 1938, box 24, "No Location" folder, Wilson-Welles Papers.

91. See Mrs. L. Sibert to WBBM, Nov. 3, 1938, box 23, "Indiana" folder (13/54); Rose Meyer to Orson Wells [sic], Oct. 30, 1938, box 24, "Missouri" folder (24/54), both Wilson-Welles Papers.

92. See A. W. Smithies to the Federal Radio Commission [sic], Oct. 30, 1938; Warner Ogden to the Federal Radio Communications Commission [sic], Oct. 30, 1938; Mrs. J. R. Ray to Frank R. McNinch, Nov. 1, 1938, all box 238, NARA; and Mrs. M. Carrcini to Orson Wells [sic], Oct. 30, 1938, box 24, "NYC & boroughs" folder 1 (33/54); Ruth S. Wadeson to Orson Welles, Nov. 1, 1938, box 24, "Ohio" folder (39/54); Mary Reilly to Orson Welles, Oct. 30, 1938, box 24, "New York, NYC & boroughs" folder 2 (30/54), all Wilson-Welles Papers.

93. Mary E. Ferguson to the FCC, Oct. 31, 1938, box 238, NARA.

94. Charles Nelson Coon to Orson Wells [sic], Nov. 1, 1938, box 24, "NYC & boroughs" folder 1 (33/54), Wilson-Welles Papers.

95. Amis Cooper to Orson Welles, Oct. 31, 1938, box 24, "Pennsylvania" folder 1 (42/54), Wilson-Welles Papers.

96. Heart attacks: "A Citizen" to F. R. McNinch, Oct. 30, 1938; Morris N. Kertzer to the Federal Radio Commission [sic], Oct. 31, 1938; Frank H. Warren to the FCC, Oct. 30, 1938; L. C. Miller to the Federal Radio Commission [sic], Oct. 31, 1938; John Groener to Frank McNinch, Oct. 31, 1938; Iva Collins to the FCC, Nov. 1, 1938; Ed R. Grisell to Frank R. McNinch, Nov. 1, 1938; H. Walker to the Federal Radio Commission [sic], Nov. 3, 1938, all box 238, NARA; and Therese Kelly to the Mercury Theatre, Oct. 30, 1938, box 24, "Pennsylvania" folder 2 (43/54); Aline M. Racken to the FCC, Oct. 31, 1938, box 23, "Connecticut" folder (6/54), both Wilson-Welles Papers. Doctors and hospitals: A. P. Bussman to Frank R. McNinch, n.d.; A. M. Thompson to the Radio Communications Commission [sic], Oct. 30, 1938; C. C. Linstroth to CBS, Nov. 12, 1938; Millard Boggs to the Federal Radio Commission [sic], Nov. 1, 1938; Bernard J. Lamin to Frank R. McNinch, Nov. 1, 1938; Paul R. Scheffey to CBS, Nov. 1, 1938, all box 238, NARA; and Martin Golda to the Mercury Theatre, Oct. 30, 1938, box 24, "New Jersey" folder 1 (29/54); Garrett Duryea to the Mercury Theater [sic], Oct. 30, 1938, box 24, "New York (state)" folder 1 (36/54), both Wilson-Welles Papers. See also Goodman, *Radio's Civic Ambition*, p. 273.

97. On Nov. 13, 1938, the Associated Press reported that sixty-year-old Samuel Shapiro of Baltimore had suffered a heart attack from listening to *War of the Worlds*. His family said that he had collapsed while preparing to flee the invaders. Shapiro was hospitalized and died on Nov. 12, almost two weeks after the show. With the relative lack of information surrounding Shapiro's death, and the fact that it occurred so long after the show, it seems impossible to tie it directly to *War of the Worlds*. Apparently, no major newspapers outside of Baltimore gave the story much coverage. If a direct link

had been proved, it almost certainly would have received greater attention. ("Jeweler Dies from Stroke Suffered After Radio Play," *Baltimore Sun*, Nov. 13, 1938, p. 22. "Death Blamed on Radio Scare," *Los Angeles Times*, Nov. 13, 1938, p. 3. "'Mars Invasion' Heart Attack Fatal to Baltimore Man," *Washington Post*, Nov. 13, 1938, p. M8.) One woman also wrote to the FCC that a friend of hers had died of a heart attack two days after being frightened by the broadcast. But, again, a direct link is impossible to prove. (Justine J. Roseman to Frank R. McNinch, Nov. 13, 1938, box 238, NARA.)

98. See Mrs. Ethel York to the Federal Radio Commission [*sic*], Oct. 31, 1938; R. M. Horner to the FCC, Oct. 31, 1938; Freda Schwartz to the Federal Radio Commission [*sic*], Oct. 31, 1938; Carl J. Baumann to the Communications Commission [*sic*], Oct. 31, 1938; Arthur J. Birkner to Frank R. McNinch, Oct. 31, 1938; Mrs. Frank Handlon to F. R. McNinch, Oct. 31, 1938; Hannah McGovern Wall to Frank P. [*sic*] McNinch, Oct. 31, 1938; Paul B. Eaton to Frank P. [*sic*] McNinch, Oct. 31, 1938; Claude L. Stewart to the FCC, Oct. 31, 1938; Lilla Wood Daniels to the FCC, Oct. 31, 1938; Evelyn R. McDonald to the FCC, Oct. 31, 1938; Warner Ogden to the Federal Radio Communications Commission [*sic*], Oct. 30, 1938; O. R. Lambert to Frank P. [*sic*] McNinch, Nov. 1, 1938; Elizabeth Brighton to C. R. [*sic*] McNinch, Oct. 31, 1938; Charles Merserau to Franklin D. Roosevelt, Oct. 30, 1938, all box 238, NARA; and Mrs. Seiner to Orson Welles, Oct. 30, 1938, box 24, "Pennsylvania" folder 2 (43/54); Ruthe B. Cohen to the Mercury Theatre, Oct. 31, 1938, box 24, "Pennsylvania" folder 2 (43/54); "A Listener" to the Mercury Theatre, Oct. 30, 1938, box 23, "Florida" folder (9/54); George E. Harris to Orson Wells [*sic*], Oct. 31, 1938, box 23, "California" folder (4/54); Aline M. Racken to the FCC, Oct. 31, 1938, box 23, "Connecticut" folder (6/54); Florence Benedetto to Orson Welles, Oct. 31, 1938, box 24, "New York, NYC & boroughs" folder 2 (34/54); Mary Parente to Orson Welles, Oct. 31, 1938, box 24, "New York (state)" folder 1 (36/54); Mrs. Max Boggs to CBS, n.d., box 23, "California" folder (4/54); B. E. Malloy to Orson Welles, Oct. 31, 1938, box 24, "Pennsylvania" folder 2 (43/54); Esther Belville to H. B. [*sic*] Wells, Oct. 31, 1938, box 23, "Indiana" folder (13/54); Martin Zeller to the Mercury Theather [*sic*], Oct. 31, 1938, box 24, "New Jersey" folder 1 (29/54), all Wilson-Welles Papers.

99. Perhaps the most serious case of fright found in the letters is one written to Welles by an Illinois man more than a month after the broadcast, claiming that his wife had not been able to work after suffering "a nervous collapse" during the program. He requested that CBS pay her lost wages (Arch E. Colburn to Orson Welles, Dec. 1, 1938, box 23, "Illinois" folder [12/54], Wilson-Welles Papers).

100. Fled: Mr. and Mrs. Fred Baker to Orton [*sic*] Welles, Oct. 30, 1938, box 23, "Michigan" folder (21/54); Estelle Paultz to Orson Wells [*sic*], Oct. 31, 1938, box 24, "NYC & boroughs" folder 1 (33/54); Anna Farrell to Orson Welles, Nov. 2, 1938, box 24, "New York, NYC & boroughs" folder 2 (34/54); Lewis Hong to Orson Wells [*sic*], Oct. 30, 1938, box 24, "Virginia" folder (51/54); Julia Summons to Orson Welles, Nov. 7, 1938, box 24, "New Jersey" folder 2 (30/54); J. Byron Morgan to Orson Welles, Oct. 30, 1938, box 24, "Virginia" folder (51/54), all Wilson-Welles Papers. Considered fleeing: Florence Turner to Orson Wells [*sic*], n.d., box 24, "No Location" folder; Alice Adams to Orson Welles, n.d., box 24, "No Location" folder; Benjamin Danish to Orson Welles, Oct. 30, 1938, box 24, "Pennsylvania" folder 2 (43/54); Donald Newhard to the Mercury Theatre, Oct. 30, 1938, box 24, "Pennsylvania" folder 1 (42/54); H. T. Miller to H. G. Wells [*sic*], Oct. 30, 1938, box 24, "Pennsylvania" folder 1 (42/54); J. Ford to Orson Welles, Oct. 30, 1938, box 24, "Pennsylvania" folder 1 (42/54); Marie Hahn to Orson Welles, Oct. 30, 1938, box 24, "Pennsylvania" folder 2 (43/54); Mrs. William Drumheller to Orson Welles, Oct. 30, 1938, box 24, "Pennsylvania" folder 1 (42/54); James H. Barnett to the Mercury Theatre, Oct. 30, 1938, box 24, "Pennsylvania" folder 1 (42/54); Mrs. Ethel Ristoni to the Mercury Theatre, n.d., box 24, "NYC & boroughs"

folder 1 (33/54); John King et al. to CBS, Oct. 30, 1938, box 24, "NYC & boroughs" folder 1 (33/54); Harold Greenhalgh to Orson Welles, Oct. 30, 1938, box 24, "New York (state)" folder 1 (36/54); Charles Nelson Coon to Orson Wells [sic], Nov. 1, 1938, box 24, "NYC & boroughs" folder 1 (33/54), all Wilson-Welles Papers.

101. Fled: Vernon R. Brien to the FCC, Oct. 31, 1938; Willard Shahart to the Federal Radio Commission [sic], Oct. 30, 1938; Anna Weber to the FCC, Nov. 1, 1938; O. Ceranes to the FCC, Oct. 30, 1938; E. J. Tembroeke to Frank R. McNinch, Oct. 31, 1938, all box 238, NARA. Clipping: Ingval Lynner to Frank R. McNinch, Nov. 5, 1938, box 238, NARA.

102. Mr. and Mrs. Fred Baker to Orton [sic] Welles, Oct. 30, 1938, box 23, "Michigan" folder (21/54), Wilson-Welles Papers.

103. Thomas E. Rhodes to Frank R. McNinch, Oct. 31, 1938, box 238, NARA. This may very well be the same incident reported in *The Washington Post* that same day ("Men of Mars Riding Meteor Terrorize U.S.," *Washington Post*, Oct. 31, 1938, p. 12).

104. Alvesta C. Flanagan to Orson Welles, Oct. 30, 1938, box 24, "Pennsylvania" folder 2 (43/54), Wilson-Welles Papers.

105. Gerta S. Brown to the Mercury Theater [sic], Nov. 2, 1938, box 24, "New York (state)" folder 2 (37/54), Wilson-Welles Papers. See also Florence Rohm to Frank R. McNinch, Oct. 31, 1938, box 238, NARA.

106. William Manchester, *The Death of a President: November 20–November 25, 1963* (New York: Harper & Row, 1967), p. 525.

107. See Mrs. N. D. Inman to the Radio Commission [sic], Oct. 30, 1938; Mrs. Philip Artese to Frank R. McNinch, Oct. 31, 1938; Mrs. G. Nesbith to the Federal Radio Commission [sic], Nov. 1, 1938; M. A. Hoeschen to Frank R. McNinch, Oct. 31, 1938; Doris Hurley to Frank R. McNinch, Oct. 31, 1938; Mrs. M. W. Durham to Frank McNinch, n.d., all box 238, NARA; and Mrs. M. Carrcini to Orson Wells [sic], Oct. 30, 1938, box 24, "NYC & boroughs" folder 1 (33/54); Lucile McLain to Orson Welles, Oct. 30, 1938, box 24, "Oregon" folder (41/54); Mrs. Butts to Orson Wells [sic], Oct. 30, 1938, box 24, "Pennsylvania" folder 2 (43/54); Mrs. Seiner to Orson Welles, Oct. 30, 1938, box 24, "Pennsylvania" folder 2 (43/54); George Weeden to the Mercury Theater [sic], Oct. 30, 1938, box 24, "Wisconsin" folder (54/54); Ingeborg Zimmer to CBS, Oct. 31, 1938, box 24, "New Jersey" folder 1 (29/54); Robert C. Bust to Orson Wells [sic], Oct. 30, 1938, box 24, "Pennsylvania" folder 1 (42/54); Bertha E. Boughton to Orson Wells [sic], n.d., box 24, "New York (state)" folder 1 (36/54); "Mr. & Mrs. A.K. and family and friends" to the Mercury Theatre, Oct. 30, 1938, box 23, "California" folder (4/54); Earl H. Stuart to WBBM, Oct. 30, 1938, box 23, "Illinois" folder (12/54); Esther Belville to H. B. [sic] Wells, Oct. 31, 1938, box 23, "Indiana" folder (13/54); Mrs. Charles Scheel to the Mercury Theatre, Oct. 31, 1938, box 23, "Maryland" folder (19/54); Unsigned to "Mr. Wells and Mr. Orson," n.d., box 24, "Ohio" folder (39/54); Merle Jennings to WBBM, Oct. 30, 1938, box 23, "Illinois" folder (12/54); Mr. and Mrs. Fred Baker to Orton [sic] Welles, Oct. 30, 1938, box 23, "Michigan" folder (21/54); Lois Davenport to Orson Welles, Oct. 30, 1938, box 23, "Minnesota" folder (22/54); Vicky Hunter to Orson Welles, Oct. 30, 1938, box 24, "NYC & boroughs" folder 1 (33/54); Mary Campbell to Orson Welles, Oct. 30, 1938, box 24, "No Location" folder; J. Stanley Ebb to Orson Welles, Oct. 30, 1938, box 24, "Virginia" folder (51/54); Sue Madison Richards to Orson Welles, Oct. 30, 1938, box 24, "Virginia" folder (51/54); Esther L. Hoadley to the Mercury Theater [sic], Oct. 31, 1938, box 23, "Illinois" folder (12/54); Agnes Riners to Orson Welles, Oct. 31, 1938, box 24, "New York, NYC & boroughs" folder 3 (35/54); Albert M. Fowler to Orson Welles, Nov. 6, 1938, box 24, "New Jersey" folder 1 (29/54); John F. Powers to Orson Wells [sic], Oct. 30, 1938, box 23, "Massachusetts" folder (20/54), all Wilson-Welles Papers.

108. See "A Citizen" to the "Radio Commission Secretary [sic]," Oct. 30, 1938; Paul H. Taylor to the FCC, Oct. 31, 1938; Fred J. Maser to the Radio Commission [sic], Oct. 31,

1938; A. C. Patterson to the Radio Commission [sic], Oct. 30, 1938; Frederick Samuels, Jr., to the Federal Bureau of Radio [sic], Oct. 30, 1938; Helen Degen to Frank P. [sic] McNinch, Oct. 31, 1938; J. Philip Schaefer to the FCC, Oct. 31, 1938; S. F. Bauer to the FCC, Oct. 31, 1938; Margaret C. Craig to Frank R. McNinch, Oct. 31, 1938; Arthur C. Gillette to Dorothy Thompson, Nov. 2, 1938; Justine J. Roseman to Frank R. McNinch, Nov. 13, 1938; Helen K. Matthew to F. P. [sic] McNinch, n.d., all box 238, NARA; and Sylvia Katz to Orson Welles, Oct. 30, 1938, box 24, "New Jersey" folder 2 (30/54); J. Ford to Orson Welles, Oct. 30, 1938, box 24, "Pennsylvania" folder 1 (42/54); Josephine Bowman to the Mercury Theatre, Oct. 30, 1938, box 24, "Pennsylvania" folder 1 (42/54); Gloria L. Skipper to WABC, Oct. 30, 1938, box 24, "New Jersey" folder 2 (30/54); Josephine O'Cone to Orson Welles, Oct. 31, 1938, box 24, "New Jersey" folder 3 (31/54); Lillian Spear to Orson Welles, Oct. 30, 1938, box 24, "New York, NYC & boroughs" folder 3 (35/54); Gerta S. Brown to the Mercury Theater [sic], Nov. 2, 1938, box 24, "New York (state)" folder 2 (37/54); A. Lee Schichtel to Orson Welles, Oct. 30, 1938, box 24, "New Jersey" folder 1 (29/54); Alvesta C. Flanagan to Orson Welles, Oct. 30, 1938, box 24, "Pennsylvania" folder 2 (43/54); Lulie Hard McKinley to Orson Welles, Oct. 30, 1938, box 23, "Alabama" folder (1/54); Betty Scymansky to Orson Welles, Oct. 30, 1938, box 24, "New Jersey" folder 1 (29/54); Mr. and Mrs. Edward Gee to the Mercury Theater [sic], Oct. 30, 1938, box 23, "California" folder (4/54); Iris A. Sebree to the Mercury Theater [sic], Oct. 30, 1938, box 23, "Florida" folder (9/54); Alfred C. Prime to Orson Welles, n.d., box 24, "Pennsylvania" folder 2 (43/54); Willson Bader to "Austin" Welles, n.d., box 24, "New Jersey" folder 1 (29/54), all Wilson-Welles Papers. For nonfrightened people told by frightened ones, see Alvin J. Bogart to the FCC, Oct. 31, 1938, box 237, NARA; and Mary D. Owen to H. G. Wells [sic], Oct. 31, 1938, box 24, "Ohio" folder (39/54); Luther John Binkley to Orson Welles, Nov. 1, 1938, box 24, "Pennsylvania" folder 2 (43/54); Sydney Marschalk Powell to Orson Welles, Nov. 3, 1938, box 24, "Texas" folder (48/54), all Wilson-Welles Papers.
109. Melissa Hanson to Orson Welles, Oct. 30, 1938, box 23, "Maryland" folder (19/54), Wilson-Welles Papers.
110. Campbell, *Getting It Wrong*, pp. 27, 38–41. See also Cantril, *Invasion*, pp. 140–143.
111. Anna Farrell to Orson Welles, Nov. 2, 1938, box 24, "New York, NYC & boroughs" folder 2 (34/54), Wilson-Welles Papers.
112. Johanna Wilizenski to Franklin D. Roosevelt, Nov. 1, 1938, box 238, NARA.
113. "Those terrified were not the ones who heard the fake news dispatches, but those who were told about it with such additions of emotion as may have been induced. If one susceptible, neurotic or simply credulous persons [sic] heard that a meteor had killed a lot of people and that all were in danger of a celestial bombardment, instead of listening to the rest of the program he might have rushed out to tell a dozen others, who told others, the total of those informed running up swiftly into the hundreds of thousands. I doubt if 1% of those who were panicked actually heard the broadcast or any part of it." (Henry Edward Warner to Frank McNinch, Oct. 31, 1938, box 238, NARA.)
114. Eleanor Buikema to the Mercury Theater [sic] of the Air, Oct. 30, 1938, box 24, "New Jersey" folder 3 (31/54), Wilson-Welles Papers.
115. Frederick Samuels, Jr., to the Federal Bureau of Radio [sic], Oct. 30, 1938, box 238, NARA.
116. Morris N. Kertzer to the Federal Radio Commission [sic], Oct. 31, 1938, box 238, NARA. Wesleyan Freshmen to Orson Wells [sic], Oct. 30, 1938, box 23, "Georgia" folder (10/54); Betty Krueger to Orson Wells [sic], Oct. 30, 1938, box 24, "Missouri" folder (24/54); La May Allen to Austin Wells [sic], Oct. 30, 1938, box 24, "North Carolina" folder (38/54); Janet K. Low to Orson Welles, Oct. 30, 1938, box 24, "Ohio" folder (39/54); Henry Ciemnolonski to Orson Wells [sic], Oct. 30, 1938, box 24, "Pennsylvania" folder 1; James H. Barnett et al. to the Mercury Theatre, Oct. 30, 1938, box 24,

"Pennsylvania" folder 1 (42/54); Phi Mu Delta Fraternity to WABC, Oct. 30, 1938, box 24, "Pennsylvania" folder 2 (43/54), all Wilson-Welles Papers. One letter ("A Group of West Va Univ Students" to Orson Wells [sic], Oct. 30, 1938, box 24, "West Virginia" folder [53/54], Wilson-Welles Papers) is quoted, with minor changes, in Cantril, *Invasion*, p. 53. For New Jersey, see Paul Bradbury to Orson Welles, Oct. 31, 1938, box 24, "New Jersey" folder 3 (31/54), Wilson-Welles Papers; Doris Kearns Goodwin, *The Fitzgeralds and the Kennedys: An American Saga* (New York: St. Martin's, 1977), p. 582. Peggy Daub of the University of Michigan's Special Collections Library also shared with me a letter, describing a similar disturbance at St. Joseph's College in Indiana, written by the student Sam Cartwright and kindly provided by his sister-in-law, Betty Wannamacher. See also "Radio War Drama Creates a Panic," p. 4; "Invasion Play on Radio Sends U.S. into Panic," *Baltimore Sun*, Oct. 31, 1938, p. 2.

117. Emmet Riordan to Orson Wells [sic], Oct. 30, 1938, box 24, "Oregon" folder (41/54), Wilson-Welles Papers.

118. Robert Keplinger to Orson Wells [sic], Oct. 30, 1938, box 23, "Kansas" folder (15/54), Wilson-Welles Papers.

119. Mary Cougedo to Orson Wells [sic], Oct. 30, 1938, box 24, "New Jersey" folder 2 (30/54), Wilson-Welles Papers. See also Alfred C. Prime to Orson Welles, n.d., box 24, "Pennsylvania" folder 2 (43/54); J. William Althaus to the Mercury Theatre, Oct. 30, 1938, box 24, "Ohio" folder (39/54), both Wilson-Welles Papers.

120. Fred Elliott to Orson Welles, Nov. 2, 1938, box 23, "Michigan" folder (21/54), Wilson-Welles Papers.

121. Cantril, *Invasion*, pp. 140–43.

122. See Campbell, *Getting It Wrong*, p. 39.

123. Arthur C. Gillette to Dorothy Thompson, Nov. 2, 1938, box 238, NARA.

124. Murray M. Allen to Orson Welles, Oct. 31, 1938, box 23, "California" folder (4/54), Wilson-Welles Papers.

125. Harry W. Clifford to Orson Welles, Oct. 30, 1938, box 24, "New Jersey" folder 1 (29/54); Betty Scymansky to Orson Welles, Oct. 30, 1938, box 24, "New Jersey" folder 1 (29/54), both Wilson-Welles Papers.

126. Peter Van Wyk to Orson Wells [sic], Oct. 31, 1938, box 24, "New Jersey" folder 1 (29/54), Wilson-Welles Papers.

127. Mildred Jepsen and Marion Martinsen to Orson Wells [sic], Oct. 30, 1938, box 24, "South Dakota" folder (46/54), Wilson-Welles Papers.

128. Mrs. Seiner to Orson Welles, Oct. 30, 1938, box 24, "Pennsylvania" folder 2 (43/54), Wilson-Welles Papers. See also Earl H. Stuart to WBBM, Oct. 30, 1938, box 23, "Illinois" folder (12/54); Esther Belville to H. B. [sic] Wells, Oct. 31, 1938, box 23, "Indiana" folder (13/54); Mr. and Mrs. Fred Baker to Orton [sic] Welles, Oct. 30, 1938, box 23, "Michigan" folder (21/54), all Wilson-Welles Papers.

129. "AT&T Operators Recall War of the Worlds Broadcast—AT&T Archives" (2012), 6:23, YouTube, http://youtu.be/R29BTsoIHpQ (accessed May 17, 2013). *The Battle Over Citizen Kane* (1996), *American Experience* (WGBH Boston), *Citizen Kane* DVD, disc 2, directed by Michael Epstein and Thomas Lennon (Atlanta: Turner Home Entertainment, 2001). "Radio Listeners in Panic, Taking War Drama as Fact," *New York Times*, Oct. 31, 1938, pp. 1, 4. Gosling, *Waging the War*, pp. 46, 49–50. Brown, *Manipulating the Ether*, p. 221. Robert E. Bartholomew and Benjamin Radford, *The Martians Have Landed! A History of Media-Driven Panics and Hoaxes* (Jefferson, N.C.: McFarland, 2012), p. 17. Howard Koch, *The Panic Broadcast: Portrait of an Event* (Boston: Little, Brown, 1970), pp. 22, 29. Campbell, *Getting It Wrong*, pp. 35–36. I am skeptical of the claim (advanced by Miller [*Collective Behavior*, p. 143] and Campbell [p. 36], among others) that many of these calls were from nonfrightened listeners calling friends and relatives to talk excitedly about the show. There is little evidence of

such behavior in the letters, or anywhere else. Though a handful of people may have done this, it seems highly unlikely that they made up a significant portion of the sudden flood of calls. All evidence suggests that the bulk of the calls were from frightened listeners.

130. Cantril, *Invasion*, p. 60. "F.C.C. Inquiry Is Ordered into Radio War Play," p. 19. "U.S. Body Demands War Scare Script," *New York Sun*, Oct. 31, 1938, p. 3. "Some St. Louisans Fall for 'Men from Mars' Yarn," *St. Louis Post-Dispatch*, Oct. 31, 1938, p. 3A.

131. "Sidelights on the Mars Scare," *New York Sun*, Oct. 31, 1938, p. 3. See also Gosling, *Waging the War*, p. 50.

132. Frank Hurst to Orson Welles, Nov. 20, 1938, box 24, "Pennsylvania" folder 2 (43/54), Wilson-Welles Papers.

133. "Radio War Drama Creates a Panic," p. 4. Gosling, *Waging the War*, p. 49.

134. "Radio Play Causes Panic: Thousands Plunged into Hysteria," *San Francisco Examiner*, Oct. 31, 1938, p. 9.

135. Paul Morton to the FCC, Oct. 31, 1938, box 238, NARA.

136. Cantril, *Invasion* p. 60.

137. Ibid., pp. 43–44. O. J. Kelchner to the FCC, Nov. 2, 1938, box 238, NARA. One of the affiliates that frequently interrupted the show was station WJR in Detroit. See Harry S. Goodwin, Jr., to Orson Welles, Nov. 2, 1938; and William Hossick to Orson Welles, Oct. 30, 1938, both box 23, "Michigan" folder (21/54), Wilson-Welles Papers.

138. "Hysteria Grips East Coast After Fake Radio Bulletins," *Detroit Free Press*, Oct. 31, 1938, p. 2. "Thousands Flee, Pray and Weep as Radio War Play Panics U.S.," *Baltimore Sun*, Oct. 31, 1938, p. 1. "Listeners Weep and Pray, Prepare for End of World When Radio Puts On Show," New Orleans *Times-Picayune*, Oct. 31, 1938, p. 3. See also Gosling, *Waging the War*, p. 50.

139. Campbell, *Getting It Wrong*, p. 36.

140. Edith B. Slack to Frank R. McNinch, Nov. 1, 1938, box 238, NARA.

141. "Some St. Louisans Fall for 'Men from Mars' Yarn," p. 3A. See also "Thousands Flee, Pray and Weep," p. 2. "Radio Play Causes Panic," p. 9.

142. "Many Baltimoreans, Near Hysteria, Are Persuaded Not to Flee Homes," *Baltimore Sun*, Oct. 31, 1938, p. 2.

143. Quoted in Gosling, *Waging the War*, p. 64.

144. "Attack from Mars in Radio Play Puts Thousands in Fear," *New York Herald Tribune*, Oct. 31, 1938, p. 1. See also "War: Maryland Sector," *Baltimore Sun*, Oct. 31, 1938, pp. 1–2.

145. See "Radio Listeners in Panic," pp. 1, 4. "'Mars Invasion' Broadcast Creates Panic over Nation," *Atlanta Constitution*, Oct. 31, 1938, pp. 1, 7. "Radio Story of Mars Raid Causes Panic," *Los Angeles Times*, Oct. 31, 1938, p. 1. "Worried Listeners Ask News of Globe," p. 10. "Invasion Play on Radio," p. 2.

146. "Listeners Inquire About 'Catastrophe,'" New Orleans *Times-Picayune*, Oct. 31, 1938, p. 3.

147. See "Radio War Drama Creates a Panic," p. 4.

148. Kathryn A. Kraemer to the FCC, Oct. 30, 1938, box 238, NARA.

149. Kathryn Erniston to Orson Wells [sic], Oct. 30, 1938, box 23, "Florida" folder (9/54), Wilson-Welles Papers.

150. Jean L. Masterson to Orson Welles, Nov. 2, 1938, box 24, "Pennsylvania" folder 1 (42/54), Wilson-Welles Papers.

151. Miller, *Collective Behavior*, pp. 142–43. Robert E. Bartholomew, *Little Green Men, Meowing Nuns and Head-Hunting Panics: A Study of Mass Psychogenic Illness and Social Delusion* (Jefferson, N.C.: McFarland, 2001), pp. 18–19. Gosling, *Waging the War*, pp. 75–76.

152. Koch, *Panic Broadcast*, p. 24.

153. "Fake Radio 'War' Stirs Terror Through U.S.," New York *Daily News*, Oct. 31, 1938, p. 1.

154. Campbell, *Getting It Wrong*, p. 32.

155. See Joe Nickell, "Shootout with Martians: In the Wake of the 1938 Broadcast Panic," *Skeptical Inquirer*, vol. 20, no. 4 (Dec. 2010), www.csicop.org/sb/show/shootout_with _martians_in_the_wake_of_the_1938_broadcast_panic/ (accessed Jan. 16, 2014).

156. See, for example, Howard Koch's visit to Grover's Mill thirty-one years after the broadcast, in Koch, *Panic Broadcast*, pp. 115-33. See also Campbell, *Getting It Wrong*, p. 37.

157. Cantril, *Invasion*, pp. 55-58.

158. Lillian Spear to Orson Welles, Oct. 30, 1938, box 24, "New York, NYC & boroughs" folder 3 (35/54), Wilson-Welles Papers.

159. Mrs. J. R. McCalla to Orson Wells [*sic*], Oct. 31, 1938, box 23, "Georgia" folder (10/54), Wilson-Welles Papers.

160. Houseman, *Run-Through*, p. 403.

161. Strunk and Cantril, eds., *Public Opinion*, p. 717.

162. "Divided Reaction to Mars Broadcast," *Broadcasting*, Nov. 15, 1938, p. 28.

163. Cantril, *Invasion*, p. 201.

164. Lucile McLain to Orson Welles, Oct. 30, 1938, box 24, "Oregon" folder (41/54), Wilson-Welles Papers.

165. See Miss K. Doyle to Orson Welles, Oct. 30, 1938, box 24, "Rhode Island" folder (44/54), Wilson-Welles Papers.

166. George Weeden to the Mercury Theater [*sic*], Oct. 30, 1938, box 24, "Wisconsin" folder (54/54), Wilson-Welles Papers.

167. "A TAX PAYER" to the Mercury Theatre, Oct. 30, 1938, box 24, "No Location" folder, Wilson-Welles Papers.

168. A. G. Kennedy to Orson Wells [*sic*], Nov. 1, 1938, box 1, "Mercury Theatre on the Air. 'War of the Worlds' (10/30/38). Fan mail, 1938" folder, Welles-Kodar Collection. Also in Correspondence box 1, "1938. May-Dec." folder, Welles mss.

169. Hannah McGovern Wall to Frank P. [*sic*] McNinch, Oct. 31, 1938, box 238, NARA. See also Mrs. Ed Myers to the FCC, n.d., box 238, NARA.

170. Lydia Hank to Orson Welles, Oct. 30, 1938, box 24, "New Jersey" folder 2 (30/54), Wilson-Welles Papers.

171. J. William Althaus to the Mercury Theatre, Oct. 30, 1938, box 24, "Ohio" folder (39/54), Wilson-Welles Papers.

172. Miss K. Doyle to Orson Welles, Oct. 30, 1938, box 24, "Rhode Island" folder (44/54), Wilson-Welles Papers.

173. Mary Campbell to Orson Welles, Oct. 30, 1938, box 24, "No Location" folder, Wilson-Welles Papers. See also Vicky Hunter to Orson Welles, Oct. 30, 1938, box 24, "NYC & boroughs" folder 1 (33/54), Wilson-Welles Papers.

174. "FCC to Scan Script of 'War' Broadcast," *New York Times*, Nov. 1, 1938, p. 26.

175. "F.C.C. Orders Inquiry into Radio Scare," *New York Herald Tribune*, Nov. 1, 1938, p. 1.

176. Carl Kleve to Orson Welles, Nov. 3, 1938, box 24, "Ohio" folder (39/54), Wilson-Welles Papers.

177. Dorothy Springer to the Mercury Theater [*sic*], Nov. 3, 1938, box 24, "Wisconsin" folder (54/54), Wilson-Welles Papers.

178. John H. Dent to Frank McNinch, Oct. 31, 1938, box 238, NARA. See also Mrs. L. A. Bernard to the FCC, Oct. 31, 1938, box 238, NARA.

179. Barnouw, *Golden Web*, p. 72. Robert T. Elson, *Time Inc.: The Intimate History of a Publishing Enterprise, 1923-1941*, ed. Duncan Norton-Taylor (New York: Atheneum, 1968), p. 183. Raymond Fielding, *The March of Time, 1935-1951* (New York: Oxford

University Press, 1978), p. 19. See also Cantril and Allport, *Psychology of Radio*, p. 96. Goodman, *Radio's Civic Ambition*, pp. 98, 268.

180. Mrs. Andrew J. Mauney to Frank R. McNinch, Nov. 3, 1938, box 237, NARA.
181. "Radio War Drama Creates a Panic," p. 4.
182. Quoted in Brady, *Citizen Welles*, p. 173.

5. "Public Frightener No. 1"

1. Joe Smith to Frank McNish [*sic*], Oct. 31, 1938, box 237, NARA.
2. David A. Crespy, *Richard Barr: The Playwright's Producer* (Carbondale: Southern Illinois University Press, 2013), pp. 16–17. See also Richard Barr, interviewed by Frank Beacham, p. 3, box 14, "*Theatre of the Imagination* (1988). Interviews [transcripts]. 1988" folder, Wilson-Welles Papers.
3. See John Houseman, *Run-Through: A Memoir* (New York: Simon & Schuster, 1972), pp. 398–403.
4. Ibid., pp. 402–403. Interview with John Houseman, in *Theatre of the Imagination: The Mercury Company Remembers*, audio documentary written and produced by Frank Beacham, narrated by Leonard Maltin (Santa Monica: Voyager Company, 1988), in *Theatre of the Imagination: Radio Stories by Orson Welles and the Mercury Theatre* laserdisc, side 2, analog track 2, chap. 14.
5. "Dracula," *The Mercury Theatre on the Air*, CBS (New York, NY: WABC, July 11, 1938), CD (Radio Spirits).
6. Orson Welles, interviewed by Peter Bogdanovich, in *This Is Orson Welles* (New York: Harper Audio, 1992), tape 4, side 7.
7. A letter written to the secretary of the interior about the broadcast (Thomas Brosnan to Harold Ickes, Nov. 2, 1938, box 238, NARA) quotes a news article in which Taylor says he "went to the broadcasting room and tried to induce Welles to change his ending when he was supposed to announce that the broadcast was a Hallowe'en prank." The name of the paper is not given, so I have been unable to find the source of the quote, but I have no reason to doubt its veracity. It's a much more reasonable explanation for Taylor's behavior than those that other sources have inferred, such as that he was trying to stop the broadcast. See also William Alland's description of this exchange in *The Battle Over Citizen Kane* (1996), *American Experience* (WGBH Boston), *Citizen Kane* DVD, disc 2, directed by Michael Epstein and Thomas Lennon (Atlanta: Turner Home Entertainment, 2001); Robert J. Brown, *Manipulating the Ether: The Power of Broadcast Radio in Thirties America* (Jefferson, N.C.: McFarland, 1998), p. 226.
8. Richard Barr, the source of this anecdote, was apparently sure the call came from Michigan, but he alternately gave the location as Flint, Detroit, or Ann Arbor (Crespy, *Richard Barr*, p. 17). Richard Barr, interviewed by Frank Beacham, p. 3, box 14, "*Theatre of the Imagination* (1988). Interviews [transcripts]. 1988" folder, Wilson-Welles Papers. It's unclear if this is the same call that Houseman described in his memoirs as coming from "the mayor of some Midwestern city, one of the big ones," but it seems likely (Houseman, *Run-Through*, p. 404).
9. Orson Welles and Peter Bogdanovich, *This Is Orson Welles*, ed. Jonathan Rosenbaum (New York: Da Capo Press, 1998), p. 18. Frank Brady, *Citizen Welles: A Biography of Orson Welles* (New York: Scribner, 1989), p. 170. There has been some doubt that there actually were police in the studio that night, as Welles claimed (see David Thomson, *Rosebud: The Story of Orson Welles* [New York: Vintage Books, 1996], p. 103). But other members of the Mercury who were there that night, including William Alland, Richard Barr, William Herz, John Houseman, Paul Stewart, and Richard Wilson, all later said they saw the officers as well. See Barnouw, *Golden Web*, p. 87; Simon Callow, *Orson Welles: The Road to Xanadu* (New York: Viking, 1995), p. 404; Crespy, *Richard*

Barr, p. 17; Houseman, *Run-Through*, p. 404; *The Battle Over Citizen Kane*; Michael Ogden, "RE: Were the Mercury players aware of the panic?" posting to oldradio.net, Oct. 23, 2009, http://jeff560.tripod.com/wotw.html (accessed Feb. 19, 2013).

10. Barnouw, *Golden Web*, p. 87. Brady, *Citizen Welles*, p. 170.

11. "Radio War Drama Creates a Panic," *New York Times*, Oct. 31, 1938, p. 4. "Listeners Weep and Pray, Prepare for End of World, When Radio Puts On Show," New Orleans *Times-Picayune*, Oct. 31, 1938, p. 3. "Nation-Wide Panic Caused by Radio Play," *San Francisco Examiner*, Oct. 31, 1938, p. 1. Brady, *Citizen Welles*, p. 170.

12. Houseman, *Run-Through*, p. 404. Howard Koch, interviewed by Joe Bevilacqua, in *We Take You Now to Grover's Mill: The Making of the War of the Worlds Broadcast* (Napanoch, N.Y.: Waterlogg Productions, 2011).

13. Quoted in Callow, *Road to Xanadu*, p. 404. See also Crespy, *Richard Barr*, p. 17.

14. Houseman, *Run-Through*, p. 404.

15. Interview with John Houseman, in *Theatre of the Imagination: The Mercury Company Remembers*, written and produced by Frank Beacham, narrated by Leonard Maltin (Santa Monica: Voyager Company, 1988), *Theatre of the Imagination: Radio Stories by Orson Welles and the Mercury Theatre* laserdisc, side 2, analog track 2, chap. 14. Houseman, interviewed by Bevilacqua, in *We Take You Now to Grover's Mill*. See also Houseman, *Run-Through*, p. 404. John Houseman, introduction to Howard Koch, *As Time Goes By: Memoirs of a Writer* (New York: Harcourt Brace Jovanovich, 1979), p. xiv.

16. Ben Gross, *I Looked and Listened: Informal Recollections of Radio and TV* (New York: Random House, 1954), p. 199.

17. "U.S. Investigates Radio War Drama," *New York World-Telegram*, Oct. 31, 1938, p. 8, box 27, "Radio. Mercury Theatre on the Air. War of the Worlds. Articles & Clippings, 1938" folder, Welles-Kodar Collection. See also "Sidelights on the Mars Scare," *New York Sun*, Oct. 31, 1938, p. 3.

18. See "Radio Listeners in Panic, Taking War Drama as Fact," *New York Times*, Oct. 31, 1938, pp. 1, 4. "'Mars Invasion' Broadcast Creates Panic over Nation," *Atlanta Constitution*, Oct. 31, 1938, pp. 1, 7. "Radio Story of Mars Raid Causes Panic," *Los Angeles Times*, Oct. 31, 1938, p. 1. "Worried Listeners Ask News of Globe," *Boston Globe*, Oct. 31, 1938, p. 10. "Invasion Play on Radio Sends U.S. into Panic," *Baltimore Sun*, Oct. 31, 1938, p. 2.

19. "Radio War Drama Creates a Panic," *New York Times*, Oct. 31, 1938, p. 4.

20. "Worried Listeners," p. 10.

21. John Gosling, *Waging the War of the Worlds: A History of the 1938 Radio Broadcast and Resulting Panic* (Jefferson, N.C.: McFarland, 2009), pp. 60, 62.

22. "F.C.C. Inquiry Is Ordered into Radio War Play," *New York Herald Tribune*, Nov. 1, 1938, p. 19.

23. "Geologists at Princeton Hunt 'Meteor' in Vain," *New York Times*, Oct. 31, 1938, p. 4. Gosling, *Waging the War*, p. 62. W. Joseph Campbell, *Getting It Wrong: Ten of the Greatest Misreported Stories in American Journalism* (Berkeley: University of California Press, 2010), p. 38.

24. "F.C.C. Inquiry Is Ordered," p. 19. See also "Geologists at Princeton Hunt," p. 4. "Men of Mars Riding Meteor Terorrize U.S.," *Washington Post*, Oct. 31, 1938, p. 12. "Hysteria Grips East Coast After Fake Radio Bulletins," *Detroit Free Press*, Oct. 31, 1938, p. 2. "'Where Is Safe?': Incidents, Sad and Funny, in Wake of Broadcast," *Milwaukee Journal*, Oct. 31, 1938, p. 3. Campbell, *Getting It Wrong*, pp. 37–38.

25. See "Radio Listeners in Panic," pp. 1, 4. "'Mars Invasion' Broadcast," pp. 1, 7. "Radio Story of Mars Raid," p. 1. "Worried Listeners," p. 10.

26. "Radio War Drama Creates a Panic," p. 4. See also Marshall Andrews, "Monsters of Mars on a Meteor Stampede Radiotic America," *Washington Post*, Oct. 31, 1938, p. X1.

27. See "Air Sketch Spreads Fright Through Homes in Detroit," *Detroit Free Press*, Oct. 31, 1938, p. 1.

28. "Hysteria Grips East Coast," p. 2. "Thousands Flee, Pray and Weep as Radio War Play Panics U.S.," *Baltimore Sun*, Oct. 31, 1938, p. 1. "Listeners Weep and Pray, Prepare for End of World," p. 3.

29. "Radio War Drama Creates a Panic," p. 4. See also "War's Over: How U.S. Met Mars," New York *Daily News*, Oct. 31, 1938, p. 2, box 2, "Clippings and Articles, 1936–1940" folder (2 of 4), Welles-Feder Collection; "Sidelights on the Mars Scare," p. 3; Campbell, *Getting It Wrong*, pp. 34–35.

30. Campbell, *Getting It Wrong*, pp. 34–35.

31. Gross, *I Looked and Listened*, p. 201.

32. Andrews, "Monsters of Mars," p. X1.

33. "Radio Story of Mars Raid," p. 1.

34. "Mass Hysteria Seizes East Coast After Fake Radio News Bulletins Report Chaos Following Invasion," *Detroit Free Press*, Oct. 31, 1938, p. 1. See also "Listeners Weep and Pray, Prepare for End of World," p. 3; "'Mars Invasion' Broadcast," p. 1. "Radio Play Terrifies Nation," *Boston Globe*, Oct. 31, 1938, p. 1; Campbell, *Getting It Wrong*, p. 35.

35. See Campbell, *Getting It Wrong*, pp. 31–33.

36. "Radio War Drama Creates a Panic," p. 4. See also "Men of Mars Riding Meteor," p. 12; "Hysteria Grips East Coast," p. 2; "'Mars Invasion' Broadcast," p. 7; "Radio Play Terrifies Nation," p. 10; "Mars Invasion in Radio Skit Terrifies U.S.," *New York Herald Tribune*, Oct. 31, 1938, p. 26.

37. "Radio War Drama Creates a Panic," p. 4. See also "Men of Mars Riding Meteor," p. 12; "Hysteria Grips East Coast," p. 2; "'Mars Invasion' Broadcast," pp. 1, 7; "Radio Play Terrifies Nation," pp. 1, 10; "U.S. Body Demands War Scare Script," *New York Sun*, Oct. 31, 1938, p. 3; "Radio Play Causes Panic," p. 9.

38. "Radio War Drama Creates a Panic," p. 4. Campbell, *Getting It Wrong*, pp. 39–40.

39. Campbell, *Getting It Wrong*, pp. 33–38.

40. See "Worried Listeners," p. 10; "Air Sketch Spreads Fright," p. 1; "Detroit Gets Jitters Listening to Radio," *Detroit News*, Oct. 31, 1938, pp. 1–2, box 2, "Clippings and Articles, 1936–1940" folder (2 of 4), Welles-Feder Collection; "Radio Story of Invasion by Mars Upsets Nation," *Los Angeles Times*, Oct. 31, 1938, p. 2; "Listeners Inquire About 'Catastrophe,'" New Orleans *Times-Picayune*, Oct. 31, 1938, p. 3; "Examiner Gets 'Disaster' Calls," *San Francisco Examiner*, Oct. 31, 1938, p. 9.

41. "Milwaukee Laughs at Charlie's Quips as 'Martian Monsters' Spread Fear," *Milwaukee Journal*, Oct. 31, 1938, p. 1.

42. "Radio Listeners in Panic," p. 1.

43. "Listeners Weep and Pray," p. 3.

44. "Hysteria Grips East Coast," p. 2.

45. "Radio Listeners in Panic," pp. 1, 4.

46. Ibid. "Radio Story of Mars Raid," p. 1.

47. George Dixon, "Fake 'War' on Radio Spreads Panic over U.S.," New York *Daily News*, Oct. 31, 1938, p. 2, box 2, "Clippings and Articles, 1936–1940" folder (2 of 4), Welles-Feder Collection. See also "Radio Story of Attack from Mars Causes Hysteria," *St. Louis Post-Dispatch*, Oct. 31, 1938, p. 3A.

48. "Men of Mars Riding Meteor," p. 12. See also "Radio War Drama Creates a Panic," p. 4; "'End of World' Broadcast Quiz Started by FCC," *Chicago Daily Tribune*, Nov. 1, 1938, p. 17; "Federal Board Asks for Script of Wells Play," *New York Sun*, Oct. 31, 1938, p. 1; "Invasion Play on Radio," p. 2; "Radio Listeners Alarmed by Fictional Broadcast of Attack by Men from Mars," *St. Louis Post-Dispatch*, Oct. 31, 1938, p. 1.

49. "Milwaukee Laughs at Charlie's Quips," p. 1.

50. "Men of Mars Riding Meteor," p. 12. "Hysteria Grips East Coast," p. 2.

51. Hadley Cantril with Hazel Gaudet and Herta Herzog, *The Invasion from Mars: A Study in the Psychology of Panic* (New York: Harper & Row, 1966), p. 210.
52. Erika Kinetz, "Is Hysteria Real? Brain Images Say Yes," *New York Times*, Sept. 26, 2006, www.nytimes.com/2006/09/26/science/26hysteria.html (accessed Jan. 21, 2014).
53. Lydel Sims to Frank P. [sic] McNinch, Oct. 31, 1938, box 238, NARA. Also in Correspondence box 1, "1938. May-Dec." folder, Welles mss. See also Magdalene Lehrer to Orson Welles, Oct. 31, 1938, box 23, "Michigan" folder (21/54), Wilson-Welles Papers.
54. Welles and Bogdanovich, *This Is Orson Welles*, p. 19. Orson Welles, interviewed by Tom Snyder, *Tomorrow with Tom Snyder*, NBC, Sept. 1975, Paley Center for Media iCollection for Colleges, catalog ID T:35495. Todd Tarbox, *Orson Welles and Roger Hill: A Friendship in Three Acts* (Albany, Ga.: BearManor Media, 2013), p. 53.
55. Houseman, *Run-Through*, pp. 404–405. John Houseman, interviewed by Leonard Maltin, April 22, 1988, p. 10, box 14, "Theatre of the Imagination (1988). Interviews [transcripts]. 1988" folder, Wilson-Welles Papers. Houseman, interviewed by Bevilacqua, in *We Take You Now to Grover's Mill*.
56. Campbell, *Getting It Wrong*, pp. 27, 41–43. See also Jefferson Pooley and Michael Socolow, "The Myth of the *War of the Worlds* Panic," *Slate*, Oct. 28, 2013, www.slate.com /articles/arts/history/2013/10/orson_welles_war_of_the_worlds_panic_myth_the _infamous_radio_broadcast_did.html (accessed Dec. 17, 2013). The only researcher to treat this idea with any real skepticism is John Gosling (*Waging the War of the Worlds*, pp. 56–60, 67).
57. Paul W. White, *News on the Air* (New York: Harcourt, Brace, 1947), p. 30. Brown, *Manipulating the Ether*, pp. 136–38.
58. Quoted in Barnouw, *Tower in Babel*, p. 278.
59. Francis Chase, Jr., *Sound and Fury: An Informal History of Broadcasting* (New York: Harper & Brothers, 1942), pp. 133–34. See also Barnouw, *Tower in Babel*, p. 138; Brown, *Manipulating the Ether*, pp. 132–33; Gwenyth L. Jackaway, *Media at War: Radio's Challenge to the Newspaper, 1924–1939* (Westport, Conn.: Praeger, 1995), pp. 14–15.
60. Jackaway, *Media at War*, pp. 14–19. See also Chase, *Sound and Fury*, pp. 134–36; Michael Stamm, "The Sound of Print: Newspapers and the Public Promotion of Early Radio Broadcasting in the United States," in *Sound in the Age of Mechanical Reproduction*, ed. David Suisman and Susan Strasser (Philadelphia: University of Pennsylvania Press, 2010), pp. 230–31; Susan J. Douglas, *Listening In: Radio and the American Imagination* (Minneapolis: University of Minnesota Press, 2004), p. 167.
61. Chase, *Sound and Fury*, pp. 134–35. Jackaway, *Media at War*, pp. 19–20, 85. White, *News on the Air*, p. 34. Hadley Cantril and Gordon Allport, *The Psychology of Radio* (New York: Harper & Brothers, 1935), p. 240.
62. Barnouw, *Tower in Babel*, p. 267. Barnouw, *Golden Web*, p. 18. Brown, *Manipulating the Ether*, pp. 30, 136. Douglas, *Listening In*, pp. 166–67. Jackaway, *Media at War*, pp. 20–24. White, *News on the Air*, pp. 35–36.
63. "A.P. and A.N.P.A. Declare War on Radio," *Broadcasting*, May 1, 1933, pp. 5–6. Barnouw, *Golden Web*, pp. 18–19. Brown, *Manipulating the Ether*, pp. 136–37. Douglas, *Listening In*, p. 167. Jackaway, *Media at War*, pp. 24–25. White, *News on the Air*, p. 36.
64. Barnouw, *Golden Web*, pp. 19–20. Brown, *Manipulating the Ether*, p. 137. Chase, *Sound and Fury*, p. 136. Jackaway, *Media at War*, pp. 25–27. White, *News on the Air*, pp. 38–40.
65. Barnouw, *Golden Web*, p. 20. Brown, *Manipulating the Ether*, p. 137.
66. Quoted in White, *News on the Air*, p. 41.
67. Barnouw, *Golden Web*, pp. 20–21. Brown, *Manipulating the Ether*, p. 137. Chase, *Sound and Fury*, p. 136. Douglas, *Listening In*, pp. 167–68. Jackaway, *Media at War*, pp. 27–29. White, *News on the Air*, pp. 41–42.

68. Jackaway, *Media at War*, pp. 29–34. See also Barnouw, *Golden Web*, p. 21; Brown, *Manipulating the Ether*, p. 137; Chase, *Sound and Fury*, p. 136; Douglas, *Listening In*, p. 168; White, *News on the Air*, pp. 43–44.

69. "Newspapers End Antagonism to Rādio," *Broadcasting*, May 1, 1937, p. 15.

70. Ibid. Barnouw, *Golden Web*, p. 22. Brown, *Manipulating the Ether*, pp. 138, 172. Jackaway, *Media at War*, p. 32. Stamm, "Sound of Print," pp. 223, 232–33.

71. Bruce Robertson, "ANPA Moves Toward Harmony with Radio," *Broadcasting*, May 1, 1939, pp. 11, 68.

72. Brown, *Manipulating the Ether*, p. 172. Cantril and Allport, *Psychology of Radio*, p. 98.

73. Paul F. Lazarsfeld, *Radio and the Printed Page: An Introduction to the Study of Radio and Its Role in the Communication of Ideas* (New York: Duell, Sloan and Pearce, 1940), pp. 261–64. Chase, *Sound and Fury*, p. 134. Stamm, "Sound of Print," pp. 222, 234–35.

74. Lazarsfeld, *Radio and the Printed Page*, pp. 246–50. See also Douglas, *Listening In*, pp. 174–75.

75. "War Service a Radio High Spot," *Broadcasting*, Oct. 15, 1938, p. 62.

76. Chase, *Sound and Fury*, p. 145.

77. "War Service a Radio High Spot," p. 62. Douglas, *Listening In*, p. 161.

78. Lazarsfeld, *Radio and the Printed Page*, pp. 263–64.

79. Bruce Robertson, "ANPA Moves Toward Harmony," p. 68.

80. Lazarsfeld, *Radio and the Printed Page*, pp. 264–65, 276. Cantril and Allport, *Psychology of Radio*, pp. 32–33. Chase, *Sound and Fury*, pp. 137, 145. Stamm, "Sound of Print," pp. 236–38. White, *News on the Air*, pp. 29–30.

81. Stamm, "Sound of Print," pp. 232–36.

82. Lazarsfeld, *Radio and the Printed Page*, pp. 272–76.

83. "Peter Quill Returns for New Mutual Series Next Friday," *Chicago Tribune*, Feb. 19, 1939, p. W5.

84. Special Agent, "Crimson Wizard," *Chicago Tribune*, Oct. 2, 1938, pp. G1, G3.

85. No recordings of *The Crimson Wizard* are known to exist, so this summary of the show is based on the recap printed in the following Sunday's *Chicago Tribune* (ibid., pp. G1, G3, G9).

86. "Hundreds Call Police to Ask of Peter Quill," *Chicago Daily Tribune*, Oct. 1, 1938, p. 1.

87. Jackaway, *Media at War*, p. 14. Leonard Maltin, *The Great American Broadcast: A Celebration of Radio's Golden Age* (New York: Dutton, 1997), p. 4. Stamm, "Sound of Print," pp. 224–29.

88. Karl H. Schadow, "Peter Quill, the Crimson Wizard: America's Radio Hunchback Hero," *Radio Recall*, Oct. 2004, www.mwotrc.com/rr2004_10/quill.htm (accessed Jan. 18, 2014). Special Agent, "Crimson Wizard," p. G1. WGN and the *Tribune* had a history of similar cross-promotions, beginning with the radio series *Sam 'n' Henry*—which later became *Amos 'n' Andy* (Stamm, "Sound of Print," pp. 226–28).

89. "Hundreds Call Police," p. 1.

90. "The Government Pursues 'The Red Circle,'" *Chicago Tribune*, Oct. 9, 1938, p. 16.

91. Newspapers published on that date and available for review at the Harold Washington Library Center in Chicago include the *Chicago American*, *The Chicago Daily News*, the *Chicago Daily Times*, and the Chicago *Herald Examiner*.

92. "Realistic Radio Broadcast Gives Public a Scare,'" *Chicago Daily Tribune*, Oct. 31, 1938, p. 3.

93. Claude W. Morris to the Federal Radio Commission [*sic*], Nov. 2, 1938, box 238, NARA.

94. White, *News on the Air*, p. 23.

95. H. B. Summers, ed., *Radio Censorship*, Reference Shelf series, vol. 12, no. 10 (New York: H. W. Wilson, 1939), pp. 27–29. See also Cantril, *Invasion*, p. 61.

96. Cantril, *Invasion*, pp. 61–62. Campbell, *Getting It Wrong*, p. 32.

97. One paper that did was *The Washington Post*, after printing a short article about a supposed panic on a military base. Their source was "a young leatherneck" who, it later turned out, had made the whole thing up as a prank on his comrades. ("Quantico Marines Wept and Prayed During 'Invasion,'" *Washington Post*, Nov. 1, 1938, p. X4. "Marines Deny Mars' Monsters Made Them Quail," *Washington Post*, Nov. 2, 1938, p. X4.) The following day, the *Post* also printed a letter to the editor, criticizing their coverage of the broadcast. Its author walked through downtown Washington during the broadcast and "observed nothing whatsoever of the absurd supposed 'terror of the populace.'" This appears to be the only editorial commentary in any major newspaper that took the story with even a grain of salt. (A. McK. Griggs, "Reactions to the Radio Panic," *Washington Post*, Nov. 3, 1938, p. X10.)

98. Cantril, *Invasion*, p. 55.

99. For example, *The Boston Globe*, somewhat ironically, used the panic to remind listeners that they should take all information, in print and on the radio, skeptically ("Radio and Skepticism," *Boston Globe*, Nov. 1, 1938, p. 14).

100. "Phantasmagoria," *New York Herald Tribune*, Nov. 1, 1938, p. 20. See also "What Radio Cannot Do," *St. Louis Post-Dispatch*, Nov. 1, 1938, p. 2C; Orrin E. Dunlap, Jr., "Message from Mars: Radio Learns That Melodrama Dressed Up as a Current Event Is Dangerous," *New York Times*, Nov. 6, 1938, p. 184.

101. See Campbell, *Getting It Wrong*, pp. 42–43.

102. "Radio's Cruel Hoax," *The Detroit News*, Oct. 31, 1938, p. 1, box 2, "Clippings and Articles, 1936–1940" folder (2 of 4), Welles-Feder Collection.

103. "The Gullible Radio Public," *Chicago Tribune*, Nov. 10, 1938, p. 16. See also "Great American Jitters," *Washington Post*, Nov. 1, 1938, p. X10.

104. "A Foolhardy Radio Stunt," *Milwaukee Journal*, Nov. 1, 1938, p. 10.

105. "Spankings in Order," *Detroit Free Press*, Nov. 1, 1938, p. 6.

106. "Terror by Radio," *New York Times*, Nov. 1, 1938, p. 22.

107. Stamm, "Sound of Print," pp. 239–40.

108. "Phantasmagoria," p. 20. See also "Radio and Skepticism," p. 14.

109. Joseph Bulgatz, *Ponzi Schemes, Invaders from Mars & More Extraordinary Popular Delusions and the Madness of Crowds* (New York: Harmony Books, 1992), pp. 142–50; quote on p. 148. See also Robert E. Bartholomew and Benjamin Radford, *The Martians Have Landed!: A History of Media-Driven Panics and Hoaxes* (Jefferson, N.C.: McFarland, 2012), pp. 79–83; Zack Stiegler and Brandon Szuminsky, "Mediating Misinformation: Hoaxes and the Digital Turn," in *War of the Worlds to Social Media: Mediated Communication in Times of Crisis*, ed. Joy Elizabeth Hayes, Kathleen Battles, and Wendy Hilton-Morrow (New York: Peter Lang, 2013), pp. 168–69.

110. Quoted in Bulgatz, *Ponzi Schemes*, p. 149. See also Bartholomew and Radford, *Martians*, pp. 81–82; Stiegler and Szuminsky, "Mediating Misinformation," p. 169.

111. Gosling, *Waging the War*, p. 55.

112. Charles Jackson, "The Night the Martians Came," in *The Aspirin Age: 1919–1941*, ed. Isabel Leighton (New York: Simon & Schuster, 1949), p. 437. See also Brady, *Citizen Welles*, p. 173; Orson Welles, interviewed by Tom Snyder, *Tomorrow with Tom Snyder*, NBC, Sept. 1975, Paley Center for Media iCollection for Colleges, catalog ID T:35495. Sources disagree as to whether Welles actually saw the sign himself. Richard Barr later claimed that he, and not Welles, brought several cast members from *Danton's Death* to Times Square, in order to prove what had happened. (See Callow, *Road to Xanadu*, p. 404; Richard Barr, interviewed by Frank Beacham, p. 4, box 14, "Theatre of the Imagination (1988). Interviews [transcripts]. 1988" folder, Wilson-Welles Papers.) However, I have elected to go with the version published soonest after the actual event.

113. Callow, *Road to Xanadu*, p. 404. Richard Barr, interviewed by Frank Beacham, p. 4, box 14, "*Theatre of the Imagination* (1988). Interviews [transcripts]. 1988" folder, Wilson-Welles Papers.

114. Arlene Francis, interviewed by Frank Beacham, p. 2, box 14, "*Theatre of the Imagination* (1988). Interviews [transcripts]. 1988" folder, Wilson-Welles Papers.

115. Steven C. Smith, *A Heart at Fire's Center: The Life and Music of Bernard Herrmann* (Berkeley: University of California Press, 2002), p. 67.

116. Houseman, *Run-Through*, pp. 404–405.

117. Quoted in Brian Holmsten and Alex Lubertozzi, eds., *The War of the Worlds: Mars' Invasion of Earth, Inciting Panic and Inspiring Terror from H. G. Wells to Orson Welles and Beyond* (Naperville, Ill.: Sourcebooks, 2001), p. 20.

118. Houseman, *Run-Through*, p. 405. See also Holmsten and Lubertozzi, eds., *War of the Worlds*, pp. 9, 13.

119. "'Horrors! What Have I Done?'" *Detroit News*, Oct. 31, 1938, p. 2, box 2, "Clippings and Articles, 1936–1940" folder (2 of 4), Welles-Feder Collection.

120. Edith Iannucci to Orson Welles, Nov. 1, 1938, box 24, "New Jersey" folder 1 (29/54), Wilson-Welles Papers.

121. Mina Sutherland to Orson Welles, Nov. 2, 1938, box 24, "Oregon" folder (41/54), Wilson-Welles Papers.

122. Dixon, "Fake Radio 'WAR,'" p. 1, box 2, "Clippings and Articles, 1936–1940" folder (2 of 4), Welles-Feder Collection.

123. "Radio Play Terrifies Nation," p. 1.

124. Alvin T. Sapinsley, Jr., to Orson Welles, Oct. 31, 1938, box 23, "Connecticut" folder (6/54), Wilson-Welles Papers.

125. See Wilha Young to Orson Welles, Nov. 3, 1938, box 23, "Michigan" folder (21/54); Ralph B. Perkins to the Mercury Theatre, Oct. 31, 1938, box 23, "Michigan" folder (21/54), both Wilson-Welles Papers.

126. Ena B. Kind to Orson Welles, Nov. 3, 1938, box 23, "Illinois" folder (12/54), Wilson-Welles Papers.

127. Molly P. W. Schumacher to Orson Welles, Oct. 31, 1938, box 24, "New York, NYC & boroughs" folder 2 (34/54), Wilson-Welles Papers.

128. See Elmer Warren to the Mercury Theatre, Nov. 2, 1938, box 24, "North Carolina" folder (38/54); J. Hallingsworth to Orson Welles, Oct. 31, 1938, box 24, "Pennsylvania" folder 2 (43/54), both Wilson-Welles Papers; and Beverley R. Jouett to the Radio Commission [*sic*], Nov. 3, 1938, box 237, NARA.

129. "Sidelights on the Mars Scare," p. 3.

130. "'Men of Mars' to Stay on Mars, CBS Decides," *Detroit News*, Oct. 31, 1938, p. 1, box 2, "Clippings and Articles, 1936–1940" folder (2 of 4), Welles-Feder Collection.

131. Paul Fritsch to Orson Welles, Nov. 1, 1938, box 24, "Ohio" folder (39/54), Wilson-Welles Papers. See also J. S. Thomburg to Orson Welles, Nov. 1, 1938, box 23, "District of Columbia" folder (8/54); Austin King to Orson Welles, n.d., box 24, "NYC & boroughs" folder 1 (33/54); J. T. Matyas to the Mercury Theatre, Oct. 31, 1938, box 24, "New York, NYC & boroughs" folder 2 (34/54); H. J. Dauney to Orson Welles, Nov. 3, 1938, box 24, "Canada" folder, all Wilson-Welles Papers; and William T. Zusag to Frank R. McNinch, Nov. 4, 1938; Joan Woolworth Tyson to the FCC, Nov. 1, 1938; C. G. Abbey to the FCC, Nov. 2, 1938; Joe Smith to Frank McNish [*sic*], Oct. 31, 1938, all box 237, NARA.

132. Doris Hurley to Frank R. McNinch, Oct. 31, 1938, box 238, NARA.

133. "U.S. Investigates Radio Drama of Invasion by Martians That Threw Nation into Panic," *New York World-Telegram*, Oct. 31, 1938, p. 1, box 27, "Radio. Mercury Theatre on the Air. War of the Worlds. Articles & Clippings, 1938" folder, Welles-Kodar Collection.

6. "Air Racketeers"

1. James A. Higgins to Frank R. McNinch, Oct. 31, 1938, box 238, NARA.
2. Howard Koch, *The Panic Broadcast: Portrait of an Event* (Boston: Little, Brown, 1970), p. 16.
3. Ibid.
4. Ibid., p. 24.
5. Howard Koch, "Orson Welles—Some Reminiscences," in *Orson Welles on the Air: The Radio Years* (New York: Museum of Broadcasting, 1988), p. 30. Frank Brady, *Citizen Welles: A Biography of Orson Welles* (New York: Scribner, 1989), p. 173.
6. "FCC to Scan Script of 'War' Broadcast," *New York Times*, Nov. 1, 1938, p. 26. "F.C.C. Inquiry Is Ordered into Radio War Play," *New York Herald Tribune*, Nov. 1, 1938, p. 19.
7. The Digital Implosion, "George Orson Welles Apologizes for the War of the Worlds Broadcast (Oct. 31 1938)," 7:06, YouTube, http://youtu.be/uuEGiruAFSw (accessed Feb. 26, 2014).
8. "FCC to Scan Script," p. 26. See also John Gosling, *Waging the War of the Worlds: A History of the 1938 Radio Broadcast and Resulting Panic* (Jefferson, N.C.: McFarland, 2009), pp. 78–80.
9. "FCC to Scan Script," p. 26. See also "U.S. Body Demands War Scare Script," *New York Sun*, Oct. 31, 1938, p. 3.
10. Hadley Cantril, with Hazel Gaudet and Herta Herzog, *The Invasion from Mars: A Study in the Psychology of Panic* (New York: Harper & Row, 1966), pp. 43–44.
11. W. O. Harington to Frank R. McNinch, Nov. 1, 1938, box 238, NARA.
12. Orson Welles and Peter Bogdanovich, *This Is Orson Welles*, ed. Jonathan Rosenbaum (New York: Da Capo Press, 1998), p. 19.
13. Quoted in Brady, *Citizen Welles*, p. 175.
14. James D. Secrest, "Martian Invasion by Radio 'Regrettable,' Says McNinch," *Washington Post*, Nov. 1, 1938, p. 4.
15. Alan Gallop, *The Martians Are Coming!: The True Story of Orson Welles' 1938 Panic Broadcast* (Gloucestershire: Amberley Publishing, 2011), p. 103.
16. John Houseman, *Run-Through: A Memoir* (New York: Simon & Schuster, 1972), p. 405.
17. "FCC to Scan Script," p. 1.
18. Nick Antonelli to Orson Welles, n.d., box 24, "Rhode Island" folder (44/54), Wilson-Welles Papers. See also Mrs. M. Hingesoll to WABC, Oct. 31, 1938, box 24, "New York, NYC & boroughs" folder 3 (35/54); Mr. Howard Kerns and family to Orson Welles, Oct. 30, 1938, box 24, "Ohio" folder (39/54); Therese Kelly to CBS, Oct. 30, 1938, box 24, "Pennsylvania" folder 2 (43/54); Mary Kirby to Orson Welles, Oct. 30, 1938, box 24, "Wisconsin" folder (54/54), all Wilson-Welles Papers.
19. Anonymous to Orson Wells [*sic*], Oct. 30, 1938, box 24, "New Jersey" folder 1 (29/54), Wilson-Welles Papers.
20. James Browne to Austin Wells [*sic*], Oct. 30, 1938, box 24, "New Jersey" folder 2 (30/54), Wilson-Welles Papers.
21. "FCC to Scan Script," p. 26. "Rewriting Outrages H. G. Wells but Radio Scare Booms Book," *New York Herald Tribune*, Nov. 2, 1938, p. 21. "U.S. Body Demands Script," p. 3.
22. "Run on Book at Library," *Baltimore Sun*, Nov. 1, 1938, p. 6.
23. H. G. Wells, *The War of the Worlds* (New York: Dell, 1938).
24. Brady, *Citizen Welles*, p. 175. Charles Jackson, "The Night the Martians Came," in *The Aspirin Age: 1919-1941*, ed. Isabel Leighton (New York: Simon & Schuster, 1949), p. 437. Simon Callow, *Orson Welles: The Road to Xanadu* (New York: Viking, 1995), pp. 405–407. Gosling, *Waging the War*, p. 48. Charles Higham, *Orson Welles: The Rise and Fall of an American Genius* (New York: St. Martin's, 1985), p. 128. Houseman, *Run-Through*, p. 405. Barbara Leaming, *Orson Welles: A Biography* (New York: Viking, 1985), pp. 162-63. Orson Welles, interviewed by Tom Snyder, *Tomorrow with*

Tom Snyder, NBC, Sept., 1975, Paley Center for Media iCollection for Colleges, catalog ID T:35495.

25. Norton Russell, "Astounding Outcome of the 'Martian Scare,'" *Radio Mirror*, Feb. 1939, p. 17. See also Paul W. White, *News on the Air* (New York: Harcourt, Brace, 1947), pp. 47–48.

26. R. H. McBride and R. A. Springs, Jr., "Orson Welles Calls Broadcast 'Terribly Shocking Experience,'" *Daily Princetonian*, Nov. 1, 1938, p. 1.

27. Gosling, *Waging the War*, p. 78. Paul Heyer, *The Medium and the Magician: Orson Welles, the Radio Years, 1934-1952* (Lanham, Md.: Rowman & Littlefield, 2005), pp. 97–98. David Thomson, *Rosebud: The Story of Orson Welles* (New York: Vintage Books, 1996), p. 105.

28. "U.S. Is Probing Hoax on Radio," *Detroit Free Press*, Nov. 1, 1938, p. 5.

29. See Heyer, *Medium and Magician*, pp. 97–98.

30. "Panic! This Is the Orson Welles Broadcast That Hoaxed America," *Radio Guide*, Nov. 19, 1938, p. 4.

31. "Radio War Drama Creates a Panic," *New York Times*, Oct. 31, 1938, p. 4. See also "U.S. Body Demands Script," p. 3.

32. "Panic!," p. 4.

33. Digital Implosion, "George Orson Welles Apologizes for the War of the Worlds Broadcast." See also "FCC to Scan Script," p. 26.

34. "Panic!," p. 4.

35. Digital Implosion, "George Orson Welles Apologizes for the War of the Worlds Broadcast."

36. See R. J. Henry to Franklin Roosevelt, Oct. 31, 1938; W. J. Young to the National Board of Radio Control [*sic*], Oct. 31, 1938; Mary E. Ferguson to the FCC, Oct. 31, 1938; Marie Goodman to the Federal Bureau of Investigation, Oct. 31, 1938; M. Carl Jones to the Federal Radio Commission [*sic*], Oct. 31, 1938; Judge James W. Smith to the Federal Radio Commission [*sic*], Oct. 31, 1938; Robert E. Stoner to the Federal Radio Commission [*sic*], Oct. 31, 1938; Ethel York to the Federal Radio Commission [*sic*], Oct. 31, 1938; Edith B. Slack to Frank R. McNinch, Nov. 1, 1938; Helen K. Matthew to F. P. [*sic*] McNinch, n.d., all box 238, NARA; and Johnas Kranley to Orson Welles, Oct. 30, 1938, box 24, "No Location" folder, Wilson-Welles Papers. See also David Goodman, *Radio's Civic Ambition: American Broadcasting and Democracy in the 1930s* (Oxford: Oxford University Press, 2011), p. 281.

37. Mable Clements to F. R. McNinch, Nov. 2, 1938, box 238, NARA.

38. Communications Act of 1934, sec. 325 (a).

39. See Anonymous to Orson Welles, n.d., box 24, "No Location" folder; Gerta S. Brown to the Mercury Theater [*sic*], Nov. 2, 1938, box 24, "New York (state)" folder 2 (37/54), both Wilson-Welles Papers; and Anonymous to the FCC, n.d.; Thomas Brosnan to Harold I. Ickes, Nov. 2, 1938; Rhea Johnson to the FCC, Oct. 30, 1938, all box 238, NARA.

40. Justin Levine, "A History and Analysis of the Federal Communications Commission's Response to Radio Broadcast Hoaxes," *Federal Communications Law Journal*, vol. 52, no. 2 (March 2000), p. 276.

41. James G. Gill to the FCC, Nov. 1, 1938, box 238, NARA. See also "A. Citizen" to the Radio Communications Committee [*sic*], Oct. 31, 1938; Stuart McCarthy to the FCC, Oct. 30, 1938; E. A. Hackett to Frank P. [*sic*] McNinch, Nov. 1, 1938, all box 238, NARA; and Annette M. Ham to Orson Welles, Oct. 31, 1938, box 24, "Rhode Island" folder (44/54), Wilson-Welles Papers.

42. Lilla Wood Daniels to the FCC, Oct. 31, 1938, box 238, NARA. See also Henry Edward Warner to Frank McNinch, Oct. 31, 1938; R. M. Horner to the FCC, Oct. 31, 1938; Mrs. Johanna Wilizens to Franklin Roosevelt, Nov. 1, 1938; Wendall F. Little to the Federal

Radio Communications Bureau [sic], Nov. 1, 1938, all box 238, NARA; and D.C.S. to Orson Welles, Nov. 1, 1938, box 24, "New Jersey" folder 1 (29/54), Wilson-Welles Papers.

43. See David L. Reifer to Frank W. [sic] McNinch, Oct. 31, 1938; Frank R. Bean to the Federal Communications Bureau [sic], Oct. 30, 1938; Mrs. Arthur Hunter to the FCC, Nov. 1, 1938; Walter Schmidt to the FCC, Oct. 30, 1938; C. J. Coven to "The Commissioner of Radio Broadcasting," Oct. 31, 1938; Murray S. Parker to the Federal Radio Communications Commission [sic], Nov. 1, 1938; Paul Schwarzwalder to the FCC, Oct. 31, 1938; A. L. Stebbins to the FCC, Nov. 1, 1938 [?]; Carl J. Baumann to the Communications Commission [sic], Oct. 31, 1938; E. J. Tembroeke to Frank R. McNinch, Oct. 31, 1938; J. B. Foster to the FCC, Oct. 31, 1938; Robert C. Harhsberger to the FCC, Oct. 31, 1938; J. Douglas to the Federal Radio Commission [sic], Oct. 31, 1938; Edward Gibson to the Federal Radio Commission [sic], n.d., all box 238, NARA; and Neil H. Jenkins to Frank P. [sic] McNinch, Oct. 31, 1938, box 237, NARA; and John V. Leinmiller to the Mercury Theatre of the Air, Oct. 30, 1938, box 24, "Pennsylvania" folder 2 (43/54); Alethea G. Snokos to Orson Wells [sic], Oct. 30, 1938, box 24, "New Jersey" folder 3 (32/54); George E. Harris to Orson Wells [sic], Oct. 31, 1938, box 23, "California" folder (4/54), all Wilson-Welles Papers.

44. Mrs. H. D. Graham to Frank R. McNinch, Nov. 1, 1938, box 238, NARA. See also Marie Helen Ovany to James A. Farley, Oct. 31, 1938, box 238, NARA.

45. See Warner Ogden to the Federal Radio Communications Commission [sic], Oct. 30, 1938; Louis F. Heidenrich to the FCC, Oct. 31, 1938; Christine Parascondolo to the FCC, Oct. 31, 1938, all box 238, NARA; Goodman, Radio's Civic Ambition, pp. 281, 283.

46. Mrs. F. M. Dekker to the Federal Radio Communications Commission [sic], Oct. 31, 1938, box 238, NARA.

47. See Marie Burns to the U.S. Federal Radio Commission [sic], Oct. 31, 1938, box 238, NARA.

48. Ethel York to the Federal Radio Commission [sic], Oct. 31, 1938, box 238, NARA.

49. Charles Merserau to Franklin Roosevelt, Oct. 30, 1938, box 238, NARA.

50. D.C.S. to Orson Welles, Nov. 1, 1938, box 24, "New Jersey" folder 1 (29/54), Wilson-Welles Papers.

51. O. R. Lambert to Frank P. [sic] McNinch, Nov. 1, 1938, box 238, NARA.

52. Stanley Cohen, Folk Devils and Moral Panics: The Creation of the Mods and Rockers, 3rd ed. (London: Routledge, 2002), pp. xvii, 1.

53. George E. Dimmick to Orson Welles, Nov. 3, 1938, box 24, "New York (state)" folder 2 (37/54), Wilson-Welles Papers.

54. "Farmers: Rural Revelry," Time, Sept. 9, 1935, p. 13. "Herring, Clyde LaVerne, (1879–1945)," Biographical Directory of the United States Congress, http://bioguide.congress.gov/scripts/biodisplay.pl?index=H000543 (accessed March 1, 2014). Michael Kramme, "Herring, Clyde LaVerne," in The Biographical Dictionary of Iowa, ed. David Hudson, Marvin Bergman, and Loren Horton (Iowa City: University of Iowa Press, 2008), p. 233.

55. "Invasion Play on Radio Sends U.S. into Panic," Baltimore Sun, Oct. 31, 1938, p. 2. "Senator to Ask Air Censorship," Detroit Free Press, Oct. 31, 1938, p. 2. "Senator Proposes Curb of Abuses," Los Angeles Times, Oct. 31, 1938, p. 2. "U.S. Requests Radio Record," Milwaukee Journal, Oct. 31, 1938, p. 3. "Radio Listeners Alarmed by Fictional Broadcast of Attack by Men From Mars," St. Louis Post-Dispatch, Oct. 31, 1938, p. 1. "Ban on Radio 'Scares' Looms," San Francisco Examiner, Oct. 31, 1938, p. 1. "Stricter Federal Rule of Air Seen," San Francisco Examiner, Nov. 1, 1938, p. 2.

56. Dewey L. Fleming, "Panic Brings New Demand to Curb Radio," Baltimore Sun, Nov. 1, 1938, pp. 1, 6. See also "Senator to Ask Air Censorship," p. 2; "U.S. Requests Radio Record," p. 3; Clyde L. Herring, "Is Radio Censorship Necessary?," in Radio Censorship,

ed. H. B. Summers, Reference Shelf series, vol. 12, no. 10 (New York: H. W. Wilson, 1939), pp. 221–26; Robert J. Brown, *Manipulating the Ether: The Power of Broadcast Radio in Thirties America* (Jefferson, N.C.: McFarland, 1998), p. 242; Goodman, *Radio's Civic Ambition*, p. 262.

57. "Senator to Ask Air Censorship," p. 2. "U.S. Requests Radio Record," p. 3.

58. For the full text of the Motion Picture Production Code, see Thomas Doherty, *Pre-Code Hollywood: Sex, Immorality, and Insurrection in American Cinema, 1930–1934* (New York: Columbia University Press, 1999), pp. 347–64.

59. "U.S. Requests Radio Record," p. 3. "Panic!," p. 5.

60. Leona Smith to Orson Welles, Oct. 31, 1938, box 24, "No Location" folder, Wilson-Welles Papers. See also Bruno Rabus to Orson Welles, Oct. 31, 1938, box 24, "North Carolina" folder (38/54); Janice Marx to Orson Welles, n.d., box 24, "No Location" folder, both Wilson-Welles Papers.

61. John C. Culver and John Hyde, *American Dreamer: A Life of Henry A. Wallace* (New York: W. W. Norton, 2000), pp. 180, 197, 209–10.

62. "NBC Head Defends Its Radio Record," *New York Times*, Jan. 16, 1938, p. 26. "Herring for Radio Censorship," *New York Times*, Jan. 23, 1938, p. 3. Walter Brown, "Bill to Clap Stiff Censorship on Broadcasts Being Drafted," *Broadcasting*, Feb. 1, 1938, p. 28. Dewey L. Fleming, "Panic Brings New Demand," pp. 1, 6.

63. Herring, "Is Radio Censorship Necessary?," p. 223.

64. "Senator to Ask Air Censorship," p. 2. "U.S. Requests Radio Record," p. 3.

65. Herring, "Is Radio Censorship Necessary?," p. 223.

66. See Jon D. Swartz and Robert C. Reinehr, *Handbook of Old-Time Radio: A Comprehensive Guide to Golden Age Radio Listening and Collecting* (Metuchen, N.J.: Scarecrow Press, 1993), p. 340; "Radio: Listen Flatfoot...," *Time*, April 8, 1940, p. 48. For an in-depth analysis of *Gang Busters*, see Elena Razlogova, *The Listener's Voice: Early Radio and the American Public* (Philadelphia: University of Pennsylvania Press, 2011), pp. 1–2, 115–31.

67. "Do You Want Radio Censorship?," *Look*, Feb. 14, 1939, in *Radio Censorship*, ed. Summers, p. 260. Herring, "Is Radio Censorship Necessary?," p. 223.

68. Garth S. Jowett, Ian C. Jarvie, and Kathryn H. Fuller, *Children and the Movies: Media Influence and the Payne Fund Controversy* (Cambridge: Cambridge University Press, 1996), pp. 17–29. Shearon A. Lowery and Melvin L. DeFleur, *Milestones in Mass Communication Research: Media Effects*, 3rd ed. (White Plains, N.Y.: Longman, 1995), pp. 21–24. Melvin L. DeFleur, *Mass Communication Theories: Explaining Origins, Processes, and Effects* (New York: Allyn & Bacon, 2010), pp. 122, 138–39.

69. Jowett, Jarvie, and Fuller, *Children and the Movies*, pp. 57–59, 91. Lowery and DeFleur, *Milestones*, pp. 24–42. DeFleur, *Mass Communication*, pp. 139–40.

70. Jowett, Jarvie, and Fuller, *Children and the Movies*, pp. 7–9, 102–108; quote on p. 103.

71. Henry James Forman, *Our Movie Made Children* (New York: Macmillan, 1933), pp. 38, 104, 111. See also "Child's Reactions to Movies Shown," *New York Times*, May 28, 1933, p. E7.

72. Jowett, Jarvie, and Fuller, *Children and the Movies*, pp. 7–8, 94–96, 103–108, 110–11. See also DeFleur, *Mass Communication*, p. 140.

73. "Broadcasters Act to Curb 'Bogyman,'" *New York Times*, Feb. 28, 1933, p. 21. See also "Education: Mothers v. Curdlers," *Time*, March 13, 1933, p. 24; "Parents Are Wondering If It Is Wise to Give Children a Free Hand in Choice of Broadcasts," *New York Times*, Nov. 25, 1934, p. X13; "Protest: Adults Condemn Air Hair-Raisers for Youngsters," *News-Week*, Dec. 1, 1934, in *Radio Censorship*, ed. Summers, pp. 36–37.

74. "Teacher Shot by Boy to File No Charges," *New York Times*, Sept. 26, 1937, p. 21. See also "Boy's Shooting of His Teacher a 'Gang Crime,'" *Chicago Daily Tribune*, Sept. 25, 1937, p. 3; "Radio Gangs and Puppy Love Blamed for School Shooting," *Detroit Free Press*, Sept. 25, 1937, p. 3; "Wounded Teacher Forgives Pupil, 12," *Detroit Free Press*, Sept. 26, 1937, p. 2; Mr. V. E. McAran et al. to the Federal Radio Commission [sic], Oct. 1938, box 238, NARA.

75. Herring, "Is Radio Censorship Necessary?," p. 222.
76. A. A. Martin to the FCC, Oct. 31, 1938, box 238, NARA.
77. See "Education: Mothers v. Curdlers," p. 24; "Parents Are Wondering," p. X13; "Protest: Adults Condemn Air Hair-Raisers," p. 37; Hadley Cantril and Gordon Allport, *The Psychology of Radio* (New York: Harper & Brothers, 1935), pp. 235-36; Francis Chase, Jr., *Sound and Fury: An Informal History of Broadcasting* (New York: Harper & Brothers, 1942), pp. 244-45.
78. Charles W. Whinston, "Terror in the Bedtime Stories," Letter to the Editor, *New York Times*, March 12, 1938, p. X10. "Protest: Adults Condemn Air Hair-Raisers," p. 36. Cantril and Allport, *Psychology of Radio*, pp. 235-37. Chase, *Sound and Fury*, pp. 243-45.
79. Summers, ed., *Radio Censorship*, p. 26. John Dunning, *On the Air: The Encyclopedia of Old-Time Radio* (New York: Oxford University Press, 1998), p. 403. Cantril and Allport, *Psychology of Radio*, pp. 63-64. Bruce Smith, *The History of Little Orphan Annie* (New York: Ballantine, 1982), pp. 38-42.
80. Agnes M. Hersey to Orson Welles, Oct. 31, 1938, box 23, "Massachusetts" folder (20/54), Wilson-Welles Papers.
81. Jim Palmer to the FCC, Nov. 1, 1938, box 237, NARA.
82. A. L. Stebbins to the FCC, Nov. 1, 1938, box 238, NARA. See also Mr. V. E. McAran et al. to the Federal Radio Commission [sic], Oct. 1938, box 238, NARA.
83. See Lawrence H. Harm to the Federal Radio Commission [sic], Oct. 31, 1938; A. A. Martin to the FCC, Oct. 31, 1938; C. R. Kennan to Frank McNinch, Oct. 31, 1938; Mrs. G. Nesbith to the Federal Radio Commission [sic], Nov. 1, 1938; Maude Wiard to Frank McNinch, Nov. 1, 1938; Earle S. Russell to the FCC, Nov. 1, 1938, all box 238, NARA; and J. W. Cunningham to Frank R. McNinch, Nov. 1, 1938, box 237, NARA.
84. Edith B. Slack to Frank R. McNinch, Nov. 1, 1938, box 238, NARA. See also S. G. Toll, Monroe Sims, M. W. Gardner, et al. to the FCC, Nov. 2, 1938, box 238, NARA.
85. See Ethel S. Cohen to Frank McNinch, Nov. 1, 1938; Carrie M. Roesink to the FCC, Oct. 31, 1938; J. R. McGirr to the FCC, Oct. 31, 1938; Emil Heinlein to Frank P. [sic] McNinch, Nov. 1, 1938, all box 238, NARA; and Charles Stumpp to Frank McNinch, Oct. 31, 1938; Aug. C. Metz to the FCC, Nov. 2, 1938; R. K. Antz to the FCC, Nov. 3, 1938; Thomas E. Rhodes to Frank R. McNinch, Oct. 31, 1938; Owen Kraft to the FCC, Nov. 2, 1938; Frank O'Hearn to the FCC, Nov. 2, 1938; Eleanor Potter to the Radio Commission [sic], n.d., all box 237, NARA.
86. Mrs. George J. Newport to the United States Radio Commission [sic], n.d., box 238, NARA.
87. "Radio Listeners in Panic, Taking War Drama as Fact," *New York Times*, Oct. 31, 1938, p. 1. "Phantasmagoria," *New York Herald Tribune*, Nov. 1, 1938, p. 20. "Yellow Journalism of the Air," *St. Louis Post-Dispatch*, Oct. 31, 1938, p. 2C. See also Richard B. O'Brien, "Unmasking a Hobgoblin of the Air," *New York Times*, Oct. 29, 1939, p. X12; James A. Higgins to Frank R. McNinch, Oct. 31, 1938, box 238, NARA.
88. "Spankings in Order," *Detroit Free Press*, Nov. 1, 1938, p. 6. See also Ex-Listener, "Critic of Program Hopes for End of Horror Hours," *Detroit Free Press*, Nov. 2, 1938, p. 6.
89. See Cantril and Allport, *Psychology of Radio*, pp. 10, 233, 238-39.
90. Murray S. Parker to the Federal Radio Communications Commission [sic], Nov. 1, 1938, box 238, NARA.
91. Alva Johnston and Fred Smith, "How to Raise a Child: The Disturbing Life—to Date—of Orson Welles," *Saturday Evening Post*, Feb. 3, 1940, p. 38. See also Welles's comments in Orson Welles, interviewed by Peter Bogdanovich, *This Is Orson Welles* (New York: Harper Audio, 1992), tape 4, side 8.
92. In general, very few children wrote letters to broadcasters, except when responding to an offer for some kind of gift. See Kenneth M. Goode, *What About Radio?* (New York: Harper & Brothers, 1937), p. 103.

93. Pro-Welles letters with no evidence of fright: Nicholas Carr to Orson Welles, Oct. 31, 1938, box 23, "Illinois" folder (12/54); Dorothy Smith to Orson Welles, Nov. 1, 1938, box 23, "Illinois" folder (12/54); Jane Corwin to Orson Welles, Nov. 5, 1938, "Michigan" folder (21/54); Esther Langman to Orson Wells [sic], Oct. 31, 1938, box 23, "Minnesota" folder (22/54); Rose Dellini to Orson Wells [sic], Nov. 1938 (n.d.), box 24, "New Jersey" folder 1 (29/54); Thelma Iramucci to Orson Welles, Nov. 1, 1938, box 24, "New Jersey" folder 2 (30/54); Claire Horn to the Mercury Theatre, Nov. 3, 1938, box 24, "New York, NYC & boroughs" folder 3 (35/54); Milton A. Klasfeld to Orson Welles, n.d., box 24, "New York (state)" folder 1 (36/54); Cameron Hollyer to Orson Welles, Nov. 1, 1938, box 24, "New York (state)" folder 1 (36/54); John R. Snyder to Orson Welles, Nov. 8, 1938, box 24, "New York (state)" folder 1 (36/54); Lola Hunter to Orson Welles, Nov. 1, 1938, box 24, "Pennsylvania" folder 1 (42/54); Jessica Stoner to the Mercury Theatre, Nov. 7, 1938, box 24, "Tennessee" folder (47/54), all Wilson-Welles Papers; and Clifford Sickles to the FCC, Nov. 22, 1938; Merritt H. Junior Swick to the FCC, Nov. 21, 1938, both box 237, NARA. Neutral with no evidence of fright: Martin Johnson to the FCC, Nov. 21, 1938, box 237, NARA; and Irwin Heffner to WABC, Oct. 31, 1938, box 24, "Ohio" folder (39/54); Ann Benner to Orson Welles, n.d., box 23, "Minnesota" folder (22/54); Ned Rosenthal to Orson Welles, Oct. 31, 1938, box 24, "NYC & boroughs" folder 1 (33/54), all Wilson-Welles Papers. Another letter, written to Welles by a ten-year-old boy from Milwaukee, makes no reference to *War of the Worlds.* ("Big Little Jack Horner" to Orson Welles, Nov. 18, 1938, box 24, "Wisconsin" folder [54/54], Wilson-Welles Papers.)
94. See Clio Weinel to CBS, Oct. 30, 1938, box 24, "South Dakota" folder (46/54); Kathryn Erniston to Orson Wells [sic], Oct. 30, 1938, box 23, "Florida" folder (9/54); Harold Greenhalgh to Orson Welles, Oct. 30, 1938, box 24, "New York (state)" folder 1 (36/54), all Wilson-Welles Papers; and Dorothy Babcock to the FCC, Nov. 27, 1938; Ralph Johnson to the FCC, Nov. 21, 1938, box 237, both NARA.
95. Clio Weinel to CBS, Oct. 30, 1938, box 24, "South Dakota" folder (46/54), Wilson-Welles Papers. See also Harold Greenhalgh to Orson Welles, Oct. 30, 1938, box 24, "New York (state)" folder 1 (36/54), Wilson-Welles Papers.
96. Mrs. Katharine Mandeville to the FCC, Nov. 22, 1938, box 237, NARA. See also Lillian M. Davenport to Frank R. McNinch, Nov. 2, 1938, box 237, NARA.
97. Cantril, *Invasion*, p. 120.
98. Esther Langman to Orson Wells [sic], Oct. 31, 1938, box 23, "Minnesota" folder (22/54), Wilson-Welles Papers.
99. Claire Horn to the Mercury Theatre, Nov. 3, 1938, box 24, "New York, NYC & boroughs" folder 3 (35/54), Wilson-Welles Papers.
100. "Radio Does U.S. a Favor," *Variety*, Nov. 2, 1938, in Koch, *Panic Broadcast*, p. 95.
101. Paul Pesch to the FCC, Nov. 1, 1938, box 237, NARA.
102. Koch, "Orson Welles—Some Reminiscences," p. 30. See also Thomson, *Rosebud*, p. 105.
103. Callow, *Road to Xanadu*, p. 407.
104. Houseman, *Run-Through*, p. 405. Brady, *Citizen Welles*, p. 176. Leaming, *Orson Welles*, pp. 162–63.
105. McBride and Springs, "Orson Welles Calls Broadcast," p. 5.
106. "Federal Board to Probe Broadcast That Sent Shivers Through Nation," *Milwaukee Journal*, Oct. 31, 1938, pp. 1, 3. "Calls for Probe of Radio Case Are Multiplied," *New Orleans Times-Picayune*, Nov. 1, 1938, p. 12. Secrest, "Martian Invasion by Radio 'Regrettable,' Says McNinch," p. 4. "Radio Listeners Alarmed by Fictional Broadcast," and "Communications Board Investigating Broadcast That Caused Hysteria," *St. Louis Post-Dispatch*, Oct. 31, 1938, p. 1. "Ban on Radio 'Scares,'" p. 1. Fleming, "Panic Brings New Demand," p. 1. "Stricter Federal Rule Seen," p. 2.
107. Jerome W. Stone to Frank R. McNinch, Oct. 31, 1938, box 237, NARA.

7. "The Public Interest"

1. Ellen B. Nash to Orson Welles, Nov. 3, 1938, box 24, "Washington" folder (52/54), Wilson-Welles Papers.
2. "Revolt Against Chairman McNinch Bursts Out in FCC as Payne and Craven Oppose His Civil Service Proposal," *Broadcasting*, Oct. 15, 1938, p. 13.
3. Warren B. Francis, "Mars Panic May Cause Radio Curbs," *Los Angeles Times*, Nov. 1, 1938, pp. 1, 2.
4. "FCC Is Perplexed on Steps to Take," *New York Times*, Nov. 1, 1938, p. 26.
5. See Louis G. Caldwell, "Legal Restrictions on Broadcasting Programs," *Air Law Review*, July 1938, in *Radio Censorship*, ed. H. B. Summers, Reference Shelf series, vol. 12, no. 10 (New York: H. W. Wilson, 1939), pp. 65-66.
6. James D. Secrest, "Martian Invasion by Radio 'Regrettable,' Says McNinch; Radio Company Won't Let It Happen Again," *Washington Post*, Nov. 1, 1938, p. 4. See also "Demand Grows for Radio Curb," *Boston Globe*, Nov. 1, 1938, p. 5; "No FCC Action Due in Radio 'War' Case," *New York Times*, Nov. 2, 1938, p. 26; "U.S. Body Demands War Scare Script," *New York Sun*, Oct. 31, 1938, p. 3; Dewey L. Fleming, "Stricter Policing in Radio Demanded," *Baltimore Sun*, Nov. 1, 1938, p. 6.
7. See "FCC Is Perplexed," p. 26; "F.C.C. Orders Inquiry into Radio Scare," *New York Herald Tribune*, Nov. 1, 1938, p. 1; "Federal Board to Probe Broadcast That Sent Shivers Through Nation," *Milwaukee Journal*, Oct. 31, 1938, p. 1; "U.S. Is Probing Hoax on Radio," *Detroit Free Press*, Nov. 1, 1938, p. 5; "Calls for Probe of Radio Case Are Multiplied," New Orleans *Times-Picayune*, Nov. 1, 1938, p. 12; "Communications Board Investigating Broadcast That Caused Hysteria," *St. Louis Post-Dispatch*, Oct. 31, 1938, p. 1; "Stricter Federal Rule of Air Seen," *San Francisco Examiner*, Nov. 1, 1938, p. 2.
8. James D. Secrest, "Martian Invasion by Radio 'Regrettable,' Says McNinch," *Washington Post*, Nov. 1, 1938, p. X1. See also "Federal Board to Probe Broadcast," p. 1; "U.S. Is Probing Hoax," p. 5; "Calls for Probe of Radio Case," p. 12.
9. Mrs. Ed Myers to the FCC, n.d., box 238, NARA. See also Helen Markham to Frank P. [sic] McNinch, Oct. 31, 1938; Helen Degen to Frank P. [sic] McNinch, Oct. 31, 1938; Frances E. Robinson to Frank R. McNinch, Oct. 31, 1938; Al Armon to Frank McNinch, Nov. 7, 1938; Elizabeth Brighton to Frank R. McNinch, Oct. 31, 1938, all box 238, NARA; and C. H. Faulkner to Orson Welles, Nov. 1, 1938, box 24, "Pennsylvania" folder 2 (43/54), Wilson-Welles Papers.
10. See Johanna Wilizenski to Franklin D. Roosevelt, Nov. 1, 1938; Franklin J. Schaefer to the U.S. Department of Commerce, Oct. 31, 1938; Marie Goodman to the Federal Bureau of Investigation, Oct. 31, 1938, all box 238, NARA.
11. See J. B. Elarth to the Radio Commission [sic], Oct. 31, 1938, box 238, NARA; Charles A. Clark to the Radio Commission [sic], Oct. 31, 1938, box 237, NARA.
12. Warner Ogden to the Federal Radio Communications Commission [sic], Oct. 30, 1938, box 238, NARA.
13. Minna F. Kassner, "Radio Censorship," *Air Law Review*, April 1937, in *Radio Censorship*, ed. Summers, p. 81.
14. Communications Act of 1934, sec. 326.
15. David Sarnoff, "The American System of Broadcasting," speech, Town Hall, New York, April 28, 1938, in *Radio Censorship*, ed. Summers, p. 102. "Sarnoff Foresees a Peril to Radio," *New York Times*, April 29, 1938, p. 19. See also Kassner, "Radio Censorship," p. 82; Henry A. Bellows, "Is Radio Censored?," *Harper's Magazine*, Nov. 1935, in *Radio Censorship*, ed. Summers, pp. 102-103; "The Broadcaster's Dilemma," *Washington Star*, Jan. 2, 1939, in *Radio Censorship*, ed. Summers, pp. 117-18.
16. See Hadley Cantril and Gordon Allport, *The Psychology of Radio* (New York: Harper & Brothers, 1935), pp. 52-55; Vita Lauter and Joseph H. Friend, "Radio and the Censors," *Forum*, Dec. 1938, in *Radio Censorship*, ed. Summers, pp. 154-68; Mitchell

Dawson, "Censorship on the Air," *American Mercury*, March 1934, in *Radio Censorship*, ed. Summers, pp. 172–78; Kassner, "Radio Censorship," pp. 184–90.

17. Dawson, "Censorship on the Air," p. 173. See also Cantril and Allport, *Psychology of Radio*, p. 55.

18. Summers, *Radio Censorship*, pp. 27–29. "Damn It to Hell, It's Dangerous!," *New York News*, n.d., in ibid., pp. 247–48. Sol Taishoff, "FCC Orders Study of Program Complaints," *Broadcasting*, Nov. 1, 1938, in ibid., pp. 107–108. James D. Secrest, "F.C.C. Actions May Lead to Congressional Investigation Next Session," *Washington Post*, Nov. 20, 1938, p. B7. "FCC Decides Against Action in 'Mars' Case," *Washington Post*, Dec. 6, 1938, p. 3. Barnouw, *Golden Web*, p. 169, n. 3.

19. "Damn It to Hell, It's Dangerous!," p. 248.

20. Secrest, "F.C.C. Actions May Lead," pp. B7, 10. "Boards & Bureaus: Fixer and Feud," *Time*, Aug. 30, 1937, pp. 14–15. "Radio: QRX," *Time*, May 16, 1938, pp. 25–26, 28. "Radio: Mopper-Upper," *Time*, Aug. 7, 1939, p. 32.

21. "Damn It to Hell, It's Dangerous!," p. 247. See also T.A.M. Craven, "Industry Must Solve Its Own Problems," speech, National Association of Broadcasters, Feb. 15, 1938, in *Radio Censorship*, ed. Summers, pp. 252–53; Secrest, "Martian Invasion by Radio 'Regrettable,' Says McNinch," p. 4; "Demand Grows for Radio Curb," p. 1.

22. "FCC Is Perplexed," p. 26. See also "Demand Grows for Radio Curb," pp. 1, 5; "U.S. Is Probing Hoax," p. 5; Francis, "Mars Panic," p. 1; "FCC to Scan Script of 'War' Broadcast," *New York Times*, Nov. 1, 1938, p. 1; "U.S. Body Demands Script," p. 3; "Radio Fake Starts U.S. Action to Bar Terrorizing Plays," *San Francisco Examiner*, Nov. 1, 1938, p. 1; Secrest, "Martian Invasion by Radio 'Regrettable,' Says McNinch," p. 4.

23. David Goodman, *Radio's Civic Ambition: American Broadcasting and Democracy in the 1930s* (Oxford: Oxford University Press, 2011), pp. 3–64.

24. "Demand Grows for Radio Curb," p. 5. "Radio Fake Starts Action," p. 1. See also "U.S. Is Probing Hoax," p. 5; Fleming, "Stricter Policing," p. 6; Secrest, "Martian Invasion by Radio 'Regrettable,' Says McNinch," p. 4.

25. "Payne, Urging Closer Control, Asserts Most Programs 'Silly and Degrading,'" *Broadcasting*, May 15, 1938, p. 44.

26. Fleming, "Stricter Policing," p. 6. "'Anti-Semitic' Radio Broadcast Inquiry Opened," *St. Louis Post-Dispatch*, Nov. 1, 1938, p. 6A. "Radio Fake Starts Action," p. 1. Secrest, "Martian Invasion by Radio 'Regrettable,' Says McNinch," p. 4. See also "Demand Grows for Radio Curb," p. 5.

27. George Henry Payne, "Need for Program Standards," speech, National Conference on Educational Broadcasting, Dec. 1, 1937, in *Radio Censorship*, ed. Summers, pp. 243–44.

28. Fleming, "Stricter Policing," p. 6. Secrest, "Martian Invasion by Radio 'Regrettable,' Says McNinch," p. 4. "'Anti-Semitic' Radio Broadcast," p. 6A. "Radio Fake Starts Action," p. 1. See also "Demand Grows for Radio Curb," p. 5.

29. "F.C.C. Orders Inquiry," p. 1.

30. "Demand Grows for Radio Curb," p. 5. "FCC Is Perplexed," p. 26. "Stricter Federal Rule Seen," p. 2. Secrest, "Martian Invasion by Radio 'Regrettable,' Says McNinch," p. 4.

31. "Federal Board to Probe Broadcast," p. 1.

32. "FCC Is Perplexed," p. 26.

33. "Radio: QRX," p. 25.

34. Walter Brown, "Frank R. McNinch: Liberal, Not Radical," *Broadcasting*, Sept. 1, 1937, pp. 10, 65. "McNinch Given Free Hand on FCC Post," *Broadcasting*, Sept. 15, 1937, p. 15. "Radio: QRX," pp. 25–26. "Radio: Delayed Purge," *Time*, Oct. 24, 1938, pp. 44–45.

35. Brown, "Frank R. McNinch," p. 10. See also Goodman, *Radio's Civic Ambition*, p. 68.

36. Charles W. Hurd, "Will the Radio Be Censored?," *New York Times*, Nov. 6, 1938, p. 81.

37. Goodman, *Radio's Civic Ambition*, pp. 10–19. See also Fleming, "Stricter Policing," p. 6.

38. "Beliefs About Radio," *New York Times*, May 1, 1938, p. 160. See also "Sarnoff Foresees a Peril," p. 19; "Paley Holds Radio Needs No Censors," *New York Times*, April 6, 1938, p. 25.
39. "McNinch Abolishes Division of the FCC," *Broadcasting*, Oct. 15, 1937, pp. 16, 80. "Boards & Bureaus: Plucked Feathers," *Time*, Oct. 25, 1937, pp. 14–15. "McNinch Finishes Major FCC Remodeling," *Broadcasting*, Nov. 15, 1938, p. 13.
40. "Business & Finance: Foot Forward," *Time*, April 11, 1938, p. 70.
41. "Business & Finance: Perturbation & Comfort," *Time*, April 18, 1938, pp. 62, 64, 66.
42. Quoted in Steve Craig, "Out of Eden: The Legion of Decency, the FCC, and Mae West's 1937 Appearance on *The Chase & Sanborn Hour*," *Journal of Radio Studies*, vol. 13, no. 2 (Nov. 2006), p. 234.
43. See "Tainting the Air," *Evangelist*, Dec. 17, 1937, in *Radio Censorship*, ed. Summers, p. 29.
44. Summers, *Radio Censorship*, pp. 28–29. Craig, "Out of Eden," pp. 232–33.
45. Craig, "Out of Eden," pp. 232–33, 235–38, 243–44.
46. "FCC Issues Rebuke for Mae West Skit," *Broadcasting*, Jan. 15, 1938, p. 13.
47. Craig, "Out of Eden," pp. 242, 244. John Gosling, *Waging the War of the Worlds: A History of the 1938 Radio Broadcast and Resulting Panic* (Jefferson, N.C.: McFarland, 2009), p. 68.
48. Summers, ed., *Radio Censorship*, pp. 28–29.
49. "FCC Attacked by Newspaper Writers For Rebuke to NBC in Mae West Case," *Broadcasting*, Feb. 1, 1938. See also Craig, "Out of Eden," pp. 242–43.
50. "McNinch Warns Industry to Toe Mark," *Broadcasting*, Feb. 15, 1938, p. 104.
51. David L. Reifer to Frank W. [*sic*] McNinch, Oct. 31, 1938, box 238, NARA.
52. "FCC to Scan Script," p. 1. Secrest, "Martian Invasion by Radio 'Regrettable,' Says McNinch," p. 4. See also Warren B. Francis, "Mars Broadcast Hysteria May Cause Curbs on Radio," *Los Angeles Times*, Nov. 1, 1938, p. 2. "Demand Grows for Radio Curb," p. 5. "U.S. Is Probing Hoax," p. 5. Dewey L. Fleming, "Panic Brings New Demand to Curb Radio," *Baltimore Sun*, Nov. 1, 1938, p. 1. "Stricter Federal Rule," Nov. 1, 1938, p. 2.
53. Brown, "Frank R. McNinch," p. 10.
54. "FCC Is Perplexed," p. 26. See also "'End of World' Broadcast Quiz Started by FCC," *Chicago Daily Tribune*, Nov. 1, 1938, p. 17. "U.S. Is Probing Hoax," p. 5. "Federal Board to Probe Broadcast," p. 1. Francis, "Mars Panic May Cause Radio Curbs," p. 1. "F.C.C. Orders Inquiry," p. 1. "Federal Board Asks for Script of Wells Play," *New York Sun*, Oct. 31, 1938, p. 1. "Communications Board Investigating Broadcast," p. 1. Fleming, "Stricter Policing," p. 6. Secrest, "Martian Invasion by Radio 'Regrettable,' Says McNinch," pp. 1, 4.
55. See James G. Gill to the FCC, Nov. 1, 1938, box 238, NARA.
56. "FCC Is Perplexed," p. 26. See also "'End of World' Broadcast Quiz," p. 17. "U.S. Is Probing Hoax," p. 5. "Federal Board to Probe Broadcast," p. 1. Francis, "Mars Panic May Cause Radio Curbs," p. 1. "F.C.C. Orders Inquiry," p. 1. "Federal Board Asks for Script," p. 1. Fleming, "Stricter Policing," p. 6. "Stricter Federal Rule Seen," p. 2. Secrest, "Martian Invasion by Radio 'Regrettable,' Says McNinch," pp. 1, 4.
57. "Demand Grows for Radio Curb," p. 1. See also "Radio Fake Starts Action," p. 1.
58. Francis, "Mars Panic May Cause Radio Curbs," p. 1.
59. Ena B. Kind to Orson Welles, Nov. 3, 1938, box 23, "Illinois" folder (12/54), Wilson-Welles Papers.
60. W. J. Crehan and Frances Crehan to Orson Welles, Nov. 2, 1938, box 24, "No Location" folder, Wilson-Welles Papers.
61. David H. Schwartz to Orson Welles, Oct. 31, 1938, box 24, "NYC & boroughs" folder 1 (33/54), Wilson-Welles Papers. See also Beatrice D. Dobbin to Orson Welles, Oct. 31, 1938, box 23, "Maryland" folder (19/54), Wilson-Welles Papers.
62. Nicholas Carr to Orson Welles, Oct. 31, 1938, box 23, "Illinois" folder (12/54), Wilson-Welles Papers. See also Claire Horn to the Mercury Theatre, Nov. 2, 1938, box 24, "New York, NYC & boroughs" folder 3 (35/54), Wilson-Welles Papers.

63. See Dwight L. Bolinger to the Federal Radio Commission [*sic*], Oct. 31, 1938; Isabelle M. Parks to Frank R. McNinch, Nov. 1, 1938; William T. Zusag to F. R. McNinch, Nov. 4, 1938, all box 237, NARA; and Lee E. Ellison to Orson Welles, Nov. 7, 1938, box 23, "District of Columbia" folder (8/54); Lillian A. Ettinger to Orson Wells [*sic*], Nov. 3, 1938, box 23, "Illinois" folder (12/54); K. E. Lerche to Orson Welles, Oct. 31, 1938, box 24, "New Jersey" folder 1 (29/54); Hugh Gillen to Orson Welles, Oct. 31, 1938, box 24, "New Jersey" folder 2 (30/54); Joseph A. Stauhs to Orson Welles, n.d., box 24, "New Jersey" folder 2 (30/54); David H. Schwartz to Orson Welles, Oct. 31, 1938, box 24, "NYC & boroughs" folder 1 (33/54); Ernest A. Gray to Orson Welles, Oct. 31, 1938, box 24, "New York" folder 2 (37/54); Chester S. Nagel to CBS, Nov. 1, 1938, box 24, "Pennsylvania" folder 1 (42/54); William Bennix to Orson Welles, Oct. 31, 1938, box 24, "Pennsylvania" folder 2 (43/54); Gertrude Staska to Orson Welles, Nov. 6, 1938, box 24, "South Dakota" folder (46/54); Walter H. Juniper to Orson Welles, Oct. 31, 1938, box 24, "Texas" folder (48/54), all Wilson-Welles Papers.

64. Hume V. Stephani to Orson Welles, Nov. 4, 1938, box 24, "No Location" folder, Wilson-Welles Papers. See also Beaumont and Nancy Newhall to CBS, Oct. 31, 1938; Mrs. Ralph E. Sanders to Frank R. McNinch, Nov. 1, 1938, both box 237, NARA.

65. George Reynolds to the Mercury Theatre, Oct. 31, 1938, box 24, "New York (state)" folder 2 (39/54), Wilson-Welles Papers. See also Elmer Sheets to Orson Welles, Oct. 31, 1938, box 24, "New York (state)" folder 2 (37/54); Howard S. Bradley to Orson Welles, Nov. 5, 1938, box 24, "Canada" folder, both Wilson-Welles Papers.

66. Evangeline Ensley to Frank R. McNinch, Nov. 2, 1938, box 237, NARA.

67. Eddie Cantor to Frank McNinch, Nov. 2, 1938, box 237, NARA.

68. Mary Elizabeth Calderine to Orson Wells [*sic*], Oct. 31, 1938, box 24, "Ohio" folder (39/54), Wilson-Welles Papers. See also Mildred Samars to CBS, Nov. 3, 1938, box 23, "Michigan" folder (21/54), Wilson-Welles Papers.

69. John Carson, *The Measure of Merit: Talents, Intelligence, and Inequality in the French and American Republics, 1750–1940* (Princeton: Princeton University Press, 2007), pp. 242–49. See also Paul Frederic Peifer to Frank McNinch, Oct. 31, 1938, box 237, NARA; Goodman, *Radio's Civic Ambition*, pp. 254–55, 269.

70. U.S. Department of the Interior, *Report of the Advisory Committee on Education by Radio* (Columbus, Ohio: F. J. Heer Printing Co., 1930), pp. 40–41. Frank N. Freeman, "A Radio Intelligence Test," *New York Times*, June 25, 1933, p. X7. See also Elena Razlogova, *The Listener's Voice: Early Radio and the American Public* (Philadelphia: University of Pennsylvania Press, 2011), pp. 99–101.

71. Cantril and Allport, *Psychology of Radio*, pp. 42, 97–98, 254.

72. Secrest, "F.C.C. Actions May Lead," p. B7. See also Susan J. Douglas, *Listening In: Radio and the American Imagination* (Minneapolis: University of Minnesota Press, 2004), p. 104.

73. "The Gullible Radio Public," *Chicago Daily Tribune*, Nov. 10, 1938, p. 16.

74. See Sidney Forbes to Orson Welles, Nov. 2, 1938, box 23, "California" folder (4/54); Russell N. Haas and Elmer Van Arsdall to Orson Welles, Nov. 1, 1938, box 23, "Florida" folder (9/54); Katherine Buck to Orson Welles, Nov. 1, 1938, box 23, "Maine" folder (18/54); Howard W. Littlefield to Orson Welles, n.d., box 23, "Maine" folder (18/54); G. J. Rellim to Orson Welles, Oct. 31, 1938, box 24, "New Jersey" folder 1 (29/54); Lucretia B. Forbes to Orson Welles, Nov. 3, 1938, box 24, "No Location" folder; W. H. Young to Orson Wells [*sic*], Oct. 31, 1938, box 24, "New York, NYC & boroughs" folder 2 (34/54); Barrie Winslow to Orson Welles, Oct. 31, 1938, box 24, "NYC & boroughs" folder 1 (33/54); Mrs. M. J. Liederman to Orson Wells [*sic*], Nov. 3, 1938, box 24, "New York, NYC & boroughs" folder 2 (34/54); Rachel J. Imman to Orson Welles, Oct. 31, 1938, box 24, "Ohio" folder (39/54); Frank Hartley to Orson Wells [*sic*], Nov. 3, 1938, box 23, "Michigan" folder (21/54), all Wilson-Welles Papers; and George A. Sherron to Frank R. McNinch, Nov. 1, 1938; William P. Thomas, Jr., to Frank R. McNinch, Nov. 1, 1938, both box 237, NARA.

75. William P. Gavin to Frank P. [sic] McNinch, Oct. 31, 1938, box 237, NARA. See also Joseph Menchen to CBS, Oct. 31, 1938, box 23, "California" folder (4/54), Wilson-Welles Papers; and Ernest L. Petit to Frank P. [sic] McNinch, Nov. 1, 1938, box 237, NARA; Skulda Banér to the Federal Communications Bureau [sic], Oct. 31, 1938, box 237, NARA (also in box 24, "Wisconsin" folder [54/54], Wilson-Welles Papers).

76. Frank Bayless to the Mercury Theater [sic], Nov. 1, 1938, box 24, "Texas" folder (48/54), Wilson-Welles Papers.

77. Prof. Roy K. Marshall to Frank R. McNinch, Nov. 1, 1938, box 237, NARA.

78. See Janet Roughton to Orson Welles, Nov. 3, 1938, box 24, "New York, NYC & boroughs" folder 2 (34/54); G. R. Ewing to Orson Welles, Nov. 6, 1938, box 24, "Washington" folder (52/54), both Wilson-Welles Papers.

79. Carolyn Van Ness to Orson Welles, Nov. 2, 1938, box 24, "New York, NYC & boroughs" folder 2 (34/54), Wilson-Welles Papers. See also Leonard Douglas to Arson [sic] Welles, Nov. 1, 1938, box 24, "Texas" folder (48/54); Jane Ward to Orson Welles, Nov. 1, 1938, box 24, "New Jersey" folder 2 (30/54); Beatrice D. Dobbin to Orson Welles, Oct. 31, 1938, box 23, "Maryland" folder (19/54); Jean E. Knowles to Orson Welles, Nov. 4, 1938, box 23, "Massachusetts" folder (20/54); Magdalene Lehrer to Orson Welles, Oct. 31, 1938, box 23, "Michigan" folder (21/54), all Wilson-Welles Papers; and Eva Ruark to the FCC, Nov. 4, 1938; E. D. Clampitt to F. R. McNinch, Nov. 1, 1938, both box 237, NARA.

80. J. C. Torbett to Frank R. McNinch, n.d., box 237, NARA.

81. Frank Hartley to Orson Wells [sic], Nov. 3, 1938, box 23, "Michigan" folder (21/54), Wilson-Welles Papers.

82. "Set Owners Found Against Censorship," *Broadcasting*, Feb. 15, 1938, p. 40. "Radio Public Seen Against a Censor," *New York Times*, Feb. 11, 1938, p. 4. Goodman, *Radio's Civic Ambition*, p. 281.

83. Jim R. Taylor to Orson Wells [sic], Nov. 2, 1938, box 24, "Montana" folder (25/54), Wilson-Welles Papers. See also Rowena Ferguson to Frank P. [sic] McNinch, n.d., box 237, NARA; and Chauncey D. Cowles, Jr., and Mary Beakes Cowles to Orson Welles, Oct. 31, 1938, box 24, "New York (state)" folder 1 (36/54), Wilson-Welles Papers.

84. Roland S. Biersach to the FCC, Oct. 31, 1938, box 237, NARA. See also E. Wright to Orson Welles, Nov. 3, 1938, box 24, "Missouri" folder (24/54); Evelyn Ranioille to CBS, Nov. 1, 1938, box 24, "Ohio" folder (39/54), both Wilson-Welles Papers; and Herbert O. Bergdahl to Frank McNinch, Nov. 3, 1938, box 237, NARA.

85. Barnouw, *Golden Web*, pp. 43–44. Francis Chase, Jr., *Sound and Fury: An Informal History of Broadcasting* (New York: Harper & Brothers, 1942), pp. 80–81. Donald Warren, *Radio Priest: Charles Coughlin, the Father of Hate Radio* (New York: Free Press, 1996), pp. 73–74.

86. Michael Hiltzik, *The New Deal: A Modern History* (New York: Free Press, 2011), p. 31.

87. S. Miles Bouton, "Can It Happen Here as It Happened Abroad?" *New York Times*, May 2, 1937, p. SM3.

88. Lyman Bryson, *Which Way America?* (New York: Macmillan, 1939), pp. 1–2.

89. Barnouw, *Golden Web*, pp. 44–47. Robert J. Brown, *Manipulating the Ether: The Power of Broadcast Radio in Thirties America* (Jefferson, N.C.: McFarland, 1998), pp. 84–88. Chase, *Sound and Fury*, pp. 81–82, 88–95. Irving E. Fang, *Those Radio Commentators!* (Ames: Iowa State University Press, 1977), pp. 87–103. Hiltzik, *New Deal*, pp. 218–20, 225–26. Warren, *Radio Priest*, pp. 20–39, 45–47, 50, 52, 74–81, 84–94, 112–13, 132–38, 154–56, 188–92.

90. Barnouw, *Golden Web*, pp. 48–50. Brown, *Manipulating the Ether*, pp. 82–84. Hiltzik, *New Deal*, pp. 220–22.

91. Quoted in Chase, *Sound and Fury*, p. 84.

92. Barnouw, *Golden Web*, pp. 47–51. Brown, *Manipulating the Ether*, pp. 85–88, 94–95. Fang, *Commentators!*, pp. 91–96, 98–99. Hiltzik, *New Deal*, pp. 222–26. Warren, *Radio Priest*, pp. 40–44, 62–64, 82–95.

93. Quoted in Chase, *Sound and Fury*, p. 82. See also Bouton, "Can It Happen Here," p. SM3; Barnouw, *Golden Web*, pp. 44, 48–50; Chase, *Sound and Fury*, pp. 81–87. Hiltzik, *New Deal*, pp. 223–24.

94. Hiltzik, *New Deal*, pp. 297–98. Frederick Allen, *Since Yesterday: The Nineteen-Thirties in America, September 3, 1929–September 3, 1939* (New York: Harper & Brothers, 1940), pp. 215, 254.

95. Sinclair Lewis, *It Can't Happen Here* (Garden City, N.Y.: Doubleday, Doran, 1935), p. 40.

96. Ibid., pp. 21–22.

97. John A. McCormick to Orson Wells [*sic*], Oct. 31, 1938, box 24, "New York, NYC & boroughs" folder 2 (34/54), Wilson-Welles Papers. See also George Beam to the FCC, Nov. 2, 1938, box 237, NARA.

98. Franklin Wright to Orson Welles, Nov. 4, 1938, box 23, "Maine" folder (18/54), Wilson-Welles Papers.

99. Besse P. Gephardt to CBS, Nov. 2, 1938, box 24, "Missouri" folder (24/54), Wilson-Welles Papers. See also H. M. Blum to Orson Wells [*sic*], Oct. 31, 1938, box 24, "Texas" folder (48/54), Wilson-Welles Papers.

100. Michael Stamm, "The Sound of Print: Newspapers and the Public Promotion of Early Radio Broadcasting in the United States," in *Sound in the Age of Mechanical Reproduction*, ed. David Suisman and Susan Strasser (Philadelphia: University of Pennsylvania Press, 2010), p. 238.

101. Fred French, Jr., to Orson Welles, Nov. 1, 1938, box 24, "Washington" folder (52/54), Wilson-Welles Papers.

102. William A. Aspinwall to CBS, Oct. 31, 1938, box 24, "New York, NYC & boroughs" folder 3 (35/54), Wilson-Welles Papers.

103. Walter H. Kelly to Frank McNinch, Nov. 1, 1938, box 237, NARA.

104. Goodman, *Radio's Civic Ambition*, pp. 245–47, 264–72. See also John Houseman, *Run-Through: A Memoir* (New York: Simon & Schuster, 1972), p. 400.

105. Eva Ruark to the FCC, Nov. 4, 1938, box 237, NARA.

106. Goodman, *Radio's Civic Ambition*, pp. 245–55, 264–72.

107. Edwin George to Orson Welles, Nov. 1, 1938, box 24, "Canada" folder, Wilson-Welles Papers. See also R. H. Peterson to Frank R. McNinch, Oct. 31, 1938; G. P. Dionne to the FCC, Nov. 1, 1938, both box 237, NARA.

108. W. E. Moore to the FCC, Oct. 31, 1938, box 237, NARA.

109. See Gaylord St. John to Frank R. McNinch, Nov. 1, 1938; Alfred R. Neff to the FCC, Nov. 1, 1938; Robert Collyer Hosmer to Anning S. Prall, Nov. 2, 1938; Fred Nalley, Jr., to the FCC, Nov. 3, 1938, all box 237, NARA; and Arthur R. Tomlinson to Orson Wells [*sic*], Nov. 1, 1939 [*sic*], box 23, "Connecticut" folder (6/54); Dora H. Kelley to Orson Welles, Oct. 31, 1938, box 23, "Indiana" folder (13/54); Jean Hermann and family to CBS, Oct. 31, 1938, box 23, "Indiana" folder (13/54); Mrs. Harry A. Pierson to NBC [*sic*], n.d., box 23, "Indiana" folder (13/54); Alfred R. Neff to Orson Welles, Nov. 1, 1938, box 24, "New Jersey" folder 2 (30/54), all Wilson-Welles Papers. A few other letters suggested that frightened listeners be institutionalized or, in one case, sterilized and denied the right to vote. See Stillson B. Arnquist to the FCC, Oct. 31, 1938; H. R. Katterman to the FCC, Nov. 1, 1938, both box 237, NARA; and Daniel O'Grady to Orson Welles, Oct. 31, 1938, box 23, "Indiana" folder (13/54), Wilson-Welles Papers.

110. Claude Moore to Frank C. [*sic*] McNinch, Nov. 2, 1938, box 237, NARA. See also Miriam Noll to the FCC, Nov. 2, 1938, box 237, NARA.

111. Paul Pesch to the FCC, Nov. 1, 1938, box 237, NARA.

112. "Well, Wells, Welles," *Broadcasting*, Nov. 15, 1938, p. 40.
113. See "Yellow Journalism of the Air," *St. Louis Post-Dispatch*, Oct. 31, 1938, p. 2C; "U.S. Body Demands Script," p. 3; "Setback: Radio Lost Esteem by Fake War Program," *San Francisco Examiner*, Nov. 1, 1938, p. 8; "Lesson Learned," *Baltimore Sun*, Nov. 2, 1938, p. 12; "Calm After the Storm," *Washington Post*, Nov. 2, 1938, p. X8; Orrin E. Dunlap, Jr., "Seeking a Code: Voluntary Self-Regulation of Broadcasting Is Urged to Avoid Censorship," *New York Times*, Nov. 20, 1938, p. 174; Justin Levine, "A History and Analysis of the Federal Communications Commission's Response to Radio Broadcast Hoaxes," *Federal Communications Law Journal*, vol. 52, no. 2 (March 2000), pp. 282-83.
114. "A Foolhardy Radio Stunt," *Milwaukee Journal*, Nov. 1, 1938, p. 10.
115. "Radio Riot," New York *Daily News*, Nov. 2, 1938, p. 35, box 2, "Clippings and Articles, 1936-1940" folder (2 of 4), Welles-Feder Collection.
116. Jim Palmer to the FCC, Nov. 1, 1938, box 237, NARA.
117. "No FCC Action Due," p. 26. "FCC Turns from Mars to Fascist Speech," *Washington Post*, Nov. 2, 1938, p. 3. "'Anti-Semitic' Radio Broadcast," p. 6A.
118. "No FCC Action Due," p. 26.
119. Secrest, "Martian Invasion by Radio 'Regrettable,' Says McNinch," p. 4.
120. See "FCC to Determine Its Authority in Handling Program Complaints," *New York Times*, Nov. 6, 1938, p. 184.
121. Fleming, "Panic Brings New Demand," pp. 1, 6.
122. "Networks to Curb Use of Term 'Flash,'" *New York Times*, Nov. 8, 1938, p. 25. "Program Standards Studied by FCC," *Broadcasting*, Nov. 15, 1938, p. 15. Levine, "History," p. 282.
123. Quoted in Orson Welles, interviewed by Leslie Megahey, in *The Orson Welles Story*, BBC, 1982, in *Orson Welles: Interviews*, ed. Mark W. Estrin (Jackson: University Press of Mississippi, 2002), p. 181. See also Orson Welles, interviewed by Tom Snyder, *Tomorrow with Tom Snyder*, NBC, Sept. 1975, Paley Center for Media iCollection for Colleges, catalog ID T:35495.
124. "Do You Want Radio Censorship," *Look*, Feb. 14, 1939, in *Radio Censorship*, ed. Summers, p. 258. Levine, "History," p. 284.
125. Levine, "History," p. 284, n. 55.
126. Clyde L. Herring, "Is Radio Censorship Necessary?," in *Radio Censorship*, ed. Summers, pp. 222, 226.
127. "Broadcasters Meet Here Today to Tighten Self-Censorship," *Washington Post*, Dec. 12, 1938, p. 1.
128. Earl Sparling, "Radio Gets the Jitters," *American Magazine*, March 1939, in *Radio Censorship*, ed. Summers, pp. 261-62.
129. Brown, *Manipulating the Ether*, pp. 244-45. "Radio: March Resumed," *Time*, Oct. 13, 1941, p. 56.
130. David Sarnoff, "In Favor of Self-Regulation," statement before Federal Communications Commission, Nov. 14, 1938, in *Radio Censorship*, ed. Summers, p. 232. See also Dunlap, "Seeking a Code," p. 174; "Radio Takes the Initiative," *Wall Street Journal*, Nov. 28, 1938, p. 4.
131. Barnouw, *Golden Web*, p. 169.
132. "Radio: Mopper-Upper," p. 32. "McNinch May Leave FCC for New Post," *Broadcasting*, June 15, 1939, p. 13.
133. Sol Taishoff, "James L. Fly to Become Chairman of FCC," *Broadcasting*, Aug. 1, 1939, p. 11.
134. "Freedom to Listen Basic Counterpart of Freedom of Speech, Fly Tells Club," *Broadcasting*, Oct. 4, 1943, p. 30. See also Goodman, *Radio's Civic Ambition*, p. 288.
135. Barnouw, *Golden Web*, pp. 168-73, 188.

136. Ibid., pp. 173–81, 187–90. See also Douglas, *Listening In*, p. 187.
137. Quoted in Barnouw, *Golden Web*, p. 189.
138. Leonard Maltin, *The Great American Broadcast: A Celebration of Radio's Golden Age* (New York: Dutton, 1997), pp. 147–64, especially p. 159.
139. Sparling, "Radio Gets the Jitters," pp. 262–65.
140. "Radio Playing It Safe," *Variety*, Feb. 15, 1939, in *Radio Censorship*, ed. Summers, pp. 201–202.
141. Cantril and Allport, *Psychology of Radio*, pp. 233–34.
142. Simon Callow, *Orson Welles: The Road to Xanadu* (New York: Viking, 1995), pp. 370–71.
143. Neil Verma, *Theater of the Mind: Imagination, Aesthetics, and American Radio Drama* (Chicago: University of Chicago Press, 2012), pp. 81–83. See also Razlogova, *The Listener's Voice*, pp. 97, 108–14.
144. Maltin, *Great American Broadcast*, p. 305.

8. "The Story of the Century"

1. Mrs. Michael Conovich to the FCC, Nov. 1, 1938, box 237, NARA.
2. John Gosling, "Grover's Mill," *War of the Worlds Invasion: The Historical Perspective*, www.war-ofthe-worlds.co.uk/grovers_mill.htm (accessed March 20, 2014).
3. Howard Koch, *The Panic Broadcast: Portrait of an Event* (Boston: Little, Brown, 1970), pp. 115–33.
4. "F.C.C. Inquiry Is Ordered into Radio War Play," *New York Herald Tribune*, Nov. 1, 1938, p. 19.
5. Quoted in Joe Nickell, "Shootout with Martians: In the Wake of the 1938 Broadcast Panic," *Skeptical Inquirer*, vol. 20, no. 4 (Dec. 2010), www.csicop.org/sb/show/shootout_with_martians_in_the_wake_of_the_1938_broadcast_panic/ (accessed March 21, 2014).
6. Quoted in John Gosling, *Waging the War of the Worlds: A History of the 1938 Radio Broadcast and Resulting Panic* (Jefferson, N.C.: McFarland, 2009), p. 62. Newspapers variously gave the witness's name as "Philip Wassun" and "William Wassum," and also disagree on whether the men he met were state troopers or National Guardsman. But it seems likely that they were the same state troopers dispatched from Trenton, according to the *Trenton Evening Times*. See also "F.C.C. Inquiry Is Ordered," p. 19.
7. "Hoax Spreads Terror Here; Some Pack Up," *Trenton Evening Times*, Oct. 31, 1938, p. 1, www.war-ofthe-worlds.co.uk/trenton_times_page1p2.htm (accessed March 20, 2014).
8. "Pseudo–Heavenly Body Shakes Burghers as Congregation Prepares for World's End," *Daily Princetonian*, Oct. 31, 1938, p. 1.
9. "Hoax Spreads Terror," p. 1.
10. See "F.C.C. Inquiry Is Ordered," p. 19; "Geologists at Princeton Hunt 'Meteor' in Vain," *New York Times*, Oct. 31, 1938, p. 4; "Pseudo–Heavenly Body," p. 1; "Radio Story of Attack from Mars Causes Hysteria," *St. Louis Post-Dispatch*, Oct. 31, 1938, p. 3A; "U.S. Body Demands War Scare Script," *New York Sun*, Oct. 31, 1938, p. 3. The traffic jam around Grover's Mill that night is well attested. See also Gosling, *Waging the War*, pp. 60–62; W. Joseph Campbell, *Getting It Wrong: Ten of the Greatest Misreported Stories in American Journalism* (Berkeley: University of California Press, 2010), pp. 37–38; Chris Jordan, " 'War of the Worlds' Radio Broadcast Turns 75," *USA Today*, Oct. 29, 2013, www.usatoday.com/story/news/nation/2013/10/29/war-of-the-worlds-75th-anniversary-new-jersey/3306975/ (accessed March 20, 2014).
11. "Pseudo–Heavenly Body," p. 1.
12. Alan Gallop, *The Martians Are Coming!: The True Story of Orson Welles' 1938 Panic Broadcast* (Gloucestershire: Amberley Publishing, 2011), pp. 95–97; quote on p. 96.
13. Koch, *Panic Broadcast*, pp. 117–19, 121, 125–27, 131.

14. "F.C.C. Inquiry Is Ordered," p. 19. Koch, *Panic Broadcast*, pp. 119, 121. Gosling, *Waging the War*, p. 63. Koch (*Panic Broadcast*, p. 119) describes Dock as the mill's owner, but that is untrue.

15. Brian Holmsten and Alex Lubertozzi, eds., *The War of the Worlds: Mars' Invasion of Earth, Inciting Panic and Inspiring Terror from H. G. Wells to Orson Welles and Beyond* (Naperville, Ill.: Sourcebooks, 2001), p. 7. Koch (*Panic Broadcast*, p. 119) and others claim that Dock was photographed in the old mill, but in 2011, the researcher Bruce Clark conclusively proved that the photo was actually taken in the warehouse across the street. See Brian Bingaman, "Clearing the Record About 'War' Photo," *Reporter*, Oct. 30, 2011, www.thereporteronline.com/article/20111030/TMP08/310309972/clearing -the-record-about-war-photo (accessed March 21, 2014).

16. "Speaking of Pictures . . . This Terror Has Box Office," *Life*, Nov. 14, 1938, p. 3.

17. Brian Bingaman, "Clearing the Record."

18. Nickell, "Shootout with Martians."

19. Roy Thomas, Gene Colan, and Mike Gustovich, "The Crimson Avenger" in *Secret Origins* 5 (New York: DC Comics, Aug. 1986), p. 20. Gosling, *Waging the War*, pp. 174–75.

20. Dan Harper to Orson Welles, Nov. 1, 1938, box 24, "New York, NYC & boroughs" folder 3 (35/54), Wilson-Welles Papers. See also Evelyn Toole to Orson Welles, Oct. 31, 1938, box 24, "New York, NYC & boroughs" folder 2 (34/54); Arthur Davison Ficke to Orson Welles, Nov. 3, 1938, box 24, "New York (state)" folder 1 (36/54), both Wilson-Welles Papers.

21. Joseph Haltier to Orson Welles, Oct. 31, 1938, box 24, "New York (state)" folder 1 (36/54), Wilson-Welles Papers.

22. Mrs. S. Shirley to CBS, Nov. 1, 1938, box 23, "Michigan" folder (21/54), Wilson-Welles Papers. See also Joseph Toniutti to Orson Welles, Nov. 1, 1938, box 24, "Tennessee" folder (47/54); Paul F. Peifer to Orson Wells [*sic*], Oct. 31, 1938, box 23, "Illinois" folder (12/54); Mrs. Charles E. Brown to Orson Welles, Nov. 3, 1938, box 24, "Texas" folder (48/54), all Wilson-Welles Papers.

23. Jess Kuttuer to Orson Wells [*sic*], Nov. 1, 1938, box 24, "NYC & boroughs" folder 1 (33/54), Wilson-Welles Papers. See also Paul Pesch to the FCC, Nov. 1, 1938; D. Russell Barnes to Frank R. McNinch, Nov. 1, 1938; E. D. Clampitt to F. R. McNinch, Nov. 1, 1938; Kennett K. Allen to Frank P. [*sic*] McNinch, Nov. 2, 1938; R. N. Lamberson to the FCC, Nov. 2, 1938; Malcolm L. Moore to the FCC, Nov. 2, 1938, all box 237, NARA; and Mabel Clemens to Frank R. McNinch, Nov. 2, 1938; Florence Taylor to Frank R. McNinch, Nov. 20, 1938; Lynn Montross to the Communications Commission [*sic*], Nov. 1, 1938; Laura V. Smith to the FCC, Oct. 31, 1938, all box 238, NARA.

24. Francis Chase, Jr., *Sound and Fury: An Informal History of Broadcasting* (New York: Harper & Brothers, 1942), p. 154. Robert J. Brown, *Manipulating the Ether: The Power of Broadcast Radio in Thirties America* (Jefferson, N.C.: McFarland, 1998), pp. 153, 168–69.

25. See William P. Thomas, Jr., to Frank R. McNinch, Nov. 1, 1938; Beatrice Henning Shaw to Frank R. McNinch, Nov. 1, 1938; Malcolm L. Moore to the FCC, Nov. 2, 1938, all box 237, NARA; and Mrs. E. M. Wheelock to Orson Welles, n.d., box 23, "Massachusetts" folder (20/54); W. C. McPhee to Orson Welles, n.d., box 24, "New Jersey" folder 2 (30/54); Garland Bailey to Orson Welles, Nov. 2, 1938, box 24, "Texas" folder (48/54), all Wilson-Welles Papers.

26. Mrs. G. Herbert Taylor to Orson Welles, Nov. 1, 1938, box 24, "New Jersey" folder 2 (30/54), Wilson-Welles Papers. See also Mrs. S. Shirley to CBS, Nov. 1, 1938, box 23, "Michigan" folder (21/54), Wilson-Welles Papers; and Miriam Noll to the FCC, Nov. 2, 1938; Mrs. R. H. Ragland to Frank P. [*sic*] McNinch, Nov. 1, 1938; Lillian M. Davenport to Frank R. McNinch, Nov. 2, 1938; D. Russell Barnes to the FCC, Nov. 1, 1938; Paul Pesch to the FCC, Nov. 1, 1938, all box 237, NARA. And see "Charlie Saved Us," *Baltimore Sun*, Nov. 1, p. 10.

27. "Europe Laughs at Radio Panic," *San Francisco Examiner*, Nov. 2, 1938, pp. 1, 6.

28. "What German Press Made of U.S. Scare," *New York Sun*, Oct. 31, 1938, p. 2. Gallop, *Martians*, p. 118.

29. "Reich Heaps Ridicule on U.S. for Its Panic," *San Francisco Examiner*, Nov. 2, 1938, p. 6. See also Gosling, *Waging the War*, pp. 96–97; Holmsten and Lubertozzi, eds., *War of the Worlds*, p. 25; James D. Secrest, "Martian Invasion by Radio 'Regrettable,' Says McNinch," *Washington Post*, Nov. 1, 1938, p. 4.

30. "Hitler's 'Only Claim' On Britain and France: Colonies Yet to Be Agreed On," *Manchester Guardian*, Nov. 9, 1938, p. 14. See also Goodman, *Radio's Civic Ambition*, p. 267.

31. Richard R. McCombs to Orson Welles, Oct. 31, 1938, box 24, "Pennsylvania" folder 1 (42/54), Wilson-Welles Papers. Major George Fielding Eliot, an author and U.S. intelligence officer, made a similar prediction in the *San Francisco Examiner*: "You may rest assured that any power in Europe that may be laying up trouble for us has carefully filed away last night's scare for future reference." (A. F. McCullough, "Radio Scare Declared Vital Lesson to U.S.," *San Francisco Examiner*, Nov. 1, 1938, p. 2.) See also Reginald Fox Carmody to Frank McNinch, Oct. 31, 1938, box 238; William C. McIntire to Frank R. McNinch, Oct. 31, 1938, box 237, both NARA; and D. S. Ripperton to Orson Welles, n.d., box 23, "Iowa" folder (14/54), Wilson-Welles Papers.

32. Lillian M. Davenport to Frank R. McNinch, Nov. 2, 1938, box 237, NARA.

33. William L. Shirer, *The Rise and Fall of the Third Reich: A History of Nazi Germany* (New York: Simon & Schuster, 1960), pp. 518–20, 594–95. See also David Jenemann, *Adorno in America* (Minneapolis: University of Minnesota Press, 2007), p. 67.

34. Shirer, *Rise and Fall*, pp. 595–96.

35. Stanley Sibelius to CBS, Nov. 1, 1938, box 23, "Connecticut" folder (6/54), Wilson-Welles Papers.

36. [Name unclear] (Brockport, N.Y.) to CBS, Oct. 31, 1938, box 237, NARA. See also Dr. Christian Lind to the FCC, Nov. 1, 1938; "Name Illegible" to Frank R. McNinch, Nov. 1, 1938, both box 237, NARA; and Charles L. Thorpe to Orson Welles, Nov. 1, 1938, box 23, "Connecticut" folder (6/54); E. Wright to Orson Welles, Nov. 3, 1938, box 24, "Missouri" folder (24/54); Louis Ruzieba to Orson Welles, Nov. 1, 1938, box 24, "New Jersey" folder 2 (30/54); John A. McCormick to Orson Wells [*sic*], Oct. 31, 1938, box 24, "New York, NYC & boroughs" folder 2 (34/54); William Kunitch to Orson Wells [*sic*], Oct. 31, 1938, box 24, "New York, NYC & boroughs" folder 2 (34/54); Elizabeth Salk to Orson Welles, Nov. 1, 1938, box 24, "New York (state)" folder 2 (37/54); F. B. Butterfield to Orson Welles, Oct. 31, 1938, box 24, "Pennsylvania" folder 1 (42/54); Ray L. Cramer to Orson Welles, Oct. 31, 1938, box 24, "Virginia" folder (51/54), all Wilson-Welles Papers.

37. Frederick Lewis Allen, *Since Yesterday: The Nineteen-Thirties in America, September 3, 1929–September 3, 1939* (New York: Harper & Brothers, 1940), pp. 318–27. See also E. E. Petit to Orson Wells [*sic*], Nov. 1, 1938, box 24, "South Carolina" folder (45/54); Claude M. Bretz to Orson Welles, Oct. 31, 1938, box 24, "Pennsylvania" folder 2 (43/54), both Wilson-Welles Papers; and Bernice Anderson to Frank P. [*sic*] McNinch, Nov. 2, 1938; George A. Sherron to CBS, Nov. 1, 1938, box 237, NARA.

38. See Mrs. N. G. DeWeend to Orson Wells [*sic*], Oct. 31, 1938, box 23, "Michigan" folder (21/54), Wilson-Welles Papers; Paul J. Holsen to Frank McNish [*sic*], Nov. 1, 1938, box 237, NARA.

39. Mrs. A. Gulloth to Frank R. McNinch, Nov. 1, 1938, box 237, NARA. See also R. H. Peterson to Frank R. McNinch, Oct. 31, 1938, box 237, NARA; D. S. Ripperton to Orson Welles, n.d., box 23, "Iowa" folder (14/54), Wilson-Welles Papers. Goodman (*Radio's Civic Ambition*, pp. 270–71) noticed a similar trend in the FCC letters.

40. Louis M. Benepe, III, to Orson Welles, Nov. 2, 1938, box 23, "Minnesota" folder (22/54), Wilson-Welles Papers. See also Clara Clifford to Frank R. McNinch, Nov. 1,

1938, box 237, NARA; George Knight to Orson Welles, Oct. 31, 1938, box 23, "Louisiana" folder (17/54), Wilson-Welles Papers.

41. See Frank J. Young to Frank P. [sic] McNinch, Nov. 1, 1938; James H. Jennings to the Radio Commission [sic], Nov. 1, 1938, both box 237, NARA; and Edward Sereda to Orson Wells [sic], Oct. 31, 1938, box 24, "New Jersey" folder 2 (30/54); Victor Mangeney to Orson Wells [sic], Oct. 31, 1938, box 24, "NYC & boroughs" folder 1 (33/54); Mr. and Mrs. J. McCarthy to Orson Welles, Oct. 31, 1938, box 23, "NYC & boroughs" folder 1 (33/54); Alice C. Heinke to Orson Wells [sic], Nov. 1, 1938, box 24, "New Jersey" folder 3 (31/54); "A woman physician" to Orson Welles, Nov. 1, 1938, box 24, "No Location" folder, all Wilson-Welles Papers.

42. Cadet Alfred C. Prime to Orson Welles, n.d., box 24, "Pennsylvania" folder 2 (43/54), Wilson-Welles Papers. See also Gerald Johnson, Jr., to Orson Welles, Oct. 31, 1938, box 23, "Georgia" folder (10/54), Wilson-Welles Papers.

43. See Mrs. N. Reilly to Orson Welles, Nov. 2, 1938, box 23, "California" folder (4/54); Victor Mangeney to Orson Wells [sic], Oct. 31, 1938, box 24, "New Jersey" folder 1 (29/54); Louis Ruzieba to Orson Welles, Nov. 1, 1938, box 24, "New Jersey" folder 2 (30/54); Amy Armour Smith to Orson Welles, Oct. 31, 1938, box 24, "New York (state)" folder 2 (37/54); Stephen S. Crause to Orson Welles, Nov. 1, 1938, box 24, "Ohio" folder (39/54); Clarence A. Hammond to Orson Welles, Oct. 31, 1938, box 24, "West Virginia" folder (53/54), all Wilson-Welles Papers; and [Name unclear] (Altoona, Pa.) to Frank R. McNinch, Oct. 31, 1938; John P. Chrenko to Franklin Delano Roosevelt, Nov. 1, 1938, both box 237, NARA. One biographer has suggested that "Welles secretly intended" to reveal America's vulnerability to invasion with the *War of the Worlds,* but there is absolutely no evidence to back this notion up (Charles Higham, *Orson Welles: The Rise and Fall of an American Genius* [New York: St. Martin's, 1985], pp. 128–29).

44. Vera Stanley to WABC, Nov. 1, 1938, box 24, "New Jersey" folder 3 (31/54), Wilson-Welles Papers. See also Bernice Anderson to Frank P. [sic] McNinch, Nov. 2, 1938; Mildred and Norman Banks to Frank McNinch, Oct. 31, 1938, both box 237, NARA; and Edward J. Longtim to Orson Welles, Nov. 1, 1938, box 23, "Minnesota" folder (23/54); Howard F. Thomas to Orson Welles, Nov. 4, 1938, box 24, "Pennsylvania" folder 2 (43/54); Muriel Tempest to Orson Welles, Oct. 31, 1938, box 23, "Illinois" folder (12/54); Fred L. Robinson to Orson Welles, Oct. 31, 1938, box 23, "Michigan" folder (21/54), all Wilson-Welles Papers. And see Brown, *Manipulating the Ether,* p. 249.

45. "Federal Board Studies Action on Radio Scare," *San Francisco Examiner,* Nov. 2, 1938, p. 6.

46. Hugh S. Johnson, "'Mars Panic' Useful," United Features Syndicate, Nov. 2, 1938, in Koch, *Panic Broadcast,* p. 95.

47. "Lesson for Real War Furnished by Drama," *Baltimore Sun,* Nov. 1, 1938, p. 6. Brown, *Manipulating the Ether,* pp. 248–50.

48. "Radio Does U.S. a Favor," *Variety,* Nov. 2, 1938, in Koch, *Panic Broadcast,* p. 95.

49. Chester S. Nagel to Frank McNinch, Nov. 1, 1938, box 237, NARA. See also Dr. Christian Lind to the FCC, Nov. 1, 1938, box 237, NARA; and Arthur Davison Ficke to Orson Welles, Nov. 3, 1938, box 24, "New York (state)" folder 1 (36/54); John A. McCormick to Orson Wells [sic], Oct. 31, 1938, box 24, "New York, NYC & boroughs" folder 2 (34/54); L. Fay Dix to Orson Welles, Nov. 6, 1938, box 24, "New York (state)" folder 2 (37/54); Edward J. Gelbruth to Orson Welles, Nov. 1, 1938, box 24, "No Location" folder; Isabel Elling to Orson Welles, Oct. 31, 1938, box 24, "Ohio" folder (39/54); E. E. Petit to Orson Wells [sic], Nov. 1, 1938, box 24, "South Carolina" folder (45/54), all Wilson-Welles Papers.

50. Allen (*Since Yesterday,* pp. 155–57) notes that the Depression decade saw a decline in religious observance. This made some listeners even more grateful for the results of Welles's broadcast. See Hardie C. Bass to Orson Welles, Nov. 2, 1938, box 23, "Mississippi" folder

(23/54); "An Observer" to Orson Welles, Oct. 30, 1938, box 24, "No Location" folder; Mrs. Caldwell to Orson Wells [sic], n.d., box 24, "North Carolina" folder (38/54); Mary E. Oliver to Orson Welles, Nov. 4, 1938, box 24, "Pennsylvania" folder 2 (43/54); Emma Howard to Orson Welles, Nov. 10, 1938, box 24, "Pennsylvania" folder 2 (43/54); Hugh E. Kennedy to Orson Wells [sic], Nov. 10, 1938, box 23, "Minnesota" folder (22/54); Ola Creeve to Orson Welles, n.d., box 24, "North Carolina" folder (38/54); Adelbert Bodman to Orson Welles, Oct. 31, 1938, box 24, "Ohio" folder (39/54); Russell N. Haas and Elmer Van Arsdall, Nov. 1, 1938, box 23, "Florida" folder (9/54); Frances Hardin to Orson Welles, Nov. 2, 1938, box 23, "Arkansas" folder (3/54); Neva Jones Maudlin to Orson Welles, Nov. 6, 1938, box 24, "Oklahoma" folder (40/54); Minnie J. Engle to Orson Wells [sic], Nov. 3, 1938, box 24, "Pennsylvania" folder 1 (42/54); Fay Etta Robinson to CBS, Oct. 30, 1938, box 23, "Illinois" folder (12/54), all Wilson-Welles Papers.
51. Judge B. V. Chapman to Orson Welles, Nov. 3, 1938, box 24, "South Carolina" folder (45/54), Wilson-Welles Papers. See also J. H. Keffer to Orson Welles, Oct. 31, 1938, box 24, "New Jersey" folder 1 (29/54); Frances S. Womack to Orson Welles, Oct. 31, 1938, box 24, "Virginia" folder (51/54); Wilmer Trexel to CBS, Oct. 31, 1938, box 24, "Pennsylvania" folder 1 (42/54); Marguerite de Francesco to Orson Wells [sic], Nov. 4, 1938, "Pennsylvania" folder 1 (42/54); Betty Down to Orson Welles, Nov. 3, 1938, box 24, "South Carolina" folder (45/54); Eleanor F. McKean to Orson Wells [sic], n.d., box 24, "No Location" folder, all Wilson-Welles Papers.
52. A. Rideout to Orson Welles, Nov. 11, 1938, box 24, "NYC & boroughs" folder 1 (33/54), Wilson-Welles Papers. See also George A. Sherron to Frank R. McNinch, Nov. 1, 1938; Chester S. Nagel to Frank McNinch, Nov. 1, 1938, both box 237, NARA; and Laura A. Barto to Orson Welles, Nov. 1, 1938, box 23, "Florida" folder (9/54); R. M. McLeod, Sr., to Orson Wells [sic], Nov. 2, 1938, box 23, "Florida" folder (9/54); H. M. Pierce to CBS, Nov. 1, 1938, box 23, "Michigan" folder (21/54), all Wilson-Welles Papers.
53. Quoted in Irving E. Fang, *Those Radio Commentators!* (Ames: Iowa State University Press, 1977), p. 132.
54. Ibid., pp. 132, 134–42.
55. Ibid., pp. 140–41.
56. Dorothy Thompson, "On the Record: Mr. Welles and Mass Delusion," *New York Herald Tribune*, Nov. 2, 1938, p. 21.
57. Ibid.
58. Arthur C. Gillette to Dorothy Thompson, Nov. 2, 1938, box 237, NARA.
59. Thompson, "Mr. Welles and Mass Delusion," p. 21.
60. Quoted in Fang, *Commentators!*, p. 146.
61. "Orson Welles Recalls the 'War of the Worlds' Broadcast," CD, track 5, in *War of the Worlds*, eds. Holmsten and Lubertozzi. Koch, *Panic Broadcast*, p. 24. Paul Heyer, *The Medium and the Magician: Orson Welles, the Radio Years, 1934–1952* (Lanham, Md.: Rowman & Littlefield, 2005), p. 228, n. 26.
62. After Thompson's column ran, some listeners noted in their letters how much they agreed with it. See Annie L. Black to Orson Welles, Nov. 2, 1938, box 23, "Connecticut" folder (6/54); Arthur J. Mann to Orson Welles, Nov. 2, 1938, box 23, "Connecticut" folder (6/54); Dorothy Mills to Orson Welles, Nov. 2, 1938, box 23, "Massachusetts" folder (20/54); J. Hammett to Orson Wells [sic], box 23, Nov. 2, 1938, "Massachusetts" folder (20/54); Edith Wipper to Orson Welles, Nov. 2, 1938, box 24, "New York, NYC & boroughs" folder 2 (34/54); Helen Misicka to Orson Wells [sic], Nov. 4, 1938, box 24, "New York, NYC & boroughs" folder 2 (34/54); Mr. & Mrs. Joe McClellan to Orson Welles, Nov. 5, 1938, box 24, "Washington" folder (52/54), all Wilson-Welles Papers.
63. Thompson, "Mr. Welles and Mass Delusion," p. 21.
64. Alexandre José de Seabra to Orson Welles, Oct. 31, 1938, box 24, "Pennsylvania" folder 2 (43/54), Wilson-Welles Papers. See also Dr. L. L. Stern to Orson Welles, Oct. 31, 1938,

box 24, "New Jersey" folder 2 (30/54); Robert Nibley, Loye Harmon, Ben Williams, and Rufus P. Spalding, Jr., to Orson Welles, Oct. 31, 1938, box 23, "California" folder (4/54); Mary Alice Gresham to Orson Welles, Oct. 31, 1938, box 24, "New Jersey" folder 3 (31/54); Paul W. Hetterstrom to Orson Welles, Oct. 30, 1938, box 23, "Kansas" folder (15/54); Flora duBeque Hart to Orson Welles, Oct. 31, 1938, box 23, "District of Columbia" folder (8/54); Spahr Hull to Orson Welles, Oct. 31, 1938, box 24, "Pennsylvania" folder 2 (43/54); Mrs. J. E. Darys to Orson Welles, Nov. 3, 1938, box 23, "California" folder (4/54), all Wilson-Welles Papers. For contemporary cartoons lampooning the panic, see Koch, *Panic Broadcast*, pp. 98–101; Gallop, *Martians*, pp. 98–99.

65. Dr. George Gallup, "Voters Call Czech Crisis No. 1 Story," *Washington Post*, Dec. 25, 1938, p. B1. "Czech Crisis Led News," *New York Times*, Dec. 29, 1938, p. 7.
66. "Orson Welles Recalls." Orson Welles, interviewed by Tom Snyder, *Tomorrow with Tom Snyder*, NBC, Sept. 1975, Paley Center for Media iCollection for Colleges, catalog ID T:35495.
67. Martha R. White to Orson Welles, Nov. 4, 1938, box 24, "Pennsylvania" folder 1 (42/54), Wilson-Welles Papers.
68. Peter Del Morris to Orson Welles, n.d., box 24, "New York, NYC & boroughs" folder 2 (34/54), Wilson-Welles Papers. See also Mrs. Ronald A. Druilhet to CBS, Oct. 31, 1938, box 23, "Louisiana" folder (17/54); Cornelia Dakine to Orson Welles, n.d., box 24, "No Location" folder, both Wilson-Welles Papers.
69. Quoted in Orson Welles and Peter Bogdanovich, *This Is Orson Welles*, ed. Jonathan Rosenbaum (New York: Da Capo Press, 1998), p. 18.
70. Gosling, *Waging the War*, p. 83.
71. See Simon Callow, *Orson Welles: The Road to Xanadu* (New York: Viking, 1995), pp. 408–11; John Houseman, *Run-Through: A Memoir* (New York: Simon & Schuster, 1972), p. 407.
72. Richard Watts, Jr., "The Theaters," *New York Herald Tribune*, Nov. 3, 1938, p. 16.
73. Houseman, *Run-Through*, pp. 407–408.
74. Ibid., p. 408. Higham, *Orson Welles*, pp. 130–31.
75. Houseman, *Run-Through*, p. 408.
76. Clinton Heylin, *Despite the System: Orson Welles Versus the Hollywood Studios* (Chicago: Chicago Review Press, 2005), p. 258. Callow, *Road to Xanadu*, p. 445.
77. Houseman, *Run-Through*, p. 409. Callow, *Road to Xanadu*, p. 445.
78. Houseman, *Run-Through*, pp. 412–13. Callow, *Road to Xanadu*, p. 417.
79. Interview with John Houseman, in *Theatre of the Imagination: The Mercury Company Remembers*, audio documentary written and produced by Frank Beacham, narrated by Leonard Maltin (Santa Monica: Voyager Company, 1988), in *Theatre of the Imagination: Radio Stories by Orson Welles and the Mercury Theatre* laserdisc, side 2, analog track 2, chap. 14. See also Leonard Maltin, *The Great American Broadcast: A Celebration of Radio's Golden Age* (New York: Dutton, 1997), p. 160.
80. Houseman, *Run-Through*, p. 413. Callow, *Road to Xanadu*, pp. 418–23, 461–63. Higham, *Orson Welles*, pp. 136–37. Frank Brady, *Citizen Welles: A Biography of Orson Welles* (New York: Scribner, 1989), pp. 221–26. Maltin, *Great American Broadcast*, pp. 160–61.
81. Howard Koch, *As Time Goes By: Memoirs of a Writer* (New York: Harcourt Brace Jovanovich, 1979), pp. 3, 9–11.
82. Houseman, *Run-Through*, pp. 432, 435–37. Callow, *Road to Xanadu*, pp. 449–53, 460–61. Higham, *Orson Welles*, pp. 134–37. Barbara Leaming, *Orson Welles: A Biography* (New York: Viking, 1985), pp. 167–69, 176–77. Brady, *Citizen Welles*, pp. 198–99. David Thomson, *Rosebud: The Story of Orson Welles* (New York: Vintage Books, 1996), pp. 112–13, 118–19, 129–30.
83. Houseman, *Run-Through*, pp. 432–37. Callow, *Road to Xanadu*, pp. 452–53, 457–81. Higham, *Orson Welles*, pp. 134–43. Leaming, *Orson Welles*, pp. 168–84. Brady, *Citizen Welles*, pp. 199–221, 226. Thomson, *Rosebud*, pp. 119–21, 125–34.

84. John J. Murray to Orson Welles, Nov. 1, 1938, box 24, "Ohio" folder (39/54), Wilson-Welles Papers.

85. Mrs. W. K. Baker to the Federal Communications Committee [*sic*], Oct. 31, 1938, box 238, NARA. See also "a disgusted listener" to the Mercury Theatre, Oct. 31, 1938, box 24, "Oregon" folder (41/54); Anonymous to Orson Welles, n.d., box 24, "No Location" folder, both Wilson-Welles Papers; and James W. Kilpatrick to the Federal Radio Commission [*sic*], Oct. 31, 1938; Florence Rohm to Frank R. McNinch, Oct. 31, 1938; Mary E. Ferguson to the FCC, Oct. 31, 1938; Paul B. Eaton to Frank P. [*sic*] McNinch, Oct. 31, 1938; L. R. Demond to the Federal Radio Commission [*sic*], Oct. 30, 1938; Arthur C. Gillette to Dorothy Thompson, Nov. 2, 1938; H. G. Phair to the FCC, Oct. 31, 1938; A. A. Martin to the Radio Commission [*sic*], Oct. 31, 1938; Kathryn A. Kraemer to the FCC, Oct. 30, 1938; Robert W. [last name unclear] to the Federal Radio Commission [*sic*], Oct. 31, 1938; F. C. Adams to the FCC, Oct. 31, 1938; "a thoroughly disgusted Lansing listener" to the Federal Communications Bureau [*sic*], Oct. 30, 1938; Henry Edward Warner to Frank McNinch, Oct. 31, 1938, all box 238, NARA. And see Brown, *Manipulating the Ether*, pp. 250–51.

86. See Brown, *Manipulating the Ether*, pp. 173–93, 250–51.

87. Bill Finger, art by Bob Kane and Jerry Robinson, *Batman* #1 (Spring 1940), in *Batman: The Dark Knight Archives*, vol. 1 (New York: DC Comics, 1992), p. 13. See also Gosling, *Waging the War*, pp. 169, 226.

88. Brown, *Manipulating the Ether*, pp. 190–91. Susan J. Douglas, *Listening In: Radio and the American Imagination* (Minneapolis: University of Minnesota Press, 2004), pp. 187–88. Joe Garner, *We Interrupt This Broadcast: The Events That Stopped Our Lives . . . from the Hindenburg Explosion to the Attacks of September 11* (Naperville, Ill.: Sourcebooks, 2002), pp. 8–9.

89. Brown, *Manipulating the Ether*, pp. 250–51. Listeners' doubts also appeared in two films about Pearl Harbor made during the 1940s, in which characters disbelieve the news because of *War of the Worlds* (see Welles and Bogdanovich, *This Is Orson Welles*, p. 20).

90. Welles and Bogdanovich, *This Is Orson Welles*, p. 20. Learning, *Orson Welles*, pp. 230–31. Orson Welles, interviewed by Dick Cavett, *The Dick Cavett Show*, ABC, Sept. 14, 1970, Paley Center iCollection for Colleges, catalog ID T84:0258. Gosling (*Waging the War*, p. 97) neatly disproves Welles's claim. Welles actually performed on a patriotic program, *We Hold These Truths*, aired in response to Pearl Harbor, shortly after the attacks. For deails on that show, see Neil Verma, *Theater of the Mind: Imagination, Aesthetics, and American Radio Drama* (Chicago: University of Chicago Press, 2012), pp. 77–81.

91. William Manchester, *The Death of a President: November 20–November 25, 1963* (New York: Harper & Row, 1967), p. 200.

92. "Well, Wells, Welles," *Broadcasting*, Nov. 15, 1938, p. 40.

93. "Radio Takes the Initiative," *Wall Street Journal*, Nov. 28, 1938, p. 4.

94. "'War' Broadcast Studied," *New York Times*, Dec. 20, 1938, p. 29. General Education Board Grant GE-GA-3821, Nov. 28, 1938, General Education Board Archives, ser. 1.2, box 361, folder 3723, Rockefeller Archive Center, Sleepy Hollow, N.Y.

9. "A Matter of Psychology"

1. Chapter title is from Lee E. Ellison to Orson Welles, Nov. 7, 1938, box 23, "District of Columbia" folder (8/54), Wilson-Welles Papers. Epigraph is from Emmet Riordan to Orson Wells [*sic*], Oct. 30, 1938, box 24, "Oregon" folder (41/54), Wilson-Welles Papers.

2. "Pseudo-Heavenly Body Shakes Burghers as Congregation Prepares for World's End," *Daily Princetonian*, Oct. 31, 1938, pp. 1, 3.

3. Kirk LeMoyne Billings to Kathleen Kennedy, quoted in Doris Kearns Goodwin, *The Fitzgeralds and the Kennedys: An American Saga* (New York: Simon & Schuster, 1987), p. 582.
4. Donald Mulford to Orson Welles, Oct. 31, 1938, box 24, "New Jersey" folder 3 (31/54), Wilson-Welles Papers. See also "FCC to Scan Script of 'War' Broadcast," *New York Times*, Nov. 1, 1938, p. 26.
5. "Welles' Broadcast Aids Psychologists," *Daily Princetonian*, Nov. 2, 1938, p. 1.
6. Jean M. Converse, *Survey Research in the United States: Roots and Emergence, 1890-1960* (Berkeley: University of California Press, 1987), p. 144.
7. Hadley Cantril to J. Douglas Brown, June 16, 1955, Hadley Cantril Personnel File (1937-1967), Faculty and Professional Staff Files, Princeton University Archives, Department of Rare Books and Special Collections, Princeton University Library.
8. Hadley Cantril Personnel File (1937-1967). Albert H. Cantril, "Cantril, Hadley," in *Public Opinion and Polling Around the World: A Historical Perspective*, ed. John G. Geer (Santa Barbara: ABC-CLIO, 2004), p. 387.
9. See W. H. Atwood and T. M. Longcope III, "National Assertions of Racial Superiority Debunked on Scientific Grounds by Cantril," *Daily Princetonian*, Jan. 13, 1939, p. 1; Recommendation for Promotion, Feb. 1, 1945, and Recommendation for Change in Salary, April 9, 1951, Hadley Cantril Personnel File (1937-1967).
10. "Welles' Broadcast Aids Psychologists," *Daily Princetonian*, Nov. 2, 1938, p. 1.
11. "'Martian Invasion' Treated by Cantril," *Daily Princetonian*, Nov. 3, 1938, pp. 1, 3.
12. Shearon A. Lowery and Melvin L. DeFleur, *Milestones in Mass Communication Research: Media Effects*, 3rd ed. (White Plains, N.Y.: Longman, 1995), pp. 12-14. Arthur Asa Berger, *Essentials of Mass Communication Theory* (Thousand Oaks, Calif.: SAGE Publications, 1995), pp. 111, 174. Melvin L. DeFleur, *Mass Communication Theories: Explaining Origins, Processes, and Effects* (New York: Allyn & Bacon, 2010), pp. 122-32.
13. Quoted in Gobind Behari Lal, "Today's Science: Martian Radio Alarm Called Mob Hysteria," *San Francisco Examiner*, Nov. 3, 1938, p. 13. See also Susan J. Douglas, *Listening In: Radio and the American Imagination* (Minneapolis: University of Minnesota Press, 2004), p. 165.
14. Lowery and DeFleur, *Milestones*, pp. 12-14. DeFleur, *Mass Communication*, pp. 137-38.
15. Quoted in Lal, "Today's Science," p. 13.
16. "The Aftermath of Mars: An Interview with Professor Hadley Cantril," *Princeton News*, Feb. 9, 1939, p. 5.
17. See Hadley Cantril, "The Unseeing Eye," *Daily Princetonian*, Jan. 28, 1938, p. 2; "Psychology Group Hits Discrimination," *Daily Princetonian*, Jan. 10, 1939, p. 1; Atwood and Longcope, "National Assertions," p. 1.
18. David Goodman, *Radio's Civic Ambition: American Broadcasting and Democracy in the 1930s* (Oxford: Oxford University Press, 2011), p. 248. Fred Turner, *The Democratic Surround: Multimedia & American Liberalism from World War II to the Psychedelic Sixties* (Chicago: University of Chicago Press, 2013), pp. 21-22.
19. Untitled article, *Princeton Alumni Weekly*, Nov. 12, 1937, Hadley Cantril Personnel File (1938-1951), Faculty and Professional Staff files, Princeton University Archives, Department of Rare Books and Special Collections, Princeton University Library.
20. "First Institute Letter Describes Propaganda," *Daily Princetonian*, Nov. 5, 1937, Hadley Cantril Personnel File (1938-1951). Untitled article, *Princeton Alumni Weekly*, Nov. 12, 1937. Goodman, *Radio's Civic Ambition*, pp. 248-52. Turner, *Democratic Surround*, pp. 21-22.
21. Goodman, *Radio's Civic Ambition*, p. 283.
22. Hadley Cantril, *The Human Dimension: Experiences in Policy Research* (New Brunswick, N.J.: Rutgers University Press, 1967), p. 22. Converse, *Survey Research*, pp. 146-48.

23. Hadley Cantril and Gordon Allport, *The Psychology of Radio* (New York: Harper & Brothers, 1935), pp. 3-4, 19-21. See also Douglas, *Listening In*, pp. 131-36.

24. Cantril and Allport, *Psychology of Radio*, pp. vii-viii, 270-72.

25. See Douglas, *Listening In*, pp. 124-25.

26. Frank Stanton, "Checking the Checkers," *Advertising & Selling*, Dec. 19, 1935, box 3A, "Correspondence: Stanton, Frank II" folder, Lazarsfeld Papers. Michael J. Socolow, "The Behaviorist in the Boardroom: The Research of Frank Stanton, Ph.D.," *Journal of Broadcasting and Electronic Media*, vol. 52, no. 4 (Dec. 2008), pp. 527, 530-36. Christopher H. Sterling, ed., *Biographical Encyclopedia of American Radio* (New York: Routledge, 2011), p. 361. Douglas, *Listening In*, pp. 125, 135-38. Neil Verma, *Theater of the Mind: Imagination, Aesthetics, and American Radio Drama* (Chicago: University of Chicago Press, 2012), pp. 119-20. Elena Razlogova, *The Listener's Voice: Early Radio and the American Public* (Philadelphia: University of Pennsylvania Press, 2011), pp. 82-83.

27. Frank Stanton to Paul Lazarsfeld, April 23, 1935; H. H. Maynard to Frank Stanton, April 23, 1936; Paul Lazarsfeld to Frank Stanton, April 29, 1936, all box 26, "Princeton Radio Research Project" folder 10, Lazarsfeld Papers. Frank Stanton, interviewed by Mary Marshall Clark, Oral History Research Office, Columbia University, pp. 102-105 (session #3, March 14, 1991), www.columbia.edu/cu/lweb/digital/collections/nny/stantonf/transcripts/stantonf_1_3_104.html (accessed April 21, 2014).

28. "The Essential Value of Radio to All Types of Listeners," April 9, 1937, Rockefeller Foundation records, projects, RG 1.1, ser. 200.R, box 271, folder 3234, *100 Years: The Rockefeller Foundation*, http://rockefeller100.org/items/show/3882 (accessed April 21, 2014). See also Razlogova, *The Listener's Voice*, pp. 101-102.

29. Frank N. Stanton, "The Outlook for Listener Research," p. 8, box 3A, "Correspondence: Stanton, Frank II" folder, Lazarsfeld Papers. See also pp. 1-2, 7-8, 10-13.

30. "School to Make Study on Effect of Wireless," *Daily Princetonian*, Oct. 20, 1937, p. 1.

31. Stanton, interviewed by Clark, p. 105. Socolow, "Behaviorist in the Boardroom," p. 536.

32. Cantril, *Human Dimension*, pp. 22-24. Converse, *Survey Research*, pp. 148-49.

33. Stanton, interviewed by Clark, pp. 105-108. Paul F. Lazarsfeld, "An Episode in the History of Social Research: A Memoir," in *The Intellectual Migration: Europe and America, 1930-1960*, eds. Donald Fleming and Bernard Bailyn (Cambridge, Mass.: Harvard University Press, 1969), pp. 304-305. Douglas, *Listening In*, p. 130. Converse, *Survey Research*, p. 149. Sterling, *Biographical Encyclopedia*, p. 229. Socolow, "Behaviorist in the Boardroom," p. 536. Bruce Lenthall, *Radio's America: The Great Depression and the Rise of Modern Mass Culture* (Chicago: University of Chicago Press, 2007), pp. 144, 146-48. David Jenemann, *Adorno in America* (Minneapolis: University of Minnesota Press, 2007), pp. 5, 8.

34. Lazarsfeld, "Episode in the History," pp. 272-76, 302-308, 311-12, 319-20. Converse, *Survey Research*, pp. 131-49. Lenthall, pp. 143-48. Sterling, *Biographical Encyclopedia*, pp. 229-30. Jefferson Pooley and Michael J. Socolow, "War of the Words: The *Invasion from Mars* and Its Legacy for Mass Communication Scholarship," in *War of the Worlds to Social Media: Mediated Communication in Times of Crisis*, ed. Joy Elizabeth Hayes, Kathleen Battles, and Wendy Hilton-Morrow (New York: Peter Lang, 2013), p. 38. Douglas, *Listening In*, pp. 125-30, 139.

35. Lazarsfeld, "Episode in the History," pp. 304-307.

36. Hadley Cantril to Paul Lazarsfeld, Aug. 9, 1937, box 26, "Princeton Radio Research Project" folder 10, Lazarsfeld Papers.

37. Stanton, interviewed by Clark, pp. 105-106.

38. Elisabeth M. Perse, "Herta Herzog (1910-)," in *Women in Communication: A Biographical Sourcebook*, ed. Nancy Signorielli (Westport, Conn.: Greenwood, 1996), p. 206.

39. Douglas, *Listening In*, pp. 137-39. Lazarsfeld, "Episode in the History," pp. 312-27. Converse, *Survey Research*, pp. 135-44. Jenemann, *Adorno*, pp. 8-11, 18-27. Socolow,

"Behaviorist in the Boardroom," p. 536. Verma, *Theater of the Mind*, p. 120. Peter Simonson and Lauren Archer, "Methods for Studying Mass Media: Lazarsfeld-Stanton Program Analyzer," *Out of the Question*, http://outofthequestion.org/Media-Research -of-the-1940s/Methods.aspx#LSPA (accessed April 23, 2014).

40. Stanton, interviewed by Clark, pp. 108–17.
41. Douglas, *Listening In*, p. 139.
42. Lazarsfeld, "Episode in the History," pp. 299, 310. Converse, *Survey Research*, pp. 150–51.
43. Lazarsfeld, "Episode in the History," pp. 310–11, 313–16. See also Converse, *Survey Research*, pp. 131–32; Jenemann, *Adorno*, pp. 9–11.
44. Converse, *Survey Research*, pp. 267–302. Jenemann, *Adorno*, pp. 9–11; quote on p. 10. Razlogova, *The Listener's Voice*, pp. 101–103.
45. Douglas, *Listening In*, p. 136. For critiques of the commercialism of Lazarsfeld's research, see also Jenemann, *Adorno*, pp. 9–10; Verma, *Theater of the Mind*, p. 121. Razlogova, *The Listener's Voice*, pp. 83, 101–105, 108–14.
46. Stanton, interviewed by Clark, pp. 115–16. Hadley Cantril, with Hazel Gaudet and Herta Herzog, *The Invasion from Mars: A Study in the Psychology of Panic* (New York: Harper & Row, 1966), p. 77. See also Michael J. Socolow, "The Hyped Panic Over 'War of the Worlds,'" *Chronicle of Higher Education*, vol. 55, no. 9 (Oct. 24, 2008), "The Chronicle Review," sect. B, p. 16. Socolow, "Behaviorist in the Boardroom," p. 526. Pooley and Socolow, "War of the Words," pp. 35–36.
47. Lazarsfeld, "Episode in the History," p. 313. Herta Herzog, "Why Did People Believe in the 'Invasion from Mars'?," in *The Language of Social Research: A Reader in the Methodology of Social Research*, eds. Paul F. Lazarsfeld and Morris Rosenberg (New York: Free Press, 1955), p. 420. Perse, "Herta Herzog," pp. 206–207.
48. Stanton, interviewed by Clark, pp. 115–16. See also Cantril, *Invasion*, pp. 77–78.
49. Herzog, "Why Did People Believe," p. 420.
50. Perse, "Herta Herzog," pp. 204–206. Peter Simonson and Lauren Archer, "Herta Herzog Massing," *Out of the Question*, http://outofthequestion.org/Women-in-Media-Research/Office-of-Radio-Research-Bureau-of-Applied-Social-Research.aspx#herzog (accessed April 23, 2014).
51. Copies of telegrams between Hadley Cantril and Paul Lazarsfeld, box 3A, "Correspondence: Stanton, Frank & Cantril, Hadley" folder, Lazarsfeld Papers. Hadley Cantril to Paul Lazarsfeld, Aug. 9, 1937, box 26, "Princeton Radio Research Project" folder 10, Lazarsfeld Papers.
52. Perse, "Herta Herzog," p. 206. Douglas, *Listening In*, pp. 139, 144–47.
53. Herzog, "Why Did People Believe," p. 420. For the location of the Radio Project's offices, see Lazarsfeld, "Episode in the History," p. 309.
54. Herzog, "Why Did People Believe," p. 420.
55. Converse, *Survey Research*, pp. 137–38.
56. Cantril, *Invasion*, p. 211 (for the questions used in later interviews, see pp. 211–20). Peter Simonson and Lauren Archer, "Methods for Studying Mass Media: In-Depth /Focused Interviewing," *Out of the Question*, http://outofthequestion.org/Media-Research-of-the-1940s/Methods.aspx (accessed April 24, 2014).
57. Douglas, *Survey Research*, p. 139.
58. See "Inter-Office Memorandum (Orson Welles Broadcast)," n.d., General Education Board Archives, ser. 1.2, box 361, folder 3723, Rockefeller Archive Center, Sleepy Hollow, N.Y. Lazarsfeld later published an edited version of this memo as Herzog, "Why Did People Believe," pp. 420–28.
59. "Inter-Office Memorandum," pp. 2–4, 13. Herzog, "Why Did People Believe," pp. 421–23.
60. "Inter-Office Memorandum," pp. 4–6. Herzog, "Why Did People Believe," pp. 423–24.

61. "Inter-Office Memorandum," pp. 7, 13.

62. Ibid., pp. 8, 13. See also Herzog, "Why Did People Believe," pp. 424-25.

63. Herzog, "Why Did People Believe," p. 427. The final published study quotes this interview at length, with the name changed to "Sylvia Holmes." See Cantril, *Invasion*, pp. 53-54.

64. "Inter-Office Memorandum," p. 10. Herzog, "Why Did People Believe," pp. 426-27.

65. "Inter-Office Memorandum," pp. 9-10. See also Herzog, "Why Did People Believe," pp. 425-27.

66. "Inter-Office Memorandum," p. 13.

67. Cantril, *Invasion*, pp. xiv-xv. Perse, "Herta Herzog," pp. 206-209. Peter Simonson and Lauren Archer, "Pioneering Women in Media Research," *Out of the Question*, http://outofthequestion.org/Women-in-Media-Research.aspx (accessed April 24, 2014). Peter Simonson and Lauren Archer, "The Bureau of Applied Social Research," *Out of the Question*, www.outofthequestion.org/Media-Research-of-the-1940s/BASR.aspx (accessed April 24, 2014). Pooley and Socolow, "War of the Words," pp. 36-37, 39, 50-53.

68. Hadley Cantril, "Proposed Study of 'Mass Hysteria,'" pp. 1-4, General Education Board Archives, ser. 1.2, box 361, folder 3723, Rockefeller Archive Center, Sleepy Hollow, N.Y.

69. Theodor W. Adorno, Else Frenkel-Brunswik, Daniel J. Levinson, and R. Nevitt Sanford, *The Authoritarian Personality*, Studies in Prejudice (New York: Harper & Row, 1950), p. 10. See also Turner, *Democratic Surround*, pp. 171-73.

70. General Education Board Grant GE-GA-3821, Nov. 28, 1938, General Education Board Archives, ser. 1.2, box 361, folder 3723, Rockefeller Archive Center, Sleepy Hollow, N.Y.

71. "Memorandum of Welles Study," n.d., pp. 1-2, box 26, "Princeton Radio Research Project" folder 6, Lazarsfeld Papers. "Outline for Welles Study," Nov. 30, 1938, p. 2, box 26, "Princeton Radio Research Project" folder 6, Lazarsfeld Papers. See also Cantril, "Proposed Study," p. 1.

72. Cantril, *Invasion*, pp. 55-58.

73. Ibid., pp. 55-58. Mildred Strunk and Hadley Cantril, eds., *Public Opinion: 1935-1946* (Princeton: Princeton University Press, 1951), p. 717. The number of people polled is recorded in Hadley Cantril, *The Invasion from Mars* (draft), chap. 2, p. 9, General Education Board Archives, ser. 1.2, box 361, folder 3724, Rockefeller Archive Center, Sleepy Hollow, N.Y.

74. Cantril, *Invasion*, p. 56.

75. Paul Heyer, *The Medium and the Magician: Orson Welles, the Radio Years, 1934-1952* (Lanham, Md: Rowman & Littlefield, 2005), pp. 100-101. Cantril (*Invasion*, p. 58) admits the same possibility. See also Socolow, "Hyped Panic," p. 17; Jefferson Pooley and Michael Socolow, "The Myth of the *War of the Worlds* Panic," *Slate*, Oct. 28, 2013, www.slate.com/articles/arts/history/2013/10/orson_welles_war_of_the_worlds _panic_myth_the_infamous_radio_broadcast_did.html (accessed Dec. 17, 2013).

76. Cantril, *Invasion*, p. 56.

77. One percent gave no answer (Strunk and Cantril, *Public Opinion*, p. 717). Cantril (*Invasion*, p. 58) states that 28 percent of respondents believed in the show, but the poll data in Strunk and Cantril (p. 717) give that figure as 26 percent. The latter is perhaps more reliable: when combined with the percentage of people who knew it was fiction (68 percent) and who gave no answer (6 percent), it adds up to 100 percent.

78. Cantril, *Invasion*, pp. 57-58. See also Strunk and Cantril, *Public Opinion*, p. 717.

79. See Cantril, *Invasion*, p. 107.

80. "Memorandum of Welles Study," pp. 2-4. "Outline for Welles Study," pp. 1-4.

81. Cantril, *Invasion*, p. 103. To understand why some people panicked and others did not, the researchers only sought people who tuned in late and, however briefly, believed the broadcast to be true. Even the nonfrightened listeners they talked to all initially

thought that the show was real (ibid., pp. 101–103). This meant that the study only focused on a small sliver of the audience, instead of accurately capturing how listeners as a whole responded to *War of the Worlds*.

82. "Outline for Welles Study," pp. 3–4. See also "Memorandum of Welles Study," p. 2.
83. Cantril, *Invasion*, p. xiv.
84. Cantril appears to have operated under the dubious assumption that frightened listeners behaved in essentially the same way no matter where they lived. The Rockefeller Foundation archives include a working draft of *The Invasion from Mars* that is very close to the published version; in all probability, it was the penultimate draft before publication. Under a heading for "Miscellaneous Information" (defined as "certain findings . . . that should be included here for the sake of the record"), Cantril included a very brief section on "Proximity to scene of invasion," noting that people who lived closer to Grover's Mill might be more likely to be frightened. His brief treatment of this idea, and its position in "Miscellaneous Information" (between a section on farmers' supposedly being more skeptical than other people and the predictions of social scientists on what they thought might have caused the panic) indicate that he gave little thought to it. (Cantril, *Invasion from Mars* [draft], chap. 6, pp. 22, 25–26.) In a memo commenting on that draft, Hazel Gaudet suggested that he reconsider. "Proximity to the scene of the invasion might well be a miscellaneous factor," she wrote, "but it would certainly fit into the section on factors contributing to the realism of the broadcast." (Hazel Gaudet, memo to Hadley Cantril ["Chapter VI—Orson Welles"], Jan. 26, 1940, box 26, "Princeton Radio Research Project" folder 6, Lazarsfeld Papers.) Cantril took some note of this advice. In the published version, he either cut or moved most of the "Miscellaneous Information" to an appendix, but he kept the proximity section in the main body of the text. He also expanded it slightly, including information from the CBS survey showing that people farther from New Jersey tended to be less frightened. But the geographical differences in fright remained only tangential to his work, producing another serious blind spot in the study. (Cantril, *Invasion*, pp. 147–48.)
85. Cantril, *Invasion*, pp. 77–78, 103. Although the CBS survey was more representative than Cantril's interviews, its interviewees were not selected scientifically, either. The investigators talked to a larger percentage of frightened people than would probably be found in a scientific sample (see ibid., p. 78).
86. Expense report, "Princeton University—RADIO RESEARCH—Study of Public Reactions to Orson Wells [sic] Broadcast," June 21, 1939, General Education Board Archives, ser. 1.2, box 361, folder 3723, Rockefeller Archive Center, Sleepy Hollow, N.Y.
87. "Memorandum of Welles Study," p. 4. Cantril racked up relatively hefty phone bills and traveling expenses in the first few months of 1939, perhaps staying in contact with the Newark office (expense report, "Princeton University—RADIO RESEARCH").
88. Perse, "Herta Herzog," p. 206.
89. Cantril, *Invasion*, p. xiii.
90. Hadley Cantril to John Hausman [sic], March 20, 1939; Augusta Weissberger to Hadley Cantril, March 22, 1939; Hadley Cantril to Augusta Weissberger, March 27, 1939; Augusta Weissberger to Hadley Cantril, April 5, 1939, all Correspondence box 1, "1939. Jan.–July" folder, Welles mss.
91. Hazel Gaudet, memo to Herta Herzog ("Orson Welles study"), Dec. 15, 1938, box 26, "Princeton Radio Research Project" folder 6, Lazarsfeld Papers. Hazel Gaudet, memo to Herta Herzog ("Orson Welles study"), Dec. 16, 1938, box 26, "Princeton Radio Research Project" folder 6, Lazarsfeld Papers.
92. Gaudet, memo to Herzog, Dec. 15, 1938, Lazarsfeld Papers.
93. Gaudet, memo to Herzog, Dec. 16, 1938, Lazarsfeld Papers.
94. Cantril, *Invasion*, p. xiii.
95. See ibid., pp. 154–64, 191–97, 202–203.

96. Ibid., pp. 131–33. For the questions asked, see pp. 218–19.

97. "*The Aftermath of Mars*: An Interview with Professor Hadley Cantril," *Princeton News*, Feb. 9, 1939, p. 5.

98. Cantril, *Invasion*, pp. 163, 203.

99. The year after the *War of the Worlds* study was published, Cantril explored how economic and other insecurities gave rise to the Nazi Party in his next book, *The Psychology of Social Movements*. In it, Cantril explores various mass movements with many of the same analytical tools that he applied to the broadcast, such as "critical ability" and "standards of judgment." The book references *War of the Worlds* more than once, and gives particular attention to the influence of economic insecurity on social movements (especially lynch mobs). This further suggests that Cantril treated the panic as evidence of potential susceptibility to fascism, because he treated both subjects in much the same way. See Hadley Cantril, *The Psychology of Social Movements* (New York: John Wiley, 1963 [orig. 1941]), pp. 10, 19–29, 64–77, 83–85, 221–32.

100. See Cantril, *Invasion*, pp. 202–205.

101. Cantril's myopic view of the panic is best demonstrated in the eighth chapter of the published study (*Invasion*, pp. 167–85), where he contrasts lengthy case studies of frightened and nonfrightened listeners to show what factors supposedly led to panic. In the first two of these case studies, he focuses almost exclusively on individual mental attitudes and ignores the fact that these people heard the broadcast under entirely different circumstances. In both cases, the frightened listeners were surrounded by other agitated people, and experienced things that seemed to corroborate the broadcast (like jammed telephone lines). The nonfrightened listeners, by contrast, tuned in late under more sedate circumstances and saw no evidence of panic. Although Cantril ascribes these listeners' behavior entirely to their own mental capacities, it seems very likely that their listening situations were just as important, if not more so. See ibid., pp. 168–79.

102. Lazarsfeld, "Episode in the History," pp. 310, 326–29. Converse, *Survey Research*, pp. 150–51. Pooley and Socolow, "War of the Words," pp. 41–47.

103. Quoted in David E. Morrison, *The Search for a Method: Focus Groups and the Development of Mass Communication Research* (Bedfordshire: University of Luton Press, 1998), pp. 73–74.

104. Stanton, interviewed by Clark, pp. 110–12.

105. See Hadley Cantril, "Proposed Study," pp. 3–4; Robert J. Havighurst, interview with Hadley Cantril and Paul Lazarsfeld, Nov. 22, 1938; D. C. Poole to Robert Havighurst, Nov. 22, 1938; General Education Board Grant GE-GA-3821; Robert J. Havighurst, interview with Violet Edwards, Dec. 1, 1938; John Marshall to Hadley Cantril, May 6, 1939; Hadley Cantril to Robert Havighurst, Jan. 6, 1939; Hadley Cantril to Robert Havighurst, July 17, 1939, all in General Education Board Archives, ser. 1.2, box 361, folder 3723, Rockefeller Archive Center, Sleepy Hollow, N.Y. See also Cantril's comments in "The Aftermath of Mars," p. 5.

106. Hadley Cantril to Paul Lazarsfeld, Nov. 25, 1939, box 26, "Princeton Radio Research Project" folder 6, Lazarsfeld Papers. See also Hadley Cantril to Robert Havighurst, July 17, 1939, General Education Board Archives, ser. 1.2, box 361, folder 3723, Rockefeller Archive Center, Sleepy Hollow, N.Y.

107. Douglas, *Listening In*, p. 143. See also Goodman, *Radio's Civic Ambition*, pp. 234–36.

108. Hazel Gaudet, memo to Hadley Cantril ("OW first draft"), Aug. 17, 1939, p. 4, box 26, "Princeton Radio Research Project" folder 6, Lazarsfeld Papers.

109. Cantril's working draft of the book includes a brief section claiming, "Farmers seem skeptical." He notes that according to the Gallup poll, "farmers were less likely to take the broadcast as news than people living in towns or than people in other occupational groups." For Cantril, this is more proof that neurotic people were likely to be

frightened and self-confident people were not. "The farmer . . . is likely to be more self-sufficient and independent," he wrote, "and thus have greater emotional security." Another explanation is that perhaps in rural areas with low population density, news of the invasion failed to spread the way it did in urban areas. In her comments on this draft, Gaudet called this section "AWFULLY miscellaneous," noting that it "stands out like a sore thumb to me," and Cantril cut it from the published version. (Cantril, *Invasion from Mars* [draft], chap. 6, p. 25. Hazel Gaudet, memo to Hadley Cantril ["Chapter VI—Orson Welles"], Jan. 26, 1940, box 26, "Princeton Radio Research Project" folder 6, Lazarsfeld Papers.)

110. Hazel Gaudet, memo to Hadley Cantril ("OW first draft"), Aug. 17, 1939, pp. 2, 4, box 26, "Princeton Radio Research Project" folder 6, Lazarsfeld Papers.

111. Ibid., pp. 3, 6.

112. Paul F. Lazarsfeld, memo to Hadley Cantril ("Analysis of Check-Ups in Orson Welles Study"), Oct. 12, 1939, box 26, "Princeton Radio Research Project" folder 6, Lazarsfeld Papers.

113. Hadley Cantril to Paul Lazarsfeld, Nov. 25, 1939, box 26, "Princeton Radio Research Project" folder 6, Lazarsfeld Papers. Hadley Cantril to Herbert Drake, Oct. 3, 1939, Correspondence box 1, "1939. Oct. 1–15" folder; Hadley Cantril to Alva Johnston, Oct. 19, 1939, Correspondence box 1, "1939. Oct. 16–31" folder, both Welles mss.

114. Hadley Cantril to Paul Lazarsfeld, n.d. ("Tuesday"), box 26, "Princeton Radio Research Project" folder 6, Lazarsfeld Papers.

115. Cantril, *Invasion*, pp. 111, 130.

116. See ibid., pp. 111–24, 127–39, 203–205.

117. Ibid., pp. 139–48; quote on p. 149.

118. Herbert J. Gans, *Popular Culture & High Culture: An Analysis and Evaluation of Taste*, rev. ed. (New York: Basic Books, 1999), p. 63.

119. Michael Denning, *The Cultural Front: The Laboring of American Culture in the Twentieth Century* (London: Verso, 2010), p. 555, n. 39.

120. Cantril, *Invasion*, p. 49; see also pp. 47–54.

121. Indeed, Cantril's imagined ideal listener—well educated, rational, self-confident—seems like a self-portrait. When discussing how education corresponds to "critical ability," his working draft includes a line cut from the published version that makes this even clearer. "A Harvard man would, on the whole, be expected to differ in his reactions from a graduate of a barber college," wrote Cantril—himself a Harvard man. (Cantril, *Invasion from Mars* [draft], chap. 5, p. 15. Cf. Cantril, *Invasion*, p. 122.)

122. Ralph Thompson, "Books of the Times," *New York Times*, April 15, 1940, p. 20.

123. "Book by Hadley Cantril Will Go on Sale Today," *Daily Princetonian*, April 10, 1940, p. 1.

124. Louella O. Parsons, "Robert Taylor Awarded Star Role Opposite Vivien Leigh," *San Francisco Examiner*, Jan. 15, 1940, p. 18.

125. Advertisement for *The Invasion from Mars*, in *Princeton Alumni Weekly*, April 12, 1940, p. 623, Hadley Cantril Personnel File (1938–1951).

126. Thompson, "Books of the Times," p. 20.

127. Cantril, *Invasion*, p. 47. At least four of these were drawn from the Mercury letters, with slight changes in wording and detail to disguise their source. For example, Cantril quotes "an unskilled laborer in Massachusetts" who spent $3.25 on a train ticket to escape the invaders. This listener had planned to use that money to buy "a pair of black shoes, size 9-B," and supposedly wrote to Cantril asking for reimbursement (ibid., p. 54). In fact, he lived in Virginia, and wrote to the Mercury asking for $3.37 "to buy an Arrow shirt and tie." Whether he was actually "an unskilled laborer," as Cantril suggests, is anyone's guess. But the story of his spending his savings on a train ticket and going seventy-five miles before realizing his mistake is true. The others undoubtedly are as well. See Lewis Hong to Orson Wells [sic], Oct. 30, 1938, box 24,

"Virginia" folder (51/54), Wilson-Welles Papers. See also Margery Sem to Orson Wells [sic], Oct. 30, 1938, box 24, "Washington" folder (52/54) (cf. Cantril, *Invasion*, p. 48); Johnas Kranley to Orson Welles, n.d., box 24, "No Location" folder (cf. Cantril, *Invasion*, pp. 49–50); "A Group of West Va Univ Students" to Orson Welles, Oct. 30, 1938, box 24, "West Virginia" folder (53/54) (cf. Cantril, *Invasion*, p. 53) all Wilson-Welles Papers; and Herzog, "Why Did People Believe," pp. 421, 427 (cf. Cantril, *Invasion*, pp. 53–54).

128. Cantril, *Invasion*, pp. 47–55. In Cantril's penultimate draft, he describes these as "typical reactions" to the broadcast, but this line was removed from the published version (Cantril, *Invasion from Mars* [draft], chap. 2, p. 1).

129. Hazel Gaudet, memo to Hadley Cantril ("OW first draft"), Aug. 17, 1939, p. 1, box 26, "Princeton Radio Research Project" folder 6, Lazarsfeld Papers.

130. Cantril's prose furthers this misconception. Although he is careful to note that *War of the Worlds* "did not affect more than a small minority of the listeners" (Cantril, *Invasion*, p. 67), he rarely misses an opportunity for artful hyperbole. His working draft of the book includes this line: "Long before the broadcast had ended, people scattered all over the United States were praying, crying, fleeing frantically to escape death from the Martians" (Cantril, *Invasion from Mars* [draft], chap. 2, p. 1). This is a slight exaggeration, perhaps, but it still gives the proper scale of the panic. In the published version, however, the word "scattered" has been deleted—implying that the panic was much more widespread than it really was (Cantril, *Invasion*, p. 47). The next chapter opens with an even more misleading statement, that *War of the Worlds* had "several million American families all over the country gathered around their radios listening to reports of an invasion from Mars" (p. 67). By Cantril's own math, "several million American families" may have *heard* the broadcast, but relatively few of them panicked or even believed.

131. Cantril, *Invasion from Mars* (draft), chap. 7, p. 14 (unnumbered). In the published version, Cantril only briefly mentions that more than a fourth of the frightened listeners believed the show to be about a foreign attack. See Cantril, *Invasion*, p. 159.

132. DeFleur, *Mass Communication*, pp. 141–42. Lowery and DeFleur, *Milestones*, pp. 66–67. Pooley and Socolow, "War of the Words," pp. 37, 52. Socolow, "Hyped Panic," pp. 16–17.

133. Cantril, *Invasion*, pp. 67–68, 115–21, 175, 178, 185.

134. Cantril, *Psychology of Social Movements*, pp. 19–29; quote on p. 29.

135. Paul F. Lazarsfeld, Bernard Berelson, and Hazel Gaudet, *The People's Choice: How the Voter Makes Up His Mind in a Presidential Campaign*, 3rd ed. (New York: Columbia University Press, 1968), pp. vi, xxv–xxvi, xxxv–xxxvi, 1, 40, 49–51, 60–61, 73–104, 120–58; quote on p. 158. See also Lowery and DeFleur, *Milestones*, pp. 83–91; Berger, *Essentials of Theory*, pp. 22, 67–68, 181; Socolow, "Hyped Panic," p. 17; DeFleur, *Mass Communication*, pp. 140–47, 172–82.

136. Jefferson Pooley, Michael Socolow, and others have cast doubt on Cantril's authorship of *The Invasion from Mars*, noting the key contributions made by Herzog and Gaudet and later statements from Lazarsfeld and Stanton that Cantril did little or none of the actual work. (Pooley and Socolow, "War of the Words," pp. 50–51. See also Socolow, "Hyped Panic," p. 17; Goodman, *Radio's Civic Ambition*, p. 283.) Although Cantril does get too much credit for the study itself, archival evidence strongly suggests that he wrote (and rewrote) the book on his own. On Jan. 26, 1940, Gaudet sent a memo to Cantril on chapter VI of his working draft of the book. This draft survives in the Rockefeller Foundation Archives, and, apart from a few emendations, it closely matches the published version. Gaudet's comments make clear that she considered the book to be Cantril's work. (Hazel Gaudet, memo to Hadley Cantril ["Chapter VI—Orson Welles"], Jan. 26, 1940, box 26, "Princeton Radio Research Project" folder 6, Lazarsfeld Papers. Cantril, *Invasion from Mars* [draft].)

137. See Lazarsfeld's comments in Herzog, "Why Did People Believe," p. 420; Lazarsfeld, "Episode in the History," p. 313. See also Pooley and Socolow, "War of the Words," pp. 50-51.
138. Quoted in Ann K. Pasanella, *The Mind Traveller: A Guide to Paul F. Lazarsfeld's Communication Research Papers in the Columbia University Library* (New York: Freedom Forum Media Studies Center, 1994), p. 30.
139. Lazarsfeld, "Episode in the History," p. 329.
140. Converse, *Survey Research*, pp. 149-50, 152. See also Pooley and Socolow, "War of the Words," pp. 50-51.
141. Cantril, *Human Dimension*, pp. 1-5, 16-20, 23-123, 129-43, 149-61. See also Converse, *Survey Research*, pp. 152-54.
142. Douglas, *Listening In*, pp. 10, 125, 131, 159-60. See also Converse, *Survey Research*, pp. 267-302.
143. Perse, "Herta Herzog," p. 207. Simonson and Archer, "Herta Herzog Massing," *Out of the Question*.
144. For modern use of the Program Analyzer, see Jenemann, *Adorno*, pp. 25-26.
145. Socolow, "Hyped Panic," pp. 16-17. See also Pooley and Socolow, "War of the Words," p. 52.
146. See Howard Koch, *The Panic Broadcast: Portrait of an Event* (Boston: Little, Brown, 1970), pp. 88-89, 96-97, 102-11; John Houseman, *Run-Through: A Memoir* (New York: Simon & Schuster, 1972), pp. 395-98.
147. "Orson Welles' Sketchbook episode 5," transcript, Wellesnet, www.wellesnet.com /sketchbook5.htm (accessed April 7, 2014).
148. Benjamin L. Alpers, *Dictators, Democracy, & American Public Culture: Envisioning the Totalitarian Enemy, 1920s-1950s* (Chapel Hill: University of North Carolina Press, 2003), p. 123.

10. "The Horror Man"

1. Margaret C. Brockmeyer to Orson Welles, Oct. 31, 1938, box 23, "Maryland" folder (19/54), Wilson-Welles Papers.
2. Orson Welles to Hadley Cantril, March 26, 1940, Correspondence box 1, "1940, Mar." folder, Welles mss. See Hadley Cantril, with Hazel Gaudet and Herta Herzog, *The Invasion from Mars: A Study in the Psychology of Panic* (Princeton: Princeton University Press, 1940), pp. v, xiv-xv, 3.
3. Orson Welles to Hadley Cantril, March 26, 1940, Correspondence box 1, "1940. Mar." folder, Welles mss.
4. Hadley Cantril to Orson Welles, April 6, 1940, Correspondence box 1, "1940. Apr." folder, Welles mss.
5. Orson Welles to Hadley Cantril, April 6, 1940, Correspondence box 1, "1940. Apr." folder, Welles mss.
6. Simon Callow, *Orson Welles: The Road to Xanadu* (New York: Viking, 1995), pp. 490-92.
7. John Houseman, *Run-Through: A Memoir* (New York: Simon & Schuster, 1972), pp. 436-37. Charles Higham, *Orson Welles: The Rise and Fall of an American Genius* (New York: St. Martin's, 1985), pp. 135-40, 142-49. Barbara Leaming, *Orson Welles: A Biography* (New York: Viking, 1985), pp. 168-85. Frank Brady, *Citizen Welles: A Biography of Orson Welles* (New York: Scribner, 1989), pp. 203-21, 226, 228-50. Callow, *Road to Xanadu*, pp. 457-92. David Thomson, *Rosebud: The Story of Orson Welles* (New York: Vintage Books, 1996), pp. 126-29, 134-40. Clinton Heylin, *Despite the System: Orson Welles Versus the Hollywood Studios* (Chicago: Chicago Review Press, 2005), pp. 14-37.
8. Houseman, *Run-Through*, pp. 437-44, 470-74. Leaming, *Orson Welles*, pp. 183-85, 212-13. See also Higham, *Orson Welles*, pp. 143-47, 165-74; Brady, *Citizen Welles*,

pp. 235, 294–96; Callow, *Road to Xanadu*, pp. 477–80, 487–89, 539–55; Thomson, *Rosebud*, pp. 134–35, 138–40, 189–90.

9. Houseman, *Run-Through*, pp. 441–42.

10. Callow, *Road to Xanadu*, pp. 490–92; quote on p. 490.

11. "Book by Hadley Cantril Will Go on Sale Today," *Daily Princetonian*, April 10, 1940, p. 1.

12. Hadley Cantril to Orson Welles, April 11, 1940, Correspondence box 1, "1940. Apr." folder, Welles mss.

13. Quoted in William A. C. Roethke, Appellee's Brief, *Orson Welles v. Columbia Broadcasting System, Inc., et al.*, U.S. Court of Appeals, 9th Circuit, Vol. 3264, No. 17518 (1962), p. 3. See also Howard Koch deposition, June 7, 1960, in Transcript of Record, *Orson Welles v. CBS*, pp. 171–72, 176–77; Orson Welles deposition, July 8, 1960, in ibid., pp. 77–79, 113–14.

14. Koch deposition, in Transcript of Record, *Orson Welles v. CBS*, p. 164. Howard Koch, *As Time Goes By: Memoirs of a Writer* (New York: Harcourt Brace Jovanovich, 1979), p. 8.

15. Welles deposition, in Transcript of Record, *Orson Welles v. CBS*, pp. 75–79, 106–108, 112–13. Hadley Cantril to Orson Welles, April 11, 1940, Correspondence box 1, "1940. Apr." folder, Welles mss.

16. See "Book by Hadley Cantril Will Go on Sale Today," *Daily Princetonian*, April 10, 1940, p. 1; Ralph Thompson, "Books of the Times," *New York Times*, April 15, 1940, p. 20; "The Public and the Martian Invasion," *New York Times*, April 28, 1940, p. 83.

17. Advertisement for *The Invasion from Mars* in *Princeton Alumni Weekly*, April 12, 1940, p. 623, Hadley Cantril Personnel File (1938–1951), Faculty and Professional Staff Files, Princeton University Archives, Department of Rare Books and Special Collections, Princeton University Library.

18. Welles deposition, in Transcript of Record, *Orson Welles v. CBS*, p. 79.

19. Quoted in Leaming, *Orson Welles*, p. 186; Callow, *Road to Xanadu*, p. 451. See also Brady, *Citizen Welles*, pp. 201, 251; Callow, *Road to Xanadu*, p. 464; Jonathan Rosenbaum, "Welles' Career: A Chronology," in Orson Welles and Peter Bogdanovich, *This Is Orson Welles*, ed. Jonathan Rosenbaum (New York: Da Capo Press, 1998), p. 357.

20. Evans Plummer, "Hollywood," *Movie Radio Guide*, Nov. 23, 1940, p. 39.

21. Callow, *Road to Xanadu*, pp. 520–21. John Gosling, *Waging the War of the Worlds: A History of the 1938 Radio Broadcast and Resulting Panic* (Jefferson, N.C.: McFarland, 2009), p. 95. Alan Gallop, *The Martians Are Coming!: The True Story of Orson Welles' 1938 Panic Broadcast* (Gloucestershire: Amberley Publishing, 2011), pp. 129–34. Rosenbaum, "Welles' Career," p. 361.

22. All quotes from interview cited in video found in David Haglund, "Orson Welles Talks to H. G. Wells, 1940," *Slate*, Oct. 31, 2011, www.slate.com/blogs/browbeat/2011/10/31/orson_welles_and_h_g_wells_the_radio_interview_1940.html (accessed May 20, 2014).

23. Leaming, *Orson Welles*, p. 288.

24. Unsigned to Hadley Cantril, Oct. 21, 1939, Correspondence box 1, "1939. Oct. 16–31" folder, Welles mss.

25. Rick Altman, "Deep-Focus Sound: *Citizen Kane* and the Radio Aesthetic," in *Perspectives on Citizen Kane*, ed. Ronald Gottesman (New York: G. K. Hall, 1996), pp. 94–114. Tom Nolan, "Rosebud and the Radio," *Wall Street Journal*, Sept. 13, 2011, http://online.wsj.com/news/articles/SB10001424053111904140604576498493526329666 (accessed April 6, 2014). See also Higham, *Orson Welles*, pp. 116, 160; Callow, *Road to Xanadu*, pp. 524–27, 565; Thomson, *Rosebud*, pp. 164–65.

26. Brady, *Citizen Welles*, pp. 250, 271. Callow, *Road to Xanadu*, pp. 523–24. Raymond Fielding, *The March of Time, 1935-1941* (New York: Oxford University Press, 1978), pp. 258–60. Welles and Peter Bogdanovich, *This Is Orson Welles*, pp. 74–76. Welles

initially used the fake newsreel idea in his script for *The Smiler with a Knife* and brought it over to *Kane* after that project fell apart—further evidence of his continued interest in fake news. (See Brady, *Citizen Welles*, p. 235; Welles and Bogdanovich, *This Is Orson Welles*, p. 74; Heylin, *Despite the System*, p. 48.)

27. See Callow, *Road to Xanadu*, pp. 561-65, 570-71; Thomson, *Rosebud*, pp. 165, 170, 182-87.

28. Leaming, *Orson Welles*, pp. 230, 283, 388-89.

29. *Citizen Kane* souvenir program (New York: RKO, 1941), p. 2; reproduced in *Citizen Kane: 70th Anniversary* Blu-Ray set (Burbank, Calif.: Warner Home Video, 2011). See also Callow, *Road to Xanadu*, pp. 572-74.

30. Quoted in Leaming, *Orson Welles*, p. 217. See also Thomson, *Rosebud*, p. 192.

31. Higham, *Orson Welles*, pp. 178-79. Leaming, *Orson Welles*, pp. 216-17. Brady, *Citizen Welles*, pp. 310-11. Callow, *Road to Xanadu*, p. 575. Thomson, *Rosebud*, p. 192. Welles and Bogdanovich, *This Is Orson Welles*, pp. 86-88.

32. Quoted in Higham, *Orson Welles*, p. 179.

33. Higham, *Orson Welles*, pp. 178-79. Leaming, *Orson Welles*, pp. 216-17. Brady, *Citizen Welles*, pp. 309-11. Callow, *Road to Xanadu*, pp. 562-65, 575. Thomson, *Rosebud*, pp. 192-93.

34. Brady, *Citizen Welles*, pp. 310-11.

35. Higham, *Orson Welles*, p. 11. Brady, *Citizen Welles*, pp. 349-50. Simon Callow, *Orson Welles: Hello Americans* (New York: Viking, 2006), pp. 18, 138-39.

36. Higham, *Orson Welles*, p. 196. Leaming, *Orson Welles*, pp. 239-40. Brady, *Citizen Welles*, pp. 324-25. Thomson, *Rosebud*, pp. 214-15. Callow, *Hello Americans*, pp. 86-87. Welles and Bogdanovich, *This Is Orson Welles*, p. 116.

37. Quoted in Welles and Bogdanovich, *This Is Orson Welles*, p. 121.

38. Quoted in Brady, *Citizen Welles*, p. 325; Welles and Bogdanovich, *This Is Orson Welles*, p. 118.

39. Quoted in Welles and Bogdanovich, *This Is Orson Welles*, p. 117. See also Callow, *Hello Americans*, pp. 87-88; Heylin, *Despite the System*, p. 118.

40. Heylin, *Despite the System*, pp. 117-19. Callow, *Hello Americans*, pp. 86-89, 111-12.

41. Higham, *Orson Welles*, pp. 10-11, 196-97, 203-204. Leaming, *Orson Welles*, pp. 240-42. Brady, *Citizen Welles*, pp. 325-27, 349-50. Thomson, *Rosebud*, pp. 216-17. Welles and Bogdanovich, *This Is Orson Welles*, pp. 119-26. Heylin, *Despite the System*, pp. 119-24. Callow, *Hello Americans*, pp. 90-91, 107-12, 123-25, 138-39.

42. Quoted in Brady, *Citizen Welles*, p. 325; Callow, *Hello Americans*, p. 89; Welles and Bogdanovich, *This Is Orson Welles*, p. 119.

43. Alva Johnston and Fred Smith, "How to Raise a Child: The Disturbing Life—to Date—of Orson Welles," *Saturday Evening Post*, Feb. 3, 1940, p. 38.

44. "The Hitchhiker," *Suspense*, CBS, Sept. 2, 1942, in *The Best of Suspense*, CD (Radio Spirits).

45. Callow, *Hello Americans*, p. 235; see also pp. 170, 212, 252, 323-24. And see "Those Men from Mars," *Newsweek*, Nov. 27, 1944, p. 89.

46. Higham, *Orson Welles*, pp. 179-81, 190-203. Leaming, *Orson Welles*, pp. 231-33, 235-39, 246-51. Brady, *Citizen Welles*, pp. 332-46. Thomson, *Rosebud*, pp. 197-98, 208-13, 218-22. Welles and Bogdanovich, *This Is Orson Welles*, pp. 149-50. Heylin, *Despite the System*, pp. 126-41. Callow, *Hello Americans*, pp. 44-46, 53-77, 91-103, 112-15, 120-21. Catherine L. Benamou, *It's All True: Orson Welles's Pan-American Odyssey* (Berkeley: University of California Press, 2007), pp. 27-58, 141, 237-38, 244-50, 328 n. 58.

47. Benamou, *It's All True*, pp. 130-33, 276-81. See also Leaming, *Orson Welles*, pp. 252-57, 261-62, 300, 328. Brady, *Citizen Welles*, pp. 346-49. Thomson, *Rosebud*, pp. 223-24, 236-38. Heylin, *Despite the System*, pp. 141-44, 153-62. Callow, *Hello Americans*, pp. 122-38, 140-50.

48. Leaming, *Orson Welles*, pp. 309, 493–94. Welles and Bogdanovich, *This Is Orson Welles*, pp. 148–51. Callow, *Road to Xanadu*, pp. 576–77.

49. Callow, *Road to Xanadu*, p. 575. Altman, "Deep-Focus Sound," p. 114.

50. Welles received a thousand-dollar advance for *Invasion from Mars: Interplanetary Stories*. After the book earned out its advance, he received a royalty payment of $93.08. See R. S. Callender to Richard Wilson, Oct. 13, 1949, box 1, "*Invasion from Mars: Interplanetary Stories*: selected by Orson Welles, correspondence, 1949" folder, Wilson-Welles Papers; Jonathan Rosenbaum, "Welles' Career," p. 403.

51. Orson Welles, ed., *Invasion from Mars: Interplanetary Stories* (New York: Dell, 1949), pp. 5–6. Anthony Boucher, "Expedition," in *Invasion from Mars: Interplanetary Stories*, ed. Welles, p. 67.

52. "Black Magic on Mars," *Superman* 62 (Jan.–Feb. 1950), in *Superman: From the Thirties to the Seventies* (New York: Bonanza Books, 1971), pp. 210–21. See also Brady, *Citizen Welles*, p. 423. Gosling, *Waging the War*, pp. 170, 226. Gallop, *Martians*, pp. 136–39.

53. Quoted in Heylin, *Despite the System*, p. 269. See also Leaming, *Orson Welles*, p. 396; Brady, *Citizen Welles*, p. 481; Rosenbaum, "Welles' Career," pp. 417–18; Gosling, *Waging the War*, p. 83; Ben Walters, "Orson's TV Revolution That Never Was," *Guardian*, Dec. 17, 2009, www.theguardian.com/film/filmblog/2009/dec/17/orson-welles-television (accessed April 6, 2014).

54. "Orson Welles' Sketchbook episode 5," transcript, Wellesnet, www.wellesnet.com/sketchbook5.htm (accessed April 7, 2014). See also Robert J. Brown, *Manipulating the Ether: The Power of Broadcast Radio in Thirties America* (Jefferson, N.C.: McFarland, 1998), p. 227; Brian Holmsten and Alex Lubertozzi, eds., *The War of the Worlds: Mars' Invasion of Earth, Inciting Panic and Inspiring Terror from H. G. Wells to Orson Welles and Beyond* (Naperville, Ill.: Sourcebooks, 2001), p. 22; Gosling, *Waging the War*, p. 83; Gallop, *Martians*, p. 135.

55. "Orson Welles' Sketchbook episode 5," transcript, Wellesnet. See also Brown, *Manipulating the Ether*, p. 227; Holmsten and Lubertozzi, eds., *War of the Worlds*, p. 22; Gosling, *Waging the War*, p. 83; Gallop, *Martians*, p. 135.

56. See Higham, *Orson Welles*, pp. 284–86; Leaming, *Orson Welles*, pp. 393–94; Brady, *Citizen Welles*, pp. 471–74; Thomson, *Rosebud*, pp. 323–24; Welles and Bogdanovich, *This Is Orson Welles*, p. 237; Rosenbaum, "Welles' Career," pp. 416–17; Heylin, *Despite the System*, pp. 269–77.

57. See Orson Welles, interviewed by Tom Snyder, *Tomorrow with Tom Snyder*, NBC, Sept. 1975, Paley Center for Media iCollection for Colleges, catalog ID T:35495; "Orson Welles Recalls the 'War of the Worlds' Broadcast," CD, track 5, in *War of the Worlds*, eds. Holmsten and Lubertozzi; Gosling, *Waging the War*, pp. 83–84; Todd Tarbox, *Orson Welles and Roger Hill: A Friendship in Three Acts* (Albany, Ga.: BearManor Media, 2013), p. 124. Simon Callow (*Hello Americans*, p. 232) casts some doubt on the idea that Welles and Barrymore really knew each other as well as this anecdote implies.

58. See Callow, *Road to Xanadu*, p. 407.

59. See Welles and Bogdanovich, *This Is Orson Welles*, pp. 18–20; Brown, *Manipulating the Ether*, pp. 226–27; Orson Welles, interviewed by Tom Snyder, *Tomorrow with Tom Snyder*, NBC, Sept. 1975.

60. See Brady, *Citizen Welles*, p. 175; Orson Welles, interviewed by Tom Snyder, *Tomorrow with Tom Snyder*, NBC, Sept. 1975.

61. Welles deposition, in Transcript of Record, *Welles v. CBS*, pp. 80–81, 121. Koch deposition, in ibid., p. 155. Val Adams, "N.B.C. Will Carry Sugar Bowl Game," *New York Times*, Sept. 11, 1957, p. 67.

62. *Orson Welles v. Columbia Broadcasting System, Inc., et al.*, Appellees, 308 F.2d 810 (U.S. Court of Appeals, 9th Circuit), Oct. 3, 1962. See also Thomson, *Rosebud*, p. 108; Gosling, *Waging the War*, pp. 98, 171–72.

63. Koch, *As Time Goes By*, p. 8. In a recorded interview with Peter Bogdanovich, Welles complained about "pirated" recordings of the *War of the Worlds* broadcast, from which he had received no royalties (Orson Welles, interviewed by Peter Bogdanovich, in *This Is Orson Welles* [New York: Harper Audio, 1992], tape 4, side 7).

64. Koch, *As Time Goes By*, pp. 42–43, 71–84, 163–70, 178–81.

65. Leaming, *Orson Welles*, p. 387. John Houseman, *Unfinished Business: A Memoir* (London: Chatto & Windus, 1986), pp. 322–26.

66. Houseman, *Run-Through*, p. 402.

67. Thomson, *Rosebud*, p. 107. See also Joseph McBride, *What Ever Happened to Orson Welles?: A Portrait of an Independent Career* (Lexington: University Press of Kentucky, 2006), p. 31.

68. *F for Fake* (1975), DVD, directed by Orson Welles (New York: Criterion Collection, 2005). Orson Welles, interviewed by Leslie Megahey, in *The Orson Welles Story*, BBC, 1982, in *Orson Welles: Interviews*, ed. Mark W. Estrin (Jackson: University Press of Mississippi, 2002), p. 181.

69. The Mercury Theatre preserved a clippings file on later radio hoaxes that drew comparisons to *War of the Worlds*. See box 24, "War of the Worlds. Clippings. 1938–1950" folder, Wilson-Welles Papers.

70. "Those Men from Mars," *Newsweek*, Nov. 27, 1944, p. 89. Gosling, *Waging the War*, pp. 99–101.

71. "'Martian Invasion' Terrorizes Chile," *New York Times*, Nov. 14, 1944, p. 1. "Those Men from Mars," p. 89. Joseph Bulgatz, *Ponzi Schemes, Invaders from Mars & More Extraordinary Popular Delusions and the Madness of Crowds* (New York: Harmony Books, 1992), p. 137. Gosling, *Waging the War*, pp. 102–3. Robert E. Bartholomew and Benjamin Radford, *The Martians Have Landed!: A History of Media-Driven Panics and Hoaxes* (Jefferson, N.C.: McFarland, 2012), pp. 23–24.

72. Gosling, *Waging the War*, p. 102.

73. "'Martian Invasion' Terrorizes Chile," p. 1. "Those Men from Mars," p. 89. Gosling, *Waging the War*, p. 101.

74. Bulgatz, *Ponzi Schemes*, p. 137. Bartholomew and Radford, *Martians*, p. 23.

75. Bulgatz, *Ponzi Schemes*, p. 137. Bartholomew and Radford, *Martians*, pp. 23–24.

76. "Those Men from Mars," Nov. 27, 1944, p. 89. Gosling, *Waging the War*, p. 102.

77. José Villamarín Carrascal, "La noche que los marcianos invadieron Cotocallao," *La Hora*, Feb. 2003, www.dlh.lahora.com.ec/paginas/temas/caleidoscopio28.htm (accessed via Internet Archive Wayback Machine capture of Aug. 21, 2003).

78. "'Martian Invasion' Terrorizes Chile," p. 1. "Those Men from Mars," p. 89. Bulgatz, *Ponzi Schemes*, p. 137. Gosling, *Waging the War*, pp. 102–3.

79. "15 Killed When Ecuador Radio Emulates Orson Welles' Stunt," Philadelphia *Bulletin*, Feb. 14, 1949, box 24, "War of the Worlds. Clippings. 1938–1950" folder, Wilson-Welles Papers. "Ecuador City Is Enraged by 'Mars Invasion,'" *New Orleans Item*, Feb. 14, 1949, box 24, "War of the Worlds. Clippings. 1938–1950" folder, Wilson-Welles Papers. "War of the Worlds," *Radiolab*, NPR (New York: WNYC, March 7, 2008), www.radio lab.org/story/91622-war-of-the-worlds/ (accessed April 12, 2014). Bartholomew and Radford, *Martians*, p. 24.

80. "War of the Worlds," *Radiolab*, NPR.

81. Gosling, *Waging the War*, pp. 103–104, 108–109. Jim Wyss, "In Ecuador, After the Green Men from Mars Invaded, the Real Tragedy Began," *Miami Herald*, Feb. 21, 2014, www .miamiherald.com/2014/02/21/3952039/in-ecuador-after-the-green-men.html (accessed April 10, 2014). Carrascal, "La noche que los marcianos invadieron Cotocallao." Holmsten and Lubertozzi, eds., *War of the Worlds*, p. 84.

82. "'Mars Raiders' Cause Quito Panic; Mob Burns Radio Plant, Kills 15," *New York Times*, Feb. 14, 1949, p. 7. Carrascal, "La noche que los marcianos invadieron Cotocallao."

Gosling, *Waging the War*, pp. 104–105. Wyss, "In Ecuador, After the Green Men from Mars Invaded."

83. "'Mars Raiders' Cause Quito Panic," p. 7.
84. Carrascal, "La noche que los marcianos invadieron Cotocallao." Gosling, *Waging the War*, p. 104.
85. Bulgatz, *Ponzi Schemes*, p. 139. Holmsten and Lubertozzi, eds., *War of the Worlds*, p. 84.
86. Gosling, *Waging the War*, p. 108. Bulgatz, *Ponzi Schemes*, p. 138. Carrascal, "La noche que los marcianos invadieron Cotocallao."
87. Cecilia Alvear, "Martians Land in Quito," *Huffington Post*, Feb. 13, 2009, www.huffingtonpost.com/cecilia-alvear/martians-land-in-quito_b_166776.html (accessed April 9, 2014). Gosling, *Waging the War*, p. 110.
88. Bulgatz, *Ponzi Schemes*, p. 138.
89. Wyss, "In Ecuador, After the Green Men from Mars Invaded."
90. "'Mars Raiders' Cause Quito Panic," p. 7. "Wolf, Wolf," *Newsweek*, Feb. 21, 1949, p. 44.
91. "Six Killed in Counter-Attack on 'Invaders from Mars,'" *Pittsburgh Press*, Feb. 14, 1949, box 24, "War of the Worlds. Clippings. 1938–1950" folder, Wilson-Welles Papers. "Quito Riot: Broadcast Causes 21 Deaths," *Broadcasting*, Feb. 21, 1949, p. 49.
92. Like the 1938 broadcast, the Ecuadorean *War of the Worlds* gave rise to a fair amount of stories—such as priests giving absolution en masse, and panicked adulterers confessing in front of their wives—that are probably urban legends. Newspaper accounts of the day describe many half-dressed people, wearing only their nightclothes, rushing into the streets in a panic because of the broadcast. ("'Mars Raiders' Cause Quito Panic," p. 1. "Wolf, Wolf," p. 44.) Like the reports of people fleeing their New Jersey homes with washcloths over their faces, this probably did happen, but on a much smaller scale than the press implied. Elsewhere in Quito, things remained quiet despite the show. Sixty years later, one Ecuadorean journalist who had heard part of the broadcast as a child recalled turning it off in boredom and going to sleep soon after. Her whole household, she wrote, slept peacefully through the night, entirely unaware of what was happening elsewhere in the city. (Cecilia Alvear, "Martians Land in Quito.") For the probable urban legends, see Carrascal, "La noche que los marcianos invadieron Cotocallao"; "War of the Worlds," *Radiolab*, NPR; Gosling, *Waging the War*, p. 113.
93. "'Mars Raiders' Cause Quito Panic," p. 7. "Quito Riot: Broadcast Causes 21 Deaths," p. 49. Bulgatz, *Ponzi Schemes*, p. 138. Holmsten and Lubertozzi, eds., *War of the Worlds*, p. 85. Carrascal, "La noche que los marcianos invadieron Cotocallao." "War of the Worlds," *Radiolab*, NPR. Gosling, *Waging the War*, p. 106. Bartholomew and Radford, *Martians*, p. 24.
94. "Six Killed in Counter-Attack."
95. "'Mars Raiders' Cause Quito Panic," pp. 1, 7. Bartholomew and Radford, *Martians*, p. 24.
96. "'Mars Raiders' Cause Quito Panic," pp. 1, 7. "Six Killed in Counter-Attack."
97. Bulgatz, *Ponzi Schemes*, p. 138.
98. Gosling, *Waging the War*, p. 106.
99. "'Mars Raiders' Cause Quito Panic," pp. 1, 7. "Six Killed in Counter-Attack."
100. Carrascal, "La noche que los marcianos invadieron Cotocallao."
101. "'Mars Raiders' Cause Quito Panic," pp. 1, 7.
102. "Six Killed in Counter-Attack."
103. Carrascal, "La noche que los marcianos invadieron Cotocallao." Some reports said that Páez, trapped on the third floor, wrapped himself in newsprint and leapt into the street. He landed, according to the United Press, on a crush of people and managed to escape, badly hurt but alive. But this account later turned out to be inaccurate. See "Six Killed in Counter-Attack."

104. Gosling, *Waging the War*, p. 107.
105. Carrascal, "La noche que los marcianos invadieron Cotocallao." "War of the Worlds," *Radiolab*, NPR.
106. Holmsten and Lubertozzi, eds., *War of the Worlds*, p. 86.
107. Wyss, "In Ecuador, After the Green Men from Mars Invaded."
108. "War of the Worlds," *Radiolab*, NPR.
109. "'Mars Raiders' Cause Quito Panic," p. 7.
110. Ibid. "Six Killed in Counter-Attack."
111. Carrascal, "La noche que los marcianos invadieron Cotocallao." "'Mars Raiders' Cause Quito Panic," p. 7.
112. "20 Dead in the Quito Riot," *New York Times*, Feb. 15, 1949, p. 5. "Wolf, Wolf," p. 44.
113. "'Mars Raiders' Cause Quito Panic," pp. 1, 7. "Quito Riot: Broadcast Causes 21 Deaths," p. 49.
114. "'Mars Raiders' Cause Quito Panic," p. 1. Bartholomew and Radford, *Martians*, p. 25.
115. "'Mars Raiders' Cause Quito Panic," p. 1. "20 Dead in Quito Riot," p. 5. "Quito Riot: Broadcast Causes 21 Deaths," p. 49.
116. Bulgatz, *Ponzi Schemes*, pp. 138–39. Carrascal, "La noche que los marcianos invadieron Cotocallao."
117. Gosling, *Waging the War*, p. 104. Wyss, "In Ecuador, After the Green Men from Mars Invaded."
118. Gosling, *Waging the War*, pp. 111–12. See also Carrascal, "La noche que los marcianos invadieron Cotocallao"; Wyss, "In Ecuador, After the Green Men from Mars Invaded."
119. Untitled clipping, *Washington Post*, Feb. 17, 1949, box 24, "War of the Worlds. Clippings. 1938–1950" folder, Wilson-Welles Papers.
120. Editorial, *Broadcasting*, Feb. 21, 1949, p. 46.
121. Gosling, *Waging the War*, p. 112.
122. Holmsten and Lubertozzi, eds., *War of the Worlds*, pp. 87–88. Bob Kosinski, "WKBW and the 'War of the Worlds,'" *Buffalo History Works*, www.buffalohistoryworks.com/broadcasters/hist_kbwow.asp (accessed April 11, 2014). Gosling, *Waging the War*, pp. 131–42.
123. "Thirty Years Later," *Broadcasting*, Nov. 4, 1968, p. 10. Holmsten and Lubertozzi, eds., *War of the Worlds*, p. 87. Kosinski, "WKBW and the 'War of the Worlds.'" Gosling, *Waging the War*, p. 137.
124. Holmsten and Lubertozzi, eds., *War of the Worlds*, p. 87. Kosinski, "WKBW and the 'War of the Worlds.'" Gosling, *Waging the War*, p. 137.
125. "Thirty Years Later," p. 10. Other sources (such as Holmsten and Lubertozzi, eds., *War of the Worlds*, p. 88) give a larger number of calls and claim that the "Canadian National Guard" was called up to fight the Martians, but Gosling (*Waging the War*, p. 138) nicely debunks these exaggerations.
126. Kosinski, "WKBW and the 'War of the Worlds.'" Holmsten and Lubertozzi, eds., *War of the Worlds*, p. 88. Gosling, *Waging the War*, p. 142.
127. Justin Levine, "A History and Analysis of the Federal Communications Commission's Response to Radio Broadcast Hoaxes," *Federal Communications Law Journal*, vol. 52, no. 2 (March 2000), pp. 286–89. See also Gosling, *Waging the War*, pp. 149–53. In their defense, WPRO argued that their *War of the Worlds* had caused only minor confusion. They noted, for example, that no crowd had formed where the Martians were supposed to have landed. The FCC dismissed that argument with the wry observation "that the last place those people misled by the broadcast would want to gather is at the Martian landing site" (quoted in Levine, "History," p. 288, n. 71). But, of course, that is exactly what happened in 1938: confused listeners went looking for the fallen meteor.

128. Other Martian broadcasts aired in Brazil in 1971 and Portugal in 1955, 1988, and 1998. Each followed the Welles format, and each caused some frightened phone calls and a few minor disturbances. (Gosling, *Waging the War*, pp. 120–29, 143–48, 156–63.)

129. Hadley Cantril, in preface, Hadley Cantril with Hazel Gaudet and Herta Herzog, *The Invasion from Mars: A Study in the Psychology of Panic* (New York: Harper & Row, 1966), p. vii. See also Stephen King, *Danse Macabre* (New York: Berkeley Books, 1981), pp. 119–21; Susan J. Douglas, *Listening In: Radio and the American Imagination* (Minneapolis: University of Minnesota Press, 2004), pp. 19–20; Gosling, *Waging the War*, pp. 130, 138; Zack Stiegler and Brandon Szuminsky, "Mediating Misinformation: Hoaxes and the Digital Turn," in *War of the Worlds to Social Media: Mediated Communication in Times of Crisis*, ed. Joy Elizabeth Hayes, Kathleen Battles, and Wendy Hilton-Morrow (New York: Peter Lang, 2013), p. 172.

130. Orrin E. Dunlap, Jr., "Message from Mars: Radio Learns that Melodrama Dressed Up as a Current Event Is Dangerous," *New York Times*, Nov. 6, 1938, p. 184.

131. According to *The New York Times*, *Special Bulletin* was one of that evening's top-rated programs in many media markets. But NBC affiliates in the country's biggest cities—New York, Chicago, Los Angeles, Washington, and Cleveland—received only around twenty-two hundred calls about the show in total. These calls were mostly critical, but not necessarily from people who were frightened. Of the 731 viewers who called WNBC-TV in New York, only forty-three wanted to know if *Special Bulletin* was real. In Chicago, 121 out of 710 callers had the same concern. (Sally Bedell, "NBC Nuclear-Terror Show Criticized," *New York Times*, March 22, 1983, p. C15. See also Bartholomew and Radford, *Martians*, pp. 37–39.)

132. Bartholomew and Radford, *Martians*, p. 38.

133. Brown, *Manipulating the Ether*, p. 253. Gosling, *Waging the War*, pp. 177, 228–29. Bartholomew and Radford, *Martians*, p. 40.

134. Bartholomew and Radford, *Martians*, p. 41.

135. Bill Carter, "Were Asteroids Falling? Few Viewers Cared," *New York Times*, Nov. 1, 1994, p. C18.

136. Bartholomew and Radford, *Martians*, p. 41.

137. *F for Fake*, DVD. The film also includes a parody of the "News on the March" sequence from *Citizen Kane*, which was itself a parody of the *March of Time* newsreel series, continuing Welles's fascination with fake news. See Joseph McBride, *Orson Welles*, rev. ed. (New York: Da Capo Press, 1996), pp. 181–84.

138. Houseman, *Unfinished Business*, pp. 340–42. Leaming, *Orson Welles*, pp. 401–402.

139. Thomson, *Rosebud*, p. 400. Max Allan Collins, *The War of the Worlds Murder* (New York: Berkeley Prime Crime, 2005), p. 240.

140. Peter Bogdanovich, "My Orson," introduction to Welles and Bogdanovich, *This Is Orson Welles*, pp. xxii–xxiii.

141. Houseman, *Unfinished Business*, pp. 459–61, 466–68, 470–82.

142. Peter Biskind, ed., *My Lunches with Orson: Conversations Between Henry Jaglom and Orson Welles* (New York: Metropolitan Books, 2013), p. 275.

143. Biskind, ed., *My Lunches*, pp. 227–28. Tarbox, *Welles and Hill*, pp. 157–58. Robert Leiter, "A New Look at the 'Cradle' That Rocked Broadway," *New York Times*, May 1, 1983, www.nytimes.com/1983/05/01/theater/a-new-look-at-the-cradle-that-rocked-broadway.html (accessed April 5, 2014).

144. Higham, *Orson Welles*, pp. 329–30.

145. Biskind, ed., *My Lunches*, pp. 272, 275. See also Tarbox, *Welles and Hill*, p. 162.

146. Leaming, *Orson Welles*, pp. 512–14. Brady, *Citizen Welles*, pp. 582–83. Jonathan Rosenbaum, afterword, *The Cradle Will Rock: An Original Screenplay* by Orson Welles (Santa Barbara: Santa Teresa Press, 1994), pp. 113–14. Biskind, ed., *My Lunches*, pp. 220–29, 248; quote on p. 221. Tarbox, *Welles and Hill*, p. 157.

147. Leaming, *Orson Welles*, pp. 512–14. Brady, *Citizen Welles*, pp. 582–83. Biskind, ed., *My Lunches*, p. 221. Tarbox, *Welles and Hill*, pp. 157, 161–62, 193.

148. Rosenbaum, afterword, *Cradle Will Rock*, p. 118.

149. Welles, *Cradle Will Rock*, pp. 32, 110.

150. Welles, interviewed by Megahey, *Orson Welles Story*, p. 209.

151. Tarbox, *Welles and Hill*, p. 217.

152. Brady, *Citizen Welles*, p. 583. Rosenbaum, afterword, *Cradle Will Rock*, p. 117. Tarbox, *Welles and Hill*, pp. 191–93, 199–200, 203.

153. Tarbox, *Welles and Hill*, p. 200.

154. Rosenbaum, afterword, *Cradle Will Rock*, p. 117. Tarbox, *Welles and Hill*, pp. 215–16.

155. Tarbox, *Welles and Hill*, p. 216.

156. Brady, *Citizen Welles*, pp. 582–91. Rosenbaum, afterword, *Cradle Will Rock*, pp. 117–18. Tarbox, *Welles and Hill*, pp. 215–17, 265, 292.

157. Brady, *Citizen Welles*, p. 591. Thomson, *Rosebud*, pp. 3–5, 421.

158. John T. Caldwell, *Televisuality: Style, Crisis, and Authority in American Television* (New Brunswick, N.J.: Rutgers University Press, 1995), pp. 4–13.

159. John Houseman, interviewed by Leonard Maltin, April 22, 1988, p. 18, box 14, "Theatre of the Imagination (1988). Interviews [transcripts]. 1988" folder, Wilson-Welles Papers.

160. See *Orson Welles on the Air: The Radio Years* (New York: Museum of Broadcasting, 1988).

161. Edward Oxford, "Night of the Martians," *American History Illustrated*, vol. 23, no. 6 (Oct. 1988), p. 48. Jo Astrid Glading, "Welles' Martians Get a Warmer Welcome in Grovers [sic] Mill This Time," *Item*, Oct. 30, 1988, p. 5D. Holmsten and Lubertozzi, eds., *War of the Worlds*, pp. 29–30.

162. Marilyn Berger, "John Houseman, Actor and Producer, 86, Dies," *New York Times*, Nov. 1, 1988, www.nytimes.com/learning/general/onthisday/bday/0922.html (accessed March 10, 2014).

Conclusion

1. Esther Langman to Orson Welles, Oct. 31, 1938, box 23, "Minnesota" folder (22/54), Wilson-Welles Papers.

2. Barnouw, *Tower in Babel*, pp. 97–99, 189–231.

3. There is a large and growing body of scholarship assessing the influence that listeners exerted on what went over the airwaves in the interwar period. For a particularly in-depth analysis of the content and impact of listener letters in the network era, see Elena Razlogova, *The Listener's Voice: Early Radio and the American Public* (Philadelphia: University of Pennsylvania Press, 2011), especially pp. 2–4, 8–9, 55–74, 81–97.

4. Charlene Simmons, "Dear Radio Broadcaster: Fan Mail as a Form of Perceived Interactivity," *Journal of Broadcasting & Electronic Media*, vol. 53, no. 3 (2009), pp. 444–56. David Goodman, *Radio's Civic Ambition: American Broadcasting and Democracy in the 1930s* (Oxford: Oxford University Press, 2011), pp. 97–99. Bruce Lenthall, *Radio's America: The Great Depression and the Rise of Modern Mass Culture* (Chicago: University of Chicago Press, 2007), pp. 74–75. Razlogova, *The Listener's Voice*, pp. 2–4, 8–9, 81–97.

5. Neil Verma, *Theater of the Mind: Imagination, Aesthetics, and American Radio Drama* (Chicago: University of Chicago Press, 2012), p. 118. Razlogova, *The Listener's Voice*, pp. 97, 108–114, 122–23.

6. Verma, *Theater of the Mind*, pp. 81–83.

7. See Barnouw, *Golden Web*, pp. 88–89; Goodman, *Radio's Civic Ambition*, pp. 3–64.

8. Joy Elizabeth Hayes and Kathleen Battles, "Exchange and Interconnection in U.S. Network Radio: A Reinterpretation of the 1938 *War of the Worlds* Broadcast," in *War of the Worlds to Social Media*, ed. Joy Elizabeth Hayes, Kathleen Battles, and Wendy Hilton-Morrow (New York: Peter Lang, 2013), pp. 21–23, 28–31.

9. Zack Stiegler and Brandon Szuminsky, "Mediating Misinformation: Hoaxes and the Digital Turn," in *War of the Worlds to Social Media*, eds. Joy Hayes, Battles, and Hilton-Morrow, pp. 174–81.

10. See Edward D. Miller, *Emergency Broadcasting and 1930s American Radio* (Philadelphia: Temple University Press, 2003), pp. 186–87.

11. Stiegler and Szuminsky, "Mediating Misinformation," pp. 174, 177.

12. Julian Miglierini, "Mexico 'Twitter Terrorism' Charges Cause Uproar," BBC News, Sept. 6, 2011, www.bbc.com/news/world-latin-america-14800200 (accessed May 19, 2014). Jo Adetunji, " 'Twitter Terrorists' Face 30 Years After Being Charged in Mexico," *Guardian*, Sept. 4, 2011, www.theguardian.com/world/2011/sep/04/twitter-terrorists -face-30-years (accessed May 19, 2014).

13. " 'Twitter Terrorists' Face 30 Years." "Mexico 'Twitter Terrorism' Charges Dropped," BBC News, Sept. 21, 2011, www.bbc.com/news/world-latin-america-15010202 (accessed May 19, 2014).

14. In September 2011, the same month in which English-language news media reported the Mexican "Twitter panic," there were two other minor Twitter scares in North America alone. Both drew comparisons to Welles's *War of the Worlds*. The first occurred in Canada, as a real NASA satellite fell to Earth. The aspiring filmmaker Sebastian Salazar tweeted lines from the broadcast's script, falsely claiming that the defunct satellite had landed in Alberta. According to *The Vancouver Sun*, reporters in the United States, England, and Japan believed the tweets to be real and called the Royal Canadian Mounted Police about the supposed crash. (Bryce Forbes, "Aspiring Filmmaker Behind Alberta Falling-Satellite Hoax," *Vancouver Sun*, Sept. 26, 2011, www.vancouversun.com/news /Aspiring+filmmaker+behind+Alberta+falling+satellite+hoax/5461351/story.html [accessed Sept. 26, 2011].) The second incident occurred less than a week later, when the satirical newspaper *The Onion* tweeted that several congressmen were holding a group of schoolchildren hostage at the U.S. Capitol. They used the names of real government officials, in order to satirize the gridlock in Congress. But some Twitter users took the tweets seriously, causing a minor uproar. Those who fell for the stunt received a fair amount of derision for believing in *The Onion*; one blogger even compared them to "Orson Welles' radio audience in 1938." But, in the post-9/11 world, they should perhaps be forgiven for taking seriously a tweet that reads "BREAKING: Witnesses reporting screams and gunfire heard inside Capitol building," regardless of its source. (Alexandra Petri, "The Onion Attacks Congress! Or Something," *Washington Post*, Sept. 29, 2011, www.washingtonpost.com/blogs/compost/post/the-onion-attacks -congress-or-something/2011/09/29/gIQAy0Yj7K_blog.html [accessed Sept. 30, 2011]. Megan Friedman, "Is The Onion Going Too Far with Its #CongressHostage Twitter Satire?," *Time*, Sept. 29, 2011, http://newsfeed.time.com/2011/09/29/is-the-onion -going-too-far-with-its-congresshostage-twitter-satire/ [accessed Sept. 29, 2012].)

15. Emmet Rensin, "The Great Satirical-News Scam of 2014," *New Republic*, June 5, 2014, www.newrepublic.com/article/118013/satire-news-websites-are-cashing-gullible -outraged-readers (accessed August 14, 2014).

16. Paul Vigna, "Stocks Plunge, Quickly Recover, on Fake Tweet," *Wall Street Journal*, April 23, 2014, http://blogs.wsj.com/moneybeat/2013/04/23/stocks-plunge-quickly -recover-on-fake-tweet/ (accessed May 21, 2014). Gary Strauss, Adam Shell, Roger Yu, and Byron Acohido, "SEC, FBI Probe Fake Tweet That Rocked Stocks," *USA Today*, April 24, 2013, www.usatoday.com/story/news/nation/2013/04/23/hack-attack-on -associated-press-shows-vulnerable-media/2106985/ (accessed May 21, 2014). Paul Vigna, "From 'War of the Worlds' to the Hack Crash," *Wall Street Journal*, April 24, 2013, http://blogs.wsj.com/moneybeat/2013/04/24/from-war-of-the-worlds-to-the-hack -crash/ (accessed May 21, 2014).

17. Vigna, "From 'War of the Worlds.' "

18. Elizabeth M. Imre to Frank R. McNinch, n.d., box 237, NARA.
19. Federal Communications Commission, "In the Matter of Editorializing by Broadcast Licensees" (13 FCC 1257-1258, 1949), http://transition.fcc.gov/Bureaus/Mass_Media /Databases/documents_collection/490608.pdf (accessed Aug. 13, 2014).
20. Ibid., 13 FCC 1255 (1949).
21. Robert D. Hershey, Jr., "F.C.C. Votes Down Fairness Doctrine in a 4–0 Decision," The New York Times, Aug. 5, 1987, www.nytimes.com/1987/08/05/arts/fcc-votes-down-fair ness-doctrine-in-a-4-0-decision.html (accessed Aug. 13, 2014).
22. Geoffrey Baym, From Cronkite to Colbert: The Evolution of Broadcast News (Boulder, Colo.: Paradigm Publishers, 2010), pp. 2–24, 79–99, 145–76.
23. Quoted in Joseph McBride, What Ever Happened to Orson Welles?: A Portrait of an Independent Career (Lexington: University Press of Kentucky, 2006), p. 247.
24. Baym, From Cronkite to Colbert, pp. 101–76. "Daily Show Viewers Knowledgeable About Presidential Campaign, National Annenberg Election Survey Shows," Annenberg Public Policy Center press release, Philadelphia, Pa., Sept. 21, 2004, www.annenbergpublic policycenter.org/Downloads/Political_Communication/naes/2004_03_late-night -knowledge-2_9-21_pr.pdf (accessed Aug. 13, 2014). Pew Research Center, "Public Knowledge of Current Affairs Little Changed by News and Information Revolutions," summary of findings, April 15, 2007, www.people-press.org/2007/04/15/public-knowledge -of-current-affairs-little-changed-by-news-and-information-revolutions/ (accessed Aug. 15, 2014). Bruce W. Hardy, Jeffrey A. Gottfried, Kenneth M. Winneg, and Kathleen Hall Jamieson, "Stephen Colbert's Civics Lesson: How Colbert Super PAC Taught Viewers About Campaign Finance," Mass Communication and Society, vol. 17, no. 3 (2014), pp. 329–53, http://dx.doi.org/10.1080/15205436.2014.891138 (accessed Aug. 13, 2014).
25. Jon Stewart, "Rally to Restore Sanity Announcement," The Daily Show With Jon Stewart, Comedy Central, Sept. 16, 2010, 11:10, http://thedailyshow.cc.com/video-playlists /pj77i8/daily-show-15117/mkk1sq (accessed Aug. 13, 2014).
26. "Stewart: 'We Live in Hard Times, Not End Times,'" CBS News, Oct. 30, 2010, 4:17, www .youtube.com/watch?v=FNKUPvzAkFY (accessed May 16, 2014).
27. Brian Montopoli, "Jon Stewart Rally Attracts Estimated 215,000," CBS News, Oct. 30, 2010, www.cbsnews.com/8301-503544_162-20021284-503544.html (accessed Aug. 8, 2011).
28. Kelvin Robinson, "'Dueling Rallies' Spike Hotel Bookings," NBC Washington, Oct. 25, 2010, www.nbcwashington.com/the-scene/events/Dueling-Rallies-Spike-Hotel -Bookings-103892163.html (accessed Oct. 17, 2011). Brian Stelter, "Transit Frustrations at Rally to Restore Sanity and/or Fear," New York Times, Oct. 30, 2011, http://the caucus.blogs.nytimes.com/2010/10/30/transit-frustrations-at-rally-to-restore -sanity-andor-fear/ (accessed Oct. 17, 2011). "News Release: Metro Sets New Record for Highest Saturday Metrorail Ridership," Washington Metropolitan Area Transit Authority, Oct. 31, 2010, www.wmata.com/about_metro/news/PressReleaseDetail .cfm?ReleaseID=4717 (accessed Oct. 17, 2011).
29. Jerome Socolovsky, "Tens of Thousands Rally for Laughs, Activism in Washington," Voice of America, Oct. 30, 2010, www.voanews.com/english/news/Political-Rally-in-US -Capital-Draws-Thousands-106371909.html (accessed Aug. 8, 2011).
30. Mike Isaac, "The Tech Behind the Rally to Restore Sanity: How Social Media Sparked a Parodic Revolution," Forbes, Oct. 29, 2010, www.forbes.com/sites/mikeisaac/2010/10 /29/the-tech-behind-the-rally-to-restore-sanity-how-social-media-sparked -a-parodic-revolution/ (accessed May 16, 2014).
31. Quoted in Katla McGlynn, "The Funniest Signs from the Rally to Restore Sanity and/or Fear! (PHOTOS)," Huffington Post, May 25, 2011, www.huffingtonpost.com/2010 /10/30/the-funniest-signs-at-the_n_776490.html#s169297&title=Really (accessed May 17, 2014).

A Note on Sources

1. Letters counted only once: Warner Ogden to the Federal Radio Communications Commission [sic], Oct. 30, 1938, and Warner Ogden to the Secretary of the Interior, Oct. 30, 1938, both box 238 (anti-Welles); Mrs. W. D. Nesbitt to the FCC, Nov. 1, 1938, and Mrs. W. D. Nesbitt to Frank McNinch, Nov. 1, 1938, both box 237 (pro-Welles); E. M. Moody to Frank R. McNinch, Oct. 31, 1938, and E. M. Moody to CBS, Oct. 31, 1938, both box 238 (anti-Welles); Owen A. McNiff to the FCC, Oct. 30, 1938, and Owen A. McNiff to Franklin D. Roosevelt, Oct. 30, 1938, both box 238 (anti-Welles); Arthur M. and Clara Lassner to the Federal Radio Communications Bureau [sic], Oct. 30, 1938, and Arthur M. and Clara Lassner to Franklin D. Roosevelt, Oct. 30, 1938, both box 238 (anti-Welles); and two multi-page petitions from various cities in Minnesota (mostly Minneapolis), n.d., box 237 (pro-Welles), all NARA. Like the collection as a whole, two-thirds of these letters criticize Welles, and one-third support him.

2. David A. Crespy, *Richard Barr: The Playwright's Producer* (Carbondale: Southern Illinois University Press, 2013), p. 17. Richard Barr, interviewed by Frank Beacham, pp. 4, 19, box 14, "*Theatre of the Imagination* (1988). Interviews [transcripts]. 1988" folder, Wilson-Welles Papers.

3. The letters preserved among the Wilson-Welles Papers at the University of Michigan are organized alphabetically by location. Currently, there are sheets of paper keeping the letters separate, but the imprint of the preceding letter is frequently visible on the one below it, suggesting that the letters have been kept in this order for some time.

4. See Hadley Cantril to John Hausman [sic], March 20, 1939; Augusta Weissberger to Hadley Cantril, March 22, 1939; Hadley Cantril to Augusta Weissberger, March 27, 1939; Augusta Weissberger to Hadley Cantril, April 5, 1939; all Correspondence box 1, "1939. Jan.–July" folder, Welles mss.

5. Michael Ogden, "RE: Were the Mercury Players Aware of the Panic?," posting to oldradio .net, Oct. 23, 2009, http://jeff560.tripod.com/wotw.html (accessed Feb. 19, 2013).

6. Joseph McBride, *What Ever Happened to Orson Welles?: A Portrait of an Independent Career* (Lexington: University Press of Kentucky, 2006), p. 231, note.

7. A. G. Kennedy to Orson Wells [sic], Nov. 1, 1938; Sol Eisenberg to Orson Welles, Nov. 28, 1938, both box 1, "Mercury Theatre on the Air. 'War of the Worlds' (10/30/38). Fan mail. 1938" folder, Welles-Kodar Collection. Another copy of the Kennedy letter is in Correspondence box 1, "1938. May–Dec" folder, Welles mss. Kennedy also sent a copy of this same letter to Frank McNinch and the FCC (A. G. Kennedy to Frank P. [sic] McNinch, Nov. 5, 1938, box 238, NARA). Therefore, Kennedy has the distinction of being the only person with letters preserved at each of the institutions holding mail from *War of the Worlds*. Welles's name is spelled "Wells" in the original letter, as preserved among the Welles-Kodar Collection, and the copy sent to McNinch, but is spelled correctly in all other copies. This suggests that someone at the Mercury made the copies.

8. FCC copies: J. E. Gallagher to Frank R. McNinch, Oct. 31, 1938; Frank S. Levy to Frank McNinch, Oct. 31, 1938; Lydel Sims to Frank P. [sic] McNinch, Oct. 31, 1938; Leon Ackinson to Frank R. McNinch, Nov. 1, 1938; H. G. Blaising to Frank R. McNinch, Nov. 1, 1938; Harry Wright, Jr., to Frank R. McNinch, Nov. 1, 1938, Correspondence box 1, "1938. May–Dec" folder, Welles mss. An exact copy of the De Brueys letter (a telegram) can be found in box 24, "Texas" folder (48/54), Wilson-Welles Papers. As with the duplicate NARA letters, I have only counted this telegram once. Additionally, one man sent a telegram to Welles informing him that he had written a letter about the broadcast to the FCC (Joseph K. Howard to Orson Welles, Oct. 31, 1938, Correspondence box 1, "1938. May–Dec" folder, Welles mss.) Winchell copies: Mort Hall to Walter Winchell, Nov. 1, 1938; Anonymous to Walter Winchell, Nov. 1, 1938, both Correspondence box 1, "1938. May–Dec" folder, Welles mss.

9. When the writer's gender could be determined, 49 percent of the FCC letters had at least one male author, and 30 percent had at least one female author. For the Mercury letters, 40 percent had at least one male author, and 43 percent had at least one female author. In each collection, letters with multiple authors of both genders were counted twice. Anonymous letters, or those that only gave the writer's initials, were not counted unless they gave specific evidence of the writer's gender, such as a reference to "my husband" or "my wife."

10. Jeannette Sayre, "Progress in Radio Fan-Mail Analysis," *Public Opinion Quarterly*, vol. 3, no. 2 (1939), p. 276.

11. Hadley Cantril and Gordon Allport, *The Psychology of Radio* (New York: Harper & Brothers, 1935), p. 95.

12. In his analysis of the FCC letters, David Goodman argues that the pro-Welles letters came largely from people of "elite status," and the anti-Welles letters typically came from "less elite" listeners. This may be broadly true, but it seems dangerous to generalize, because there are many counterexamples in both collections. At the very least, it further suggests that the *War of the Worlds* letters represent the opinions of a broad swath of Americans. (David Goodman, *Radio's Civic Ambition: American Broadcasting and Democracy in the 1930s* [Oxford: Oxford University Press, 2011], pp. 272, 275.)

13. Hadley Cantril, with Hazel Gaudet and Herta Herzog, *The Invasion from Mars: A Study in the Psychology of Panic* (Princeton: Princeton University Press, 1940), pp. 57, 59.

14. The Mercury received 171 letters from New Jersey, 304 from New York (203 of which came from just New York City), and 113 from Pennsylvania. The federal government received 64 letters from New Jersey, 108 from New York (62 of which came from just New York City), and 51 from Pennsylvania.

15. Cantril, *Invasion*, p. 58.

16. Ibid., pp. 60–61.

17. In a press release sent out in Dec. 1938, the FCC stated that it had "received 372 protests against the broadcast and 255 letters and petitions favoring it," or a total of 627 letters (quoted in Justin Levine, "A History and Analysis of the Federal Communications Commission's Response to Radio Broadcast Hoaxes," *Federal Communications Law Journal*, vol. 52, no. 2 [March 2000], p. 286). David Goodman (*Radio's Civic Ambition*, p. 268) cites an internal FCC memo (which I have not been able to locate at the National Archives) that puts the total number of letters received by the FCC at 625.

18. In a letter to John Houseman, Cantril wrote that he had already copied some of Welles's letters and returned the rest to the Mercury Theatre by late March 1939 (Hadley Cantril to John Hausman [sic], March 20, 1939, Correspondence box 1, "1939. Jan.–July" folder, Welles mss.). Several of the case studies presented in *The Invasion from Mars* are slightly modified quotes from letters in the University of Michigan's Wilson-Welles Papers. See Lewis Hong to Orson Wells [sic], Oct. 30, 1938, box 24, "Virginia" folder (51/54) (cf. Cantril, *Invasion*, p. 54); Margery Sem to Orson Wells [sic], Oct. 30, 1938, box 24, "Washington" folder (52/54) (cf. Cantril, *Invasion*, p. 48); Johnas Kranley to Orson Welles, n.d., box 24, "No Location" folder (cf. Cantril, *Invasion*, pp. 49–50); "A Group of West Va Univ Students" to Orson Welles, Oct. 30, 1938, box 24, "West Virginia" folder (53/54) (cf. Cantril, *Invasion*, p. 53), all Wilson-Welles Papers.

19. Cantril, *Invasion*, p. 61.

Acknowledgments

I first heard about the *War of the Worlds* letters less than a week after attending the Rally to Restore Sanity. At the time, I was in my junior year at the University of Michigan at Ann Arbor, double-majoring in history and screen arts and culture. One day in early November, a librarian named Phil Hallman visited one of my film classes to talk about the various library resources available to students. After describing the databases and other sources we could use to write our papers, Phil happened to mention that the university had recently acquired two large collections of Orson Welles's papers. Among those materials, he said, were hundreds of letters written to Welles by ordinary Americans about *War of the Worlds*, and no one had read them in over six decades.

That offhand comment changed the course of my life. I grew up listening to old-time radio; I was a childhood insomniac, and my parents used cassettes of shows like *The Shadow* and *The Lone Ranger* to try to get me to sleep. I had first heard Welles's *War of the Worlds* as a kid, and I knew very well the legend surrounding it. Phil's remark immediately fired my imagination, and I cannot thank him enough for providing the initial spark that led to this book. Throughout this journey, I have benefitted tremendously from his constant support and friendship.

This project is only possible because of the late Richard Wilson, former member of the Mercury Theatre and tireless advocate for Welles's work, who preserved the *War of the Worlds* letters for almost six decades. His son, Christopher Wilson, donated those letters to the University of Michigan in 2005, along with a mountain of other documents illuminating every aspect of Welles's career. I am deeply grateful to the Wilsons for ensuring the survival of this material, and to Dr. Catherine L. Benamou for bringing it to Michigan, where researchers like me continue to delve into it.

This book began as my senior honors thesis, and I am indebted to the department of history at Michigan for providing me with the rare opportunity to conduct self-directed original research as an undergrad. The insightful guidance of my thesis adviser, Dr. John Carson, greatly honed my skills as a writer and scholar. His advice struck the perfect balance, giving me free rein to explore but challenging my thinking when I deserved it. This project could never have proceeded this far without his wisdom and encouragement.

Dr. Derek Peterson gave me my initial grounding in research methodology, and encouraged me to pursue *War of the Worlds* as a thesis topic. Jim Burnstein instilled in me unshakable writing discipline, and played an instrumental role in turning me into a professional writer. Several other professors and instructors at the University of Michigan contributed to this project in myriad ways, including Charles Gentry, Mark Kligerman, Dr. Sheila Murphy, Dr. Derek Vaillant, and Dr. Michael Witgen. Very early on, Rebecca Sestili saw potential in my thesis, and gave generously of her time in helping me pursue publication. The young scholars from the 2012 History Honors cohort at Michigan provided a wonderfully supportive environment as I pursued my research. In particular, my reading-group partners, Shannon Elliott and Ethan Sachs, deserve my thanks (and my apologies) for slogging through my ridiculously long chapter drafts and managing to give excellent feedback.

Funding grants from the university's Honors Program, through the generosity of Mr. and Mrs. Jerome Fine, and from the history department helped me conduct research in archives outside the state. Following completion of my thesis, several university awards provided additional funding to pursue my work, including the Arthur Fondiler History Award for Best Thesis (Highest Honors) from the history department, the Undergraduate Research Award from the U-M Library, and the Robert Hayden Humanities Award from the College of Literature, Science and the Arts. This assistance made it possible for me to devote time to turning my thesis into a book. I am deeply grateful to these departments for their recognition, and to the donors for their generosity.

The staff of the University of Michigan's Special Collections Library were tremendously helpful and accommodating when I moved into their reading room in the summer of 2011 to work with the Welles collections. Kate Hutchens and Peggy Daub provided particular assistance that summer and in the following years, ensuring that my research and my transition from thesis to book could proceed as smoothly as possible. I'm also indebted to the helpful and obliging archivists at the National Archives II facility in College Park, Maryland; the Wisconsin Historical Society Archives in Madison, Wisconsin; the Lilly Library at Indiana University; and the Rare Book and Manuscript Library at Columbia University. Margaret Hogan kindly facilitated my research at the Rockefeller Archive Center in Sleepy Hollow, New York. The staffs of the Mudd Manuscript Library at Princeton University and the Billy Rose Theatre Collection at the New York Public Library were very helpful in letting me conduct research long-distance. The Capital Area District Library, the Michigan Electronic Library system, and the libraries of the University of Michigan and Michigan State University kept me well stocked with every book I needed, no matter how obscure.

In the midst of transitioning from writing a thesis to writing a book, I was fortunate enough to co-write an episode of the PBS series *American Experience* on *War of the Worlds*. I'm grateful to the executive producer, Mark Samels, for that opportunity, and to everyone at *American Experience* for letting me contribute to a series I've long admired. Cathleen O'Connell, director/producer, and Michelle Ferrari, my co-writer, deserve special recognition for making a delightful and insightful film that I'm proud to have been a part of. The cast and crew, especially the actors who brought some of the letters to life, consistently blew me away with their talent and attention to detail.

My editor, Alex Star, has my deepest gratitude for seeing promise in my proposal, and for giving me the chance to bring my honors thesis to the greatest publishing house in New York. His keen eye and perceptive comments have sharpened my writing immeasurably and pushed my thinking in exciting new directions. My thanks as well to Alex's assistant, Laird Gallagher, for critiquing the manuscript and tracking down the answers to my unending list of questions.

My agent, Ross Harris, has proved to be my greatest discovery since Orson Welles's fan mail. He immediately impressed me with his enthusiasm for the project, and expertly guided me throughout this process. I have benefitted enormously from his knowledge, sagacity, and friendship. I'm also indebted to Stuart Krichevsky and Shana Cohen of the Stuart Krichevsky Literary Agency for bringing me on board, and for everything they have done to bring this book to print.

My managers, Ava Jamshidi and Micah Klatzker of Industry Entertainment, cannot be thanked enough for shepherding this project from academia to publishing. I'm grateful for their advice, encouragement, and support. Doug Wick, Lucy Fisher, and Charlie Morrison of Red Wagon Entertainment gave me entrée into the writing game, and they have my thanks for the best summer internship I ever had. Max Allan Collins continues to set a great career example for me to pursue, and I'm proud to follow in his footsteps by publishing my first book.

For permission to quote from the script of the *War of the Worlds* broadcast, I'm grateful to Peter Koch, son of the late Howard E. Koch; Buddy Thomas and Jared Weber of ICM Partners; and Norman Rudman. Nicholas George Skroumbelos shared with me his memories of the fiftieth-anniversary celebrations in Grover's Mill, and graciously let me reprint one of his photographs from the occasion. Michael Socolow kindly reviewed the manuscript and suggested ways it could be improved at the very last minute.

This list can never be anything but incomplete, since space will not permit me to thank everyone who contributed to the project in ways large and small. Those who do not find their names here have not been forgotten; they have my appreciation and my apologies. But I must recognize three Okemos High School teachers who set me on the path that led to this book. I did my first research project on *War of the Worlds* in Matthew Morrison's ninth-grade U.S. history class, and almost a decade later I'm still drawing on the knowledge I first picked up then. Studying journalism with Joyce Haner in the eleventh and twelfth grades helped me develop my research, writing, and editorial skills. Christopher Smith's AP U.S. history course gave me my first experience working with primary sources, and his passion for history convinced me to pursue the subject at the college level. I have been extremely fortunate in working with them and other brilliant educators throughout my career, and I wouldn't be doing what I am now without them.

Finally, my parents, Dennis and Nancy Austin Schwartz, deserve my most profound thanks for contributing to this project in a million different ways. They had no idea quite what they were getting into when they gave me those cassette tapes of old radio shows many years ago, but they have tolerated four years of Wellesiana with more good humor than most parents could manage. As I worked on first my thesis and then this book, they greatly assisted my research, carefully and perceptively edited each draft, and gave me a roof to work and sleep under. They've allowed me to write the best book on *War of the Worlds* that I possibly could. I only hope the result can validate, in some small way, their inexhaustible faith in me.

Index